NATURAL HISTORY MUSEUM
ANIMAL RECORDS

MARK CARWARDINE

First published by the Natural History Museum, Cromwell Road, London SW7 5BD
© Natural History Museum, London, 2007
Reprinted with updates 2010

ISBN 978 0 565 09248 1

Cover design by Ruth Hope
Designed by seagulls.net
Reproduction by Saxon Digital Services
Printed by C&C Offset, China

Front cover
Eagle: © Frank Leung/Istockphoto
Tree frog: © Sascha Burkard/Istockphoto
Giraffe: © Istockphoto
Polar bear: © Michel de Nijs/Istockphoto

Back cover
Rattlesnake: © Dave Rodriguez/Istockphoto
Angelfish: © Dirk-Jan Mattaar/Istockphoto

CONTENTS

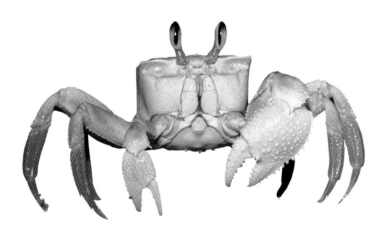

FOREWORD

The Natural History Museum aims to engage people's curiosity of the natural world and encourage its enjoyment and responsible use for the future of our planet. With the help of Mark Carwardine's painstaking research, which lies at the core of this book, and the additional input from many scientists at the Museum, I hope that *Natural History Museum Animal Records* contributes to that aim. At 256 pages it could never cover all the amazing and exceptional animals we share the Earth with, but the selection we have made introduces readers to some of the most awe-inspiring and intriguing of these animals and will, I hope, whet the appetite to find out more about the world around us.

Each of the major animal groupings (mammals, birds, reptiles, amphibians, fishes and invertebrates) has its own section. Then, where appropriate, these sections are further divided up into orders and families and species – this is the basis of the science the Museum carries out, identifying and naming species and organising them into systems of classification. *Natural History Museum Animal Records* includes different records for the different groupings, so instead of being a completely comprehensive guide, it aims to include the records that are most relevant and interesting for each type of animal. Throughout the book there are special boxes which highlight some of the top record holders and there is also a special star treatment for animals that are exceptional in some way or other.

One of the saddest things about the state of the world today is how many of the record-breaking animals featured in this book are critically endangered, if not on the verge of extinction. *Natural History Museum Animal Records* does not dwell on the plight of those endangered species. This is partly because the situation changes so rapidly that this type of information risks being inaccurate almost as soon as a book is published, and can therefore be more effectively communicated through other media. It is also because the main aim of this book is to celebrate the wonders of the natural world and particularly its diversity, even though this diversity is under greater threat now than it has ever been previously.

However, if you want to find out more about endangered animals the best source of information is the World Conservation Union (IUCN) at www.iucn.org. Through its Species Survival Commission (SSC), IUCN has for more than four decades been assessing the conservation status of species, subspecies, varieties and even selected subpopulations on a global scale in order to highlight species threatened with extinction, and therefore promote their conservation. The species assessed for the IUCN Red List are the bearers of genetic diversity and the building blocks of ecosystems, and information on their conservation status and distribution provides the foundation for making informed decisions about conserving biodiversity from local to global levels.

I hope that *Natural History Museum Animal Records* will excite a feeling of wonder at some of the amazing animals we share this planet with, and inspire readers to get involved in the discovery, understanding, enjoyment and responsible use of the natural world to ensure the diversity of life on earth continues.

Michael Dixon

Director, October 2007

MAMMALS

Tiger
Panthera tigris in close up.

AARDVARK

Tubulidentata

★ BURROWING

The aardvark or ant bear (*Orycteropus afer*), which lives in the grasslands, scrub and open woodland of sub-Saharan Africa, is one of the fastest burrowing animals in the world. With its long, spoon-shaped claws and enormously powerful legs, it can dig a burrow in soft earth faster than several people with shovels. In fact, if it is unable to run away from its enemies, it will often dig an instant hole and hide instead; in exceptional cases, a complete burrow several metres (yards) long can be completed in under five minutes. Even hard, sun-baked earth is not an obstacle, although it does make the burrowing take a little longer. When they are burrowing, aardvarks fold their ears back and close their nostrils to keep out the dirt and to ensure that ants and

termites don't get inside. Baby aardvarks are able to dig their own burrows when they are about six months old.

★ MOST BURROWS

The aardvark (*Orycteropus afer*) is an elusive, nocturnal animal and often the only sign of its presence is its burrowing. Some individuals dig a large number of burrows: the record is 60 entrances in one small area approximately 300 m (1000 ft) x 100 m (330 ft). Since the majority

of these entrances remain unused for long periods of time, many other animals take advantage of the aardvark's digging prowess and take up residence instead.

Aardvark
Aaardvark means 'earthpig' in Afrikaans although its resemblance to a pig is only superficial. It is so peculiar anatomically that it has been designated an entire order of mammals —Tubulidentata — all to itself. It is very elusive and one of the least-known mammals in the world.

ARTIODACTYL

Animals with hooves are called ungulates, and artiodactyls are ungulates with an even number of toes. Their weight is borne equally by the third and fourth toes.

Most depend on plants for their food, although some such as the pigs may also eat meat. Artiodactyls have complex digestive systems to help them process their food.

ANTELOPES & WILD CATTLE

Antilocapridae Bovidae

143 species including: pronghorn antelopes, kudu, buffalo, duiker, oryx, wildebeest, gazelles, chamois, sheep and goats

★ LARGEST

A number of bovids are known to attain a height at the shoulder of nearly 2 m (6 ft 7 in) and a weight approaching 1000 kg (2205 lb). These include the wild yak (*Bos mutus*), gaur (*Bos gaurus*), American bison (*Bison bison*), wild water buffalo (*Bubalus arnee*) and domestic cattle (*Bos taurus*). The tallest of all the wild species is probably the gaur, by a narrow margin because of the male's large shoulder hump; it has a head-body length of 2.5–3.3 m (8 ft 2 in–10 ft 10 in);

a tail length of 70–100 cm (27$\frac{1}{2}$–39$\frac{1}{2}$ in); a shoulder height of 1.6–2.2 m (5 ft 3 in–7 ft 3 in); and a weight of 650–1000 kg (1433–2205 lb). However, the heaviest bovid of all is probably the wild water buffalo (*Bubalus arnee*), which is found in India, Nepal, Bhutan and Thailand, and is the ancestor of the domestic water buffalo (*Bubalus bubalis*); it has a head-body length of 2.4–3 m (7 ft 10 in–9 ft 10 in); a tail length of 60–100 cm (23$\frac{1}{2}$–39 in); a shoulder height of 1.5–1.9 m (4 ft 11 in–6 ft 3 in);

and a weight of 700–1200 kg (1543–2646 lb). The largest of all the antelopes is the giant eland (*Taurotragus derbianus*) of western and central Africa. It has a head-body length of 1.8–3.5 m (6–11$\frac{1}{2}$ ft); a tail length of 50–90 cm (19$\frac{3}{4}$–35$\frac{1}{2}$ in); a shoulder height of 1.3–1.83 m (51–72 in); and a weight of 350–940 kg (772–2072 lb).

The common eland (*Taurotragus oryx*) of eastern and southern Africa is a similar size but does not have such impressive horns; there is one record of a 1.65 m (5 ft 5 in) common eland bull shot in Malawi *c.* 1937 that weighed 943 kg (2078 lb).

★ LARGEST DOMESTIC

The heaviest domestic cattle (*Bos taurus*) on record was a Holstein-Durham cross named Mount Katahdin, which from 1906 to 1910 frequently weighed 2267 kg (5000 lb). He stood 1.88 m (6 ft 2 in) at the shoulder and had a girth measuring 3.96 m (13 ft). The animal was exhibited by A. S. Rand of Maine, USA, and died in a barn fire *c.* 1923.

The largest domestic goat ever recorded was a British Saanen named *Mostyn Moorcock*, owned by Pat Robinson of Ewvas Harold, Hereford and Worcester, UK, which reached a weight of 181.4 kg (400 lb), a shoulder height of 1.12 m (44 in) and length of 1.68 m (66 in). He died in 1977 at the age of

Common wildebeest
Seen here in the Serengeti National Park, Tanzania, wildebeest form part of one of the largest gatherings of hoofed mammals in the world today, with as many as 1.69 million wildebeest in the herd (now 1.3 million).

four. The largest domestic sheep ever recorded was a Suffolk Whisper 23H, owned by Joseph and Susan Schallberger of Boring, Oregon, USA, which weighed 247.2 kg (545 lb) and stood 1.09 m (43 in) tall in March 1991.

★ SMALLEST

The royal antelope (*Neotragus pygmaeus*) of western Africa is the smallest bovid and one of the smallest of all hoofed mammals (after certain chevrotains or mouse deer in the family *Tragulidae*). About the size of a large brown hare (*Lepus europaeus*) it has a head-body length of 45–55 cm (17¾–21¾ in); a tail length of about 4–5 cm (1½–2 in); a shoulder height of 25–30.5 cm (9¾–12 in); and a weight of 1.5–3 kg (3 lb 5 oz–6 lb 10 oz).

★ SMALLEST DOMESTIC

The smallest breed of domestic cattle (*Bos taurus*) is the Ovambo of Namibia, with bulls and cows averaging 225 kg

(496 lb) and 160 kg (353 lb) respectively. The smallest breed of sheep is the Ouessant, from the Ile d'Ouessant, Brittany, France, at 13–16 kg (29–35 lb) in weight and standing 45–50 cm (18–20 in) at the shoulder.

★ LARGEST HERDS

The largest gathering of hoofed mammals today has long been thought to take place in the Serengeti-Mara ecosystem, in Tanzania and neighbouring Kenya. During the rainy season, from November to May, this area may harbour as many as 1.69 million common wildebeest or white-bearded gnus (*Connochaetes taurinus*), some 200,000 Burchell's zebras (*Equus burchellii*), more than 250,000 Thomson's gazelles (*Eudorcas thomsonii*) and Grant's gazelles (*Nanger granti*) as well as common eland (*Taurotragus oryx*), topi (*Damaliscus korrigum*), hartebeest (*Alcelaphus buselaphus*) and a variety of other species (plus all their attendant predators). There is a general movement

MAMMALS

off the plains as soon as the grasses lose their green flush, at the beginning of the long, dry season in May or June. During this migration, herds of wildebeest up to 40 km (25 miles) long have been seen from the air.

In January 2007 scientists witnessed a migration in Southern Sudan which could even exceed that in the Serengeti-Mara ecosystem. They observed a column of animals 80 km (50 miles) long and 50 km (30 miles) across, mainly made up of white-eared kob (*Kobus kob*), Mongollla gazelle (*Gazella thomsonii albontata*) and tiang antelope (*Damaliscus lunatus tiang*).

Spectacular herds of hoofed mammals once gathered in many parts of the world (particularly in Africa and North America) even during the last century. The largest on record were those of the springbok (*Antidorcus marsupialis*) on migration across the plains of the western parts of southern Africa in the 19th century. In 1849 John (later Sir John) Fraser observed a *trekbokken* that took three days

to pass through the settlement of Beaufort West, Cape Province, South Africa. Another herd seen moving near Nels Poortje, Cape Province, in 1888, was estimated to contain 100 million head, although 10 million is probably a more realistic figure. A herd estimated to be 24 km (15 miles) wide and more than 160 km (100 miles) long was reported from Karree Kloof, Orange River, South Africa, in July 1896. These unbroken herds were so enormous that other animals met on the way were either trampled or had to move along with them.

★ LONGEST HORNS

The longest horns grown by any living animal are those of the wild water buffalo (*Bubalus arnee*) which lives in India,

Nepal, Bhutan and Thailand, and is the ancestor of the domestic water buffalo (*Bubalus bubalis*). The average spread is about 1 m (3 ft 3 in), but one bull shot in 1955 had horns measuring 4.24 m (13 ft 11 in) from tip to tip along the outside curve across the forehead.

★ SHORTEST HORNS

All adult male (and some female) bovids carry horns. The shortest horns of any member of the family belong to the royal antelope (*Neotragus pygmaeus*). Present only in the male, they are normally 1.2–2.5 cm (1/2–1 in) long.

Among domestic cattle (*Bos taurus*), a record spread of 3.2 m (10 ft 6 in) was recorded for a Texas longhorn steer on exhibition at the Heritage Museum, Big Springs, Texas, USA.

★ MOST HORNS

The male four-horned antelope (*Tetracerus quadricornis*), which lives in India and Nepal, is the only mammal with four horns. The front pair are often poorly

Wild water buffalo
The wild water buffalo of India, Nepal, Bhutan and Thailand is probably the heaviest of all the bovids and has the longest horns of any living animal.

10

WORLD RECORD HOLDER

Fastest over a long distance

The pronghorn or American antelope (*Antilocapra americana*) of the western United States, southwest Canada and parts of northern Mexico is the fastest land animal over a sustained distance (the cheetah (*Acinonyx jubatus*) is the fastest over a short distance). It has been observed to run at 56 km/h (35 mph) for 6 km (4 miles), at 67 km/h (42 mph) for 1.6 km (1 mile) and 88.5 km/h (55 mph) for 0.8 km (½ mile). There are claims of speeds of up to 113 km/h (70 mph), but these are considered unlikely (at least one such claim was the result of a faulty speedometer).

Recent research has revealed some of the pronghorn's physiological secrets. Most important of all, it is able to consume oxygen with more than three times the expected efficiency of an animal of the same size. It has spectacularly large lungs and a big heart to pump more blood; the blood itself is unusually rich in haemoglobin (which means that more oxygen can be delivered to the muscles in less time); and the muscle cells are densely-packed with mitochondria, the little power houses that use oxygen to supply energy.

The fastest of the other bovids are the gazelles. Species such as the springbok (*Antidorcas marsupialis*) have a top speed of 82–89 km/h (51–55 mph). They can dodge and turn sharply when running flat out and can make long (but not high) jumps to escape still faster cheetahs (*Acinonyx jubatus*). However, they are relatively poor runners over long distances and overheat easily.

American antelope
The antelope needs both its speed and endurance to escape from wolves and other predators on the wide open prairies where there is nowhere to hide.

developed but average 2–5 cm (¾–2 in) in length, the rear pair are a slightly longer 8–12 cm (3–4¾ in).

★ HORN SHEDDING

The pronghorn or American antelope (*Antilocapra americana*) combines several characteristics of both antelopes (family Bovidae) and deer (family Cervidae), but none more striking than its horns. Male, and most female, pronghorns possess short horns. These consist of a bony core covered by an outer keratin sheath, like bovid horns, but they are shed annually after the breeding season like deer antlers. Consequently, it is the only mammal with true horns to shed them every year.

★ HIGHEST LIVING

The highest-living large mammal in the world is the yak (*Bos mutus*), which lives in China, India and Nepal (it is believed to be extinct in Bhutan and Afghanistan). It roams at high altitudes in the mountains of the Himalayas and the Tibetan plateau and is believed to reach a height of 6100 m (20,000 ft) when foraging (only the Asian large-eared pika (*Ochotona macrotis*) goes higher). A bull shot in 1899, in the Himalayas, was found at an altitude of 5639 m (18,500 ft).

★ MOST RAPID DECLINE

An estimated 50–60 million American bison or buffalo (*Bison bison*) roamed the great plains of North America in the early 1800s. Their vast migrating herds were the economic mainstay of the local Indians: they ate the meat and used the hides to make clothes, tepees and canoes; but they killed relatively small numbers and had no long-term effect on the bison population.

However, when European settlers arrived on the continent and, particularly, when they began to sweep westwards in the 1860s, a mass slaughter began. The white men killed bison (on foot, on horseback and, later, even from the comfort of passenger trains) specifically to deprive the Indians of their wild herds, but also to free the land for farming, to obtain the animals' tongues and hides, and for sport. At the peak of the slaughter, some 2.5 million bison were killed annually from 1870 to 1875 and the legendary 'Buffalo Bill' Cody claimed to have killed 4862 of the animals in one year alone.

By the late 1890s there were no more than 800 left on the entire North American continent and the species was on the point of extinction in the wild. Fortunately, a few hundred had been taken into captivity and, with strenuous conservation efforts, the bison managed to survive. The total population today is about 350,000.

MAMMALS

Springbok
The springbok, a species of gazelle found mainly in south and southwestern Africa is known for doing a series of repeated high jumps. This one is in Etosha National Park in Namibia.

★ BEST JUMPER

Springboks (*Antidorcas marsupialis*) are well known for their 'pronking' (showing off in Afrikaans) or 'stotting'. These are bouts of repeated high leaps up to 4 m (12 ft) high, although they seem more like bounces as they leap back into the air as soon as their feet touch the ground.

★ MOST INQUISITIVE

The pronghorn or American antelope (*Antilocapra americana*) of the western United States, south-western Canada and parts of northern Mexico is renowned for its insatiable curiosity and must be one of the most inquisitive animals in the world. It will approach from a considerable distance to inspect moving objects (including people, vehicles and even predators) with no apparent concern for the potential risks involved. Early settlers took advantage of this unlikely behaviour by 'flagging' – tying handkerchiefs to poles and waving them in the air – to attract the inquisitive animals within gunshot range. Flagging is now illegal but overhunting by early settlers, coupled with habitat loss, was the primary cause of a massive population decline in the pronghorn. Its numbers dropped from 35–50 million in 1850 to just 13,000 by 1920. Strenuous conservation efforts have since helped the species to recover and the population now stands at a much more healthy 700,000, although there is concern that oil exploration and strip mining for coal pose serious threats to the relatively little remaining habitat that remains.

CAMELS & LLAMAS

Camelidae

Six species: llama, alpaca, guanaco, vicuña, dromedary and Bactrian camel; three of these (dromedary, llama and alpaca) are domesticated and do not normally live independent of people

★ EARLIEST DOMESTICATION

The earliest domestication of llamas (*Lama glama*) and alpacas (*Lama pacos*), for their highly valued wool, meat and milk, and as beasts of burden, took place in Peru approximately 4000–5000 years ago – either in the Lake Titicaca region, or on the Junin Plateau, about 100 km (60 miles) to the northwest.

The two camels were domesticated independently. The dromedary (*Camelus dromedarius*) was first domesticated in central or southern Arabia some 4000–6000 years ago; it is believed to have become extinct in the wild about 2000 years ago. The Bactrian camel (*Camelus bactrianus*) was first domesticated on the plateaux of northern Iran and southwestern Turkestan about 4500 years ago.

★ HIGHEST LIVING

The vicuña (*Vicugna vicugna*) and the domesticated alpaca (*Lama pacos*) both live on alpine grasslands at heights of 3700–4800 m (12,150–15,750 ft) and 4400–4800 m (14,450–15,750 ft) respectively, where the air is too thin for most mammals to live. The highest authenticated record is for a vicuña, which was found above the snowline at 5486 m (18,000 ft) in the Peruvian Andes.

★ LARGEST

The largest member of the Camelidae is the dromedary or one-humped camel

(*Camelus dromedarius*), which is a native of the Middle East but survives today only as a feral animal in Australia and as a domestic animal elsewhere. It is also the largest artiodactyl or even-toed hoofed mammal, with a head-body length of 2.3–3.5 m (7½–11½ ft); a tail length of 55 cm (21¾ in); a shoulder height of 1.8–2.1 m (6–7 ft) (maximum 2.4 m (7 ft 11 in)) and a weight of 450–690 kg (992–1521 lb).

The Bactrian or two-humped camel (*Camelus bactrianus*), which survives in the wild only in the remote deserts of Mongolia and northern China, and as a domestic animal elsewhere, is marginally smaller.

★ SMALLEST

The smallest member of the Camelidae is the vicuña (*Vicugna vicugna*), which lives in the high Andes of South America. It has a head-body length of 1.3–1.9 m (4¼–6¼ ft); a tail length of 15–25 cm (6–9¾ in); a shoulder height of 70–110 cm (27½–43 in); and a weight of 35–65 kg (77–143 lb).

★ DESERT ADAPTATIONS

Both species of camel – the dromedary (*Camelus dromedarius*) and the Bactrian

(*Camelus bactrianus*) – are better adapted to life in the desert than almost any other mammal. Contrary to popular belief, camels do not store water in their humps, but energy-rich fat. This can be broken down in the body to produce energy, carbon dioxide

Camel dung is so dry that it can be used as fuel as soon as it leaves the animal.

and water, and helps them to survive long periods of up to several months without food. A well-fed camel has a large hump (an individual weighing 500 kg (1100 lb) can store more than 50 kg (110 lb) of fat in its hump) but a camel that has had little or nothing to eat may have no hump at all.

Camels have a number of record-breaking adaptations to

help conserve water. They do not begin to sweat until their body temperature reaches 40.5°C (105°F) – a high fever in a human; they have the ability to accumulate heat slowly within the body during the day, as the outside temperature rises, and then to dissipate it in the cool of the night; their thick coat restricts water loss through evaporation; their highly efficient kidneys ensure that the water content of their urine is kept to a minimum; they produce dry dung; and they can survive a water loss of up to 40% of their body weight without harm (compared with less than 14% in a human). They are also able to go for long periods without drinking (at least a week when working in very high temperatures and several months at

Vicuña
The smallest member of the camel family, the vicuña, is also the highest living and has been recorded at an altitude of 5486 m (18,000 ft) in the Peruvian Andes.

other times) and then, when the opportunity arises, can drink huge quantities – up to 60 litres (13 gallons) – in a matter of minutes.

Camels are unique among mammals in having elliptical (rather than round) red blood cells; this prevents their blood from thickening with a rise in temperature. They also have webbed feet, which stop them from sinking into soft sand, long, thick lashes which keep wind-blown sand out of their eyes, and nostrils that can be kept tight shut to keep out the sand.

• Dromedary camels
Camels are better adapted to life in the desert than almost any other mammal; they store energy-rich fat in their humps which can be broken down to release energy, carbon dioxide and water. These dromedary camels were photographed in the Moroccan Sahara desert.

DEER & DEER-LIKE ANIMALS

Cervidae, Moschidae and Tragulidae
Cervidae: 51 species and several times that number of sub-species
Moschidae: seven species (musk deer). Tragulidae: eight species (chevrotains)

★ EARLIEST
Deer are believed to have evolved from forest-dwelling animals (not unlike modern chevrotains or mouse deer in the family Tragulidae) during the Oligocene, some 30 million years ago. The earliest true, antler-shedding deer was a genus called *Dicrocerus*, which first appeared in Europe about 20 million years ago.

★ LARGEST PREHISTORIC
The extinct Irish elk *Megaloceros* (formerly *Megoceros*) *giganteus* was a giant among deer. It was at least as tall and heavy as the modern moose (*Alces alces*) and had even larger antlers. Despite its name, it was not an elk and did not live exclusively in Ireland (although more fossil remains have been found in Ireland than anywhere else). Fossil evidence and some remarkably good cave paintings suggest that it reached a height of at least 2 m (6 ft 7 in) at the shoulders and looked rather like a giant fallow deer (*Dama dama*). The Irish elk lived in the grassland and open woodland areas of Europe, ranging as far east as Siberia. It became extinct in Ireland around 12,700 years ago, but probably survived in central Asia until about 8000 years ago.

★ SMALLEST
The smallest true deer (family Cervidae) is the southern pudu (*Pudu puda*), which is 33–38 cm (13–15 in) tall at the shoulder and weighs 6.3–8.2 kg (14–18 lb). Found in Chile and Argentina, it has short antlers only 7–10 cm (2½–4 in) long. The similar but slightly larger northern pudu (*P. mephistophiles*) is found in Ecuador, Colombia and the extreme north of Peru. The lesser Malay chevrotain (*Tragulus javanicus*) is even smaller, but is not a true deer (see SMALLEST ARTIODACTYL p. 16).

★ LONGEST LIVING
Deer have a reputation for living a long time but, in reality, once they have survived the early, most vulnerable period of life, 10–20 years is a good age for most species. The oldest ever recorded is a hand-reared Scottish red deer (*Cervus elaphus scoticus*) named Bambi, owned by the Fraser family of Kiltarlity, Beauly, UK, which died in 1995 aged 31 years, seven months and 12 days. There are several records of deer exceeding 26 years in captivity. A red deer, which lived at Milwaukee Zoo, Wisconsin, USA, was 26 years and eight months old when it died in 1954. Another red deer, at the National Zoo, Washington, DC, USA, lived for 26 years, two months and two days.

And a female sambar (*Rusa unicolor*) in New York Zoological Park, USA, was 26 years, five months and six days when it died.

★ ANTLERS

Deer are the only animals in the world to possess antlers. Despite their superficial similarity to the horns of antelopes, goats and other mammals, they differ in several ways: they are made entirely of bone (horns are covered by an outer sheath of keratin); they fall off after a year and regrow the following year (horns are permanent and grow throughout life); they are found almost exclusively on male deer (in most horned species, females as well as males have horns); and, in most species, they are branched (horns may be straight, curved, coiled or spiral – but never branched).

While antlers are found almost exclusively on male deer, there are two exceptions: they are also found on female reindeer or caribou (*Rangifer tarandus*) and the Chinese water deer (*Hydropotes inermis*) has no antlers at all. Musk deer (family Moschidae) and chevrotains or mouse deer (family Tragulidae) do not have antlers, but are not regarded as true deer.

★ LARGEST ANTLERS

The size of antlers varies according to the species, the quality of food available, characters inherited from both parents, the age of the animal and other factors. On average, the longest antlers are normally those of the American wapiti (*Cervus elaphus canadensis*) and the caribou (*Rangifer tarandus*), some of which exceed 1.5 m (59 in) in length. The moose (*Alces americanus*) is a much larger animal, and its antlers are normally heavier, but they also tend to be shorter. However, the record antler spread or 'rack' for any modern species is 1.99 m (6 ft 6½ in) (skull and antlers 41 kg (91 lb)) from a moose killed near the head-waters of the Stewart River in the Yukon, Canada, in October 1897. The antlers are now on display in the Field Museum, Chicago, Illinois, USA.

★ LARGEST PREHISTORIC ANTLERS

The extinct Irish elk *Megaloceros giganteus*, found in continental Europe as recently as 8000 years ago, had the largest antlers of any known animal. One specimen recovered from an Irish bog had greatly palmated antlers measuring an amazing 4.3 m (14 ft) across and weighing 45 kg (99 lb), which corresponds to a shoulder height of 1.83 m (6 ft) and a body weight of 500 kg (1100 lb).

Red deer
The two oldest deer on record were both red deer (*Cervus elaphus*) and they also grow particularly fine antlers although not as big as those of the American wapiti or the caribou.

Moose
A moose (*Alces americanus*) in Teton National Park, Wyoming, USA. Moose are generally reckoned to have the heaviest antlers and the individual record for antler spread belongs to a moose on display in the Field Museum, Chicago.

★ MOST VALUABLE PRODUCT

The waxy substance known as musk, which is secreted by male musk deer (family Moschidae) is one of the most expensive animal products in the world. Used in the manufacture of perfumes and soaps in the West and for traditional medicines in the Far East (to treat anything from asthma and epilepsy to pneumonia and typhoid), it fetched up to US$45/g (US$1280/oz) on the international market in the mid-1980s, although the price has since dropped to about US$45/g (US$1280/oz) today (still several times the price of gold). The annual international trade was about 1400 kg (3086 lb) at the turn of the century, representing the slaughter of nearly 50,000 deer. The trade dropped to 300 kg (661 lb) by the mid-1980s (but has increased significantly since then). This decline has not been due to falling demand, but reflects the rapidly declining populations of musk deer in the wild. For comparison, the current market value of Asian rhino horn is US$100/g (US$2840/oz).

The musk is stored in a fist-sized pouch on the belly of the deer, near the tail. A single mature male carries about 30 g (1 oz) (maximum 45 g (1½ oz). It is estimated that populations in some parts of the range, especially in countries such as China, Mongolia, North and South Korea, Russia, Kazakhstan, and Kyrgystan have declined as much as 50%.

★ SMALLEST ANTLERS

The smallest antlers are found on the tufted deer (*Elaphodus cephalophus*) of Asia: they are often hidden in a tuft of hairs which grow from the forehead. The Chinese water deer (*Hydropotes inermis*) and, indeed, the females of all other species except the reindeer or caribou (*Rangifer tarandus*) have no antlers at all.

★ SMALLEST ARTIODACTYL

The world's smallest artiodactyl (even-toed hoofed mammal) is the lesser Malay chevrotain or Java mouse-deer (*Tragulus javanicus*) of Southeast Asia. Adults are no bigger than a rabbit, with a head-body length of 44–48 cm (15¾–19 in); a tail length of 6.5–8 cm (2½–3¼ in); a shoulder height of 20–25 cm (8–9 in); and a weight of 1.7–3 kg (3¾–6½ lb).

★ MUSK DEER

Despite their name and deer-like appearance, musk deer (of the genus *Moschus*) are not normally included in the deer family Cervidae: they show a number of important differences and are placed in a family of their own (Moschidae). They are small animals, with an average height at the shoulder of 50–60 cm (20–24 in) and a weight of 10–15 kg (22–33 lb). Unusually among deer, females are heavier than males. Both sexes lack antlers but, like a number of primitive members of the deer family, males have large canine tusks in the upper jaw. Found sporadically in the high altitude forests of central and eastern Asia, they take their name from the male's musk gland.

MOST POWERFUL NATURAL PERFUME

The musk produced by the male musk deer (family Moschidae) is thought to be the most powerful natural perfume in the world. A tiny amount will scent more than 50,000 m² (1.8 million ft²) of air quite distinctly.

★ MOST PRIMITIVE RUMINANT

The chevrotains or mouse-deer (family Tragulidae) are considered to be the most primitive ruminants (mammals with a four-chambered stomach containing micro-organisms that help to digest their cellulose-rich food). Providing a living link between non-ruminants and ruminants, they are thought to have remained virtually unchanged for approximately 30 million years. They share many features with ruminants, including a four-chambered stomach (although the third chamber is poorly developed); a lack of upper incisor teeth; and various behavioural patterns. They also share features with non-ruminants, including a lack of horns or antlers; four fully developed toes; and, again, various behavioural patterns. The water chevrotain (*Hyemoschus aquaticus*) is generally considered to be the most primitive of the four species.

★ LONGEST RECOVERY

Père David's deer (*Elaphurus davidianus*) was once widely distributed in eastern China. But it became extinct in the wild about 1500–2000 years ago and survived only in captivity in the Chinese Emperor's Imperial Hunting Park, outside Beijing. It was unknown to western scientists until Père Armand David, the French missionary and naturalist, found it in 1865. He sent two skins back to Europe for identification (the new species was later named after him) and then shipped a number of live animals to zoos outside China. Soon afterwards, in 1900, the entire Chinese herd was eaten by hungry soldiers during the Boxer Rebellion; so, perhaps unwittingly, Père Armand David

had saved the species from extinction. Then the Duke of Bedford, in what was probably the first conscious effort to save a mammal from extinction, gathered together all 18 available specimens of Père David's deer from zoos in Europe to create one breeding herd at Woburn Park, Bedfordshire, UK. From this small nucleus herd, established at the beginning of the century, there are now about 1500 Père David's deer distributed in parks and zoos around the world (fortunately, inbreeding does not appear to have been a problem) and a further 2500 as part of a reintroduction programme underway in China.

Java mouse-deer

The smallest of the mouse deer is the Java mouse-deer (*Tragulus javanicus*) which lives in the tropical rainforests and mangroves of Southeast Asia. The adults are no bigger than a rabbit.

Père David's deer

Père David's deer (*Elaphurus davidianus*) from China, was unknowingly saved from extinction by the missionary and naturalist Père David who rescued a few animals and shipped them out of China, before it went extinct.

GIRAFFE & OKAPI

Giraffidae
Two species: giraffe and okapi

★ SHORTEST

The okapi (*Okapia johnstoni*), which is restricted to the dense tropical rainforests of The Democratic Republic of the Congo, in central Africa, reaches an average overall height size of 1.7–1.8 m (67–72 in) – with a maximum of 2.1 m (83 in), and a height at the shoulder of 1.5–1.7 m (59–67 in) – with a maximum of 1.8 m (71 in). It weighs 200–250 kg (441–551 lb). It has a much shorter neck and shorter legs than its close relative the giraffe (*Giraffa camelopardalis*).

Nine different sub-species of giraffe are recognized and the smallest is Thornicroft's giraffe (*Giraffa camelopardalis thornicrofti*), which lives only in Luangwa Valley, Zambia. It is only slightly smaller than the others, males reaching a maximum height of about 5 m (16 ft 5 in) and females about 4.5 m (14 ft 9 in).

★ MOST RECENT DISCOVERY

The elusive okapi (*Okapia johnstoni*) is one of the few large terrestrial mammals to have become known to science for the first time relatively recently. It was first mentioned by the explorer Sir Henry Morton Stanley in his book *In Darkest Africa*, which was published in 1890. Stanley described a strange creature that was known to the Wambutti pygmies of the dense Ituri Forest (The Democratic Republic of the Congo formerly contained within Uganda's borders); they called it the o'api (the apostrophe is pronounced like a 'k') and described it as shy and donkey-like, with a long neck, vivid zebra-like stripes on its legs and an extraordinary, long blue tongue. The first incontrovertible proof of the okapi's existence came in 1901, when Swede Karl Eriksson managed to obtain a complete skin and two skulls; it was formally described and named on 18 June 1901 (after Sir Harry Johnston, Governor of Uganda at the time, who had been enthusiastically following up Stanley's information). News of this striking animal made newspaper headlines around the world and in 1982, the okapi was adopted as the official emblem of the International Society of Cryptozoology (for the study of 'hidden' animals).

★ FASTEST

Despite its great size and rather gangly shape, the giraffe (*Giraffa camelopardalis*) is far from ungainly and can attain such high speeds over short distances that in a race a horse would have difficulty keeping up. The highest speed ever recorded is 56 km/h (35 mph) for an individual

Special pressure-regulating narrow blood vessels in a giraffe's neck help control the blood supply to its head when reaching up to browse on high branches or bending down to drink at ground level.

running across open ground. For long-distance running (during which the giraffe does not tire easily) the animal usually lopes along at about 16 km/h (10 mph). When running, the giraffe's long neck tends to sway sinuously from side to side, almost in a figure of eight.

★ EYESIGHT

The giraffe (*Giraffa camelopardalis*) probably has the greatest range of vision of any mammal, thanks to its phenomenally good eyesight, its preferred open habitat and, of course, its height above the ground.

LONGEST TONGUE
Both members of the family Giraffidae have two of the longest and most mobile tongues in the animal kingdom. The giraffe (*Giraffa camelopardalis*) tongue has an average length of 45 cm (18 in). The okapi (*Okapia johnstoni*) has such a long tongue (up to 50 cm (20 in)) that it can reach up to lick and clean its own eyes.

Okapi
The strange-looking okapi has an exceptional tongue which is not only very long but also blue in colour.

Tallest

The tallest living animal is the giraffe (*Giraffa camelopardalis*), found in the dry savanna and open woodland areas of Africa, south of the Sahara. Its great height enables it to feed on the leaves of trees that are out of reach of other herbivores living on the African savanna. The average measurements for adult giraffes are: 4.7–5.3 m (15 ft 5 in–17 ft 5 in) overall height (including horns of about 15–22 cm (6–9 in)), 2.7–3.3 m (8 ft 10 in–10 ft 10 in) in height at the shoulder, and 900–1600 kg (1984–3527 lb) in weight, for the male; and 3.7–4.7 m (12 ft 2 in–15 ft 5 in) overall height, 2.5–3 m (8 ft 2 in–9 ft 10 in) in height at the shoulder, and 600–1000 kg (1323–2205 lb) in weight, for the female. Despite their long necks, giraffes have no more than the usual seven neck vertebrae found in most other mammals.

The tallest sub-species is the Masai giraffe (*Giraffa c. tippelskirchi*) and the tallest specimen ever recorded was a Masai bull named George, who was received at Chester Zoo, UK, on 8 January 1959; he had arrived from Kenya, at the age of about 18 months. His horns almost grazed the roof of the 6.1 m (20 ft) high Giraffe House when he was nine years old. George died on 22 July 1969. Another Masai bull, shot in Kenya earlier in the 20th century, measured 5.87 m (19 ft 3 in) between pegs (standing height about 5.8 m (19 ft)). Less credible and unauthenticated heights of up to 7 m (23 ft) between pegs have been claimed for several other bulls shot in the field.

Masai giraffe
The Masai giraffe (*Giraffa c. tippelskirchi*) is the tallest sub-species of giraffe. No two giraffes have exactly the same body pattern although all the ones living in a particular area tend to have similar patterns to one another.

HIPPOPOTAMUSES

Hippopotamidae

There are only two species of hippo: the common and the pygmy

★ LARGEST

The common hippopotamus (*Hippopotamus amphibius*) is one of the world's heaviest terrestrial animals, second only in weight to elephants and some rhinos. It has an average head body length of 2.8–4 m (9 ft 2 in–3 ft 1 in) plus a tail of about 35–50 cm (14–20 in), a height at the shoulder of about 1.4 m (55 in) and a weight of 1.3–2.5 tonnes. The largest recorded individuals measure about 4.6 m (15 ft 1 in) head-body length, plus a tail of about 60 cm (24in) and a height at the shoulder of 1.65 m (65 in); on rare occasions, they may weigh in excess of four tonnes.

★ SMALLEST

The pygmy hippopotamus (*Hexaprotodon liberiensis*) has an average head-body length of

1.5–1.85 m (59–73 in) plus a tail of about 15–21 cm (6–8¼ in), a height at the shoulder of 70–100 cm (27½–39½ in) and a weight of 160–275 kg (353–606 lb). There is relatively little difference between the two sexes.

★ LARGEST POPULATION

There are considerably more common hippopotamuses (*Hippopotamus amphibius*) in Zambia than in any other country in Africa (the Zambian population is estimated to be approximately 30,000–40,000). The Democratic Republic

Hippos do not have sweat glands, instead they have glands below their skin which secrete an oily pink fluid protecting the skin from sunburn. This strange fluid prompted the early, erroneous idea that hippos sweat blood.

of Congo once had the second largest population, with about 30,000 hippos but the population has plummeted in recent years to fewer than 400.

Common hippopotamus
The common hippopotamus is one of the world's heaviest terrestrial animals and the males are considerably bigger than the females of a similar age. Yawning is a form of threat display, often used during confrontations in the water.

PIGS & PECCARIES

Suidae and Tayassuidae

19 species of pig (including the domestic pig and the extinct Vietnam warty pig) and three species of peccary

★ LARGEST

The largest of the pigs and peccaries is the giant forest hog (*Hylochoerus meinertzhageni*), which lives in scattered populations across central Africa, and parts of west and east Africa. It has a head-body length of 1.3–2.1 m (51–83 in); a tail length of 30–45 cm (12–17¾ in); a shoulder height of 85–105 cm (33½–41¼ in); and a weight of 130–275 kg (287–606 lb). The wild boar (*Sus scrofa*) and the Java warty pig (*Sus verrucosus*) can attain maximum weights of 200 kg (441 lb) and 185 kg (408 lb) respectively.

In 1933, the heaviest domestic pig (*Sus domesticus*) ever recorded was a Poland-China hog named Big Bill, weighing 1157.5 kg (2552 lb). His other statistics included a height of 1.52 m (5 ft) at the shoulder and a length of 2.74 m (9 ft).

★ SMALLEST

The smallest of the pigs and peccaries is the pygmy hog (*Porcula salvanius*), which used to be fairly widespread in the foothills of the Himalayas but today survives only in Assam, India (it is thought to be extinct in Bhutan and Nepal). It has

Giant forest hog
The largest of the pigs and peccaries is the giant forest hog (*Hylochoerus meinertzhageni*).

a head-body length of 50–65 cm (20–25½ in); a tail length of 3 cm (1.2 in); a shoulder height of 25–30 cm (9.8–11.8 in); and a weight of 6–10 kg (13¼–22 lb). In 2007, this miniature mammal was given a new genus, *Porcula*, after tests revealed that its DNA is different to pigs and boars, which it was previously grouped with.

The smallest breed of domestic pig (*Sus domesticus*) is the Mini Maialino, developed by Stefano Morini of Italy, after ten years experimentation with Vietnamese pot-bellied pigs. The piglets weigh 400 g (14 oz) at birth and 9 kg (20 lb) at maturity.

★ LONGEST ABSENCE

The Chacoan peccary (*Catagonus wagneri*) was thought to have become extinct during the last Ice Age, some 10,000 years ago, and was known only from the fossil record. Since its discovery in 1930, there had been no evidence for its existence later than the Pleistocene (two million to 10,000 years ago). But it was unexpectedly discovered, in 1975, living in the dry thorn forest of the Gran Chaco region of western Paraguay.

Dr Ralph Wetzel and his colleagues at Connecticut University discovered that local inhabitants recognized the existence of three species of peccary (only two were known at the time) and, after detailed enquiries, succeeded in obtaining some skulls. Wetzel compared his skulls with the prehistoric peccary, which had been named *Platygonus wagneri*, and realized that they belonged to the same species. However, he concluded that it was more akin to members of the genus *Catagonus* than *Platygonus*, and it was later renamed.

STRANGEST TUSKS

Instead of growing out of the side of the mouth and over the lips, as with all other wild pigs, two of the four tusks of the babirusa (*Babyrousa babyrussa*) pierce the flesh and grow up through the top of the animal's muzzle, then curve backward towards the forehead.

PERISSODACTYL

The perissodactyls are ungulates which means that they are animals with hooves. They also have an odd number of toes. The middle or third toe is the longest, and they are extremely well adapted to running. They are browsing or grazing animals and they have very long and complex intestines to digest the plants they feed on.

HORSES, ASSES & ZEBRAS

Equidae

Eight living species: mountain zebra, Grevy's zebra, Burchell's zebra, African wild ass, kulan, kiang, onager and Przewalski's horse; the domestic donkey and the horse are normally considered sub-species of the African wild ass and Przewalski's horse respectively

★ EARLIEST

The evolutionary history of horses, asses and zebras is relatively well known. The earliest of the horse ancestors are popularly known collectively as dawn horses (e.g. *Cymbalophus*, *Pliolophus*), which appeared near the beginning of

the Eocene some 55 million years ago in Europe and North America; they were forest-dwellers and were about the size of a small dog. They had four hooved-toes on each fore foot and three on the hind. Their teeth tell us that they fed on soft leaves and fallen fruit.

The subsequent evolutionary history of horses was centered on North America, where the genus *Equus*, to which all living species belong, first appeared during the early Pliocene about 5 million years ago.

★ EARLIEST DOMESTICATION
The first domestication of the horse probably occurred in what is now the Ukraine approximately 6500 years ago, when paleolithic hunters tamed small numbers of wild horses (*Equus ferus*) for their flesh and milk (compared with 12,000 years ago for dogs and 9000 years ago for sheep). Evidence also from the Ukraine indicates that horses may have been ridden at about the same time.

★ LARGEST
Wild equids are generally smaller in size than domestic breeds. The largest is Grevy's zebra (*Equus grevyi*), which has an average head-body length of 2.5–2.7 m (8 ft 2 in–8 ft 10 in), a tail length of 50–70 cm (20–27½ in), a height at the shoulder of 1.5 m (59 in) and a weight of

350–430 kg (772–948 lb) – with a maximum weight of 450 kg (992 lb). As with all members of the family, males are normally 10% larger than females.

The tallest and heaviest domestic horse was the shire gelding Sampson (later renamed Mammoth), bred by Thomas Cleaver of Toddington Mills, Bedfordshire, UK. This horse (foaled 1846) measured 21.25 hands (2.19 m or 7 ft 2½ in) in 1850, and was later said to have weighed 1524 kg (3360 lb).

★ SMALLEST
The wild ass (*Equus africanus*) is the smallest of the wild equids. It has an average head-body length of 2 m (79 in), a tail length of 42 cm (16½ in) and a weight of about 275 kg (606 lb).

The smallest domesticated horse was the stallion 'Little Pumpkin' (foaled 15 April 1973), which stood 35.5 cm (14 in) and weighed 9.07 kg (20 lb) on 30 November 1975. It was owned by J. C. Williams Jr of Della Terra Mini Horse Farm, Inman, South Carolina, USA.

The smallest breed of horse is the Falabella of Argentina, which was developed by Julio Falabella of Recco de Roca. Most adult specimens stand less than 76 cm (30 in) and average 36–15 kg (80–100 lb) in weight. The smallest example was an adult mare which was 38 cm (15 in) tall and weighed 11.9 kg (26¼ lb).

Grevy's zebra
Like all horses, zebras and asses, Grevy's zebras have outstanding eyesight. They have binocular vision in front, can probably see colour and their acute night vision ranks with that of owls. No two zebras have stripes that are exactly alike; even the patterns on opposite sides of a zebra's body do not match exactly.

★ LONGEST LIVING
The greatest age reliably recorded for a domestic horse is 62 years for 'Old Billy' (foaled 1760), believed to be a cross between a Cleveland and Eastern blood, which was bred by Edward Robinson of Woolston, Lancashire, UK. In 1762/63 the horse was sold to the Mersey and Irwell Navigation Company and remained with them in a working capacity (mainly marshalling and towing barges) until 1819, when he was retired to a farm at Latchford, near Warrington, UK. He died on 27 November 1822.

The average longevity of wild equids is believed to be about 10–25 years in the wild and can be up to 35 years in captivity.

★ FASTEST
In horse racing, the highest speed record is 69.62 km/h (43.26 mph) by 'Big Racket' (20.8 seconds for 402 m (¼ mile)) at Mexico City, Mexico, on 5 February 1945; the four-year-old carried 51.7 kg (114 lb).

The record for 2414 m (1½ miles) is 60.86 km/h (37.82 mph) by three-year-old 'Hawkster', carrying 54.9 kg (121 lb) at Santa Anita Park, Arcadia, California, USA, on 14 October 1989 with a time of 2 min 22.8 s.

Wild horses (*Equus caballus*) living in an inhospitable region of Serrado, on Brazil's border with Venezuela, are reputed to accelerate faster than domestic horses and, according to Embrapa, Brazil's national agricultural research institute, can maintain a top speed of 60 km/h (37¼ mph) for much longer than a racehorse. Known as the 'wild horses of Roraima', their numbers have dwindled in recent years to no more than a few hundred.

MOST VALUABLE
The world's most valuable animals (in terms of money) are racehorses. The most paid for a thoroughbred at public auction is $16 million for a two-year-old colt at Calder Race Course, Florida, USA, 28 February 2006.

★ STRONGEST
On 23 April 1924 a shire gelding named 'Vulcan', owned by the Liverpool Corporation, registered a pull equal to a starting load of 29–47 tonnes on a dynamometer at the British Empire Exhibition at Wembley, London. At the same event, a pair of shires easily pulled a starting load of 51 tonnes, the maximum registered on the dynamometer. There is a widely reported record of a pair of draught-horses (combined weight 1587 kg (3500 lb)) which hauled a load, allegedly weighing 130.9 tonnes, on a sledge litter for a distance of 402 m (1319 ft) along a frozen road at the Nester Estate near Ewen, Michigan, USA, on 26 February 1893. However, this tonnage was exaggerated: the load, which comprised 50 logs of white pine measuring 36,055 board feet, actually weighed about 42.3 tonnes.

RHINOCEROSES

Rhinocerotidae
Five species: two in Africa and three in Asia

★ EARLIEST
Many different species of rhino (superfamily Rhinocerotoidea), belonging to nearly 100 distinct genera are known from the fossil record. The ancestral forms first appeared in the Eocene, some 50 million years ago, when they were much smaller and more lightly built than their modern relatives and lacked horns. The most primitive known was called *Hyrachyus*, which was the size of an Alsatian dog and, in common with the earliest horses, had four toes on the front feet and three on the hind. The smallest, *Rhodopagus*, was only the size of a house cat and lived in central Asia around 45 million years ago; the largest, *Paraceratherium*, living around 30 million years ago, was also the largest of all land mammals and stood 5 m (16½ ft) tall at the shoulder (*see* LARGEST PREHISTORIC p. 24). The first animals belonging to the family Rhinocerotidae to have a substantial resemblance to modern rhinos were *Trigonias* and

Black rhinoceros
All types of rhino have incredibly thick skin, about 2.5 cm (1 in) on their back and flanks, to protect them from the horns of other rhinos. A 'normal' mammal of the same weight would have skin about a sixth as thick.

MAMMALS

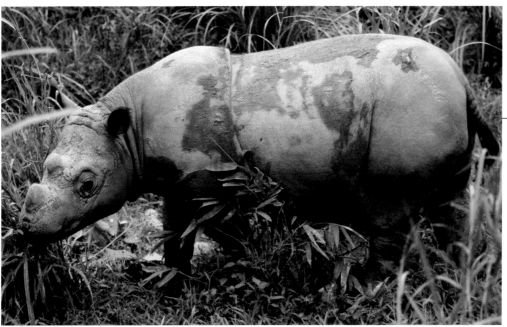

Sumatran rhino
The smallest of the rhinos is the Sumatran rhinoceros which on average is little more than 1 m (3¼ ft) at the shoulder.

Subhyracodon, which appeared in North America during the Late Eocene some 35 million years ago; they were distinctly rhinoceros-shaped, although they still lacked horns. All five modern rhino species are descended from a common ancestor, dating from the Miocene epoch; the African evolutionary line split from the Asian line about 10 million years ago.

★ MOST PRIMITIVE
The Sumatran rhinoceros (*Dicerorhinus sumatrensis*) is unusual among living rhinos as it is covered with dense, dark reddish-brown fur. It has close relatives that lived as long ago as 25 million years before the present day. It is also closely related to the extinct woolly rhinoceros (*Coelodonta antiquitatis*) a well-known species which lived during the Pleistocene Ice Age in Eurasia between about 1 million and 10,000 years ago.

★ LARGEST
The largest of the rhinos is the white or square-lipped rhinoceros (*Ceratotherium simum*), which is restricted to southern and central Africa. It can attain a height of up to 1.85 m (6 ft) at the shoulder and a length of 4.2 m (13¾ ft); the maximum weight is about 3.6 tonnes (males are heavier than females). The black

rhinoceros (*Diceros bicornis*) has been known to reach a similar height at the shoulder, 1.8 m (5 ft 11 in), but is usually shorter and considerably lighter (maximum weight about 1.45 tonnes).

★ LARGEST PREHISTORIC
The largest land mammal ever recorded was the giant 'giraffe' rhinoceros (*Paraceratherium*), a long-necked, hornless rhinocerotoid which roamed across Asia and eastern Europe during the Oligocene epoch. It is known from fossil bones which were first discovered in the Bugti Hills of Baluchistan, Pakistan, in 1907–08. A restoration in the American Museum of Natural History, New York City, USA, measures 5.41 m (17 ft 9 in) to the top of the shoulder hump and 11.27 m (37 ft) in total length. It was so tall, it had the reach of a modern giraffe and could feed on leaves high in the treetops. The most likely maximum weight of this browser was revised in 1993 to 11–20 tonnes from earlier

estimates of 34 tonnes; although there are well-established techniques for estimating the size of extinct animals from fragments of fossil bones (using living animals as a guide), rhinoceroses are deceptive because they have skeletons which are far more robust than is necessary to support their bulk. *Paraceratherium* became extinct about 25 million years ago.

★ MOST THREATENED
All five species of rhinoceros – white (*Ceratotherium simum*), black (*Diceros bicornis*), Indian (*Rhinoceros unicornis*), Sumatran (*Dicerorhinus sumatrensis*) and Javan (*Rhinoceros sondaicus*) – are threatened with extinction. No other large mammals, except possibly the tiger, give cause for greater concern. The main threat is poaching for their horn, which is used as an ingredient in traditional Chinese medicines with particular popularity.

> The population of black rhinoceroses in Africa declined by about 97.5% in just 30 years, making it one of the fastest-disappearing large mammals in the world.

in South Korea, and, to a lesser extent is carved to make dagger handles worn by many men in Yemen. Dealing in rhino horn has become as lucrative as pushing drugs and, even for local villagers at the beginning of a chain of people in the trade, the temptation to poach is irresistible.

★ SMALLEST

The smallest rhino is the Sumatran rhinoceros (*Dicerorhinus sumatrensis*), which is sparsely scattered in Southeast Asia. It can attain a maximum shoulder height of 1.5 m (4 ft 11 in) but the average is little more than 1 m (3¼ ft).

★ LONGEST HORN

The longest recorded anterior horn for a rhinoceros is one of 1.58 m (62¼ in) found on a female southern white rhinoceros (*Ceratotherium simum simum*) shot in South Africa in *c.* 1848. The posterior horn measured 57 cm (22¼ in).

TAPIRS

Tapiridae

Four species: Baird's, mountain and Brazilian tapirs in South America and the Malayan tapir in southern Asia

★ EARLIEST

Tapirs are among the most primitive large mammals in the world and, indeed, it is thought that they are still very similar to the common ancestors of all perissodactyls which lived more than 50 million years ago. The modern genus *Tapirus* first appeared in the Miocene nearly 20 million years ago.

★ LARGEST

The largest tapir is the Malayan or Asian tapir (*Tapirus indicus*), which is well known for its striking black and white markings. It has a head-body length of 2.2–2.5 m (7¼–8 ft); a tail length of 5–10 cm (2–4 in); a height at the shoulder of 95–110 cm (37½–43¼ ft); and weighs 250–360 kg (551–794 lb). One individual is reputed to have weighed 540 kg (1191 lb).

★ SMALLEST

The mountain or woolly tapir (*Tapirus pinchaque*) is the smallest member of the tapir family. It has an average head-body length of 1.8 m (71 in); a tail length of 5 cm (2 in); a shoulder height of 75 cm (29½ in); and an average weight of 225 kg (496 lb).

★ HIGHEST LIVING

The mountain tapir (*Tapirus pinchaque*) lives consistently at a height of 2000–4500 m (6560–14,760 ft) in the upper reaches of the Andes (up to 4700 m (15,400ft)). This is a region of low temperatures and almost perpetual mist and so, not surprisingly, it is the only member of the family with a long, thick coat of hair. Other tapirs live at high altitudes, but they also occur down to sea level.

Malayan tapir
The striking black and white Malayan tapir is the largest member of the tapir family.

BATS

Chiroptera

c. 1100 species. 173 Megachiroptera (herbivorous or fruit bats) and c. 920 Microchiroptera (predominantly insect eating)

★ EARLIEST

The earliest known fossil bats date from about 55 million years ago, although remains of these are rather fragmentary. The oldest complete skeleton of a bat belongs to a species called *Icaronycteris index*, which was found in ancient lake deposits in Wyoming, USA. It lived during the Eocene 53 million years ago and, according to its teeth, was insectivorous (significantly, insect-eating bats, and possibly all bats, are thought to have evolved from land-based insectivores). *Icaronycteris* was an active flier, suggesting that bats of one kind or another must have been around much earlier.

★ LARGEST

The largest bats in the world are the flying foxes (family Pteropodidae), particularly those living in Southeast Asia. Several species in the genus *Pteropus* may have a head-body length of 45 cm (17¾ in); a wingspan of at least 1.7 m (5 ft 7 in); a fore arm length of 23 cm (9 in); and a weight of 1.6 kg (3½ lb). Unfortunately, there is insufficient agreement among experts to identify the overall largest with certainty, although it is probably either the appropriately named gigantic or Indian flying fox (*Pteropus giganteus*), which lives on the Indian sub-continent and the Maldives or a population of large flying foxes (*Pteropus vampyrus*) also living on the Maldives. The other main contenders are the Bismarck or great flying fox (*Pteropus neohibernicus*) and the Samoan flying fox (*Pteropus samoensis*).

★ SMALLEST

The smallest mammal in the world is the bumblebee or Kitti's hog-nosed bat (*Craseonycteris thonglongyai*), which is confined to the deepest and darkest chambers of about 21 limestone caves (population of only about 5000) in Sai Yok National Park, Kanchanaburi Province, southwest Thailand, and in the Kayah-Karen rainforests of Myanmar. It has a head-body length of 2.9–3.3 cm (1–1⅓ in); a forearm length of 2.2–2.6 cm (¾–1 in); a wingspan of approximately 15–16 cm (6–6⅓ in); and a weight of 1.7–2 g (³⁄₅₀–⁷⁄₁₀₀ oz). It was discovered in October 1973 by the Thai mammal researcher Dr Kitti Thonglongya, who sadly died less than five months later. His sensational discovery was confirmed in 1974, when the bat was described for science bearing his name.

Bats are by far the most efficient echolocators of all terrestrial animals, using the echoes of their ultrasonic calls and clicks to detect objects as small as midges from at least 20 m (65 ft) away.

★ ECHOLOCATION

Echolocation is an extremely sophisticated form of sonar, in which an animal builds up a 'sound picture' of its surroundings by listening for the returning echoes of sounds it produces to locate objects in its path. In bats, which are by far the most efficient echolocators of all terrestrial mammals, it enables them to gather information on the distance, direction and relative velocity of an object, as well as its shape, size and texture; some species are able to detect objects as small as midges from at least 20 m (65½ ft) away.

The calls and clicks produced by echolocating bats are mostly ultrasonic (beyond the range of human hearing) and are very complex, made up of different sounds of varying frequencies. Most species use frequencies in the 20–80 kHz range, although some go as high as 120–250 kHz (the normal range of human hearing is 20 Hz to almost 20 kHz). Their ultrasonic pulses vary in duration from about 0.2 milliseconds to 100 milliseconds and are repeated at regular intervals, according to the bat's activity. A hunting bat will search using an emission rate of about 3–10 pulses per second; this

Flying fox
Flying foxes or fruit bats are the largest of the bats and live in large colonies of up to eight million individuals. This colony is in the Northern Territory, Australia.

increases to 15–50 per second once a flying insect has been detected; and, in the final approach stage, it increases still further to as much as 200 pulses per second, providing the bat with continuous information about its target. The sounds are produced in the larynx and, in most species, emitted through the open mouth; however, bats with nose leaves tend to 'call' through their nostrils (and, consequently, fly with their mouths closed).

It is presumed that all bats in the sub-order Microchiroptera are able to echolocate, although only a small number have been studied in detail. The only fruit bats or flying foxes (suborder *Megachiroptera*) known to do it are a few members of the genus *Rousettus*, such as the Egyptian fruit bat (*R. aegyptiacus*). *Rousettus* species roost in caves and need to be able to find their way in and out in total darkness; they use a very simple form of echolocation and produce orientation sounds by clicking their tongue against the side of their mouth.

★ LONGEST EARS

The spotted bat (*Euderma maculatum*), which occurs from northern Mexico through the western USA to south-western Canada, is an extraordinary-looking animal. Its ears are longer in proportion to its body than any other species of bat. An enormous 4.5–5 cm (1.8–2 in) long (compared with a head-body length of 6–7.7 cm (2½–3 in)), they make the species unmistakable. Only some related species of long-eared bats in the genus *Plecotus* have ears that are proportionally almost as large (ears up to 4 cm (1½ in) in length compared with a head-body length of 4.5–7 cm (1¾–2¾ in)).

★ FASTEST

Because of their erratic flying patterns, and therefore the great practical difficulties in obtaining accurate measurements, few data on bat speeds have been published. In one US experiment in the 1960s, using an artificial mine tunnel and 17 different species of bat, only four of them managed to exceed 20.8 km/h (13 mph) in level flight. The fastest was a big brown bat (*Eptesicus fuscus*), which reached a

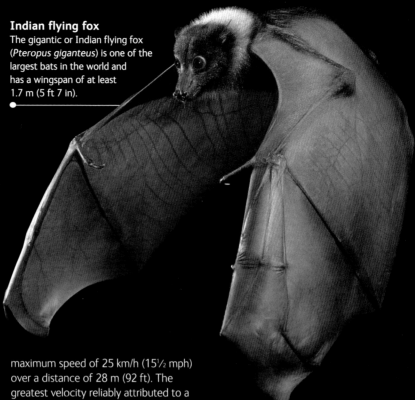

Indian flying fox
The gigantic or Indian flying fox (*Pteropus giganteus*) is one of the largest bats in the world and has a wingspan of at least 1.7 m (5 ft 7 in).

maximum speed of 25 km/h (15½ mph) over a distance of 28 m (92 ft). The greatest velocity reliably attributed to a bat is 51 km/h (32 mph) in the case of a Mexican free-tailed bat (*Tadarida brasiliensis*), but this may have been wind-assisted. Higher, unauthenticated speeds have been claimed. Fast-flying bats tend to have long, narrow wings, while agile, slow-flying species have broad wings.

★ LONGEST LIVING

Bats are relatively long-lived for their size and, once an individual has survived the most dangerous period from birth to weaning, 5–8 years is fairly typical for most species. There are a number of records of Daubenton's bats (*Myotis daubentonii*), greater horseshoe bats (*Rhinolophus ferrumequinum*), little brown bats (*Myotis lucifugus*) and gigantic or Indian flying foxes (*Pteropus giganteus*) living for about 30 years. The greatest age reliably reported for a bat is at least 41 years for a male Brandt's bat (*Myotis brandti*). Recaptured from the wild in 2006, the bat bore a numbered ring that had been attached by researchers who captured and branded 1544 bats near caves in Russia's Siberia in the 1960s. The bat was alive and well when it was released for the second time.

Why bats live for so much longer than other small mammals is a fascinating question that makes them of special interest to researchers studying the mechanisms of ageing.

★ LONGEST GESTATION PERIOD

The longest known gestation period for any bat is seven to eight months in the common vampire (*Desmodus rotundus*); the baby then suckles for a further nine months or more (changing its diet from milk to blood in stages). Several other species have exceptionally long delays between mating and birth of the young: either the egg is fertilized at mating and the development of the embryo is delayed, or fertilization itself is delayed. These long delays often coincide with hibernation. They give an 'apparent' gestation period of nine months or more in the North American little brown bat (*Myotis lucifugus*) and, indeed, most other temperate bats; however, the true period of embryonic development in each of these species is only six to eight weeks.

★ MALE LACTATION

The relatively uncommon Dayak fruit bat (*Dyacopterus spadiceus*) is the only wild mammal in which the male is known to produce milk. This remarkable discovery, which overturns a fundamental assumption about mammals, was made by a team of scientists from the New York Zoological Society, Rhode Island College and Boston University during a study of bats in the Krau Game Reserve, Pahang, Malaysia, in 1992. They happened to catch 13 male Dayak fruit bats, ten of which were sexually mature and had working mammary glands that were producing milk (albeit in small quantities). It is unknown if the bats were actually suckling young animals. Milk production by male mammals is not without precedent, but is isolated and rare and normally due to abnormalities such as extreme inbreeding in domestic animals and hormone treatment in humans.

> An inexperienced mother-to-be was helped by a roost mate who fanned her, sometimes embraced her body with spread wings and even appeared to give her instructions.

★ MIDWIFE BATS

The only bats known to give birth with the assistance of another are the rare Rodrigues fruit bat (*Pteropus rodricensis*) and the black flying fox (*Pteropus alecto*). Professor Thomas Kunz and colleagues from Boston University observed this for the first time on 5 August 1991, during a study of a small captive colony of Rodrigues fruit bats at the Lubee Foundation in Gainsville, Florida, USA. When an inexperienced mother-to-be was having problems giving birth, a female roost mate came to her aid and finally, after a rather difficult delivery lasting 1 hr 43 min, the 'midwife' even helped to manoeuvre the pup into a suckling position. Similar observations were reported soon afterwards in a captive colony of black flying foxes (*Pteropus alecto*) at a research station in Queensland, Australia. It is possible that such cooperative behaviour is common in colonial bats, and the fact that it had not been observed before may simply be because few people have ever seen a bat giving birth.

★ LARGEST LITTER

Most bats give birth to only one young at a time, although twins occur regularly in some species. The only bats which commonly have more than two young are members of the genus *Lasiurus*: the hoary bat (*L. cinereus*), northern yellow bat (*L. intermedius*), seminole bat (*L. seminolus*) and, in particular, the red bat (*L. borealis*) all produce litters of up to four. There is one report of two female red bats with

Rodrigues fruit bat
The rare Rodrigues fruit bat (*Pteropus rodricensis*) is often given help from other bats or 'mid-wives' in the roost during birth.

Little brown bat
To survive winter when there is no food and it is cold, bats either migrate to warmer climates or hibernate. The little brown bat (*Myotis lucifugus*) can hibernate for up to 86 days.

five young each, although it is possible that they were fostering orphans from other parents. The number of young varies between individuals as well as species, depending on latitude, food availability, the age and experience of the females and a variety of other factors.

Many tropical bats have more than one litter every year. Female common vampire bats (*Desmodus rotundus*) sometimes have four reproductive cycles in a year. But the record-holder is probably Wroughton's pipistrelle (*Pipistrellus minus*) which lives in Asia; the female bears twins and may have as many as three litters annually. This species reaches sexual maturity at five months, which is probably earlier than in any other bat.

★ SHORTEST GESTATION PERIOD

The shortest known gestation period in bats, by a very small margin, is probably 40–45 days in the common pipistrelle (*Pipistrellus pipistrellus*), which lives in Europe and southwestern Asia. However, many other temperate species have similarly short gestation periods.

★ LARGEST COLONIES

The largest concentration of bats anywhere in the world is a summer nursery of Mexican free-tailed bats (*Tadarida brasiliensis*) found in about a dozen caves in Texas, USA. These bats have the distinction of attaining a higher population density than any other mammal (including humans). At one time, there were estimated to be 100 million of them but, after the indiscriminate and widespread use of DDT in North America in the 1960s and vandalism, the population crashed to less than three million; their numbers have largely recovered in recent years. One particular cave (Bracken Cave near San Antonio) is probably the most populous bat cave in the world; ten million females (which have migrated some 800–1800 km (500–1200

miles) from their wintering grounds in Mexico) give birth over a 7–10 day period, resulting in ten million baby bats in one place. Several of the other caves are almost as crowded, being home to more than five million females and their young.

Since there can be as many as 3000 baby free-tailed bats per m^2 (280 per ft^2) of ceiling, and because they are always jostling one another and moving around, it can be difficult for a female to locate her own baby. After a feeding flight, she enters the dark cave and uses memory to alight to within a few feet of where she had seen it last. She calls, waits for the baby to answer and then scrambles past the other youngsters (all trying to steal a drink of milk) until she is close enough to recognize it by smell. Research has shown that the females are successful in finding their own babies 85% of the time.

Colonies of more than 1000 bats are now rare in Europe. Earlier reports suggest *c.*100,000 pipistrelles (*Pipistrellus pipistrellus*) in a cave in Romania, but one of the largest today is a group of 60,000 Schreiber's bats (*Miniopterus schreibersii*), which was discovered in the 1980s in a

cave in the northeastern Pyrenees, in Aude, France. But perhaps the most important – certainly in northern Europe – is a colony living in an old military underground tunnel system (built by the Germans before and during the Second World War) in western Poland. More than 20,000 bats of 12 different species hibernate in the tunnels of the former Miedzyrzecki Fortified Region in the Lubuskie Lake District, about 100 km

> The US Air Force at Randolph Air Force Base, Texas, USA, schedules the flights of its aircraft around the activities of Mexican free-tailed bats, which live in enormous colonies nearby.

(62 miles) west of Poznan. The tunnels comprise about 30 km (18½ miles) of reinforced concrete passages some 30 m (100 ft) below ground. The most numerous species (accounting for a little more than half the total population) is Daubenton's bat (*Myotis daubentonii*).

★ LONGEST HIBERNATION

In temperate zones, in order to survive the long, foodless winters, bats have a choice between migrating to warmer regions with a sufficient food supply or hibernating and surviving without food. Most species choose to hibernate and, indeed, some spend longer periods of time in uninterrupted hibernation than any other mammal. Under natural conditions, little brown bats (*Myotis lucifugus*) have been known to remain without movement for up to 86 days and big brown bats (*Eptesicus fuscus*) have been observed in the same state for 64–66 days. Under laboratory conditions, however, several

European noctule bat

The noctule bat (*Nyctalus noctula*), here pictured leaving a black woodpecker nest hole in a tree in Germany, is one of the species of bat to migrate to warmer southern European climates in the winter.

down costs no energy (indeed, it often continues after death) since there is a tendon that prevents the hook-like toes from straightening. Unlike many other hibernators, bats may not feed again until the following spring, but they do wake at intervals (on average every 20 days) to move to a different part of the hibernaculum or even to another site (and may eat if the opportunity arises). Waking is also essential for them to drink: they lose water by breathing and dehydrate easily. Even though bats may be awake for only 2–4% of the winter, these brief natural interludes consume more than 75% of their total energy reserves; a single forced arousal caused by disturbance uses up so

members of the genera *Nyctalus*, *Vespertilio*, *Lasiurus*, *Lasionycteris*, *Pipistrellus* and *Tadarida*. The longest true flight recorded was 2347 km (1458 miles) by a European noctule (*Nyctalus noctula*), which was ringed in August 1957 by Russian zoologist P. P. Strelkov, at Voronezh, Russia, and was found again in southern Bulgaria in January 1961. The North American red bat (*Lasiurus borealis*) migrates as far as 2000 km (1242 miles) on occasion, and Mexican free-tailed bats (*Tadarida brasiliensis*) in the south-western USA travel 1600 km (1000 miles) into the Mexican interior each autumn.

There are also a number of cases where migrating bats have been blown

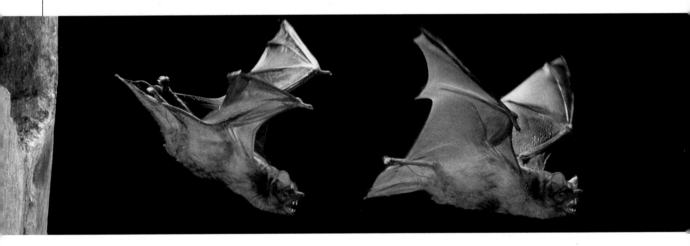

species have been kept in uninterrupted hibernation for much longer (in one exceptional case a big brown bat was kept in a controlled refrigerator for 344 days before it died of starvation).

Hibernating bats spend the autumn fattening up (increasing their total body weight by as much as 25–35%) and survive the winter on their fat reserves. They spend up to six months in a state of extended lethargy, lowering their metabolism dramatically to reduce energy consumption. Their body temperature falls to about the level of their surroundings; their heart rate may decrease to around 25 beats/min (compared with more than 1000/min while flying); and their breathing may drop to a rate of as little as one breath every 45 minutes (some individuals have been known to go for two hours between breaths). Even hanging upside

much extra energy (equivalent to up to 50 days in hibernation) that it can mean the difference between starvation and survival.

★ LOWEST BODY TEMPERATURE

Many hibernating bats can allow their bodies to cool almost to freezing point. But the North American red bat (*Lasiurus borealis*) can withstand its body tissues actually freezing into ice at temperatures well below freezing, without suffering any serious ill effects. It has the thickest fur, the lowest heart rate at low temperatures and the highest red blood cell count of any bat.

★ LONGEST MIGRATION

A number of temperate bat species undertake seasonal migrations to avoid the extremes of winter; these include

thousands of kilometres off course. The record-holder for wind-assisted flights must be the hoary bat (*Lasiurus cinereus*), which managed to reach the Hawaiian Islands, USA, located some 3700 km (2300 miles) from the American mainland at the nearest point. It has now established itself as a separate island sub-species *Lasiurus c. semotus*.

★ MOST NORTHERLY

The population of northern bats (*Eptesicus nilssonii*) living high above the Arctic Circle, in the north of Norway, is by far the most northerly population of bats anywhere in the world. One individual has even been seen at Austertana in Finnmark (70°N 25°E). Their presence is probably influenced by the Gulf Stream, which makes the climate there much warmer than in other areas at the same latitude.

★ ROOST BUILDING

Many different bat species have been recorded creating secure, dry day-time roosts, typically by turning single leaves into simple tents. But the champion is Peters' tent-making bat (*Uroderma bilobatum*), which has been studied on Barro Colorado Island, Panama, by Dr Jae Choe of Harvard University. This appropriately named species builds a sophisticated tepee-shaped tent, from as many as 14 leaves, each about 44 cm (17 in) long and 21 cm (8 in) wide, and the bats simply fly in and out of the bottom. It gives excellent protection from downpours and is spacious enough to accommodate up to three bats. No females have yet been recorded using a tepee and, since the building process has also never been observed, it is uncertain whether a single bat makes it or if several bats cooperate.

★ STRONGEST FLIER

The female red bat (*Lasiurus borealis*) is stronger in flight than any other species of bat and is capable of carrying two or even three infants (easily exceeding her own body weight) as they cling to her fur. Vampire bats (family Desmodontidae) are able to fly on exceedingly full stomachs.

★ DEEPEST

A colony of 1000 little brown bats (*Myotis lucifugus*) spends the winter at a record depth of 1160 m (3805 ft) in a zinc mine in New York, USA.

★ LONGEST ABSENCE

Bulmer's fruit bat (*Aproteles bulmerae*) was thought to have become extinct 9000–12,000 years ago and was known only from 200 incomplete fossils excavated in the 1970s in New Guinea. However, palaeontologist James I. Menzies identified some skulls left unstudied in a back room at the Australian Museum, Sydney, as belonging to Bulmer's fruit bat. When traced in 1977, it transpired that the original colony had been wiped out by local people but, in May 1992, another colony containing 137 of the bats was found in a single cave within the Hindenberg ranges. The current population is about 200 animals.

WORLD RECORD HOLDER

Blood drinking

Vampire bats (family Desmodontidae) are the only mammals that feed exclusively on blood. They have the most extreme dietary specialization of any bat and are also the only true bat parasites. There are three species, found only in Central and South America: the hairy-legged vampire (*Diphylla ecaudata*) and the white-winged vampire (*Diaemus youngi*), both of which feed almost exclusively on bird blood; and the appropriately named common vampire (*Desmodus rotundus*), which feeds almost exclusively on mammalian blood. They are fairly small bats, with a head-body length of only 65–69 cm (2½–3½ in); a wingspan of 32–35 cm (12½–13¼ in); and a weight of about 40 g (1½ oz).

The common vampire is normally active on dark, moonless nights. Once it has found a victim, it lands on the ground a few feet away and walks, runs or hops its way across (vampires are more agile on the ground than any other species of bat); if it has chosen a horse or mule it may land on the tail or mane instead. With the help of a heat sensor on its nose, it identifies an area where the blood flows close to the skin and begins to lick over an area of about 0.5 cm ($^3/_{16}$ in) in diameter. If there is fur in the way it uses its large, razor-sharp upper incisor teeth to clip it away, and then carefully removes a flap of skin – rather like a golf divot. The bite is normally painless (the victim rarely wakes up) and the vampire's saliva contains an anticoagulant that prevents the blood from clotting. Contrary to popular belief, it does not suck the blood through its 'fangs', but has a special way of licking it up as it oozes freely from the wound.

A vampire needs at least 20 g (¾ oz) of blood every day to survive (equivalent to two tablespoons or half its own body weight), and normally takes about 20 minutes to drink its fill. Within two minutes of beginning to feed, it starts to urinate to get rid of the blood plasma, which is heavy and contains no nutritive value (it is easier to fly afterwards on a less full stomach). Each bat feeds only once in a night (after feeding it returns to its roost to digest the meal) but may return night after night to the same victim (reopening the old wound on subsequent visits).

Blood loss is generally not a problem with bites caused by vampire bats, as relatively small amounts are involved. The greatest risk is from infected bats transmitting diseases such as rabies and from subsequent invasion by screw worms and other parasites.

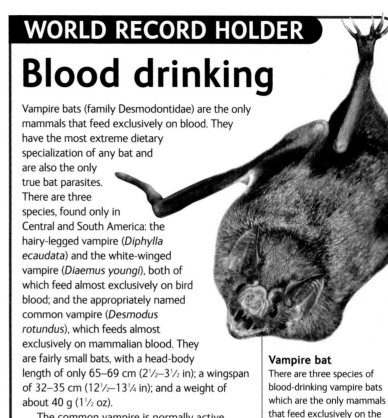

Vampire bat
There are three species of blood-drinking vampire bats which are the only mammals that feed exclusively on the blood of birds or mammals, and are the only true bat parasites. This is a common vampire bat (*Desmodus rotundus*).

CARNIVORES

Carnivores (members of the order Carnivora) are animals whose diet consists mainly but not wholly of meat, and this meat can be either living or dead. Some species, like wolves, seals, or bears may have to hunt for prey, or they may have to scavenge for it like hyenas. They typically have very large teeth which are made for grasping and tearing their food.

BEARS

Ursidae
Eight species, including giant panda (once considered to be a member of the raccoon family)

★ EARLIEST
The first real bear-like carnivore is thought to have evolved from a dog-like animal called *Cephalogale* and appeared around 5–6 million years ago. It ultimately gave rise to all other bears.

★ MOST PRIMITIVE
The most primitive bear alive today is the giant panda (*Ailuropoda melanoleuca*). Current evidence suggests that it diverged from the other bears between 18 and 25 million years ago.

The spectacled bear (*Tremarctos ornatus*) diverged from the other bears between 12 and 15 million years ago and is also very primitive. It is the only living relative of the giant short-faced bear (*Arctodus simus*), a species that became extinct about 10,000 years ago. The two animals share several characteristics: a short muzzle and similar skull proportions, and primitive auditory bullae (small projections of the skull enclosing the middle ear) and primitive teeth.

★ LARGEST
The largest bear in the world is the polar bear (*Ursus maritimus*). Adult males typically weigh 400–600 kg (880–1323 lb), although it is known that the weight of different individuals can fluctuate

Kodiak bear
The male Kodiak bear is the most heavily built bear in the world. The largest confirmed record in the wild was a male shot at English Bay, Kodiak Island, in the Gulf of Alaska, USA, in 1894; it weighed 751 kg (1656 lb) and its stretched skin measured 4.11 m (13 ft 6 in) from nose to tail.

Spectacled bear
The spectacled bear (*Tremarctos ornatus*) has the most varied diet of any bear, from deer to berries; here, it is eating a puya plant in South America.

enormously during the course of a year; they have a nose-to-tail length of 2.4–2.6 m (95–102 in); the tail itself measures 8–13 cm (3–5 in). Adult females reach a maximum length of around 2 m (80 in) and are roughly half the weight of the males. The largest polar bear on record was a male that allegedly weighed 1002 kg (2210 lb) when it was shot at the polar entrance to Kotzebue Sound, Alaska, USA, in 1960; it is now on display at Anchorage Airport, where it stands 3.4 m (11 ft 2 in) tall.

A few brown bears (*Ursus arctos*) in Alaska, USA, have been known to reach a similar size. In 1981 an unconfirmed weight of over 907 kg (2000 lb) was reported for a brown bear from Alaska, USA, on exhibition at the Space Farms Zoological Park at Beemerville, New Jersey, USA.

The male Kodiak bear (*U. a. middendorffi*), a sub-species of brown bear found on Kodiak Island and the adjacent Afognak and Shuyak islands, in the Gulf of Alaska, USA, is generally shorter in length than the polar bear but is usually more robustly built. Again, the male is usually larger than the female. Male Kodiak bears weigh 475–530 kg (1050–1170 lb) and have a nose-to-tail length of 1.7–2.8 m (5 ft 7 in–9 ft 2 in), with the tail measuring 6–21 cm (2³/₈–8¹/₄ in) they stand up to 1.5 m (4 ft 11 in) at the shoulder. The largest Kodiak bear on record was a 'cage-fat' male in the Cheyenne Mountain Zoological Park, Colorado Springs, USA, which weighed 757 kg (1670 lb) at the time of its death on 22 September 1955.

There are reports of giant bears weighing as much as 1134 kg (2500 lb) living on the Kamchatka Peninsula, Russia, but scientific evidence is virtually non-existent.

★ SMALLEST
The sun bear (*Helarctos malayanus*) of tropical forests in Southeast Asia, is the smallest of the bears, measuring 1.2–1.5 m (4–5 ft) in length and weighing 27–65 kg (60–145 lb). Males are 10–20% larger than females.

★ SMALLEST CUB
Newborn bears are extremely small compared to the newborn of other carnivores and are typically less than 1% of their mother's weight. The smallest, in actual size as well as in relation to the size of its mother, is the giant panda (*Ailuropoda melanoleuca*), which weighs only 85–140 g (3–5 oz) at birth; this is roughly the same size as an adult mole. Since the weight of a female giant panda is 70–100 kg (155–220 lb) the cub is, on average, 0.13% of the weight of its mother.

★ MOST VARIED DIET
The spectacled bear (*Tremarctos ornatus*) probably has the most varied diet of all the bears, eating from a range of over

in Wolong Natural Reserve, Sichuan Province, China, was observed to eat 3481 bamboo stems in one sitting.

★ MOST SPECIALIZED DIET

Several bear species have very specialized diets. The sloth bear (*Melursus ursinus*) is almost entirely insectivorous and feeds mainly on termites, for example, while the polar bear (*Ursus maritimus*) eats primarily ringed seals. The giant panda (*Ailuropoda melanoleuca*) feeds almost exclusively on bamboo stems, branches and leaves, which account for as much as 99% of its diet. Although as many as 30 species of bamboo are eaten throughout the panda's range, each panda usually survives on only a handful of different species. Very occasionally, it will eat other plants, such as tufted grass, crocuses and vines, the carrion of dead deer or takin, and even fish, pikas and rodents.

★ WEIGHT GAIN

Several species of bear live a continuous cycle of feast and famine: they spend most of the winter asleep and most of their waking time searching for food and eating. They do not hide the food, but store it as a thick layer of fat on their bodies; as a result, their fat deposits may constitute more than 50% of their total body weight by the end of the summer. The greatest increase in weight recorded was for an adult female polar bear (*Ursus maritimus*) weighed in western Hudson Bay, Canada; she increased her weight by a factor of five from 97 kg (2141 lb) in late November to 505 kg (1121 lb) the following August.

In the spring and early summer, polar bears (*Ursus maritimus*) feed on recently weaned ringed seal pups, which can be up to 50% fat. The seals are so plentiful from April to July that the bears sometimes eat only the layer of fat beneath the skin and leave the rest of the carcass untouched. For these few months of the year, the bears may have the highest kilojoule intake of fat of any mammal.

80 different food items, including rabbits, deer, vicuña, birds, berries, 32 species of fruit, 22 species of bromeliad, 11 species of cactus, mosses and orchid bulbs.

★ LARGEST APPETITE

The giant panda (*Ailuropoda melanoleuca*) has to spend up to 15 hours a day feeding in order to survive. It eats more food in relation to its body weight than any other bear and, unlike other members of the family with large appetites, feeds all year round. It is able to digest no more than 21% of the bamboo it eats and, consequently, every day it has to consume up to 15% of its body weight in bamboo leaves and stems (which it eats mainly during winter) or as much as 38% of its body weight in bamboo shoots (which it eats mainly in the spring); this is equivalent to 10–45 kg (22–99 lb) of food a day. One wild panda,

MOST RESOURCEFUL

An American black bear in Yosemite National Park, California, USA, specialized in stealing food from Volkswagens. It discovered they were air-tight when everything was closed and would climb on to the roof and jump up and down until it caved in: the resulting air pressure forcing the doors open.

★ WEIGHT LOSS

Brown bears (*Ursus arctos*), black bears (*Ursus americanus*) and female polar bears (*Ursus maritimus*) go into a deep sleep for the winter and survive by burning up their fat reserves. Their body weight falls dramatically during this period. Losses of more than 1 kg (2 lb 3 oz) per day have been recorded for brown bears, whose weight during the winter may halve.

★ MOST HERBIVOROUS

Most bears are predominantly herbivorous, with plant material accounting for at least 75% of their diet. The giant panda (*Ailuropoda melanoleuca*) is probably the most herbivorous member of the family and, indeed, is probably the most herbivorous of the carnivores. As much as 99% of its diet consists of bamboo stems, branches and leaves.

★ LONGEST FAST

Pregnant female polar bears (*Ursus maritimus*) in the Hudson Bay region of Canada survive entirely on their stored fat for a continuous period of about eight months. They are forced ashore in June or July, when the sea ice melts, and are unable to feed again until they return to the ice the following March or April. During this period, they walk hundreds of miles to their breeding grounds, construct a den in the snow, survive the sub-zero temperatures of the Arctic winter, give birth to one or two cubs, nurse the cubs from less than 1 kg (2 lb 3 oz) to about 10–12 kg (22–27 lb) and then, stimulated by an increase in the light shining through the den ceiling, break out and walk hundreds of miles back to their hunting grounds in the middle of the Bay

★ HIBERNATION

Bears do not hibernate in the true sense of the word: their body temperature rarely drops more than 5°C (9°F) below the normal 31–37.4°C (88–99°F) and they can wake in an instant. But four species do have a long winter sleep: American black bear (*Ursus americanus*), Asiatic black bear (*Ursus thibetanus*), brown bear (*Ursus arctos*) and polar bear (*Ursus maritimus*). During this period they have a lower metabolic rate, reduced heart and breathing rates, and they do not eat, drink, urinate or defecate; if left undisturbed, they may sleep for as long as a month without changing position.

American black bear
American black bears living in northern Canada probably sleep for longer than any of the other bears in the winter months, dozing off by October and waking in late April.

MAMMALS

★ MOST CARNIVOROUS

The polar bear (*Ursus maritimus*) lives almost exclusively on seals: primarily ringed seals but also, to a lesser degree, bearded seals. It may also eat walruses, beluga whales, narwhals and carrion. During the summer, however, it may feed on grass, berries and seaweed.

★ LARGEST PREY

An adult male polar bear (*Ursus maritimus*) has a stomach capacity of around 68 kg (150 lb) and is known to kill animals as large as walruses 500 kg (1100 lb) and beluga whales 600 kg (1320 lb). Brown bears (*Ursus arctos*) are able to kill animals as large as moose 450 kg (901 lb) and bison 500 kg (1100 lb) and, in some cases, have even been observed carrying their carcasses. Even spectacled bears (*Tremarctos ornatus*), which themselves weigh only 14–155 kg (141–342 lb) have been known to kill domestic cattle.

★ MOST DANGEROUS

All members of the bear family have been known to attack people at one time or another, though attacks are extremely rare given the large number of bear-human encounters there are. The only species that actively preys on people is the polar bear

(*Ursus maritimus*). Most attacks occur during the night and are made by hungry sub-adult males that are probably inexperienced hunters and are more likely to be driven from their normal kills by larger bears. More bears are killed in polar bear-human confrontations simply because more people carry firearms in the Arctic than in other bear habitats.

Polar bears have been seen covering their dark noses with a paw or a piece of snow when stalking seals on the open ice.

In North America, hundreds of thousands of people walk in bear country every year and close encounters are inevitable; however, there are relatively few injuries and few deaths. Since 1900 American black bears (*Ursus americanus*) have killed a total of 62 people; most attacks take place where the bears associate people with food but, on the whole, this species is not considered to be a serious threat. North American brown bears (*Ursus a. horribilis*) are

Polar bear
A polar bear (*Ursus maritimus*) at the window of a truck on the coastal plain of the Arctic National Wildlife Refuge, Alaska.

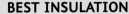

MAMMALS

estimated to injure just one in 1–2 million people.

In Japan, an average of two to three people are killed and another 10–20 injured by Asiatic black bears (*Ursus thibetanus*) and brown bears (*Ursus a yesoensis*) every year.

★ FASTEST

Bears are not really built for speed: they have few predators and rarely hunt by chasing their prey. However, they are capable of running surprisingly fast when it is necessary. The top speed reliably recorded is for a polar bear (*Ursus maritimus*) running along a road at Churchill, Canada, at a speed of 56 km/h (35 mph). It is likely that the actual top speed is higher. The brown bear (*Ursus arctos*) is capable of short bursts of speed in excess of 64 km/h (40 mph).

★ LONGEST LIVING

Bears are long-lived animals. Sunset Zoo in Manhattan, NYC, claims that its brown bear called Brownie is in his early 50s. But the oldest accurately recorded was a European brown bear (*Ursus arctos*), which died in Skansen Zoo, Stockholm, Sweden, aged 47 years. A female polar bear (*Ursus maritimus*), born in the wild in 1947, died aged 42 at Detroit Zoo, USA, on 9 September 1989. Debby a polar bear at Winnipeg's Assiniboine Park Zoo,

Canada, celebrated her 40th in August 2007. In the wild, the oldest reliably aged bear was a 32-year-old female polar bear that died on Devon Island, Canada, though there are reports of a 34-year old sow on Kodiak Island, Alaska.

★ BEST SENSE OF SMELL

It is very difficult to compare the sense of smell in different species of bear. However, it may be the most highly developed in polar bears (*Ursus maritimus*): researchers in Alaska have followed them walking in a straight line, over the tops of pressure ridges of uplifted ice and through open leads, to reach seals that they had apparently detected from up to 64 km (40 miles) away.

> Polar bears can probably detect a seal or whale carcass from as far away as 32 km (20 miles) and possibly twice as far.

★ SWIMMING

Polar bears (*Ursus maritimus*) are powerful swimmers, using their front legs to doggy-paddle and their hind legs as a rudder. They are capable of swimming distances of at least 65 km (40 ½ miles) without resting, at an average speed of 10 km/h (6 mph).

Polar bears will sometimes swim underwater to catch seabirds resting on the surface or to stalk seals that are lying on ice next to the water's edge. The longest time recorded underwater was two minutes by a polar bear stalking a seal.

★ RICHEST MILK

Milk produced by the female polar bear (*Ursus maritimus*) contains up to 48.4% fat, making it as rich as cream; this is important in building up the fat reserves of the cubs to help them survive in extremely cold conditions. In comparison, the milk produced by a female sun bear (*Helarctos malayanus*) contains only 5% fat.

★ HOMING INSTINCT

Several species of bear display an accurate homing instinct if they are removed from their home range. An adult male American black bear (*Ursus americanus*) in Michigan, USA, found its way home after being flown 250 km (156 miles) away. There are many examples of brown bears (*Ursus arctos*) finding their way home after being transplanted at least 200 km (125 miles) away.

Perhaps one of the most astonishing cases occurred in September 1973, when a young brown bear was captured near Cordova, Alaska, USA, and was moved by boat to Montague Island, Prince William Sound, some 93 km (58 miles) from its original territory. Twenty-eight days later, it was found dead just 100 m (330 ft) from where it had been captured. In order to return home, the bear had to swim 11 km (7 miles) to one island, another 1 km (½ mile) to a second island, then 3 km (2 miles) to the mainland – all the time swimming against the strong

Polar bear
Polar bears are strong swimmers. They can swim for at least 65 km (40 ½ miles) without resting and they are also happy to dive underwater in search of potential food such as seals or seabirds.

Brown bear
The brown bear is the most widespread of the bears; this individual was photographed fishing for salmon in Brooks Falls, Katmai National Park, Alaska.

tides and in the frigid waters of Prince William Sound – before walking to its original point of capture.

★ COMMONEST

The American black bear (*Ursus americanus*) is the commonest of all the bears. It is found throughout North America, from northern Alaska to the northern mountains of Mexico, inhabiting most of the continent's forested areas, and has an estimated population of 600,000–800,000. Although some populations are small and threatened, it is regarded as a game animal and many are killed illegally to supply Asian markets with gall bladders and paws.

★ MOST RESTRICTED DISTRIBUTION

The giant panda (*Ailuropoda melanoleuca*) is found only along the eastern rim of the Tibetan Plateau, in southwestern China. It is limited to six small mountainous areas in Sichuan, Shaanzi and Gansu provinces, with a total range of only 5900 km² (2277 miles²).

★ LARGEST CONCENTRATION

Bears are usually solitary creatures but there are occasions when large numbers come together. Every autumn 600–1000 polar bears (*Ursus maritimus*) gather along a 160 km (100 miles) stretch of coast between the Nelson and Churchill Rivers, on the western shores of Hudson Bay, Canada. For a few weeks, from mid-October to early November, they form the largest concentration of polar bears anywhere in the world. As soon as the ice refreezes, the bears disperse across the frozen bay to hunt for seals.

Groups of brown bears feed at garbage dumps and at salmon spawning streams in several parts of their range; at the peak of the salmon season, as many as 67 bears were recorded at one time along a 0.8 km (½ mile) stretch of the McNeil River, in Alaska. At such times they can congregate in groups of 50 or more.

★ FURTHEST NORTH

The polar bear (*Ursus maritimus*) is found throughout the Arctic. Footprints of wandering individuals have been recorded as far north as 88°N, within 2° of the North Pole, although there would be few prey animals so far north and this is clearly beyond their normal range. The furthest south they live all year round is James Bay, Canada, at about 50°N.

★ LARGEST HOME RANGE

Polar bears (*Ursus maritimus*) tend to have much larger home ranges than any other species of bear. The largest on record are for females in the Chukchi and Bering Seas, where they can be in excess of 300,000 km² (116,000 miles²). Many polar bears travel great distances: one marked individual was killed a year later some 3220 km (2000 miles) from its original release point.

A male brown bear (*Ursus arctos*) living in the Alaskan interior was recorded roaming an area of 5700 km (2200 miles). In Sweden, adult male brown bears have an average home range of 2163 km² (835 miles²); newly-independent subadults may roam over even wider areas before they settle into a more permanent home range.

★ SMALLEST HOME RANGE

Female giant pandas (*Ailuropoda melanoleuca*) studied in the Qinling Mountains, Shaanzi Province, China, had overlapping home ranges with an average size of only 4.2 km² (1½ miles²). Few giant panda home ranges are larger than 6.5 km² (2½ miles²) – and these are normally shared with other pandas.

Female black bears have an average home range of 6–26 km² (3¾–16 miles²); the males have home ranges of up to 132 km² (52 miles²). Female sloth bears (*Melursus ursinus*) that were radio-collared in Royal Chitwan National Park, Nepal, in 1990, had a home range of as little as 9 km² (3½ miles²). On Kodiak Island, Alaska, adult female brown bears have a home range of only 28–92 km² (11–36 miles²).

★ HIGHEST LIVING

During the *Daily Mail* 'Abominable Snowman Exhibition', in May 1954, expedition members reported seeing what appeared to be a brown bear (*Ursus arctos*) at a height of 5486 m (18,000 ft) on the Reipimu Glacier, in the Himalayas; they also found a fresh set of footprints which were believed to belong to this species. Sightings and tracks of the so-called 'Abominable Snowman' may well be attributable to brown bears, in which case there may well be a resident population of them living at high altitudes in the Himalayas.

Several bear species are able to live at high altitudes. The giant panda (*Ailuropoda melanoleuca*) consistently lives at 1200–3500 m (4000–11,500 ft) in the mountain forests of southwestern China; the population in Wolong, western Sichuan, spends more than 85% of its time in the forests above 2600 m (8530 ft). Panda footprints and droppings have been found as high as 4040 m (13,250 ft).

The spectacled bear (*Tremarctos ornatus*), which lives in a much wider range of habitats, has on occasion been reported at altitudes of up to 4200 m (13,800 ft) in the Andes; its preferred habitat is cloud forest from 1800–2700 m (5900–8860 ft).

The Asiatic black bear (*Ursus thibetanus*) has also been reported at an altitude of around 4000 m (13,120 ft) in the Himalayas.

CATS

Felidae
41 species

★ EARLIEST

The first cat-like carnivores were the sabre-toothed cats (family Felidae), the earliest of which was a species called *Hoplophoneus* whose 35-million-year-old fossils have been found in North America. Their powerful jaw muscles and huge upper canines (typically 20 cm (8 in) long) were specially adapted to penetrate the thick skins of bison, mammoths and other large prey.

The best-known sabre-tooth (and one of the most recent) was a species called *Smilodon fatalis*, which was similar in size to the African lion (*Panthera leo*). It lived within the past two million years, becoming extinct some 10,000 years ago.

Leopard
The most widespread big cat is the leopard, which lives in a wide variety of habitats in much of Africa, the Middle East and Asia.

★ LARGEST

The Siberian tiger (*Panthera tigris altaica*) is the largest and most massively built sub-species of tiger and, indeed, the world's largest cat. It has a total length of

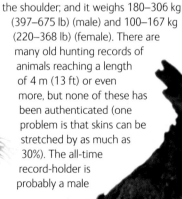

2.7–3.3 m (8 ft 10 in–10 ft 10 in) (male) and 2.4–2.75 m (7 ft 11 in–9 ft) (female), as measured between pegs from the tip of the nose to the end of the extended tail; it stands 99–107 cm (39–42 in) at the shoulder; and it weighs 180–306 kg (397–675 lb) (male) and 100–167 kg (220–368 lb) (female). There are many old hunting records of animals reaching a length of 4 m (13 ft) or even more, but none of these has been authenticated (one problem is that skins can be stretched by as much as 30%). The all-time record-holder is probably a male

Flat-headed cat
The flat-headed cat is the oddest looking cat. A secretive and poorly known animal, it appears to be largely nocturnal and feeds mainly on fish, frogs and other aquatic creatures.

weighing 384 kg (846½ lb), which was shot in 1950 in the Sikhote Alin Gory Mountains, Maritime Territory, Russian Federation. When the Siberian tiger was more numerous, it is possible that some individuals reached an even greater size.

An outsized male Bengal tiger (*P. t. tigris*) shot in northern Uttar Pradesh, India, in November 1967, measured 3.22 m (10 ft 7 in) between pegs (3.37 m (11 ft 1 in) over the curves) and weighed 389 kg (857 lb) (cf. a normal size range of 2.7–3.1 m (8 ft–10 ft 2 in) and 180–258 kg (397–569 lb) for an adult male). However, this record is a little artificial as the tiger had just killed a buffalo the previous evening and probably had an extremely full stomach (possibly adding as much as 63 kg (139 lb) to its overall weight). It is now on display at the US Museum of Natural History at the Smithsonian Institution, Washington DC, USA.

The largest tiger ever held in captivity, and the heaviest cat on record, was a nine-year-old Siberian male named Jaipur, owned by animal trainer Joan Byron Marasek of Clarksburg, New Jersey, USA. Jaipur measured 3.32 m (10 ft 11 in) in total length and weighed 423 kg (932 lb) in October 1986.

The African lion (*P. leo leo*) is the second largest of the cats; the Asiatic lion (*P. l. persica*) is slightly smaller. The average male African measures 2.4–2.8 m (7ft 11 in–9ft) overall including the tail, stands 91–97 cm (36–38 in) at the shoulder and weighs 150–189 kg (331–417 lb) (the female is considerably smaller). The heaviest wild specimen on record was a known man-eater which weighed 313 kg (690 lb) and was shot near Hectorspruit, Transvaal, South Africa,

The four largest cats (lion, tiger, jaguar, leopard) are distinguished from all the others by their ability to roar. A lion's roar can be heard up to 5 km (3 miles) away.

in 1936; this weight was so exceptional that it had to be checked several times on local railway scales before being accepted. In July 1970 a weight of 375 kg (826 lb) was reported for a black-maned lion named Simba (b. Dublin Zoo, 1959) at Colchester Zoo, Essex, UK.

★ SMALLEST
The smallest wild member of the cat family is the rusty-spotted cat (*Prionailurus rubiginosus*) of southern India and Sri Lanka, albeit by a very small margin. It has a head-body length of 35–18 cm (14–19 in); a tail length of 15–25 cm (6–10 in); and an average weight of 1.5–1.6 kg (3 lb 5 oz–3 lb 8 oz) (male).

The black-footed cat (*Felis nigripes*) of southern Africa is almost as small. It has a head-body length of 34–50 cm (13½–19½ in); a tail length of 15–20 cm (6–8 in); a shoulder height of about 25 cm (10 in); and a weight of 1.6–2.1 kg (3 lb 8 oz–4 lb 10 oz) (male). Despite its size, it has gained a reputation for ferocity among several African tribes; however, in this instance, local folklore is not taken too seriously by most experts as it claims that the black-footed cat attacks and kills animals as large as giraffes.

★ ODDEST-LOOKING
The oddest-looking cat in the world is probably the flat-headed cat (*Prionailurus*

planiceps) of the Malay Peninsula, Sumatra and Borneo. About the size of a domestic cat, its head is strangely broad and flat, with a long, sloping forehead; it has unusually small ears, set low down on each side of the head; and it has comparatively large, close-set eyes. However, the flat-headed cat is still clearly a cat and naturalists frequently consider the jaguarundi (*Puma yagouaroundi*) to look even stranger. Found from Arizona, USA, south to Argentina, this species superficially resembles a mongoose (family Herpestidae*).*

★ MOST NAMES

The puma (*Puma concolor*) has more names than any other mammal in the world and more than 40 are recognized in the English language alone. Cougar, puma, panther and mountain lion are the most commonly used, but painter, catamount (short for 'cat-of-the-mountain') and deer tiger are frequently used east of the Mississippi, USA. Some of the stranger names include mountain screamer, Indian devil and even purple feather. At the same time, as many as 29 subspecies or geographic races of the puma are recognized (12 of which live north of the Mexican/USA border) and each of these has its own name as well; for example, there is the Florida panther, Yuma cougar, eastern cougar, Wisconsin puma and Colorado cougar.

★ MOST WIDESPREAD

The wildcat (*Felis silvestris*) has three recognized sub-species which, between them, are more widely distributed than any other member of the cat family. The European wildcat (*F. s. silvestris*) is found throughout most of Europe (including the UK but excluding Scandinavia), through parts of the Middle East and into central Asia; the African wildcat (*F. s. libyca*) is found throughout Africa (except parts of west Africa) and much of the Middle East; and the Asian desert wildcat (*F. s. ornata*) lives in southwest Asia as far east as northern India. The most widespread big cat is the leopard (*Panthera pardus*), which lives in a wide variety of habitats throughout most of sub-Saharan Africa, northwest Africa, parts of the Middle East, in several areas of western Asia and through most of tropical Asia, with isolated populations in eastern Russia, northern China, North and South Korea, Sri Lanka and the Indonesian island of Java. It is also the least threatened of the big cats (although several sub-species are in serious trouble) with an estimated population of several hundred thousand.

★ EARLIEST DOMESTICATION

The first record of domestic cats comes from the ancient village of Dier el Medina, near Luxor, Egypt. In the village tombs, some 3500 years ago, people painted domestic scenes that included women sitting in their chairs with domestic cats curled up next to them; these paintings suggest that cats were common household pets at the time. Indeed, it is likely that the transition from a wild to a domestic animal took place much earlier, because dogs, cows and sheep had already been domesticated for hundreds or even thousands of years.

There is also circumstantial evidence of earlier domestication; for example, archaeologists excavating one of the earliest human settlements on Cyprus (*c.* 6000 BC) have unearthed the unmistakable remains of a cat's jawbone, although it is unknown whether the animal had actually been kept as a pet or, alternatively, whether it had been eaten. The general consensus among experts is that the domestic cat is a domesticated form of the wildcat (*Felis silvestris*) and, in particular is descended from the African wildcat (*F. s. libyca*). It is normally given the Latin name *Felis catus.*

Puma
Felis concolor has the most names attributed to it in the English language than any other mammal from puma, to cougar to catamount.

WORLD RECORD HOLDER

Fastest over a short distance

The cheetah (*Acinonyx jubatus*) is the fastest land animal over short distances (the pronghorn antelope (*Antilocapra americana*) is the fastest over long distances). Measuring the running speed of wild animals is difficult to do accurately (there is a tendency to overestimate) and considerable disagreement shrouds the cheetah's maximum speed. However, over distances of up to 500 m (1640 ft) it is widely considered to be 96–101 km/h (60–63 mph) on level ground. Tests in London, UK, in 1937 showed that, on an oval greyhound track over 316 m (1037 ft), a female cheetah's average speed during three runs was 69.8 km/h (43½ mph); but this animal was not running flat out and had great difficulty in negotiating the bends. In a study of 78 sprints in the wild, the maximum speed was 87 km/h (54 mph). Speeds of 114 km/h (71 mph), 135 km/h (84 mph) and even 145 km/h (90 mph) have been claimed, but these figures seem unlikely.

The cheetah is the only true pursuit predator in the cat family and has a longer strike distance than any other cat (90–200 m (295–650 ft)). But it has little endurance at maximum speed and appears to have evolved with a total focus on acceleration and short distance sprinting. At high speed it builds up massive amounts of heat (raising its body temperature to an almost lethal 40.6°C (105°F)) which means that it would probably die if it continued a strenuous chase over a distance much longer than 500 m (1610 ft). Most cheetahs give up after 400–500 m (1312–1640 ft) or about 60 seconds and, indeed, the average chase is no further than 200–300 m (656–984 ft) and lasts for less than 20 seconds. Afterwards, it may take a full 20 minutes of rest for the animal to cool down and to pay back its huge oxygen debt (by breathing 150–160 times/ min compared with a normal 15–20/min).

The cheetah's many anatomical specializations include exposed claws (which act like running shoes) and long legs combined with a flexible spine. Its strides are so fast and so long that all four feet are off the ground for more than 50% of the distance covered. When it is running at maximum speed it is almost literally flying.

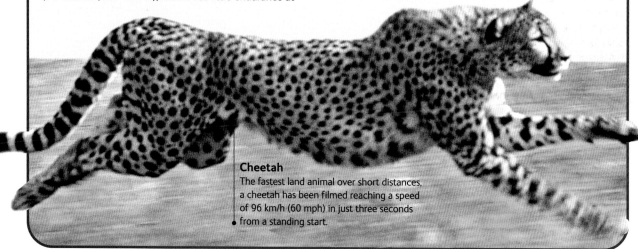

Cheetah
The fastest land animal over short distances, a cheetah has been filmed reaching a speed of 96 km/h (60 mph) in just three seconds from a standing start.

★ LONGEST GESTATION PERIOD

The longest gestation period for any member of the cat family is an average of 110 days (range 100–114 days) for the lion (*Panthera leo*). Four other species are close runners-up: snow leopard (*Uncia uncia*) with 93–110 days; jaguar (*P. onca*) with 91–111 days; leopard (*P. pardus*) with 90–105 days; and tiger (*P. tigris*) with 93–112 days.

★ SHORTEST GESTATION PERIOD

A number of small cat species have gestation periods of around 60 days or slightly less. The shortest known are 56–63 days for the African wildcat (*Felis silvestris libyca*), 56–70 for the leopard cat (*Prionailurus bengalensis*), 59–67 for the sand cat (*Felis margarita*), and 58–62 for the Asian desert cat (*Felis silvestris ornata*). There is little information on the flat-headed cat (*Prionailurus planiceps*), but one individual studied had a gestation period of 56 days. The shortest ever recorded is 50 days for a bobcat (*Lynx rufus*), but this species has an average of 62 days and a range of up to 70 days.

★ LARGEST LITTER

The European wildcat (*Felis silvestris silvestris*) has a litter size of up to eight, with an average of four (the same as in the domestic cat). Cheetah (*Acinonyx jubatus*), Canadian lynx (*Lynx canadensis*), bobcat (*Lynx rufus*) and several other species also have as many as eight, although only on rare occasions.

★ SMALLEST LITTER

Many members of the cat family have only one young in a litter at times, although the average is normally higher. The only species known to have just one consistently are the African golden cat (*Profelis aurata*), the oncilla (*Leopardus tigrinus*) and the margay (*L. wiedii*).

★ INFANTICIDE

There are scattered records of adult male pumas (*Puma concolor*), Canadian lynxes (*Lynx canadensis*), ocelots (*Leopardus pardalis*) and, in particular, tigers (*Panthera tigris*) killing kittens and cubs. But the only species in which this is known to be common and widespread is the lion (*Panthera leo*). Lions practice infanticide for two main reasons: to remove cubs sired by males they have driven away and to force the females to come into oestrus sooner. Infanticide is most common when males take over a new pride (females with dependent offspring normally lose their cubs within a month of takeover).

★ MOST SOCIAL

The majority of cats are solitary (apart from females and their dependent offspring) but lions (*Panthera leo*) are a dramatic exception to the rule. Their main social unit is the pride, which usually consists of 5–15 related adult females, and their offspring, and 1–6 adult males originally from other prides. The pride members do not spend all their time together (they are often scattered individually or in small subgroups throughout the range) but the core membership is stable and they work as a team more fully than any other member of the cat family. Uniquely among cats, they hunt cooperatively, share their prey and even help to rear each other's cubs.

★ LONGEST CANINE TEETH

The Bornean clouded leopard (*Neofelis diardi*) has the longest canine teeth relative to body size of any cat, measuring 50.8 mm (2 in). The leopard lives on the islands of Borneo and Sumatra and is a medium-sized cat whose tail can grow to be as long as its body. In 2006 the leopard was identified as being a new species of cat as its DNA is as different to the mainland clouded leopard as that of a lion to a tiger.

★ HIGHEST LIVING

A number of cat species are known to ascend to a height of at least 4000 m (13,120 ft), but only five are known to venture beyond 5000 m (16,400 ft). The highest record is of a puma (*Puma concolor*), which was recently observed at 5800 m (19,024 ft) in the Andes; however, it is quite unusual for pumas to go above 4500 m (14,760 ft). A very close runner-up is a leopard (*Panthera pardus*) whose carcass was discovered at the edge of the rim of Mt Kilimanjaro's Kibo Crater, in 1926, at a height of 5700 m (18,696 ft); there is also a population of leopards on the highest slopes of the Ruwenzori and Virunga volcanoes, central Africa, at a height of 4000–5000 m (13,120–16,400 ft). In the summer, snow leopards (*Uncia uncia*) are normally found in alpine meadows and rocky areas at a height of 2700–4500 m (8856–14,760 ft) (often below 1800 m (5904 ft) in the winter) and occasionally venture up to 5500 m (18,040 ft). The Andean cat (*Leopardus jacobitus*) is rarely found below 3000 m (9840 ft) and, in Peru at least, is known to range up to at least 5100 m (16,728 ft). Similarly, the colocolo cat (*Leopardus colocolo*) has been recorded beyond 5000 m (16,400 ft) in parts of its range in the western half of South America.

★ MOST RESTRICTED DISTRIBUTION

According to calculations done by the IUCN/ SSC Cat Specialist Group, several members of the cat family have

Snow leopard
The snow leopard holds the record for the longest jump; it has been recorded leaping over a 15 m (49 ft 2 in) wide ditch, compared to the world record for a human long-jump which is 8.95 m (29 ft 4½ in).

(49–59 ft) to the ground, and land on their feet unharmed, while the puma is able to leap upwards to a tree or ledge to a record height of 5.4 m (17 ft 8½ in).

extremely restricted distributions with a total estimated geographical range of under 1 million km² (⅓ million miles²) – roughly the size of Tanzania. These are the Spanish Lynx (*Lynx pardinus*), kodkod (*Leopardus guigna*), Bornean bay cat (*Catopuma badia*), Chinese desert cat (*Felis bieti*), black-footed cat (*Felis nigripes*), Andean cat (*Leopardus jacobitus*) and rusty-spotted cat (*Prionailurus rubiginosus*).

But the record-holder by far is the rare Iriomote cat (*Prionailurus iriomotensis*), which is confined to the 293 km² (113 miles²) Japanese island of Iriomote. This remote and mountainous island lies at the southern end of the Ryukyu Islands, southern Japan, some 2100 km (1304 miles) south of Tokyo and 200 km (124 miles) off the east coast of Taiwan. First described in 1967, the Iriomote cat has an estimated population of less than 100; it is probably the rarest cat in the world.

★ LONGEST JUMP

Two cat species are renowned for their extraordinary jumping abilities: the puma (*Puma concolor*) and the snow leopard (*Uncia uncia*). The record long jump for a puma along level ground is an outstanding 11.7 m (38 ft 4½ in).

A puma was seen jumping 3.6 m (11 ft 10 in) into the fork of a tree – with the carcass of a deer in its mouth.

But even this is overshadowed by a snow leopard, which was observed by Russian biologists leaping over a 15 m (49 ft 2 in) wide ditch. For comparison, the world record human long-jump is 8.95 m (29 ft 4½ in), achieved by Michael Anthony 'Mike' Powell (USA) in Tokyo, Japan, on 30 August 1991. Both species are also able to jump from a height of 15–18 m

★ MOST DANGEROUS

A number of wild cat species are known to attack people. The puma (*Puma concolor*), jaguar (*Panthera onca*) and leopard (*P. pardus*) have all killed on occasion, although they are not normally aggressive and rarely regard people as potential prey. The only regular man-eaters are the lion (*P. leo*) and tiger (*P. tigris*), both of which have killed thousands of people over the years. But even these two species normally try to avoid people and most attacks are the result of accidental close encounters or confrontations.

The individual man-eating record is held by a notorious tigress dubbed the 'Champawat man-eater', which operated first in Nepal and then in the Kumaon district of northern India. Such was the fear of local villagers that, towards the end of her reign of terror, they lived behind locked doors and refused to go outside. When the tigress was eventually shot, in 1911, by the legendary Jim

Pride of lions
Lions are exceptional members of the cat family in being highly social. This pride was photographed in the Masai Mara National Park, Kenya, East Africa.

Corbett, author of *Man-Eaters of Kumaon*, she was found to have damaged teeth from an earlier gunshot wound.

When records were kept by the British in India, during the early 1900s, tigers were claiming an average of 800–900 human victims per year (although many more tigers were killed by people in retribution). Even so, it was estimated at the time that no more than one in 300 tigers were ever guilty of attacking humans: a minority simply gained a bad reputation for the innocent majority.

Nowadays, man-eating tigers are rare outside two key problem areas. The worst is a vast area of mangrove forests, tidal creeks and rivers known as the Sundarbans, which is shared by Bangladesh (5980 km² (2310 miles²)) and neighbouring India (3900 km² (1505 miles²)) and is home to the largest single population of tigers in the world (as many as 400). The area has had a reputation for man-eating tigers since at least the 17th century. Most victims are honey-collectors and wood-cutters, though it is not unusual for man-eating tigers to swim out to boats to kill fishermen as well.

The tiger known as the 'Champawat man-eater' killed 436 people in a period of just eight years.

The number of deaths dropped dramatically (to fewer than 50 per year) after the introduction of boldly painted face masks, in November 1986. These were worn on the back of the head to

Siberian tiger
The Siberian tiger (*Panthera tigris altaica*) is the largest and most massively built sub-species of tiger and the world's largest cat.

confuse the tigers (which nearly always attack from behind) and there were occasions when tigers have followed people wearing the masks for up to eight hours without attacking. The masks worked for a short time, but the tigers quickly realised it was a hoax and the attacks continued. Approximately 100–250 people are currently being killed per year.

The second problem area is Dudhwa National Park, Kheri District, Uttar Pradesh, India, which is near the border with Nepal. Man-eating in Dudhwa started in 1978 and nearly 200 people were killed during the next ten years. Deaths have been more sporadic in the years since, although it was reported that a single tiger was responsible for killing four villagers in July and August 2006.

There are numerous examples of prides of man-eating African lions (*P. l. leo*) killing large numbers of people and terrorizing entire villages. The worst case was a pride of 17 lions that persistently killed and ate people around Njombe, at the northern end of Lake Malawi, southern Tanzania, over a 15-year period (1932–1947). They killed an average of nearly two people every week (a total of 1000–1500) before being shot in 1947. The most famous case involved the so-called 'man-eaters of Tsavo' which, in 1898, preyed on railworkers who were building the Mombasa to Kampala railroad, in East Africa. While the men were putting the rails and bridge over the Tsavo River, Kenya, the lions killed 28 immigrant Indians and 'dozens' of natives over a nine month period. The situation became so bad that, in the end, work had to be halted for three weeks while the lions were found and shot. Interestingly, in both these cases, the lions were found to be in good condition and, presumably, fully capable of hunting the abundant game in each area.

When leopards become man-eaters, they can be more difficult to deal with because of their stealth. The worst case was an Indian leopard known as the 'man-eater of Panar' which killed about 400 people before it was shot by Jim Corbett in 1910. But another leopard, dubbed the 'man-eater of Rudraprayag', received far more publicity. After killing its first person on 9 June 1918, it terrorized villagers for an eight-year period (1918–1926) and killed more than 125 people in total. Somehow, it survived every conceivable effort to kill it: breaking out of a box trap, surviving a poisoning campaign and trip-guns set over kills, escaping from an ambush by British army officers, and even managing to extricate itself from a leg-hold trap. Its progress was followed by the press in at least ten countries around the world and questions were even asked about it in the House of Commons, London. Eventually, soon after its last killing on 14 April 1926, and following a hunt which had lasted for several months, it was shot by Jim Corbett.

DOGS, FOXES & WOLVES

Canidae

c. 40 species, including domestic dogs, foxes, jackals, coyotes, wolves, zorros and dholes

★ EARLIEST

Canids originated in North America during the late Eocene, some 40 million years ago, when they were short-legged in appearance and more closely resembled mongooses and civets than modern species. The earliest known was the North American civet-like *Hesperocyon*, or 'dawn dog' which had an elongated muzzle, a long tail, and a fairly slender body shape; it grew to a length of about 80 cm (32 in). The oldest surviving dog is the grey fox (*Urocyon cinereoargenteus*) of North, Central and northern South America, which first appeared 6–9 million years ago; it lives much like the dawn dogs did in the late Eocene.

★ LARGEST

The largest member of the dog family is the widely distributed grey or timber wolf (*Canis lupus*), which has a head-body length of 1–1.6 m (40–63 in); a tail length of 31–51 cm (12–20 in); a shoulder height of 66–81 cm (26–32 in); and a weight of 16–80 kg (35¼–176½ lb). Males are usually about 15–20% larger than females. Size varies noticeably throughout the range, with the largest animals living in mid-latitude Canada, Alaska and Siberia, and the smallest in the Middle East. There is also a general large-to-small trend from north to south. The largest widely accepted (albeit poorly

Fennec fox
The fennec fox of northern Africa and parts of Arabia is the smallest member of the dog family, but has the largest ears in relation to body size of any carnivore.

documented) grey wolf on record is an individual from the Yukon, Canada, which reportedly weighed 103 kg (227 lb).

The maned wolf (*Chrysocyon brachyurus*) of central and eastern South America has extremely long legs and, consequently, has an impressive shoulder height of 74–87 cm (29–34¼ in), making it the tallest member of the family. However, it weighs only 20–23 kg (44–51 lb) and is therefore much smaller than the wolf in overall size. For comparison, its other measurements are: head-body length 1.24–1.32 m (48³⁄₄–52 in) and tail length 28–45 cm (11–17³⁄₄ in). With a pointed muzzle, bright chestnut coat and bushy tail, in combination with such long, slender legs, it looks rather like a red fox (*Vulpes vulpes*) on stilts. It was once believed that the maned wolf had long legs as an adaptation for running but, in fact, it has a loping gait and is not particularly fast; they are more likely to enable it to peer over the tall grass of its pampas home.

★ SMALLEST

The smallest member of the dog family is the fennec fox (*Vulpes zerda*), which lives in the deserts of northern Africa and parts of Arabia. It has a head-body length of 24–41 cm (9½–16 in); a tail length of 18–31cm (7–12¼ in); a shoulder height

of 19–21 cm (7½–8¼ in); and a weight of 1–1.5 kg (2 lb 3 oz–3 lb 5 oz).

Little is known about Blanford's fox (*Vulpes cana*), which lives in parts of southwestern Asia, the Middle East, and Arabia. It appears to be longer and taller than the fennec fox (head-body length about 42 cm (16½ in); tail length 30 cm (12 in); and shoulder height 28–30 cm (11–12 in) but specimens studied in Israel had a weight range of only 0.9–1.3 kg (2 lb–2 lb 13 oz).

The raccoon dog (*Nyctereutes procyonoides*) of Asia (and parts of Europe where it has been introduced) has such short legs that it stands only 20 cm (8 in) at the shoulder. However, it is a stocky animal with a head-body length of 50–60 cm (20–24 in); a tail length of 18 cm (7 in); and a weight of 7.5 kg (16½ lb) – six times heavier than the fennec fox.

★ MOST CARNIVOROUS

The African wild dog (*Lycaon pictus*) is the only exclusively carnivorous member of the canid family; other species feed mostly on other mammals, but invariably take invertebrates, fruit and vegetables as well.

African wild dog
The African wild dog is the most carnivorous member of the canid family, eating nothing but meat.

★ MOST VARIED DIET

Most canids eat whatever food is available in return for the least possible effort, and they vary their diets from day to day as well as from season to season. If necessary, even the grey wolf (*Canis lupus*) can live off mice and insects, or go vegetarian, until its favoured prey is more readily available. But, by a small margin, the red fox (*Vulpes vulpes*) probably has the most varied diet in the family. It will

A brown hare can run much faster than a red fox but, when it notices the fox approaching, it does not run away; instead, it stands up. Once the fox realizes that it has been seen, it does not bother to give chase and thereby saves both animals the effort of running.

eat a wide range of vertebrates, from small hoofed mammals and rodents to birds and fish; a broad selection of invertebrates, including beetles, earthworms and grasshoppers; a variety of fruit, such as blackberries and apples, and vegetables; and a mixture of carrion, human debris and other scavenged items. Absolutely nothing is wasted – to the point where even dead or dying foxes are occasionally cannibalized.

★ MOST INSECTIVOROUS

The bat-eared fox (*Otocyon megalotis*) is the most insectivorous canid. Unique among carnivores in having four to eight extra molars (which provide more chewing surfaces for feeding on insects) it is the only member of the dog family to have largely abandoned mammalian prey. Its range in southern and eastern Africa actually matches that of the harvester termite (*Hodotermes mossambicus*), which accounts for more than half of its total food intake. It will also eat adult and larval beetles and grasshoppers, as well as the occasional spider and scorpion, but vertebrate prey such as lizards, birds and mammals seldom constitutes more than 10% of its diet.

★ LARGEST EARS

In relation to body-size, the fennec fox (*Vulpes zerda*) has the largest ears of any carnivore. They measure an astonishing 15 cm (6 in) in length, almost doubling the animal's total height at the shoulder (*see* SMALLEST p. 48). Large ears give the fennec fox a rather comical appearance, but are essential to its survival: they act like radiators, dissipating heat to keep it cool in its desert home, and they help to locate termites and other prey by detecting the infinitesimally small sounds they make while scurrying underground.

Several other desert-living foxes have exceptionally large ears. The appropriately named bat-eared fox (*Otocyon megalotis*) of southern and eastern Africa has ears up to 12–13 cm (4¾–5 in) long (compared with a shoulder height of 30–40 cm (12–16 in)). It stands with its nose pointing downward and ears tilted forward, listening for insects, then

turns its head from side to side to determine their precise location.

★ LEAST TOES

The African wild dog (*Lycaon pictus*) is unique among canids in having only four toes on its front feet; as in other species it has five on its hind feet, making a total of 18 altogether. All other members of the dog family have 20 toes.

★ EARLIEST DOMESTIC

Dogs were probably domesticated for the first time about 12,000 years ago, although the earliest undisputed evidence dates from 11,000 years ago in Iran and from 9500 years ago in Yorkshire, UK. Numerous wild dog species have been domesticated at one time or another, but the grey wolf (*Canis lupus*) is generally accepted as the ancestor of all 800 modern domestic dog breeds.

Red fox
The streetwise red fox has adapted to life in towns and cities more successfully than any other member of the dog family.

★ MOST URBANIZED

Several different canids have successfully adapted to city life, but none are quite as streetwise as the red fox (*Vulpes vulpes*) which, in some parts of the world, is more numerous in towns and cities than it is in the surrounding countryside. Red foxes have even been reported raising cubs in the 54,000-seater Yankee Stadium, New York, USA, and in the attic of a four-storey office block in Bristol, UK. One enterprising vixen, also in Bristol, would enter an occupied house via the cat-flap, run down the hall and squeeze through a broken board in the kitchen to reach her cubs under the floor; a dog and a cat also lived in the house, but she persevered and managed to raise the cubs successfully.

★ LONGEST LIVING

Surprisingly little is known about the maximum lifespans of many wild members of the dog family. Most species live for less than ten years in the wild and a little longer in captivity (at least partly because the threats of shooting, trapping and poisoning are removed). The longest-lived species are the coyote (*Canis latrans*), which lives for up to 14½ years in the wild (maximum 21 years 10 months in captivity); the grey wolf (*Canis lupus*) and golden jackal (*Canis aureus*): up to 16 years in the wild (20 in captivity); the grey fox (*Urocyon cinereoargenteus*) and maned wolf (*Chrysocyon brachyurus*): up to 13 years in the wild (15 in captivity).

Most domestic dogs live for 8–15 years. Authentic records of dogs living over 20 years are rare and generally involve the smaller breeds. The oldest reliably documented was an Australian cattle-dog named Bluey, who lived to 29 years 5 months.

★ LONGEST GESTATION PERIOD

The African wild dog (*Lycaon pictus*) has a gestation period of 69–73 days, which is the longest of all the canids. The bat-eared fox (*Otocyon megalotis*) has a lower average but can range from 60–75 days.

★ SHORTEST GESTATION PERIOD

The fennec fox (*Vulpes zerda*) of northern Africa has the shortest gestation period of all the canids, typically 50–52 days. However, the cape fox (*Vulpes chama*) of southern Africa and the widely distributed red fox (*Vulpes vulpes*) both come a very close second, with 51–52 days being typical; in addition, the gestation period in the red fox can be as low as 49 days, which is the lowest recorded in the family (it ranges up to 55 days).

★ LARGEST LITTER

The African wild dog (*Lycaon pictus*) has the largest litter size in the family, with an average of 7–10 pups but as many as 19 recorded on occasion; the female has 12–14 teats (more than any other canid). The arctic fox (*Vulpes lagopus*) typically has 6–16 pups in a litter, although in good lemming years on Wrangel Island, off the coast of north-eastern Siberia, as many as 19 have been recorded; there is also an unconfirmed report of 25 pups in a single litter. As many as 18 pups have been recorded for the coyote (*Canis latrans*), but they probably represent the litters of two different females; the typical litter size for this species is six.

★ SMALLEST LITTER

A number of canid species give birth to a single pup on occasion, but in most cases the average is higher. In this respect, the maned wolf (*Chrysocyon brachyurus*) and Blanford's fox (*Vulpes cana*) probably have the smallest litter sizes, typically ranging from a single pup to a maximum of three.

★ LARGEST PACK

A number of canids live in well-structured packs. The size of these packs is extremely variable (depending on the species, the time of year and local conditions) but the largest are normally formed by grey wolves (*Canis lupus*) and African wild dogs (*Lycaon pictus*).

The largest on record are for African wild dogs during the 19th century, when packs containing more than 100 animals were not unusual and some containing as many as 500 were reported on rare occasions. Nowadays, following drastic population declines throughout Africa, the average pack size is about ten adults and their pups; packs of over 30 animals are exceedingly rare. Each pack is typically composed of a dominant breeding pair, a number of non-breeding adults, and their dependent offspring (the dominant male and female inhibit breeding in the others by physiological and behavioural means); unusually among social mammals, it is the females rather than the males that leave their natal packs on reaching maturity, to join unrelated packs.

Grey wolf packs are generally smaller. The largest occur when mature offspring fail to disperse (in times of food abundance) and where the prey is largest. Packs of 8–12 are most common, but as many as 36 animals have been reported living together. Their complex social organization is centred around a dominant breeding pair; there is a strict hierarchy among the other, non-breeding members of the pack, which help to raise the dominant pair's offspring until they are old enough to challenge the leader or his mate, or leave to begin their search for a new pack.

★ LARGEST HOME RANGE

The home range of the grey wolf (*Canis lupis*) varies greatly between packs, depending on prey availability, but can be much larger than in any other canid. The normal range is 80–2000 km^2 (31–772 miles^2), but the largest ever recorded was an amazing 13,000 km^2 (5000 miles^2) for a pack in Alaska, USA.

• **Arctic fox**
Compact size, thick fur and fur on the soles of their feet all help to contribute to the survival of the arctic fox in cold Arctic temperatures.

The African wild dog (*Lycaon pictus*) also has an exceptionally large home range. A typical pack ranges over an area of 500–1500 km² (193–579 miles²) (overlapping with other packs by 50–80%) but can have a range as large as 3900 km² (1505 miles²) – as recorded for a pack in South Africa.

★ COLDEST

The arctic fox (*Vulpes lagopus*) regularly survives colder temperatures than any other canid. Found throughout the Arctic and sub-Arctic, it is well-suited to its extreme environment, where temperatures may drop to as low as -70°C (-94°F) (captives have even survived experimental temperatures down to -80°C (-112°F)). Its main adaptations include: a compact size, and short muzzle, ears and legs, to reduce heat loss; a thick winter coat (consisting of 70% fine under-fur) which provides unbeatable insulation; an ability to reduce blood flow to the skin; fur on the soles of the feet to protect them from frostbite; and extensive fat reserves in other parts of the body. These adaptations are so effective that the arctic fox's metabolic rate does not even start to increase until the outside temperature reaches -50°C (-58°F).

★ HOTTEST

The fennec fox (*Vulpes zerda*) probably has to survive higher temperatures in its home, deep in the Sahara Desert, than any other canid. It is so well adapted to coping with the heat that, if the temperature drops to below 20°C (68°F), it starts to shiver. Mainly active at night, it escapes the worst of the daytime heat by denning up in its underground burrow. The soles of its feet are furred to provide insulation against the hot sand, and it can survive for long periods without water. Perhaps most impressive of all, it is capable of panting at an astounding 690 breaths/min when the temperature reaches c. 38°C (100°F).

The fennec fox has exceptionally large ears that help to dissipate excess heat, like miniature radiators.

★ HIGHEST LIVING

Several members of the dog family have been observed at altitudes higher than 5000 m (16,400 ft). The record-holders are: a small pack of five African wild dogs (*Lycaon pictus*) observed by a climber in the snows atop Mt Kilimanjaro, Tanzania, at 5345 m (17,532 ft); a Tibetan fox (*Vulpes ferrilata*) at 5640 m (18,500 ft); and a grey wolf (*Canis lupus*) at 5791 m (19,000 ft).

★ BEST CLIMBER

The red fox (*Vulpes vulpes*), corsac fox (*Vulpes corsac*) and several other canids are able to climb trees, but none do so as frequently or easily as the grey fox (*Urocyon cinereoargenteus*). It is an extremely agile climber, using its long claws to anchor itself to the tree trunk, and can even leap from branch to branch. The grey fox often seeks refuge in trees if it feels threatened (reversing down the trunk backwards once the danger has passed) but often climbs without provocation as well. Young cubs are able to climb trees when they are as little as one month old.

★ MOST SUCCESSFUL

Perhaps surprisingly, a number of canid species are thriving, despite heavy persecution. Two of the best examples are the North American coyote (*Canis latrans*) and the Australian dingo (*Canis lupus dingo*). The coyote is the most numerous and successful large predator in North America. While the range of most predators is shrinking, its range is expanding. In the past century, it has spread northwards and eastwards (possibly taking advantage of the decimation of wolves in many areas) and is now found throughout the continent, from Alaska to Costa Rica and from California and British Columbia to Nova Scotia and New England. There are even large populations in the centre of Los Angeles, California, and in other major cities. In many areas, the persecution continues unabated – but the coyote population apparently thrives against all the odds.

Dingoes first came to Australia some 3000–4000 years ago. They were probably brought by Southeast Asian seafarers as a live food source to vary the diet on long ocean voyages when they visited the north of the continent to trade. The dingoes were partly domesticated, but took to the wild with relish and quickly spread throughout mainland Australia. Nowadays, they thrive in a variety of habitats, from deserts to deep forest, and are found everywhere except where they are specifically excluded from sheep grazing areas by special fences. Similar forms are also found on many islands in Southeast Asia. Unfortunately, in recent years the pure dingo gene pool has been swamped by cross-breeding with domestic dogs. Unless contact between dingoes and domestic dogs is stopped, the extinction of pure dingoes may be inevitable.

★ MOST WIDESPREAD

Only a few centuries ago, the grey wolf (*Canis lupus*) had the greatest natural range of any land mammal, apart from humans. It occupied much of the northern hemisphere, from the icy wastes of Greenland to the deserts of the Arabian Peninsula, extending across North America, Europe, Asia and the Middle East. But heavy persecution has wiped out many populations and today it is mainly an inhabitant of remote wilderness areas, where it does not conflict with human interests.

The red fox (*Vulpes vulpes*) is now the most widespread wild dog, occurring throughout much of the northern hemisphere and in parts of the southern hemisphere. It is found from the Arctic tundra to the deserts of northern Africa and from British Columbia across Europe and the Asian steppes to Japan. It lives on Ellesmere Island, Northwest Territories, Canada, at a latitude of 77°N or even

MAMMALS

higher, and is found in Australia (where it was introduced last century for hunting and in an attempt to control the rabbit population) at a latitude of about 38°S. Found in woodlands, deserts, moorland, farmland, cities and almost any other habitat, it is one of the most successful and widespread mammals in the world.

★ SMALLEST RANGE

Excluding the red wolf (*Canis rufus*), which became extinct in the wild and is now being reintroduced, the island grey fox (*Urocyon littoralis*) has the smallest range of any member of the dog family. Until recently, it was believed to occur only on the six main Channel Islands, off the coast of southern California, USA; even the largest of these islands, Santa Cruz, is just 38 km (24 miles) long and 3–13 km (2–8 miles) wide. But recent evidence suggests that some nearby populations on the mainland, which were previously believed to be grey foxes (*U. cinereoargenteus*), may in fact be this species.

★ NOISIEST

Grey wolves (*Canis lupus*) make a variety of sounds, including barks, growls, whimpers and squeaks, but their howling is the best-known and noisiest. Howling serves several different functions: it advertises the presence of a pack to avoid unnecessary encounters with neighbouring wolves, it helps to maintain contact when the pack is split up or enables its members to reassemble after being separated on a long hunt, and it helps to strengthen social bonds within the pack. When a wolf howls, it is often accompanied by other members of the pack and, under ideal conditions, their combined effort can be heard from as far as 10 km (6 miles) away.

★ LARGEST PREY

Grey wolves (*Canis lupus*) have a varied mammalian diet, but will tackle prey as large as moose (200–825 kg (441–1820 lb)) and bison (350–1000 kg (772–2205 lb)), which are many times their own weight (*see* LARGEST p. 47). Typically hunting in packs, they tend to concentrate on young animals, or

> In the 1920s it was estimated that grey wolves killed about one million cattle in Russia. The resulting control programme removed 40,000–50,000 wolves a year for the next half a century.

elderly, sick or injured adults, but will occasionally tackle perfectly healthy, fully grown adults as well. Despite their indisputable hunting skills and strength, studies in North America reveal a hunting success rate of only 7–10% and, consequently, they frequently go for several weeks without food.

African wild dogs (*Lycaon pictus*) normally prey on the most abundant mammals available in the 14–45 kg (31–99 lb) weight range but, hunting in packs, will tackle prey as large as greater kudu (200–300 kg (441–661 lb)) and Burchell's zebra (350 kg (772 lb)).

★ MOST DANGEROUS

Several members of the dog family have been reported to attack people, particularly young children. But well-documented cases are extremely rare and a great deal of nonsense has been written about dangerous canids over the years. The truth is that most of them are nervous of people and, if possible, prefer to avoid close encounters.

The grey wolf (*Canis lupus*) is the only canid that represents a potential threat to people, and there is little doubt that if this species wanted to kill someone it

Grey wolf
As well as being the largest member of the dog family, the grey wolf is the noisiest and it attacks the largest prey.

Raccoon dog
The raccoon dog looks more like a raccoon than a dog and is the only dog to hibernate.

could do so quite easily. But its evil reputation as a vicious and uncompromising killer is entirely undeserved. It is certainly not dangerous in North America where, despite a great many claims to the contrary, there has never been a serious attack by an unprovoked, healthy wild wolf. Indeed, when North American biologists walk up to packs of hungry wolves on their kills, the animals walk or run away until their food has been examined, and then return to resume feeding about ten minutes after the biologists have left.

There have been a number of well-documented minor incidents, but most of these have been under unusual circumstances. There was a fatal attack on a man in northern Saskatchewan, Canada, in November 2005 – wolves were considered the most likely culprits. Another man in Saskatchewan was attacked by a wolf but survived on New Year's Eve 2005..

However, experts are divided over the situation in Europe and Asia. There is little doubt that apparently healthy, wild wolves have made unprovoked attacks on people in these regions, although there are few well-documented examples. Two exceptional cases have received considerable attention. The first concerned a rogue wolf dubbed the 'Beast of Gevauden' which, over a period of two years, attacked dozens of children and adults in the mountainous region of Lozère, France. More than 100 wolves were killed before the culprit itself was shot, on 19 June 1766; when it was cut open, the shoulder bone of a young child killed the previous day was found inside its stomach. The second case concerned a pack of wolves that suddenly appeared, in the summer of 1948, in the Darovskoye district, about 1000 km (620 miles) east of Moscow, Russia; the animals killed about 40 children and then disappeared almost as suddenly as they had arrived.

The main problem with wolves in Europe may be hybridization with large domestic dogs. The resulting dog-wolf hybrids are believed to be considerably more dangerous than pure-bred wolves, since they are often larger and more aggressive, and frequently show little fear of people. Commonly encountered in packs of 12 or more, they have become a major concern in some parts of Russia, in particular.

The greatest threat from members of the dog family is rabies. Most mammals are susceptible to this viral disease, but some canids are highly vulnerable and can become major vectors. In Europe and much of North America, the main carrier is the red fox (*Vulpes vulpes*), but it is the arctic fox (*Vulpes lagopus*) in the far north, the black-backed jackal (*Canis mesomelas*) in southern Africa, and a variety of other species elsewhere.

★ ODDEST

The raccoon dog (*Nyctereutes procyonoides*) is the least dog-like member of the canid family. As its name suggests, it looks more like a raccoon: it is roughly the same size, and has long, thick body fur and even a black face mask. Believed to be the most primitive member of the family, it lives in woodland and forested river valleys in Asia and has been introduced into western Russia and Europe.

HYENAS

Hyaenidae

Four species: spotted hyena, brown hyena, striped hyena and aardwolf

★ EARLIEST

The hyenas form the youngest of all the carnivore families. They are thought to have evolved c. 20–22 million years ago, from a civet-like creature called *Plioviverrops* that lived in Asia. However, species closely resembling modern hyenas did not emerge as dominant scavengers until c. 10 million years ago.

★ LARGEST PREHISTORIC

The largest known hyena was the now extinct cave hyena (*Crocuta c. spelaea*), which was almost twice the size of the modern spotted hyena (*Crocuta crocuta*).

★ LARGEST

The largest member of the family Hyaenidae is the spotted hyena (*Crocuta crocuta*), also known as the laughing hyena. It is one of the world's largest carnivores, with a head-body length of 1.2–1.7 m (47–67 in); a tail of 25–35 cm (10–14 in); a shoulder height of 70–90 cm (31–35½ in); and a weight of 50–80 kg (110–176 lb). Unusually, the females are normally larger than the males. It is a fairly common animal throughout the open country of sub-Saharan Africa (except for the southern reaches of South Africa and the forests of The Democratic Republic of Congo).

Spotted hyena
The spotted hyena is the most efficient mammalian scavenger, eating everything from bones and hooves to horns and hides and getting the maximum from a carcass.

★ SMALLEST

The smallest hyena is the aardwolf (*Proteles cristatus*), which lives in open country and grassland in southern Africa and East Africa. It has a head-body length of 55–80 cm (22–32 in); a tail length of 20–25 cm (8–10 in); a shoulder height of 40–50 cm (16–20 in); and a weight of 8–12 kg (17 lb 10 oz–26 lb 8 oz).

★ MOST SPECIALIZED DIET

The aardwolf (*Proteles cristatus*) has a highly specialized diet: it feeds mainly on a few species of snouted harvester termites in the genus *Trinervitermes*, with termites in the genus *Hodotermes* supplementing the diet occasionally. Although it lacks a long snout, digging forelimbs and strong claws (and therefore is unlike any of the other ant- and termite-eating mammals such as aardvarks, pangolins and anteaters) it is a highly efficient hunter. During the summer a single aardwolf will eat up to 300,000 termites (weighing about 1 kg (2¹⁄₅ lb)) a night. It locates them by sound and smell and licks them up together with copious quantities of soil by rapid movements of its long, sticky tongue.

★ MOST EFFICIENT SCAVENGER

The spotted hyena (*Crocuta crocuta*) is not only a skilful and regular hunter, but is also the world's most efficient mammalian scavenger. It utilizes the carcasses of large vertebrates such as zebras and wildebeest more efficiently than any other carnivore. Its jaw muscles and teeth are strong enough to crush large bones (the teeth exert a pressure of 800 kg/cm² (11,400 lb/in²)) and its powerful digestive system is then able to break down the organic matter of bones, hooves, horns and hides. No other animal has this ability. The few indigestible remains, such as fur and the unwanted parts of horns and hooves, are then

> A group of 38 spotted hyenas was once seen to dismember an adult zebra in less than 15 minutes, leaving little more than a few scraps behind when they had finished.

regurgitated as pellets within 24 hours. While most other carnivores tend to waste up to 40% of their kills, this remarkably efficient system enables the spotted hyena to extract the utmost nourishment from a carcass.

★ SIBLING ATTACK

According to research by biologists at the University of California, the spotted hyena (*Crocuta crocuta*) is the only wild mammal whose infants appear to be genetically programmed to attack and, in many cases, kill their siblings. The animals are born with fully developed canine teeth and an apparent determination to use them. Most spotted hyenas produce twins, but this sibling aggression means around half of all mothers are destined to bring up a single cub. In captivity, newborn cubs will attack any inanimate object that is about the same size and texture as a brother or sister, although studies in the wild suggest the killing is confined to twins of the same sex. They have even been known to attack brothers or sisters that have not yet emerged from the amniotic sac. While this behaviour is believed to be unique among mammals, sibling attack is quite common among some large birds such as eagles, herons and egrets. In birds, the dominant fledglings kill their subordinates when food is scarce. But there are believed to be more complex factors involved in hyena sibling rivalry and the precise reasons for it are still unclear.

MONGOOSES, CIVETS, GENETS & LINSANGS

c. 80 species including Herpestidae (mongooses), Viverridae (civets, palm civets, genets, linsangs), Nandiniidae (African palm civet (*Nandinia binotata*)), Eupleridae (Malagasy mongooses and civets and fossa (*Cryptoprocta ferox*))

Mongooses are not immune to snake venom; instead, they rely on their skill, agility and thick fur to avoid being bitten while they tire a snake before grabbing it from behind.

★ MOST PRIMITIVE APPEARANCE

This group closely resembles a group of animals in the extinct family Miacidae, which are believed to be the direct ancestors of modern carnivores. The miacids, as they were then known, were small mammals (similar in both size and appearance to modern genets) which evolved directly from insectivore stock soon after the dinosaurs disappeared, some 60 million years ago. Miacids lived in the forests of the northern hemisphere until, about 40 million years ago, a burst of evolution and diversification produced two major mammalian groups: the bear-like arctoids (giving rise to modern bears, seals, dogs, raccoons, pandas and mustelids) and the cat-like aeluroids (which gave rise to modern cats, hyenas, genets, civets and mongooses).

★ LARGEST

The largest member of the group is the African civet (*Civettictis civetta*), of sub-Saharan Africa. It has a head-body length of 68–89 cm (27–35 in); a tail length of 44–46 cm (17–18 in); and a weight of 7–20 kg (15½–44 lb). This makes it about 40 times heavier than the smallest member, the dwarf mongoose (*Helogale parvula*). The Celebes palm civet (*Macrogalidia musschenbroekii*) of Sulawesi (formerly Celebes), Indonesia, is longer (head-body length up to 1 m (3¼ ft) and tail length up to 60 cm (24 in)) but weighs considerably less (3.5–6.1 kg (7 lb 11 oz–13 lb 7 oz)). Similarly, the binturong (*Arctictis binturong*) of Southeast Asia has a head-body length of 61–97 cm (24–38 in) and a tail length of 56–89 cm (22–35 in), but rarely exceeds 14 kg (31 lb) (normal range 9–14 kg (20–31 lb)).

★ SMALLEST

The smallest member of this group is the dwarf mongoose (*Helogale parvula*), which lives in many parts of sub-Saharan Africa. It has a head-body length of 18–28 cm (7–11 in); a tail length of 12–20 cm (4¾–8 in); and a weight of 230–680 g (8–24 oz) (average 320 g (11¼ oz)). This species is also one of the smallest carnivores in Africa.

★ MOST PRECOCIOUS YOUNG

The falanouc (*Eupleres goudotii*) and the fanaloka (*Fossa fossana*), both of which live in the rainforests of Madagascar, are the only carnivores that produce young which are active immediately after birth. The single babies (or twins) are born with their eyes open, and in an advanced state of development, and are able to follow their mothers around on foraging expeditions within about eight days. However, they grow and mature at a slightly slower pace than other similar-sized carnivores.

★ PREHENSILE TAIL

The binturong or bear cat (*Arctictis binturong*) is the only viverrid with a long (56–89 cm (22–35 in)), thick, prehensile tail, which it uses as an extra hand to cling to branches while it moves through the trees. The only other carnivore with a truly prehensile tail is the kinkajou (*Potos flavus*) of Central and South America, which belongs to the raccoon family but has rather similar arboreal habits.

Dwarf mongoose
This is the smallest animal in the group and, indeed, one of the smallest carnivores in Africa.

MUSTELIDS & SKUNKS

c. 67 species. Two families comprise this group. The mustelid family includes the weasels, mink, martens, badgers, and otters. The mephitidae family includes skunks and stink badgers

★ LARGEST

The sea otter (*Enhydra lutris*), which lives in the North Pacific, is the heaviest of these two families. It has a head-body length of 1–1.2 m (3¼–4 ft); a tail length of 25–37 cm (10–14½ in); and a weight of 22–45 kg (48½–99 lb) (males) and 15–32 kg (33–70½ lb) (females).

The giant otter (*Pteronura brasiliensis*), which lives in South America, is the longest. It has a head-

body length of 86–140 cm (34–55 in) and tail length of 33–100 cm (13–40 in)) but is significantly lighter: (26–34 kg (57¼–75 lb) for males and 22–26 kg (48½–57¼ lb) for females).

The bear-like wolverine or glutton (*Gulo gulo*), which lives in the tundra and taiga zones of the arctic and sub-arctic, is frequently named as the world's largest mustelid. However, its robust, stocky appearance and long, dense fur can be deceptive and it has a head-body length of only 65–105 cm (26–42 in); a tail length of 17–26 cm (6¾–10¼ in); and a weight of 7–30 kg (15½–66 lb).

★ SMALLEST CARNIVORE

The world's smallest living carnivore is the least or dwarf weasel (*Mustela nivalis*), which has a wide but fragmented range in Europe, North America, Asia and northern Africa (and has been introduced to New Zealand). It has a head-body length of 11–26 cm (4⅓–10¼ in); a tail length of 1.3–8.7 cm (½–3½ in); and a weight of 30–200 g (1–7 oz). This species varies in size more than almost any other mammal – between the sexes, between populations and from one individual to another. Females are roughly half the size of males and the smallest individuals are those living in the north of the range (especially Siberia) and in the Alps. Resembling a long, slender mouse, its small size is an advantage in hunting mice, voles and other tiny mammals in their runways and burrows.

★ SMALLEST MARINE MAMMAL

The marine otter (*Lontra felina)* of western South America is the world's smallest marine mammal. With a maximum length of just 1.15 m (46 in) (from the end of the snout to the tip of the relatively short tail), and a weight of only 4–4.5 kg (8 lb 13 oz–9 lb 15 oz), it is substantially lighter and slightly shorter than the smallest seals, dolphins and porpoises. However, it is not exclusively marine: it has been reported far upstream in rivers and comes ashore to breed.

The only other mustelid confined to marine habitats is the sea otter (*Enhydra lutris*), which is equivalent in size to the smallest dolphins and porpoises. They eat and even sleep (wrapped up in mats of kelp) at sea.

Giant otter
Although not the heaviest, the giant otter is the longest animal in this group. It feeds mainly on fish, such as catfish, piranha, and perch, but also eats crab, small caiman and snakes, including small anacondas.

★ LARGEST SETT

All badgers dig burrows of one kind or another, although most of them are fairly simple. The European badger (*Meles meles*), however, spends more than half its life underground and builds record-breaking burrow systems (known as setts) that can be used for decades or even centuries, by one generation after another. More than 20 setts have been excavated, measured and mapped by researchers. The smallest of these was an outlier sett (used only sporadically), which consisted of a single entrance and a simple, blind, L-shaped tunnel only 2 m (6½ ft) long. But the largest was a main sett estimated to contain a tunnel network 879 m (2883 ft) long, with 50 under-ground chambers and 178 entrances. In another sett, the badgers had dug out 25 tonnes of soil.

The size of a European badger sett is not always related to the size of its social group. As might be expected, main setts are normally larger than outliers and they tend to be larger in regions where the soil is more easily dug. But most important of all, since the badgers are like human DIY enthusiasts and tend to go on extending their setts for as long as they are in residence, they grow larger with age.

★ STRONGEST

The strength of the wolverine or glutton (*Gulo gulo*) is legendary and probably unexcelled among mammals of a similar size. Even though it is no larger than a medium-sized dog, it has been known to pry apart steel trap jaws, drag and carry prey carcasses several times its own weight for several kilometres (miles), and to tackle prey as large as reindeer and moose. It even distracts grizzlies and black bears by biting them on the backside while they are busily eating to steal their kills. The only serious problem it has to face (apart from people) is a chance encounter with a pack of wolves, against which even the wolverine is in trouble.

Nothing is too old or frozen for a wolverine to eat. Its powerful jaws and strong teeth are uniquely adapted for eating frozen flesh in the depths of winter.

★ STRANGEST PARTNERSHIP

A mutually beneficial partnership has evolved between the honey badger (*Mellivora capensis*) and a small bird known as the greater honeyguide

Wolverine
The super strong wolverine seems to gain unlimited confidence from its strength as it has been known to drive bears and pumas from their kills.

(*Indicator indicator*). When the bird locates a bees' nest, it gives a characteristic call (that sounds like a box of matches being shaken), which attracts the attention of the badger. Continuing to call, while the badger grunts and growls in response, the honeyguide leads the way to its find. Then it waits while the badger, which is completely impervious to the inevitable stings, breaks open the nest and devours the grubs and honey; the honey guide itself feeds on the newly exposed beeswax. Honey guides sometimes try to lead other mammals in the same way, but the honey badger is normally the only one that follows.

★ DENSEST FUR

The sea otter has the densest fur of any mammal, with an average of 110,000–125,000 hairs per cm² (710,000–806,000 per in²) – which adds up to as many as 800 million individual hairs on the pelt of an adult animal. There are 60–80 underfur hairs to every guard hair. Unlike other marine mammals, it has no blubber to provide insulation – but just 1 cm (³⁄₈ in) of this thick fur is as effective an insulator as 4 cm (1⁵⁄₈ in) of fat. At the same time, the fur is waterproof and provides the animal with buoyancy in the water. Unfortunately, it is also highly valuable (last century the Russians referred to it as 'soft gold') and in the past it has proved to be the sea otter's undoing.

★ MOST WIDESPREAD

The most widespread are the ermine or stoat (*Mustela erminea*) and the least weasel (*M. nivalis*), both of which inhabit a wide variety of habitats across much of Europe, northern Asia, North America and (stoat only) parts of Greenland.

★ TOOL USING

The sea otter (*Enhydra lutris*) is one of the few tool-using mammals and indeed the only marine mammal known to use tools (although humpback whales use bubbles for fishing). It feeds primarily on abalones, mussels, clams, sea urchins and other hard-shelled prey that are too tough to break open with its teeth alone. Instead, it uses a remarkable level of dexterity to smash them with the help of a stone. The otter first collects a suitable stone from the seabed and then uses it, like a hammer, to knock the shellfish off their rocks. It returns to the surface, rolls upside down, places the stone on its chest and proceeds to smash the shell down on it, using the rock as an anvil. The first smash is usually a tentative one, perhaps to check for accuracy, but then it smashes away (testing the shell after every five or six blows) until the tasty meal inside is exposed. On average, 35 blows in six bouts are needed to break open Californian mussels, but one particularly hard shell required 88 blows in no fewer than 15 bouts. While it eats, the otter may roll over in the water at intervals to clean all the debris off its fur and then, when it has

finished, it dives again to find more food. One otter was observed feeding on mussels for a period of 86 minutes, during which time it dived 54 times and delivered 2237 blows at the surface. Favoured stones are normally quite smooth, about 15 cm (6 in) in diameter and weighing roughly 0.5 kg (11 lb). They may be used several times and otters tend to hold them under their armpit while they are diving.

★ MOST MARINE

The sea otter (*Enhydra lutris*) of the North Pacific is the only species in this

Least weasel
The world's smallest carnivore, the least weasel, has the ability to live in a wide variety of habitats from far north of Asia and Greenland to other parts of Europe.

Sea otters are very buoyant in the water and sometimes have to carry rocks when they dive, in the same way that human divers wear weight belts.

group which is exclusively marine, even though it rarely strays further than about 1 km ($\frac{1}{2}$ mile) from the shore. It can live out its entire life without ever coming to land – feeding, sleeping and breeding in the water – although some individuals and certain populations (particularly in Alaska, USA) are frequently seen hauled out on shore. Life at sea requires some ingenious adaptations. Before falling asleep, most sea otters wrap themselves in strands of kelp to avoid drifting out to sea during the night; they often sleep with their paws over their eyes. Keeping warm can also be a problem, because they do not have a thick layer of blubber like dolphins and seals; instead, they have a dense fur coat, which provides sufficient insulation by trapping a layer of air between all the hairs (*see* DENSEST FUR p. 57). In addition, they are able to maintain their body temperature by having a rapid metabolism (about $2\frac{1}{2}$ times that of a terrestrial animal of similar size). To sustain this they have a hearty appetite and have to eat more than 25–30% of their body weight every day. The female sea otter is the only member of the family to give birth in water: she seizes her newborn cub and, lying upside down on the water surface, transfers it to her chest where she begins grooming and suckling.

★ SMELLIEST

Species from both families have well-developed anal scent glands, which are used for social communication and in defence. These glands produce a thick, oily, yellow, pungent fluid called musk, which is stored in a sac that opens into the rectum. When they are threatened, some species are able to spray this unpleasant fluid out through the anus towards their attacker. The fluid varies greatly in potency from species to species, between individuals and even with the time of year – and there is little agreement about which is the most repulsive. One of the main contenders is the zorilla or striped polecat (*Ictonyx striatus*), which has a patchy distribution in sub-Saharan Africa. Also in the running are two aptly named species of stink badger in the genus *Mydaus*, which live in Southeast Asia, and the nine species of New World skunks in the genera *Mephitis*, *Spilogale* and *Conepatus*. Skunks are certainly the best known in terms of their smell. They will normally spray only under extreme provocation, preferring to strut around as a warning, with stiff legs, their backs arched, tails pointing skyward and hairs erect. Spotted skunks in the genus *Spilogale* even dramatize the effect by performing impressive handstands as well.

Spotted skunk
The spotted skunk with its vivid black and white markings warns potential predators of its unpleasant, and exceedingly effective, means of defence by doing a handstand.

Sea otter
Male sea otters obtain as much as one-third of their food by stealing from the females. Sometimes, they will even hold a cub 'hostage' until the mother gives up her catch.

If their attacker is persistent, and they do have to spray, they have an accurate range of about 2 m (6½ ft) and an overall range of some 6–7 m (20–23 ft). They discharge either an atomized spray or a stream of droplets and aim for the attacker's eyes, causing a burning sensation, severe irritation and even temporary blindness. The smell itself is sulphurous and so foul it frequently causes nausea and retching. It can be detected up to 2.5 km (1³/₅ miles) downwind. The fluid clings to the victim and releases more of its vile-smelling agents over a period of several days. It is virtually impossible to remove from clothes, which are best thrown away after a close encounter. Young skunks as little as one month old can spray – but the skunks themselves, and their dens, do not give off the same odour.

As a result of this extraordinary defence system most animals avoid skunks, although the great horned owl (*Bubo virginianus*) is a notable exception and does not seem to be bothered by the effects of the spray.

Common raccoon
The raccoon's reputation as a mischief maker isn't just due to the bandit-like strip it has across it eyes. Raccoons are highly intelligent and naturally curious animals with hands almost as dextrous as monkeys.

RACCOONS

Procyonidae & Ailuridae

19 species: seven racoons, five olingos, three coatis, one kinkajou, one ringtail, and one cacomistle (Procyonidae) and one red panda (Ailuridae)

★ LARGEST

The largest member of the raccoon family is the common or northern raccoon (*Procyon lotor*), which is found throughout much of North, Central and northern South America, and has been introduced to parts of Europe and Asia. Several of the other large species – such as the kinkajou (*Potos flavus*) and the white-nosed coati (*Nasua narica*) – are approximately the same length (or even longer, including the tail) but do not match the raccoon in maximum weight. However, there is a great deal of individual variation in many of the procyonids and it is not unusual for certain specimens to exceed the average by a large margin. The head-body length of the common raccoon is 46–71 cm (18–28 in); the tail length is 20–35 cm (8–14 in); and the weight range is normally 2.5–12 kg (5½–26½ lb). There is one record of a male raccoon in Wisconsin, USA, that weighed 28.3 kg (62½ lb).

★ SMALLEST

Several members of the raccoon family compete for this title and, unfortunately, there is too much individual variation (and, in some cases, there are too few measurements) to identify a single record-holder. The species most commonly described as the smallest is the ringtail (*Bassariscus astutus*), which lives in southern and western USA and throughout Mexico.

This graceful animal has a head-body length of 31–38 cm (12¼–15 in); a tail length of 31–44 cm (12¼–17¼ in); and a weight of 800–1100 g (1¾ lb–2½ lb).

★ MOST MISCHIEVOUS

The common raccoon (*Procyon lotor*) is frequently described as the most mischievous animal in the world (although there are several other well qualified contenders for this title).

Raccoons often raid dustbins and can unscrew jar tops and take the stoppers out of bottles.

A highly intelligent and adaptable species, it is cheeky, has an insatiable curiosity and has learnt to coexist successfully with humans (despite being a major target for hunters). Always experimenting and poking its fingers into crevices, it can use its hands almost as skillfully as monkeys use theirs. It raids people's dustbins, overturning them and stealing the contents; begs by the roadside, where it knows from experience passers-by will stop to provide scraps; and breaks into tents and cabins at campsites. It even looks the part with its unmistakable 'bandit' mask.

SEALS, SEA LIONS & WALRUS

Pinnipedia

34 species: 19 true seals, five sea lions, nine fur seals and one walrus

★ LARGEST

The largest of the pinnipeds is the southern elephant seal (*Mirounga leonina*), which lives mainly in the Southern Ocean around the Antarctic. Males typically grow up to 5.8 m (19 ft) in length from the tip of their inflatable snout to the end of their outstretched tail flippers, have a maximum girth of 3.7 m (12 ft 2 in) and weigh about 2000–3500 kg (4400–7720 lb). Females are usually much smaller, growing up to 3 m (9 ft 10 in) in length and weighing up to 400–800 kg (882–1764 lb). The largest accurately measured specimen is a male killed in the South Atlantic at Possession Bay, South Georgia, on 28 February 1913. He probably weighed at least 4000 kg (8820 lb) and measured 6.5 m (21 ft 4 in) after flensing (stripping of the skin and blubber); his original length was estimated to be 6.85 m (22 ft 6 in).

The largest recorded live specimen is a male southern elephant seal, nicknamed 'Stalin', from South Georgia, in the South Atlantic. He was recorded by members of the British Antarctic Survey and the UK-based Sea Mammal Research Unit, on 14 October 1989, with a weight of 2662 kg (5870 lb) and a length of 5.10 m (16 ft 9 in).

★ SMALLEST

The Galapagos fur seal (*Arctocephalus galapagoensis*), which breeds on seven main islands in the Galapagos archipelago, is probably the world's smallest pinniped. Adult females average 1.2 m (47 in) in length and weigh 27 kg (60 lb). Males are usually considerably larger, averaging 1.5 m (59 in) in length and weighing around 64 kg (141 lb).

★ MOST DANGEROUS

When frightened, or molested, many pinnipeds will bite or chase intruders. But the carnivorous leopard seal (*Hydrurga leptonyx*) is the only species with a reputation for apparently unprovoked attacks on people. There are a number of documented cases of leopard seals suddenly lunging through cracks in the ice to snap at people's feet; divers have been attacked on several occasions; and several people have been chased across the ice over distances of up to 100 m (330 ft). They make powerful adversaries, growing to a maximum length of 3.6 m (11 ft 10 in), weighing up to 450 kg (992 lb). However, experts generally believe that their fierce reputation is unjustified: most reported attacks seem to have been caused by the seals making a genuine mistake (from underwater, the dark vertical shape of a man is similar to the shape of an emperor penguin) or by provocation.

★ FASTEST

The fastest swimming speed recorded for a pinniped is a short spurt of 40 km/h (25 mph) by a California sea lion (*Zalophus californianus*). A leopard seal (*Hydrurga leptonyx*) of 275 kg can easily leap from water on to an ice floe 2 m (78 in) above the surface, requiring an estimated exit speed of approximately 6 m/s or 22 km/h (14 mph).

The fastest pinniped on land is the crabeater seal (*Lobodon carcinophagus*), which has been timed at 19 km/h (12 mph) across tightly packed snow on Signy Island, South Orkneys, near Antarctica, and in other instances has been estimated to be as high as 25 km/h (16 mph).

Leopard seals do occasionally attack people without provocation, although this may be because they mistake them for emperor penguins.

Leopard seal
Armed with formidable teeth and powerful jaws leopard seals are undoubtedly more dangerous than most other pinnipeds.

MAMMALS

★ DEEPEST DIVE

Elephant seals are the only pinnipeds known to dive to depths in excess of 1000 m (3300 ft). The record is for a female northern elephant seal (*Mirounga angustirostris*) which descended to 1603 m (5290 ft) and there are several examples of dives deeper than 1500 m (4950 ft). In May 1989, off the coast of San Miguel Island, California, an adult male northern elephant seal was documented on a small microprocessor-based time-depth recorder at 1529 m (5017 ft). In the same experiment, which involved recording more than 36,000 dives by six different animals, a second seal dived to 1333 m (4374 ft). In similar experiments carried out on southern elephant seals (*M. leonina*), dives of up to 1256 m (4121 ft) and 1134 m (3720 ft) deep have been recorded.

★ LONGEST DIVE

Experiments on the diving abilities of southern elephant seals (*Mirounga leonina*) in the Southern Ocean recorded a maximum dive time of 120 minutes, by a female. However, most southern elephant seal dives last for an average of 'only' 20–27 minutes. A 119-minute dive has been documented for the northern elephant seal (*Mirounga angustirostris*) and a 73-minute dive for the Weddell seal (*Leptonychotes weddellii*).

A study of northern elephant seals, in May 1989, off the coast of San Miguel Island, California, revealed that the animals rarely spent more than five

SHORTEST LACTATION PERIOD

The hooded seal (*Cystophora cristata*) has the shortest lactation period known for any mammal. On average, the pups are weaned after only 4 days of nursing. They grow at an astonishing rate, their weight doubling from roughly 25 kg (55 lb) at birth to 50 kg (110 lb) at weaning.

minutes at the surface between dives, which typically lasted 21–24 minutes. During their many months at sea, it has been estimated that the seals are submerged about 86% of the time.

★ LONGEST LACTATION PERIOD

Compared with other pinnipeds, the female walrus (*Odobenus rosmarus*) consistently has the longest period of parental care, suckling her pups for as long as 2–2½ years. The Galapagos fur seal (*Arctocephalus galapagoensis*) has a two-year lactation period and a small number of Australian fur seals (*Arctocephalus pusillus*), South American fur seals (*Arctocephalus australis*) and Steller's or northern sea lions (*Eumetopias jubatus*) suckle their pups for two or, rarely, three years, though one year is more typical.

★ LONGEST LIVING

Many pinnipeds, especially the females, have fairly long lifespans. The greatest authenticated age was recorded by

scientists at the Limnological Institute, in Irkutsk, Russia, who have estimated that the maximum lifespan of the Baikal seal (*Pusa sibirica*) is 56 years for females and 52 years for males, based on cementum layers in the canine teeth. Female Caspian seals (*Pusa caspica*) are reputed to live to 50 years, and males to 47 years. A female grey seal (*Halichoerus grypus*) shot at Shunni Wick, Shetland, on 23 April 1969 was believed to be 'at least 46 years old' based on a count of dentine rings in its teeth. A 43-year-old ringed seal (*Pusa hispida*) was reported from the eastern Canadian Arctic. In all pinnipeds, except elephant seals, the females tend to have a slightly greater longevity than the males.

The captive record is 42–43 years for a male grey seal named 'Jacob'. He was captured on 28 October 1901, at an estimated age of two years, and died at Skansen Zoo, Stockholm, Sweden, on 30 January 1942.

★ SHORTEST LIVING

The shortest-lived pinniped in the wild is probably the Australian sea lion (*Neophoca cinerea*), which has a life expectancy of around 12 years.

★ MOST SOUTHERLY

The Weddell seal (*Leptonychotes weddellii*) consistently lives further south than any other pinniped. It occurs mainly along the land-fast ice close to the Antarctic continent, moving with the ice front (north in the winter and south in the summer) but usually remaining within sight of land.

★ MOST NORTHERLY

The ringed seal (*Phoca hispida*) has the most northerly distribution of any of the pinnipeds. The commonest seal in the Arctic, it is rarely found in the open sea or on floating pack ice, but occurs wherever there is sufficient open water in the more permanent ice. It has even been recorded as far north as the North Pole.

Northern elephant seal
Only mature male northern elephant seals have this long elephant-like nose. Their nose is quite delicate, but the bigger the nose, the more mature and strong the male.

★ MOST WIDESPREAD

The common seal (*Phoca vitulina*) is probably the most widespread pinniped, since its breeding range includes four major ocean areas: mainly the temperate North Pacific and temperate North Atlantic, but also the Pacific Arctic/sub-Arctic and Atlantic Arctic/sub-Arctic.

The breeding range of the southern elephant seal (*Mirounga leonina*) includes the temperate South Pacific, temperate South Atlantic and Antarctic, but the majority of the population occurs in the sub-Antarctic. All other pinniped species occur in just one or two major ocean areas.

★ MOST LIMITED RANGE

Several pinnipeds have extremely limited ranges. Arguably, the most limited is that of the Guadalupe fur seal (*Arctocephalus townsendi*), which until recently bred along the eastern coast of Guadalupe Island, Mexico, approximately 200 km (124 miles) west of Baja California; however, in recent years small colonies have been established outside the normal breeding range – in the San Benitos

Islands, Baja California, Mexico, and in the Channel Islands, Southern California. Other species with extremely limited ranges include: the Juan Fernandez fur seal (*Arctocephalus philippii*), restricted to the Juan Fernandez and San Felix islands, both off the coast of Chile; the Galapagos fur seal (*Arctocephalus galapagoensis*), which breeds on seven islands and hauls out on two others in the Galapagos archipelago, off the coast of Ecuador; the Hawaiian monk seal (*Monachus schauinslandi*), which is found mainly on the small, mostly uninhabited, islands in the Leeward Chain, Hawaii; the Caspian seal (*Pusa caspica*), which is found only in the Caspian Sea; and the Baikal seal (*Pusa sibirica*), which is found only in Lake Baikal and, occasionally, in some of the rivers flowing into the lake.

★ LONGEST WHISKERS

All pinnipeds have whiskers on their aces, but fur seals tend to have the longest. The record is held by a male Antarctic fur seal (*Arctocephalus gazella*) whose longest whisker measured 48 cm (19 in).

Southern elephant seal

The southern elephant seal is the largest member of the whole order Carnivora. Together with the northern elephant seal it can also dive deeper and for longer than any other pinniped.

★ SHORTEST WHISKERS

The shortest and thickest whiskers belong to the walrus (*Odobenus rosmarus*); they average only 8 cm (3 in) in length and 3 mm (1/8 in) in diameter.

★ MOST WHISKERS

The walrus (*Odobenus rosmarus*) has about 300 whiskers on each side of its 'moustache' – more than in any other pinniped.

★ LONGEST NOSE

The male northern elephant seal (*Mirounga angustirostris*) has an extremely long, inflatable proboscis; when relaxed, it hangs down over the animal's mouth by about 30 cm (12 in). The proboscis begins to appear at puberty (3–4 years old) and is fully developed when the seal is about eight

years old. The male southern elephant seal (*M. leonina*) does not have such a pendulous nose: it overhangs its mouth by only about 10 cm (4 in).

★ GREATEST CONCENTRATION

One of the greatest concentrations of large mammals found anywhere in the world is a herd of northern fur seals (*Callorhinus ursinus*) in the Pribilof Islands, Alaska. The herd reached a peak of about 2.5 million in the late 1950s, but numbers have declined since (partly due to many years of intensive hunting). Commercial harvesting of the animals is currently banned (though some 2000 are still allowed to be killed annually by subsistence hunters) and, every summer, the herd now contains an estimated 1.37 million fur seals (roughly half breeding on two main islands in the Pribilof group: St George and St Paul).

★ LONGEST MIGRATION

Female northern fur seals (*Callorhinus ursinus*) leave their breeding grounds on the Pribilof Islands, Alaska, in late September and early October and swim some 5000 km (3100 miles) south to

spend the winter off the coast of California; they begin their return journey as winter ends, arriving back in the Pribilofs some time in June. The males and youngsters make a shorter journey to spend the winter in the Gulf of Alaska.

A population of hooded seals (*Cystophora cristata*) routinely undertakes a 3250 km (2000 miles) annual migration from its breeding grounds in the Gulf of St Lawrence, Canada, to its moulting grounds between 66° and 68°N in the Denmark Strait, off the southeast coast of Greenland.

Hooded seals are great wanderers and often turn up in the most unexpected places, well outside their normal Arctic and sub-Arctic range in the North Atlantic. On 23 July 1990, a fairly healthy female, estimated to be about three years old, came ashore in San Diego, California; she must have travelled at least 13,000 km (8073 miles) through the Northwest Passage, into the Bering Sea and down through much of the North Pacific to get there.

★ FURTHEST FROM THE SEA

The Baikal seal (*Pusa sibirica*) is effectively confined to Lake Baikal, a huge freshwater

Northern fur seal
Northern fur seals are found throughout the North Pacific Ocean and, in summer, more than half a million of them gather to breed on the Pribilof Islands in the southern Bering Sea, forming one of the largest concentrations of mammals in the world.

lake 630 km (395 miles) long in Russia, immediately north of Mongolia. The oldest and deepest lake in the world, Lake Baikal is approximately 1700 km (1056 miles) from the nearest coastline, which is on the Sea of Okhotsk. A single Baikal seal was recorded 400 km (248 miles) down the Angara River, which flows out of the lake's southern end, at which point it would have been approximately 1900 km (1180 miles) from the nearest coastline, on the Laptev Sea.

★ BIGGEST TEETH

The biggest pinniped teeth belong to the walrus (*Odobenus rosmarus*), which lives in the Arctic. Its two upper canines develop into long, curved tusks that protrude from its mouth and hang down well below the chin which are used for fighting and display and maneuverability. The tusks are heavier and larger in males.

Many tusks are broken, and most are fairly worn, but they have been known to reach 1 m (39 in) in length and to weigh as much as 5.4 kg (12 lb).

★ NUMBER OF TEETH

There is little variation in the number of teeth found in most pinniped species, with a total of 30–36 being typical. There are just two exceptions: the walrus (*Odobenus rosmarus*) which normally has only 18 teeth; and the California sea lion (*Zalophus californianus*) which has 34–38 teeth.

★ WEIGHT LOSS

The male northern elephant seal (*Mirounga angustirostris*) fasts for a total of four months in every year. During the breeding season, from early December to the end of February, it is unable to abandon the harem of females on shore in case another male attempts to mate with them and, consequently, is unable to enter the sea to feed. It loses up to half its body weight (in extreme cases, a much as 1000 kg (984 lb)) during this three month period. Then it fasts again during the month-long moult in late June and July. Newly weaned elephant seal pups fast for up to three months before they learn to fish for themselves, although they often try to sneak a meal from other lactating females in the harem after their natural mothers have left. In both adults and juveniles, the thick blubber layer serves as a food store during these fasting periods.

★ SIZE DIFFERENCE

The greatest size difference between the sexes is found in the southern elephant seal (*Mirounga leonina*). At birth, pups of both sexes are roughly the same size (1.3 m (51 in) long and 40–50 kg (88–110 lb) in weight) but the males

Walrus
The large and imposing tusks of the walrus are used as an anchor and as a lever to heave the animals along a rocky shore or out of the water on to floating ice.

become substantially larger as they grow older. Adult males average 4–5 m (13–16 ft) in length and weigh about 3500 kg (7720 lb); females average 2–3 m 6½ ft–10 ft) in length and weigh about 500–800 kg (1102–1764 lb). This makes males almost twice as long and over five times heavier than females.

★ MOST VARIED DIET

Many pinnipeds take a wide range of prey. The common seal (*Phoca vitulina*), for example, is known to feed on at least 50 different species of fish, as well as squid, whelks, crabs and molluscs. But the leopard seal (*Hydrurga leptonyx*) has by far the most varied diet and, indeed, has a reputation for eating almost anything that moves. It will take many species of penguins and other sea birds, fish, squid, octopus, krill, the pups of crabeater, Weddell, Ross, southern elephant and Antarctic fur seals, and even dead whales.

The stomach of one male leopard seal contained an adult duck-billed platypus and another individual regurgitated a sea snake. Leopard seals also have voracious appetites: one was observed catching and eating six penguins in 70 minutes while another had 79 kg (1741 lb) of penguin remains in its stomach.

Many pinnipeds deliberately swallow stones and pebbles. This may help allay hunger pangs during long periods of fasting, or help to grind up food in the stomach or even play a role in buoyancy control.

★ MOST SPECIALIZED DIET

Despite its name, the crabeater seal (*Lobodon carcinophagus*) feeds almost exclusively on krill. These small, shrimp-like creatures account for 94% of its diet, the remainder consisting of other invertebrates, fish and squid.

MAMMALS

★ LONGEST GESTATION PERIOD

Research on wild Australian sea lions (*Neophoca cinerea*) suggests a total gestation period of 17½ months; the gestation period in three captive individuals was estimated at 14–15 months. These figures include unknown periods of delayed implantation, during which attachment of the fertilized egg to the uterine wall is postponed. Walrus (*Odobenus rosmarus*) pups are born approximately 15 months after conception, including 4–5 months of delayed implantation. The gestation period in all other pinnipeds lasts 10–12 months, including varying periods of delayed implantation.

★ MOST PRECOCIOUS

Common seals (*Phoca vitulina*) are often born in the intertidal zone, so their pups must be ready to enter the sea soon after birth. They usually begin swimming within hours of birth but, if necessary, can cope in the water after just a few minutes. They can swim and dive efficiently almost straight away but, during the first week of their lives, will often ride on their mothers' backs if they get tired or if there is danger nearby. Recent research

suggests that the 'white coat' pups of grey seals (*Halichoerus grypus*) can also swim, although not as proficiently as the young common seals.

> It is winner takes all with northern elephant seals — some males mate with over 100 different females in a few weeks and others die without mating at all.

★ MOST POLYGAMOUS

A male northern fur seal (*Callorhinus ursinus*) living in the Pribilof Islands, Alaska, USA, was recorded mating with 161 females, making it the most polygamous pinniped and probably the most polygamous mammal. Most male northern fur seals mate with 15–30 females.

The northern elephant seal (*Mirounga angustirostris*) is also highly polygamous. A single dominant male typically mates with 40–50 females during a brief period of receptivity within a single breeding season. There are records of individuals

mating with as many as 100 different females in the space of a few weeks, but competition is fierce and with this number it is difficult for them to keep out the lower ranking males. Only one in 100 males lives to be nine or ten years old, which is the optimum age for being dominant in the social hierarchy, and many of these die without mating at all. Even the successful males, having reached their reproductive peak, can remain sufficiently dominant for no more than one or two years before they die.

★ STRANGEST

The strangest-looking pinniped is probably the hooded seal (*Cystophora cristata*) of the North Atlantic and Arctic. The adult male has an enlarged nasal cavity, which forms an inflatable hood on the top of its head: when not inflated, this is slack and wrinkled and its tip hangs down over the front of the mouth; but, when it is filled with air, it resembles a giant leathery football. The same animal

• Hooded seal

Male hooded seals have the strange ability to inflate the black sack, or 'hood', which hangs over the end of their nose. Seen here, they can also inflate the skin-like membrane in their noses so it forms a large red balloon.

is also able to blow up the internal membrane inside its nose to form a bright red or brown 'balloon' that usually extrudes from the left nostril. Both the hood and the balloon are inflated when the seal is disturbed and during courtship display, though it sometimes appears to 'play' with the hood by moving air gently from the front to the back.

★ MOST VARIABLE COLOUR

A walrus (*Odobenus rosmarus*) changes colour depending on whether it is in or out of the water. Its basic body colour is cinnamon brown. However, in the water, blood is drawn away from the skin to maintain a high core body temperature, and the walrus turns a much paler colour; it may even appear ghostly white. On land, blood is directed towards the skin to release excess heat, and the walrus turns a grey to reddish-brown colour; it may appear bright pink, as if it were sunburnt.

★ MOST ABUNDANT

The crabeater seal (*Lobodon carcinophagus*) is the world's most abundant pinniped. The total population in its Antarctic home is estimated to be well over 10 million and, according to some estimates, maybe as high as 50 million. The most widely accepted figures suggest a minimum of 9–11 million in the Weddell Sea, 1.3 million in the Amundsen and Belling-hausen Seas, 650,000 for the Oates and George V coasts, and 600,000 for the Adelie, Clairie and Banzare coasts.

Crabeater seal
The world's most abundant seal, the crabeater seal, has a total population of an incredible ten million or more.

EDENTATES

Xenarthra

31 species: including 21 armadillos, six sloths and four anteaters; found only in North, Central and South America. The word edentate literally means without teeth, although only the anteaters are genuinely toothless (armadillos and sloths possess simple, peg-like molars and pre-molars)

★ LARGEST

The giant anteater (*Myrmecophaga tridactyla*), which lives in the savannas and open woodlands of Central and South America, is the largest of the edentates. It has a head-body length of 1–1.2 m (39–47 in); a tail length of 70–90 cm (28–36 in); and a weight of 20–60 kg (44–132¾ lb). Males are typically 10–20% heavier than females.

In exceptional circumstances, giant armadillos (*Priodontes maximus*) have been known to attain a weight of 60 kg (132 lb), but these have been over-fed zoo specimens; the average head-body length for this species is 75–100 cm (30–40 in) (tail length about 50 cm (20 in)).

★ LARGEST PREHISTORIC

Modern edentates are small compared with many of their prehistoric relatives. In particular, giant ground sloths in the family Megalonychidae, such as a species called *Megatherium*, were at least the size of today's elephants. They appeared during the early Oligocene 34 million years ago, and were prevalent in North and South America and the Caribbean until between 8500 and 11,000 years ago. For many years, there have been rumours of a giant, human-sized ground sloth – the South

American equivalent of the abominable snowman – still living in the depths of the Amazon rainforest; according to Indians, rubber-tappers and illegal gold-miners, who claim to have seen the creature and call it the *mapinguari*, it gives off a cloud of noxious gas when approached. Some western scientists take the claims seriously and believe that such an animal may really exist.

★ SMALLEST

The lesser or pink fairy armadillo (*Chlamyphorus truncatus*), which lives in central Argentina, is the smallest of the edentates. It has a head-body length of 12.5–15 cm (5–6 in); a tail length of 2.5–3 cm (1–1¼ in); and a weight of 80–100 g (2¾–3½ oz). Roughly the size of a small rat, its armour is pale pink in colour.

★ SLEEPIEST

Some armadillos (family Dasypodidae) and sloths in the wild (families Bradypodidae and Megalonychidae) spend up to 50% of their lives sleeping or dozing.

Sloths have a metabolic rate that is only 40–45% of that expected for animals of their size. Subsisting entirely

The giant anteater sleeps on its side, using its huge, fluffy tail as a blanket.

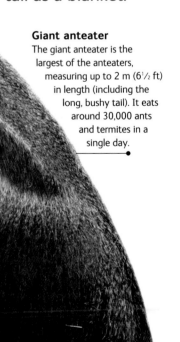

Giant anteater
The giant anteater is the largest of the anteaters, measuring up to 2 m (6½ ft) in length (including the long, bushy tail). It eats around 30,000 ants and termites in a single day.

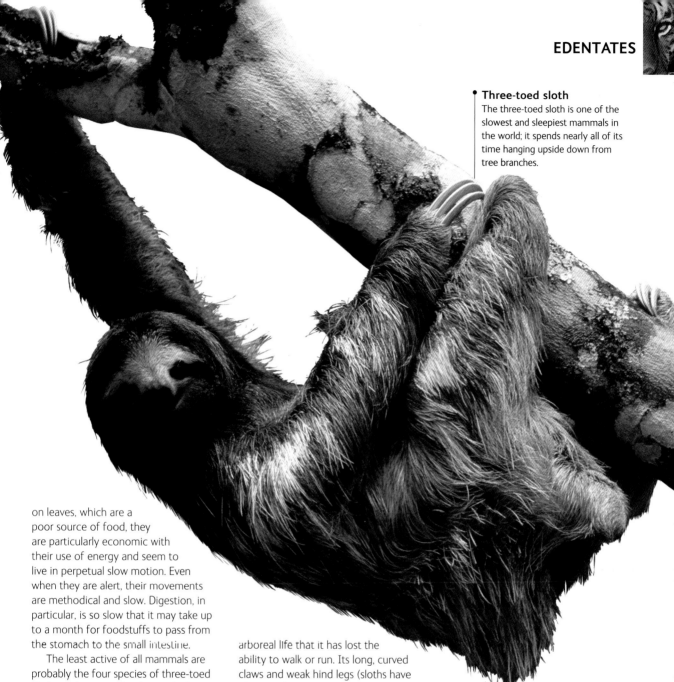

Three-toed sloth
The three-toed sloth is one of the slowest and sleepiest mammals in the world; it spends nearly all of its time hanging upside down from tree branches.

on leaves, which are a poor source of food, they are particularly economic with their use of energy and seem to live in perpetual slow motion. Even when they are alert, their movements are methodical and slow. Digestion, in particular, is so slow that it may take up to a month for foodstuffs to pass from the stomach to the small intestine.

The least active of all mammals are probably the four species of three-toed sloths in the genus *Bradypus*, which may occupy the same tree for two or more nights in a row (two-toed sloths in the genus *Choloepus* move from tree to tree as often as four times in a night).

★ SLOWEST

The three-toed sloth (*Bradypus tridactylus*) of tropical South America is probably the slowest mammal in the world, with an average ground speed of 1.8–2.4 metres per minute (6–8 feet per minute). It descends to the ground about once a week to defecate and, like all sloths, is so highly modified for its arboreal life that it has lost the ability to walk or run. Its long, curved claws and weak hind legs (sloths have about half the muscle weight of other animals of a similar size) make normal locomotion impossible, so it lies on its belly, reaches forward to get a claw-hold in the soil and literally drags itself along the ground. In the trees it can accelerate to a slightly more impressive 4.6 metres per minute (15 feet per minute); peak acceleration is probably reached during the courtship 'pursuit', when amorous males go in search of females.

Strangely, sloths are good swimmers and have considerable stamina in the water; they normally swim breast-stroke, but sometimes do an elegant front crawl.

★ MOST UPSIDE DOWN

Sloths (families Bradypodidae and Megalonychidae) probably spend more of their lives hanging upside down than any other mammals (including non-hibernating bats). They eat, sleep, travel hand-over-hand, mate and give birth in an upside down position. Indeed, even their fur grows upside down – or, at least, 'backwards' – from the wrist towards the shoulder and from the stomach towards the back. Even after they have died, they sometimes continue to hang in exactly

Three-banded armadillo
The Brazilian three-banded armadillo is endemic to Brazil and the only species of armadillo that can roll itself entirely into a ball.

the same way, firmly hooked on to a branch by their coat hanger-like 8–10 cm (3–4 in) long claws. The only times they right themselves are when climbing up or down (which they do in an upright position) or when visiting the ground briefly to defecate (about once a week).

★ QUADRUPLETS

The nine-banded armadillo (*Dasypus novemcinctus*), which lives in southern North America and Central and South America, is unique among mammals in producing litters of four chromosomally identical young. The four infants, which are all of the same sex (either male or female), are produced from a single fertilized egg that subdivides once development starts.

★ LOWEST BODY TEMPERATURE

Edentates have some of the lowest body temperatures of all mammals (excluding

species in hibernation). The two-toed sloths in the genus *Choloepus* have the lowest and most variable on record, ranging from a low of 24°C (75°F) to a high of 33°C (91°F); they move in and out of the sun in the same way that

reptiles and other cold-blooded animals do to regulate their body temperatures. The pichi (*Zaedyus pichiy*) body temperature drops to a low of 24°C (75°F), but is slightly more variable and also reaches a high of 35.2°C (95°F).

ELEPHANTS

Proboscidea

Three species: two African (bush/savanna elephant and forest elephant) and one Asian

★ EARLIEST

According to the fossil record, some 170 species of elephants and their relatives (proboscideans) have lived on Earth, on every continent except Australia and Antarctica; only two of them survive today. Remains of the earliest known proboscidean, *Phosphatherium*, have been found in Early Eocene rocks, dating from 55 million years ago in the Ouled Abdoun Basin in Morocco. The animal was roughly the size of a medium-sized dog. It is known mainly from the skull and teeth, which show that it lacked a trunk and fed on relatively soft vegetation. The first known elephant-like proboscideans were the genera *Palaeomastodon* and *Phiomia*, which appeared early in the

Oligocene of Egypt about 33 million years ago. They were roughly the size of a cow and had a medium-length trunk and downward-curving tusks. The family Elephantidae, which includes modern elephants and mammoths, first appeared in the Late Miocene about 7 million years ago; it is the only surviving family of all the proboscideans.

★ LONGEST TUSKS

Tusks are found on both male and female African elephants (*Loxodonta sp.*) but only on male Asian elephants (*Elephas maximus*), and continue to grow throughout life; in some Asian countries only a small proportion of males have tusks (5–7% in Sri Lanka, for example)

and, throughout their range, females either have no tusks at all or they are vestigial and do not protrude beyond the lip. The longest tusks from any living species are a pair from an African elephant shot in the eastern Congo at the turn of the century and preserved in the National Collection of Heads and Horns kept by the New York Zoological Society in Bronx Park, New York City, USA. The right tusk measures 3.49 m (11 ft 5½ in) along the outside curve and the left 3.35 m (11 ft); their combined weight is 133 kg (293 lb).

★ HEAVIEST TUSKS

The heaviest tusks from any animal (excluding prehistoric examples) are a pair from a bull African elephant (*Loxodonta africana*) shot at the foot of Mt Kilimanjaro, Kenya, in 1897, and now held in the Natural History Museum, UK. They originally weighed 109 kg (240 lb) (length 3.11 m (l0 ft 2½ in)) and 102 kg (225 lb) (length 3.18 m (10 ft 5½ in)) respectively, giving a total weight of 211 kg (465 lb). A single bush elephant tusk collected in Benin and exhibited at the Paris Exposition in 1900 weighed 117 kg (258 lb).

★ LONGEST LIVING

No other terrestrial mammal can match the age attained by humans (*Homo sapiens*), but the Asian elephant (*Elephas maximus*) probably comes closest. The greatest verified age is 86 years for a bull named Lin Wang, who died on 26 February 2003 at Tapei Zoo, Tawain. The

> Just as some people are left-handed or right-handed, elephants prefer to use one tusk rather than the other (usually the right).

oldest female was Modoc, a 78-year-old imported into the USA from Germany in 1898, at the age of two. She had an extraordinarily varied career, including 35 years in a circus (during which she gained notoriety by rescuing caged lions from a fire), 20 years in a roadside zoo and nine years as a TV star in programmes such as *Daktari* (for which she had to wear false ears to make her look African). She eventually died at Santa Clara, California, USA, on

17 July 1975, as a result of complications after surgery for an in-growing toenail.

★ LONGEST MEMORY

Female elephants have the amazing ability to remember the location of at least 17 family members when the herd searches for food, whether they are travelling in front, behind or in a separate group. Elephants have poor eyesight and so sniff urine-soaked earth to identify one another.

★ EARLIEST DOMESTICATION

There are records of tamed Asian elephants (*Elephas maximus*) being used as beasts of burden in the Indus Valley civilization, which thrived on the Indian sub-continent at least 4000 years ago. Since then, they have been widely used in agriculture and forestry, during wars, on

Asian elephant
The Asian elephant has the longest lifespan of any terrestrial mammal after humans. The record-holder reached a grand old age of 86 years.

WORLD RECORD HOLDER

Largest on land

The African bush elephant (*Loxodonta africana*) is the largest living land animal. The average adult stands 3–3.7 m (9 ft l0 in–12 ft) at the shoulder and weighs 4–7 tonnes; cows are considerably smaller than bulls of a similar age. The largest elephant ever recorded was a bull shot near Mucusso, southern Angola, in 1974. Lying on its side, it measured 4.16 m (13 ft 8 in) in a projected line from the highest point of the shoulder to the base of the forefoot, indicating a standing height of about 3.96 m (13 ft). Other measurements for this record-breaking individual included a length of 10.67 m (35 ft), a forefoot circumference of 1.8 m (5 ft 11 in) and a weight computed to be 12.25 tonnes.

The endangered desert elephant (a race of the African bush elephant) of Damaraland, Namibia, is the tallest elephant in the world because it has proportionally longer legs than other elephants. The tallest recorded individual was a bull shot near Sesfontein in 1978. Lying on its side, it measured 4.42 m (14½ ft) in a projected line from the shoulder to the base of the forefoot, indicating a standing height of about 4.21 m (13 ft 10 in).

The other species of African elephant, the forest elephant (*Loxodonta cyclotis*), which lives in the equatorial forests of the central African basin and West Africa, is much smaller than the savanna elephant. It has an average height at the shoulder of 2–3 m (6 ft 7 in–9 ft 10 in) and an average weight of 2–4.5 tonnes.

Asian elephants (*Elephas maximus*) are lighter and shorter than African. The majority of authenticated record-breakers belong to the Sri Lankan sub-species, *Elephas m. maximus*, which is found in Sri Lanka and southern India. The largest on record are generally bulls about 3–3.4 m (9 ft 10 in–11 ft 1 in) high at the shoulder.

The African bush elephant (*Loxodonta africana*) has larger outer ears than any other animal on Earth. Their size, however, has less to do with hearing than with temperature control. They each have a large network of blood vessels that act rather like radiator pipes: as the blood passes across the ears it loses heat; the system is so effective that there can be a difference of as much as 19°C (66°F) between the arterial blood coming from the heart and the returning venous blood. To increase temperature loss, the elephant flaps its ears or holds them out to catch the breeze; and, to decrease temperature loss, it holds them tight against the body. The African forest elephant (*Loxodonta cyclotis*) and the Asian elephant (*Elephas maximus*) have proportionately smaller ears because they live in more shady forests and do not have such a problem with over-heating.

African bush elephant
The African bush elephant has the longest tusks, which are simply enlarged incisor teeth in the upper jaw.

ceremonial occasions and, more recently, for carrying tourists. Unfortunately, since they are difficult animals to breed in captivity, most trained elephants are still obtained as youngsters from the wild.

It is a myth that African elephants (*Loxodonta sp.*) cannot be tamed and used as working animals, although they have been used less widely than their Asian relatives. The best-known example was when the Carthaginian leader, Hannibal, used them in his wars against the Romans over 2000 years ago. Until recently there were a few tamed African elephants at the Elephant Domestication Centre, in Garamba National Park, The Democratic Republic of Congo, which were used for short tourist safaris.

★ LARGEST APPETITE

Elephants have huge appetites and African bush elephants (*Loxodonta africana*) in particular spend about 18 hours a day feeding (usually in three main bouts – in the morning, afternoon and in the middle of the night – with time in between for other activities). A typical adult will consume 75–150 kg (165–330 lb) of vegetable matter every day (and will drink 80–160 litres (20–40 gallons) of water) but very large bulls may eat twice this amount.

★ TOOL USING

All species of elephant are able to use tools, but the African bush elephant (*Loxodonta africana*) is obviously the largest animal to do so (excluding humpback whales, which use bubbles as fishing nets). A recent study by Dr Suzanne Chevalier-Skolnikoff, of the University of California, and Dr Jo Liska, of the University of Colorado, in the USA,

SWIMMING

There are many accounts of elephants swimming across rivers, lakes and oceans. The largest herd swimming together was a group of 79 animals, but individuals and smaller groups have been reported swimming for as long as six hours at a time and as far as 48 km (30 miles) – without a break and without touching the bottom.

African forest elephant
African forest elephants are smaller than African bush elephants and also have smaller ears, probably because they live in more shady forests and do not have such a problem with overheating.

revealed that on average wild elephants use tools more than once an hour (captive ones use them ten times as often, perhaps because more objects are ready to hand). Most of the tool-use observed was to do with personal hygiene: for example, using vegetation to swat flies or scratch themselves, wiping cuts on their bodies with clumps of grass held in the trunk, and throwing dirt or blowing water over themselves to cool down or to relieve irritation from parasites. They also throw objects at unwanted intruders (other animals or vehicles). Some of the more unusual cases of tool-using records compiled by the researchers include a large bull picking up a young calf and throwing it against a fence to break it and captive elephants twisting hay into ropes and rings to adorn their bodies like jewellery.

ELEPHANT-SHREWS

Macroscelidea

Elephant-shrews have, at one time or another, been associated with true shrews, primates, tree shrews and even hoofed mammals. However, they possess a unique combination of features including large eyes (true shrews have little beady eyes), a long flexible trunk-like snout, and long legs (true shrews have short legs that barely lift their bellies off the ground). There are 15 species in a single family (Macroscelididae), all with their hind legs longer than their fore legs; indeed, they are the only insect-eating mammals adapted for bounding. They are widespread in Africa, but are found nowhere else in the world

Short-eared elephant shrew
This is the smallest species of elephant shrew and has the typically long snout which is responsible for them gaining their name.

★ LARGEST

The largest elephant shrews are the three members of the genus *Rhynchocyon*, known as the chequered elephant shrews. The largest of these is the golden-rumped elephant-shrew (*R. chrysopygus*), which lives in southeastern Kenya. It has a head-body length of 27–31.5 cm (10½–12½ in), a tail length of 23–26.5cm (9–10½ in), and an average adult weight of approximately 500 g (1 lb 2 oz).

★ SMALLEST

The smallest is the short-eared elephant-shrew (*Macroscelides proboscideus*) from southern Africa; it has a head-body length of 10.4–11.5 cm (4–4½ in), a tail length of 11.5–13 cm (4½–5 in), and an average adult weight of about 45 g (1½ oz).

★ FASTEST

The golden-rumped elephant-shrew (*Rhynchocyon chrysopygus*) is able to run across the open forest floor at speeds of at least 25 km/h (15½ mph), which is about as fast as a person would be able to run across similar terrain.

FLYING LEMURS

Cynocephalidae
Two species (otherwise known as colugos)

★ LARGEST

Flying lemurs are cat-sized and the largest of the two species, by a small margin, is the Malayan flying lemur (*Cynocephalus variegatus*), which is widely distributed in the rainforests and rubber plantations of Southeast Asia. It has a head-body length of 34–42 cm (13½–16½ in); a tail length of 17.5–27 cm (7–10½ in); a 'wingspan' of 70 cm (27½ in); and weighs 1–1.75 kg (2 lb 3oz–3 lb 14 oz).

★ LONGEST GLIDE

The two flying lemurs have the best-developed flying membrane of all mammals. Although few have been measured, controlled glides greater than 70 m (230 ft) are believed to be fairly common. The longest on record is a glide of 136 m (446 ft) between two trees, during which the animal lost only 10.5–12 m (34½–39½ ft) in height. Flying lemurs are primarily nocturnal and are therefore capable of launching themselves into the air, from the tops of the trees, in darkness. They have good night-time and stereoscopic vision, giving them the depth perception necessary for judging accurate landings. Indeed, they are able to determine their long, shallow glides with astonishing accuracy and normally land on a secure tree trunk selected beforehand; this may be only 3–4 m (10–13 ft) above the ground (landing on terra firma would be dangerous since they are so well adapted to life in the treetops that they are almost helpless on the ground). After landing, they climb up the tree trunk in a rather clumsy and lurching fashion, ready for another glide.

HEDGEHOGS & MOON RATS

Erinaceomorpha
24 species

★ LARGEST

The moon rat, which is found in Myanmar (formerly Burma), Thailand, Malaysia, Sumatra and Borneo, is generally considered to be the largest in this group. About the size of a rabbit, it has a head and body length of 26–46 cm (10¼–18 in), a tail length of 17–25 cm (6¾–9¾ in), and a weight of 1–2 kg (2 lb 3 oz–4 lb 6 oz). Females are slightly larger than males. The European hedgehog (*Erinaceus europaeus*) is much shorter in overall length at 20–30 cm (8–11¾ in), tail length 2–4 cm (¾–1½ in) and normally weighs 0.5–1.4 kg (1 lb 2 oz–3 lb 1 oz). However, well-fed specimens (especially captive ones with indulgent owners) can weigh as much as 2.2 kg (4 lb 14 oz).

HYRAXES

Procaviidae (otherwise known as dassies or conies)
11 species

Legend has it that the overall grip of a hyrax is so powerful that it will remain fixed to a nearly vertical surface even after it has died.

✴ EARLIEST

Hyraxes are believed to have descended from early ungulates (hoofed mammals) that were also ancestral to the elephants and sirenians, the three groups together being known as the Paenungulata. This ancestor lived about 55 million years ago. Modern hyraxes still retain many of their original features, such as teeth with a combination of crescent-shaped and straight crests. Around 35 million years ago, hyraxes were the most important medium-sized browsing ungulates in Africa. However, they began to decline in numbers some 10 million years later, when competition from antelopes that had dispersed from Eurasia forced them to live in specialized niches: in particular, around rocky outcrops, cliffs and trees.

✴ LARGEST

The largest hyrax is Johnston's rock hyrax (*Procavia johnstoni*), which grows to a maximum weight of 5.4 kg (12 lb) and has a head-body length of up to 58 cm (23 in); as with all hyraxes, it does not have an external tail. The southern tree hyrax (*Dendrohyrax arboreus*) is a bit lighter in weight (maximum about 5 kg (11 lb)) but can grow to a slightly longer head-body length of 60 cm (24 in).

✴ SMALLEST

The smallest hyrax is Bruce's yellow-spotted hyrax (*Heterohyrax brucei*), which weighs as little as 1.3 kg (2 lb 14 oz) (maximum 2.4 kg (5 lb 5 oz)) and has a minimum head-body length of 32.5 cm (12¾ in) (maximum 47 cm (18½ in)).

✴ CLIMBING

Hyraxes are the only true hoofed mammals that regularly climb trees. Although hoofed toes are not a particularly good adaptation for climbing, the soles of their feet are moist and rubbery and therefore provide excellent traction. In addition, the centre part of each sole can be pulled inward, by special muscles inside the foot, and the vacuum created by this strong 'suction cup' helps them to stick to whatever surface they happen to be climbing.

✴ DIFFERENT SPECIES LIVING TOGETHER

Two species of hyrax – Bruce's yellow-spotted hyrax (*Heterohyrax brucei*) and Johnston's hyrax (*Procavia johnstoni*) live together in harmony in the dense vegetation of the Serengeti kopjes, in Tanzania. Such a close association between different species is otherwise unknown in mammals except primates. The two different hyraxes spend the night sleeping in the same holes; they huddle together for warmth early in the morning; their newborn are greeted and sniffed enthusiastically by both species; the young animals form joint nurseries and play together; and they even use similar vocalizations to communicate with one another. There are two main reasons why they are able to coexist in this way:

they do not interbreed (their mating behaviour is different and their sexual organs are incompatible) and they do not compete for food (Bruce's yellow-spotted hyrax browses on leaves while Johnston's hyrax feeds mainly on grass). But there is no doubt about the dominant species: whenever there is a limited resource, such as a dust bath or a pool of water, the much larger Johnston's hyrax always takes precedence.

✴ HIGHEST LIVING

Several different hyraxes in the genera *Procavia* and *Dendrohyrax* live in the alpine zone of mountains and mountain ranges at heights in excess of 3500 m (11,480 ft) above sea level. The highest living species are those found on Mt Kenya, in Kenya 5199 m (17,058 ft); Mt Kilimanjaro, in Tanzania 5894 m (19,340 ft) and in the Ruwenzori Mountains, on the border between Uganda and Zaire (5119 m (16,795 ft) at Mt Stanley).

✴ LOWEST LIVING

There is a population of Abyssinian hyraxes (*Procavia habessinicus*) living at 400 m (1312 ft) below sea level along the shores of the Dead Sea.

Bruce's yellow-spotted hyrax
This is the smallest species of hyrax. Uniquely amongst hoofed mammals, hyraxes have the ability to climb trees with great success due to special adaptations on the soles of their feet.

MANATEES & DUGONG

Sirenia

Trichechidae: three species (manatees); Dugongidae: one species (dugong)

Florida manatee
Manatees thrive in warm water. At temperatures below 20°C (68°F) they start suffering which is why they take on long migrations to warmer waters in winter.

★ EARLIEST

Relatively little is known about sirenian evolution and it appears that even at their zenith there were no more than about a dozen (mostly monotypic) genera worldwide. Ancestral forms date from the early Eocene, about 55 million years ago, and the oldest known fossils belong to a species called *Protosiren*, which has been found in Jamaica. The earliest known true manatee, a species called *Potamosiren*, lived in the Middle Miocene 13–16 million years ago; the main difference between this and modern species is in the teeth: *Potamosiren* lacked the extra teeth and the tooth replacement facility that is characteristic of today's manatees (as an adaptation for eating abrasive plant materials).

★ LARGEST

The West Indian manatee (*Trichechus manatus*), which lives in the Caribbean, the Gulf of Mexico and the western Atlantic, is by a narrow margin the largest

living sirenian. It is often split into two sub-species, both of which have an average length of 3 m (9 ft 10 in) and an average weight of 500 kg (1100 lb) (males and females are similar in size); however, the sub-species known as the Florida manatee (*Trichechus m. latirostris*) reaches a larger maximum size of 3.9 m (12 ft 10 in) and 1660 kg (3650 lb) than the slightly smaller Antillean manatee (*Trichechus m. manatus*). There is an unauthenticated report of a 4.7 m (15 ft 5 in) Florida manatee, caught off the coast of Texas, USA, in 1910, but information is lacking and this figure is treated as suspect by most experts.

There is an unauthenticated record of a dugong (*Dugong dugon*) caught off India on 23 July 1959, which allegedly measured 4.06 m (13 ft 4 in) in length and weighed 1016 kg (2240 lb). However,

Manatees never run out of teeth: they possess only molars and pre-molars and these are continuously being replaced by new teeth that appear behind the 'active' row and then move forward.

the average size for this species is only 2.7 m (8 ft 10 in) and 250–350 kg (550–770 lb) and recent assessments suggest that a measurement error was made when this particular animal was examined.

★ SMALLEST

The Amazonian manatee (*Trichechus inunguis*) is the smallest sirenian and is both shorter and more slender than its relatives. The average size is about 2.5 m

(8 ft 2 in) and 350 kg (661 lb). A dwarf variety has been discovered in the Rio Arauazinho, Brazil, which is just 1.3 m (4 ft 4 ins) (most other individuals are up to 3m (9 ft 11 in)).

★ LONGEST LIVING

The normal lifespan of sirenians is not well known. But West Indian manatees (*Trichechus manatus*) have been known to live in captivity for more than 40 years and estimates of the ages of wild sirenians (by counting growth layers in the ear bones of manatees and in the tusks of dugongs) suggest a normal lifespan of 50–60 years. The record to date is 73 years in the case of a dugong (*Dugong dugon*).

★ LONGEST MIGRATION

Individual marking studies in Florida have shown that at least some Florida manatees (*Trichechus manatus latirostris*) migrate north in summer and south in winter; long-distance movements of more than 850 km (528 miles) have been recorded. There is little information on the migrations of the other two manatees, although short-range seasonal movements in response to shifts in food availability and changing weather patterns probably occur. Circumstantial evidence suggests that the dugong (*Dugong dugon*) may travel long distances. During one study, an individual equipped with a satellite transmitter travelled between two bays 200 km (124 miles) apart three times in nine weeks; there are also occasional sightings of dugongs as far south as Sydney, Australia, which is 700 km (435 miles) south of the nearest known habitat area.

★ LONGEST DIVE

The average interval between breaths for the three manatee species is estimated to be approximately 2–4 minutes and for the dugong (*Dugong dugon*) approximately $1^{1}/_{4}$ minutes (although dive times vary with activity – active animals need to breathe more frequently). The longest authenticated dive recorded for any of the four species is 24 minutes for a West Indian manatee (*Trichechus manatus*) in Florida; however, since adults frequently dive for 15–20 minutes when resting, it is likely that some manatees can hold their breath for even longer.

★ FRESHWATER LIVING

The Amazonian manatee (*Trichechus inunguis*) is the only sirenian that lives exclusively in freshwater. The dugong (*Dugong dugon*) is a marine animal, although it enters brackish or freshwater occasionally; and the West Indian manatee (*Trichechus manatus*) and West African manatee (*Trichechus senegalensis*) both live in a mixture of freshwater and saltwater habitats.

★ METABOLIC RATE

The metabolic rate of manatees is about one-third that of a typical mammal of the same weight. They are capable of rapid movement when being pursued (swimming speeds of up to 25 km/h ($15^{1}/_{2}$ mph) have been recorded) but they are normally slow in their movements.

★ LONGEST GESTATION PERIOD

All sirenians have a gestation period of approximately one year, although the dugong (*Dugong dugon*) consistently has the longest (13–14 months) by a very narrow margin (the gestation period in wild West Indian manatees (*Trichechus manatus*) is 12–13 months and in captive individuals as long as 14 months).

• Dugong
Dugongs are amongst the longest-living mammals with the oldest dugong on record reaching the grand old age of 73.

MAMMALS

MARSUPIAL MAMMALS

c. 290 species: pouch-bearing mammals that give birth to underdeveloped young used to be grouped together in the order Marsupialia. They are now divided between seven distinct orders: Diprotodontia – wombats, koala, possums, cuscus, ringtails, gliders, wallabies, kangaroos; Dasyuromorphia – thylacine, quolls, dasyures, antechinus, phascogales, dunnarts; Notoryctemorphia – marsupial moles; Didelphimorphia – opposums; Peramelemorphia – bilbies, bandicoots; Paucituberculata – caenolestids (shrew-opossums); Microbiotheria – monito del monte

★ EARLIEST

The oldest known marsupial is a skeleton of *Sinodelphys szalayi* from 125 million-year-old rocks in China. This gives us a minimum date for divergence of the marsupial and placental lineages. Most marsupial evolution during the age of the dinosaurs, however, took place in North America, the tiny jaw from the mouse-sized *Kokopellia juddi* from 100-million-year-old siltstone in Utah being the oldest. The oldest known marsupials from the southern hemisphere are about 60 million years old and include two fossil skulls belonging to *Pucadelphys andinus*

and *Mayulestes ferox*, found in Bolivia. Thus, mammals with pouches are judged to have spread from North America around the end of the Cretaceous Period, 65 million years ago, first to South America and from there to Australia via Antarctica (all three continents were united as a single landmass until about 55 million years ago).

★ LARGEST

The red kangaroo (*Megaleia rufa*) of central, southern and eastern Australia is the world's largest pouch-bearing mammal. It has a head-body length of 1.3–1.65 m (4 ft 3 in–5 ft 5 in) (male) and 85–105 cm (34–42 in) (female), a tail length of 1–1.2 m (39–48 in) (male) and 65–85 cm (26–34 in) (female) and a weight of 20–90 kg (44–198 lb) (rarely more than 55 kg (121¼ lb) in males and 30 kg (66 lb) in females). Old males may be 1.8 m (5 ft 11 in) tall when standing in the normal position, and considerably taller (up to 2.1 m (6 ft 11 in)) when standing on their toes, for example during aggressive encounters. Head-body lengths of up to 3.4 m (11 ft 2 in) and weights of up to 136 kg (300 lb) have been claimed by hunters in the past, but these are considered extremely unlikely. Old hunting reports suggest some males of the Tasmanian race of the eastern grey kangaroo (*Macropus giganteus tasmaniensis*) may rival the largest reds for size.

Red kangaroo
The largest of the marsupials is the red kangaroo which can reach up to 1.8 m (5 ft 11 in) or over 2 m (6 ft 11 in) when standing on its toes.

★ LARGEST PREHISTORIC

There were many large pouch-bearing mammals in prehistoric times. The largest known was an Australian species called *Diprotodon optatum*, which was rhinoceros-sized, but more like a bear in appearance , and belonged to the now-extinct family Diprotodontidae. It survived until about 40,000 years ago. The largest known kangaroo was the 3 m (9 ft 10 in) tall *Procoptodon goliah*.

★ SMALLEST

There are a number of very small, mouse-sized species and opinions vary over which is the smallest. All belong to the order Dasyuromorphia. The two main contenders are the rare long-tailed planigale (*Planigale ingrami*), a flat-skulled shrew-like creature found in northern Australia, and the rather similar pilbara ningaui (*Ningaui timealeyi*) from northwestern Australia. The planigale has a head and body length of 5.5–6.3 cm (2^1/$_5$–2^1/$_2$ in); a tail length of 5.7–6 cm (2^1/$_4$–2^1/$_3$ in); and a weight of 3.9–4.5 g (^{1}/$_8$–^{1}/$_6$ oz). The pilbara ningaui has a head-body length of 4.6–5.7 cm (1^7/$_8$–2^1/$_4$ in); a tail length of 5.9–7.9 cm (2^1/$_3$–3^1/$_8$ in); and a weight of 2–9.4 g (^{1}/$_{16}$–^{1}/$_3$ oz).

★ LONGEST LIVING

Despite being born in a rather vulnerable state of under-development, many larger species have fairly long potential lifespans. The greatest reliable age recorded is 26 years 22 days for a common wombat (*Vombatus ursinus*), which died in London Zoo on 20 April 1906. Large kangaroos, especially the eastern grey (*Macropus giganteus*) and red (*Megaleia rufa*), have been known to reach 20–24 years in captivity and may be able to live for as long as 28 years.

★ LONGEST JUMP

When travelling at speed, it is not unusual for large kangaroos to leap enormous distances of 8 m (26^1/$_2$ ft) or more in a single bound. Hopping is both rapid and, in terms of energy consumption, an efficient mode of travel. The record-holder may be an eastern grey kangaroo (*Macropus giganteus*) that jumped nearly 13.5 m (44 ft 8^1/$_2$ in) on the flat, although this has not been verified. A very close runner up is a female red kangaroo (*Megaleia rufa*), which made a series of exceptional bounds, including one of 12.8 m (42 ft), during a chase in New South Wales, Australia, in January 1951.

★ HIGHEST JUMP

Large kangaroos normally do not jump higher than about 1.5 m (59 in), and fences of this height will deter most animals. However, there are many records (mostly unauthenticated) of them jumping much

Tree kangaroos have been known to leap 10 m (33 ft) or more between trees and can jump to the ground from heights of up to 30 m (100 ft) without apparently harming themselves.

higher, especially when under pressure to escape from predators or human hunters. The record-holder is probably a red kangaroo (*Megaleia rufa*), which cleared a stack of timber 3.1 m (10 ft) high in a desperate bid to escape from a pack of hunting dogs in the 1960s. There is also a record of a captive male eastern grey kangaroo (*Macropus giganteus*) that reportedly cleared a 2.44 m (8 ft) fence when it was scared by a car back-firing.

★ LONGEST GESTATION PERIOD

The gestation period (the time the foetus spends developing inside the female) of all pouch-bearing mammals is relatively

Eastern grey kangaroo

The eastern grey kangaroo has the longest gestation period for a marsupial but this is only 37 days long. Newborns have been described as breathing foetuses developing more outside the womb than during the gestation period.

short. They give birth to very small, poorly developed young and the period of growth and development after birth is considerably longer than the period inside the womb. The longest gestations are 37 days in the eastern grey kangaroo (*Macropus giganteus*), 36 days in the whiptail wallaby (*M. parryi*) and 35 days in the parma wallaby (*M. parma*), swamp wallaby (*Wallabia bicolor*) and koala (*Phascolarctos cinereus*). In some species, development of the fertilized egg is delayed until the previous young leave the pouch or until there are more favourable environmental conditions. In the red kangaroo (*Megaleia rufa*), for example, this delay between mating and development can be as long as 28 weeks.

Newborns eyes and ears are embryonic and non-functional and their hind limbs are little more than short, five-lobed buds. Furthermore their skin is bare, thin and richly supplied with blood (possibly acting as a respiratory surface).

Birth is very quick: the baby simply pops out and, within a few minutes, has dragged itself through the forest of hairs on its mother's belly, into the pouch and on to a teat (it has long, powerful forelimbs with needle-sharp claws). The mother doesn't help at all, and no one knows exactly how the baby finds its way to the teat. Its good sense of smell may guide it or perhaps the fact it can detect gravitational pull is a factor. The youngster, known as a pouch embryo, closes its mouth around the teat, which enlarges so much it cannot fall off until its jaws are sufficiently developed for it to be able to release itself, which may take weeks or even months.

★ SHORTEST GESTATION PERIOD

The shortest mammalian gestation period is 12–13 days, which is common in a number of species. These include the Virginia opossum (*Didelphis virginiana*) of North America, the water opossum or yapok (*Chironectes minimus*) of Central and South America, the eastern quoll or

native cat (*Dasyurus viverrinus*) of Australia and the long-nosed bandicoot (*Perameles nasuta*), also of Australia. On rare occasions, gestation periods as short as eight days have been recorded for some of these species.

• Red kangaroo newborn
The red kangaroo has the largest newborn. It is incredibly small in comparison to a full grown adult, but it then develops outside the womb in the mother's pouch.

★ LARGEST NEWBORN

The female red kangaroo (*Megaleia rufa*) gives birth to the largest baby, but even this weighs only 0.75 g (³/₁₀₀ oz) (0.003% of the average maternal weight, compared with more than 5% in humans). It would take 36,000 of these babies to equal the weight of the mother. Interestingly, by the time the young are weaned, the ratio

between the mother's weight and the weight of the offspring (whether a litter or a single individual) is roughly the same in both mammals with pouches and placentals.

★ SMALLEST NEWBORN

All newborn pouched mammals are tiny, weighing less than 1 g (⁷/₂₀₀ oz). So it's difficult to single out the smallest. However, a strong contender is the honey possum (*Tarsipes rostratus*) of southwestern Australia, which gives birth to two, three or occasionally four young each weighing just 0.005 g (¹/₅₀₀ oz). They still weigh only 2.5 g (¹/₁₀ oz) by the time they leave the pouch (when they are eight weeks old) but, to put this into context, four of them together weigh nearly as much as their mother.

★ MOST DANGEROUS LOVE LIFE

Broad-footed mice in the genus *Antechinus* have an extremely peculiar trait: after mating frenetically over a two week period, all the exhausted males die. This remarkable phenomenon is best understood and most studied in the brown antechinus (*A. stuartii*) of eastern Australia. The male begins to change dramatically in the period leading up to the breeding season: his testes grow and grow until they make up about a quarter of his total body weight. Huge amounts of the male sex hormone testosterone enter his bloodstream and he develops an insatiable sexual appetite. For two weeks every year, the entire adult male population goes on the rampage in a desperate bid to mate with as many females as they can. They are so busy chasing females and fighting rival males they have no time (or simply forget) to eat. In a matter of days, they are all dead. Some die of

Every year all male broad-footed mice go sex mad for two weeks and then die from exhaustion

Eastern grey kangaroo
When feeling threatened, the eastern grey kangaroo is capable of hopping along at record-breaking speeds of up to 64 km/h (40 mph).

starvation, others from stomach ulcers caused by all the stress, but most succumb to disease or infection (excessive amounts of testosterone suppress the immune system). Only the pregnant females, and their unborn offspring, are left. The females live for up to three years, while most males have a life expectancy of no more than 11–12 months.

★ MOST WATERPROOF POUCH

The female South American water opossum or yapok (*Chironectes minimus*) carries her babies around in a special waterproof pouch. When she is underwater, strong sphincter muscles close the rear-opening, keeping the pouch tightly shut, while long hairs and fatty secretions create a watertight seal. Air trapped inside allows the youngsters to breathe. An accomplished swimmer, the yapok is the only such mammal highly adapted for an aquatic way of life. Its other adaptations include dense, oily, water-repellent fur and webbed hind feet.

★ LARGEST POUCH

In most of these mammals, the young are protected by a pouch of hair-covered skin, known as the marsupium. The numbat (*Myrmecobius fasciatus*) is the only one without one, and the young are carried attached to teats on the outside of the mother's belly. Other

species have little more than a fold of skin, or develop a pouch only during the breeding season.

The biggest pouches belong to the largest kangaroos in the genera *Macropus* and *Megaleia*, which normally produce only one young at a time. The baby kangaroo, or joey, remains in the pouch long after it has become detached from the teat. Even once it has begun to venture into the outside world, it frequently uses the pouch as a means of transport, a place to sleep and somewhere to dive for cover. The young

> A mother kangaroo is able to suckle two youngsters of different ages simultaneously by producing two kinds of milk: one slightly diluted for the youngest and the other more concentrated (with extra fat) for the oldest.

red kangaroo (*Megaleia rufa*) eventually leaves the pouch for good when it is about eight months old.

Species that produce large litters don't have room to carry them all for a long time. Once the youngsters have detached themselves from the teat, they are usually left in a nest while their mother is out foraging.

★ BEST GRIP

The fingertips of the feathertail glider (*Acrobates pygmaeus*) have expanded pads to give the animal extra grip while it is climbing. Each pad is microscopically grooved (as in geckos), enabling it to cling to almost any smooth surface. This is such an effective system that the feathertail is able to walk up a clean window and can even hold itself, albeit briefly, to the underside of a horizontal sheet of glass.

★ MOST FUSSY EATER

The koala (*Phascolarctos cinereus*) of eastern Australia feeds almost exclusively on the leaves of eucalyptus trees. It browses regularly on about 12 of the 500 species, prefers individual trees above others, and is even choosy about specific leaves (sometimes sifting through as much as 9 kg (20 lb) of leaves every day for the 0.5 kg (1 lb 1 oz) it eventually eats). No one knows what it is that makes one particular tree or leaf more desirable than another, especially since the choice varies between populations, between individuals and with the seasons. However, it is likely to be connected with the fact that eucalyptus leaves are not a particularly good source of food: they contain little protein, lots of difficult-to-digest fibre and essential oils that are toxic in high concentrations.

★ FASTEST

Kangaroos and wallabies are capable of attaining extremely high speeds, particularly over short distances. They hop with their two hind feet, holding their

Greater glider
The greater glider manages flight by climbing to the top of a high tree, leaping into the air and gliding a considerable distance before landing with all four feet on the trunk of another tree.

front paws up against their chests and using their big tails as counterbalances. The highest speed recorded for any pouch-bearing mammal is 64 km/h (40 mph) by a mature female eastern grey kangaroo (*Macropus giganteus*). The highest sustained speed is 56 km/h (35 mph) recorded for a large male red kangaroo (*Megaleia rufa*), which unfortunately died from its exertions after being paced for 1.6 km (1 mile) (maximum speed is normally reached only under pressure, such as when being chased by a car).

★ GLIDING

Some pouch-bearing mammals in the suborder Phalangeriformes, are capable of gliding. Within the family Pseudocheiridae, only the greater glider (*Petauroides volans*) can take to the air. In the Petauridae, six species can glide, while in the Acrobatidae only the feathertail glider (*Acrobates pygmaeus*) takes to the air. All have a membrane of skin stretched between their arms and legs which, when extended, forms a rectangular, kite-like aerofoil. Steering is achieved by altering the tension of the membrane on either side of the body, and balance by using the outstretched tail as a rudder. When not in use, the gliding membrane is folded away and may be visible as a wavy line along each side of the body. Some species can glide further than 100 m (330 ft) and are highly manoeuvrable in the air.

★ SLEEPIEST

Two species in particular are well known for their sleepy habits: the marsupial mole (*Notoryctes typhlops*) and the koala (*Phascolarctos cinereus*). Limited observations on the marsupial mole suggest it alternates without warning between periods of frenetic activity and sudden sleep. The koala's sleepy habits are a little more logical: since it has a low quality diet (*see* MOST FUSSY EATER p. 81), it spends up to 18 out of every 24 hours sleeping or dozing to conserve energy.

★ LARGEST BURROWING

The largest burrowing species is the common or coarse-haired wombat (*Vombatus ursinus*) of southeastern Australia and Tasmania, which is roughly

the same weight as an old English sheepdog. It has a head-body length of 70–120 cm (28–48 in) (the tail is almost non-existent); and a weight of 15–35 kg (33–77 lb) It is a strong and powerful digger, using its claws and trowel-like teeth to burrow through soil at an incredible rate of up to 3 m (10 ft) per hour.

★ PLAYING POSSUM

The cat-sized Virginia or American opossum (*Didelphis virginiana*) is the only pouch-bearing mammal in North America. More interestingly, it sometimes pretends to be dead when faced with danger – giving its name to the phrase 'playing possum'. The aim is to make its predators less cautious in their approach and to make them lose interest. With staring, unblinking eyes, the opossum curls up on its side, droops its head, opens its mouth

slightly and lets its tongue hang out. It is extremely convincing – especially since the opossum doesn't flinch if touched, even if bitten or shaken about in a predator's mouth. In this trance-like state, it can remain absolutely immobile for as little as less than a minute or as much as six hours. There are some physiological similarities between the opossum's behaviour and fainting in humans. But the opossum's brain remains fully operational, ready for the animal to snap back into life and seize a chance of escape the moment the predator puts it down or relaxes its grip. Death feigning has been reported in other opossums, but only rarely.

★ LARGEST LITTER

Most pouch-bearing mammals give birth to small litters of 1–10 babies, the general trend being the smaller the animal the larger the litter. The record-

Virginia opossum
The opossum is the origin of the phrase 'playing possum' because of its tendency to pretend to be dead when faced with danger.

holder is the Virginia opossum (*Didelphis virginiana*) of North America, which frequently gives birth to more offspring than can be accommodated on its teats. The female normally has 13 teats, but typically produces 21 young per litter. Not all the teats are functional and, since unfed babies soon perish, it is rare for more than eight to survive. This seems very wasteful, but competition to reach a teat ensures the mother invests her time and energy in raising only the strongest offspring. The overall record-holder is a female Virginia opossum that gave birth to an incredible 56 babies at one time, each about the size of a baked bean.

MONOTREMES

Monotremata

Five species: duck-billed platypus, eastern long-beaked echidna, Attenborough's long-beaked echidna, short-beaked echidna and western long-beaked echidna; all egg-laying

★ EARLIEST

The oldest known monotremes are represented by 110-million-year-old fossil jaw fragments from New South Wales, Australia. They belonged to two species named *Steropodon galmani* and *Kollikodon ritchiei*, which are tooth-bearing stem members of the group. Only a few other monotreme fossils have been found and these are all from much later

Australia and New Guinea, and the second oldest known monotreme fossil. A lower tooth and a second upper tooth were found in 1992. According to current theories of continental drift, the great southern continent of Gondwanaland had largely broken up by that time, but Australia was still connected to South America through Antarctica (which was much warmer than it is now). Modern

aquatic or burrowing lifestyles, superimposed on a primitive body plan. Amazingly their DNA reveals that at a genetic level the platypus is a unique amalgam of mammal and reptile.

★ LARGEST

The largest monotreme is the long-beaked echidna or spiny anteater (*Zaglossus bruijni*), which lives in the mountains of New Guinea and Salawati. The adult has a head-body length of 45–90 cm (18–35 in) (there is only a short, blunt tail) and a weight of 5–10 kg (11–22 lb); within a given population, males are normally 25% larger than females of the same age.

in the Cenozoic Era. They include the toothed platypus (*Obdurodon dicksoni*), represented by skull material from the Miocene Epoch in Queensland, and the oldest known echidna, *Megalibgwilia robusta*, from the Pliocene of New South Wales. Monotremes were always thought to have been confined to Australia and New Guinea, but a fossil tooth discovered in 1991 in the Golfo de San Jorge, on the coast of central Patagonia, Argentina, is believed to have come from an early platypus. The single upper right molar, about 1 cm (³/₈ in) long, was found in deposits laid down in a freshwater lagoon or mangrove swamp about 62 million years ago. It was the first evidence of a monotreme living outside

duck-billed platypuses (*Ornithorhynchus anatinus*) are born with teeth (indicating that their ancestors relied on them) but these are lost within a few weeks of birth.

★ MOST PRIMITIVE

The monotremes are generally assumed to be the most primitive of living mammals: they lay eggs (which is unique among mammals) and retain a number of reptilian skeletal features. The modern duck-billed platypus (*Ornithorhynchus anatinus*) is very similar to fossils found in rocks of the Mid-Miocene some 10 million years old. However, monotremes do not form a direct link between reptiles and the more advanced mammals. They represent highly specialized adaptations for either

Duck-billed platypus
The monotremes, such as this duck-billed platypus, are thought to be the most primitive of living mammals. They lay eggs and retain some reptilian features.

★ SMALLEST

The lightest monotreme is the duck-billed platypus (*Ornithorhynchus anatinus*), which lives along the eastern coast of Australia and on Tasmania. The adult male (slightly larger than the female in all respects) has a head-body length of 45–60 cm (18–24 in), a bill length of 5–7 cm (2–2³/₄ in), a tail length of 10–15 cm (4–6 in), and a weight of 1–2.4 kg (2 lb 3 oz–5 lb 5 oz). The smallest platypuses are found in northern Australia.

The short-beaked echidna (*Tachyglossus aculeatus*), which lives in Australia, Tasmania and eastern New Guinea, is considerably heavier than the platypus, but is shorter. The adult has a head-body length of 30–45 cm (12–18 in) (there is only a short, blunt tail) and a weight of 2.5–7 kg (5½–15½ lb); within a given population, males are normally 25% larger than females of the same age.

★ EGG-LAYING

The five monotreme species are the only living mammals that lay eggs. Almost everyone remained sceptical about this unlikely phenomenon for nearly a century after they were first studied, but the irrefutable fact was finally announced to a startled scientific community on 2 September 1884.

Despite their egg-laying, the reproductive system of monotremes is in most respects typically mammalian, with only a brief vestigial period of development of the young within the egg. The egg (one in echidnas and normally two in platypuses) is soft and leathery and about the size of a small grape. The female echidna incubates her egg in a small pouch for 10–10½ days before it hatches; because of her aquatic lifestyle, the female platypus does not have a pouch but incubates her eggs in a nesting chamber at the end of a 5–10 m (15–30 ft) long

FASTEST DIGGER

When frightened, an echidna digs with all four feet at once, instead of burrowing headfirst like most other mammals. It can disappear vertically into the ground in less than a minute – so rapidly that it has often been likened to a sinking ship. All that remains to be seen is a small forest of razor-sharp spines protruding through the soil.

burrow (maximum 30 m (100 ft)), curling her body around them in a half-sitting position. The incubation period is only 10–12 days and the tiny hatchlings (1.3–1.5 cm (½–⅝ in) long) are born naked and blind. The females do not have teats, but have special glands that ooze milk, which the young suck from the fur.

During courtship, a female echidna maybe followed by as many as ten hopeful males, lined up nose-to-tail, for as long as 36 days; she mates with only one of them before the two animals part company for good.

★ MOST VENOMOUS

Only two groups of mammals are venomous: certain insectivores in the families Soricidae and Solenodontidae, and the monotremes.

Slow lorises in the genus *Nycticebus* can produce a toxin which they mix with their saliva and use as protection against enemies. Of the monotremes, only the male duck-billed platypus (*Ornithorhynchus anatinus*) is capable of producing – and delivering – venom. The venom-producing gland, which is located in its thigh, is connected via a duct to a horny spur on the inner side of the ankle of each hind foot; curved and hollow, the spurs may be up to 1.5 cm (⅝ in) long and can be erected from within folds of skin. The venom itself is delivered when the platypus clasps its victim with its hind legs – so strongly that it can be almost impossible to prise off. It can kill a dingo within minutes and causes agonizing pain in people. No human deaths from platypus stings have been recorded, but the affected limb may swell to three or four times its normal size and can remain painful and useless for many months afterwards.

The female duck-billed platypus loses her spurs in infancy. The structures which produce and deliver venom are present in male echidnas, but not functional. No one knows why the male

Long beaked echidna
The largest of the monotremes is the western long-beaked echidna (*Zaglossus bruijni*) which lives in the mountains in New Guinea.

duck-billed platypus has these venomous spurs. If they are for defence, it is strange that the smaller female does not retain them; it seems unlikely that they are for catching prey, since the platypus feeds on tiny creatures such as small crustaceans, worms, tadpoles, insect larvae and the occasional small fish or frog; and, if they are for the male to hold on to the female during courtship, the venom seems to be superfluous. Since the venom glands become enlarged during the breeding season, they may be used for duels between males over females; but, even then, young animals are sometimes killed when they challenge adults, so the weaponry seems unnecessarily severe.

★ LONGEST LIVING

The natural longevity of monotremes is still largely unknown. The oldest ever recorded was a captive short-beaked echidna (*Tachyglossus aculeatus*) that lived for 49 years in Philadelphia Zoo, USA. The longest authenticated age in the wild is 16 years, for the same species. Duck-billed platypuses (*Ornithorhynchus anatinus*) have been known to live for a maximum of 20 years in captivity and 12 years in the wild.

★ DETECTING ELECTRICITY

The duck-billed platypus (*Ornithorhynchus anatinus*) is the only mammal known to be able to detect electric fields. It is totally blind and deaf underwater (its eyes and ears are sealed in a furrow of skin when it dives) and, as recently as the mid-1980s, it was believed to feel for food by rummaging around under rocks and along the river bed with its muzzle. But Australian and German scientists, working together at the Australian National University in Canberra, have discovered that the soft muzzle contains special electrical receptors, known previously only in some fish and tadpoles. These electroreceptors detect the minuscule electrical discharges produced during the muscle movements of its invertebrate prey (even if the tiny animals are under mud or stones) from a distance of about 7–10 cm (2³/₄–4 in).

PANGOLINS

Manidae

Eight species (otherwise known as scaly anteaters): four in sub-Saharan Africa and four in Asia

★ LARGEST

The giant pangolin (*Manis gigantea*), which lives in parts of sub-Saharan Africa, has a head-body length of 80–90 cm (32–36 in); a tail length of 65–80 cm (26–32 in); and a weight of 25–33 kg (55–72³/₄ lb). The male is much larger than the female.

★ SMALLEST

The long-tailed pangolin (*Manis tetradactyla*), which lives in parts of sub-Saharan Africa, has a head-body length of 30–35 cm (12–14 in); a tail length of 50–60 cm (20–24 in); and a weight of 1.2–3 kg (2 lb 10 oz–6 lb 10 oz). The female is much smaller than the male.

When alarmed, pangolins curl up into such a tight ball that they are practically impossible to unroll.

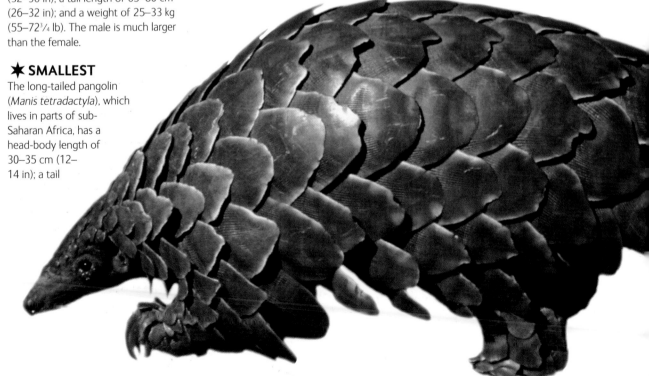

★ LONGEST TONGUE

The long tongue of the giant pangolin (*Manis gigantea*) can be extended 36–40 cm (14–16 in) beyond the end of the snout, and is some 70 cm (28 in) in total length. Coiled up inside the animal's mouth when at rest, it has muscular roots that pass down through the chest cavity and anchor to the pelvis. It is flicked in and out to catch the pangolin's favourite food – ants and termites.

★ LONGEST TAIL

The long-tailed pangolin (*Manis tetradactyla*) has no fewer than 46–47 vertebrae in its tail, which is more than in any other mammal.

★ SCALES

Pangolins are the only mammals to have an armour of horny, overlapping scales (other armoured mammals are protected by thickened skin or plates of bone with a horny covering). At first glance, the scales – which grow from the thick underlying skin – make them appear more reptilian than mammalian. They protect every part of the body except the underside and the inner surfaces of the limbs, and are shed and replaced individually.

Cape Pangolin
The cape pangolin or scaly anteater (*Manis temminckii*) pictured here has the scales typical of all pangolins, which make them appear more like reptiles than mammals.

PRIMATES

Primates

c. 400 species, including lemurs, lorises, tarsiers, marmosets, monkeys, gibbons, apes

★ EARLIEST

The first known primates belonged to the genera *Teilhardina* and *Cantius* and lived in Asia, Europe and North America at the beginning of the Eocene about 55 million years ago. *Teilhardina* was tiny and fed mainly on insects. It was probably a clinger/leaper like modern bushbabies and tarsiers. *Cantius* was larger and more like a lemur, included more fruit in its diet, and was probably adapted more for quadrupedal branch running than for leaping.

Aye-aye
When it is searching for insect larvae, hidden in hollow cavities beneath the surface of tree trunks and branches, studies have shown that the aye-aye does not use sight or smell but a form of echolocation (*see* ECHOLOCATION p. 91).

★ LARGEST PREHISTORIC

The largest primate ever known to have lived on Earth was the extinct hominid *Gigantopithecus* of the middle Pleistocene, in what is now northern Vietnam, India and southern China. From the only remains discovered to date (three partial lower jaws and more than 1000 teeth), it has been estimated that males stood about 2.74 m (9 ft) tall and weighed some 300-500 kg (660-1100 lb). However, this size will remain conjecture until further fossil evidence is uncovered, since there is a possibility that *Gigantopithecus* had a disproportionately large head, jaws and teeth in relation to its body size.

★ LARGEST

The gorilla (*Gorilla gorilla*) is the largest of all the primates, although many exaggerated reports over the years have given a false impression of its large size. It has a bipedal standing height (measured from the crown of the head to the base of the heels) of 1.4–1.8 m (4 ft 7 in–5 ft 11 in) (male) and 1.25–1.5 m (4ft 1 in–4ft 11 in) (female); a chest circumference of 1.25–1.75 m (50–70 in) (male) and 95–128 cm (38–50½ in) (female); and an average weight of 135–175 kg (298–386 lb) (male) and 68–114 kg (150–251 lb) (female). There are now considered to be two species: the western gorilla (*Gorilla gorilla*) of west and central Africa, and the eastern gorilla (*Gorilla beringei*) of The Democratic Republic of Congo, Rwanda and Uganda (mountain gorilla sub-species

(*G. b. beringei*)) and the eastern DRC (eastern lowland sub-species (*G. b. graueri*)). Of these the eastern is the biggest and the western the smallest – albeit by small margins.

The record authenticated size in the wild is a standing height of 1.95 m (6 ft 5 in); an armspan of 2.7 m (8 ft 10 in); and a weight of 219 kg (483 lb) for a male eastern gorilla collected by Commandant E Hubert and Dr Serge Freckhof in the Tchibinda Forest, northern Kivu province, The Democratic Republic of Congo, in 1938. There is also an unconfirmed (but generally accepted) report of a male eastern gorilla (reported as a mountain gorilla) shot by

Gorilla
Largest of all the primates, the gorilla can attain a standing height of up to 1.95 m (6 ft 5 in) and an impressive chest measurement of as much as 1.98 m (78 in).

Commander Attilio Gatti, in 1932, for the Royal Museum of Natural History, Florence, Italy. Also found in the Tchibinda Forest, it reputedly had a standing height of 2.06 m (6³/₄ ft) and weighed 218.6 kg (482 lb).

In captivity, gorillas tend to put on weight through lack of exercise, and they can be quite obese. The heaviest on record is a male of uncertain sub-species named N'gagi, held at San Diego Zoo, California, USA, from 5 October 1931. Weighing 310 kg (683 lb) at his heaviest in 1943, he had a bipedal standing height of 1.72 m (5 ft 7¹/₂ in) and a record-breaking chest measurement of 1.98 m (78 in).

The largest species of monkey is the mandrill (*Mandrillus sphinx*) of equatorial west Africa. The greatest reliable weight recorded is 54 kg (119 lb) for a captive male, but an unconfirmed weight of 59 kg (130 lb) has been reported (compared with an average weight of 25 kg (55 lb)). There is a high degree of sexual dimorphism and adult females are about half the size of males.

Pygmy mouse lemur
The pygmy mouse lemur (*Microcebus myoxinus*) is the world's smallest primate, and weighs about 30 g (1 oz). It is pictured here in the Kirindy forest, Madagascar.

★ SMALLEST
The world's smallest primate, the pygmy mouse-lemur (*Microcebus myoxinus*), lives in western Madagascar. First described around 200 years ago, it was thought to have become extinct until its rediscovery in 1993. Not much larger than an overweight mouse, it has a head-body length of 6.2 cm (2⁷/₁₆ in); a tail length of 13.6 cm (5⁷/₁₆ in); and a weight of 24.5–38 g (⁷/₈–1³/₈ oz). The brown mouse lemur (*Microcebus rufus*), which is found in the eastern rainforests of Madagascar, used to be considered to be the smallest. It has a head-body length of 10–12.5 cm (4–5 in); a tail length of 12.5–15 cm (5–6 in); and a weight of 45–90 g (1¹/₂–3¹/₄ oz).

★ LONGEST ARMSPAN
The longest armspan known for any non-human primate is a record-breaking 2.79 m (9 ft 2 in) for a male mountain

WORLD RECORD HOLDER
Largest tree-living

The two species of orangutan (*Pongo pygmaeus* from Borneo and *Pongo abelii* from Sumatra), surviving only on two Indonesian islands, are the largest predominantly tree-living mammals on Earth. They have an average bipedal standing height (measured from the crown of the head to the base of the heels) of 1.15 m (46 in) (female) and 1.37 m (54 in) (male) and a weight of 60–90 kg (132–198 lb) (male) and 30–50 kg (66–110 lb) (female). There is a record of an unusually large male, in Borneo, with a height of 1.8 m (6 ft); captive animals sometimes grow considerably heavier, with a record of 188 kg (415 lb). The most arboreal of the great apes, they spend nearly all their time in the trees. Gorillas (*Gorilla gorilla* and *Gorilla beringei*) are largely terrestrial. The youngsters climb regularly, and even the big silverback clambers into the trees to collect fruit, but gorilla troops always travel long distances on the ground.

gorilla (*Gorilla beringei beringei*) collected by the Percy Sladen Expedition to northern Cameroon in 1932–1933. All apes, except humans, have exceptionally long arms. The longest in relation to body length are found in the gibbons (genus *Hylobates*) and the orangutans (*Pongo pygmaeus* and *P. abelii*). The orangutan is the record holder, with an armspan of up to 2.5 m (8ft 2 in) or possibly even 3 m (9 ft 10 in) (nearly three times the head-body length of up to 97 cm (3 ft 2 in)). The siamang (*H. syndactylus*) is a close runner-up, with an armspan of up to 1.5 m (60 in) (1.7 times the maximum head-body length of 90 cm (36 in)).

Proboscis monkey
The proboscis monkey (*Nasalis larvatus*) has by far the largest nose of any primate. At its average, 10 cm (4 in), it is about a seventh of its total head-body length.

★ LONGEST NOSE

The proboscis monkey (*Nasalis larvatus*), which lives in the riverine and mangrove forests of Borneo, is named for its huge, pendulous nose. Shaped rather like a tongue, it grows until maturity and eventually droops over the mouth and chin. In elderly animals, it can reach a maximum length of 17.5 cm (7 in) (compared with a head-body length of 66–76 cm (26–30 in)). The precise function of the nose is uncertain. It has often been suggested that it may serve as a resonating organ in the production of the male's long, drawn-out honking call (it straightens out during calling), but it is more likely to be some kind of visual signal for sexual selection. Young proboscis monkeys have fairly long, rigid noses, which point forward; in females, their noses simply stop growing when the monkeys reach maturity.

★ ECHOLOCATION

The aye-aye (*Daubentonia madagascariensis*) is the only primate suspected of using a simple form of echolocation to find its food. It taps the surface of the wood cavities with its long, twig-like middle finger and then apparently listens with its extra-large ears for any change in the returning echoes when foraging for insect larvae. The system, which has been dubbed 'percussive foraging', is so efficient that the aye-aye can detect cavities as deep as 2 cm ($^3/_4$ in) below the surface and can even tell if they contain insect larvae. Whether it is listening only for reverberations inside the cavities, or whether it is aided by the sudden rustling of larvae disturbed by all the tapping, is unclear. But once it has located a grub, it quickly uses its incisor teeth to gnaw into the cavity, and then its elongated finger to probe and scoop.

Aye-ayes seem to fill a remarkably similar niche to woodpeckers, which also bore through wood (with their beaks) and probe cavities beneath the surface for insect larvae (with their long tongues). Interestingly, Madagascar is devoid of woodpeckers and it may be that aye-ayes have evolved to fill the ecological niche that woodpeckers occupy in other parts of the world.

★ NORTHERNMOST POPULATION

Japanese macaques or snow monkeys (*Macaca fuscata*) living in a mountainous area of central Honshu, Japan, known as Jigokudani, form the northernmost population of any living species of non-human primate. During the winter, temperatures drop to at least -15°C (5°F), and the ground is covered in snow. But the macaques in this particular region have learned to sit in naturally heated springs to keep warm. The water temperature can be as high as 43°C (109°F) and they test it first, with a few tentative splashes, before easing themselves into the warmth. Whole troops of snow monkeys can often be

seen taking hot baths together, with only their heads poking out of the water (sometimes with several centimetres of snow and ice balanced on top).

Snow monkeys are always careful to leave the springs in time to dry off properly before nightfall so they don't freeze to death when they sleep.

★ BEST SWIMMER

The most competent swimmer among the primates is probably the proboscis monkey (*Nasalis larvatus*), which is usually found near freshwater in the lowland rainforests and mangrove swamps of

Japanese macaques

Also known as snow monkeys, Japanese macaques are the most northern non-human primate. They overcome temperatures as low as -15°C (5°F) by bathing in naturally heated springs.

Borneo. It takes to the water readily, especially when feeling threatened or trying to escape danger, and swims both on the surface and underwater. Entire groups have been seen diving out of the trees from heights of up to 16 m (52½ ft).

★ LONGEST LIVING

Primates tend to have long lifespans compared with many other mammals. The oldest recorded non-human primate is Cheeta (aka Jiggs), who appeared in numerous movies and TV shows and starred with Johnny Weissmuller in a string

of Tarzan movies. Born 9 April, 1932 he celebrated his 75th birthday in 2007 and, whilst living at a primate sanctuary in Palm Springs, California, has adopted a new careeer as an artist. Several other chimpanzees have been known to live to their mid-50s and beyond.

A male orangutan (*Pongo sp.*) named Guas, who died in Philadelphia Zoological Garden, Pennsylvania, USA, on 9 February 1977, is reported to have reached an age of about 59 years; he was at least 13 years old on his arrival at the zoo on 1 May 1931.

The oldest gorilla (*Gorilla sp.*) was Massa, who died at Philadelphia Zoo, USA aged 54 years. An old silverback mountain gorilla named Beethoven once lived in the Virunga Volcanoes region straddling the international borders of The Democratic Republic of Congo, Rwanda and Uganda, and died in 1985 at an estimated age of late 40s–early 50s.

★ MOST PROFICIENT TOOL-USER

Orangutans (genus *Pongo*), black-capped capuchin monkeys (*Cebus apella*) and several other primates are known to use simple tools. An orangutan on Kaja island in Borneo has been seen picking up a tree branch and using it to stun a fish before eating it. Other apes have been seen trying to spear fish with sticks. However, most records are of them doing so in captivity and, in many cases, similar behaviour has not been observed in the wild. But a major exception is the chimpanzee (*Pan troglodytes*), which is by far the most proficient non-human tool-user, both in the wild and in captivity. Different communities of chimps have different repertoires of tool use (as a general rule, the more demanding the environment the more tools they use). They use stone hammers and anvils to crack open nuts; twigs as toothpicks; a handful of chewed-up leaves to form a rough sponge for soaking up water from what would otherwise be inaccessible

Chimpanzee
This chimpanzee is using a stick to fish for termites, at the Budongo Project, in Uganda.

tree hollows; and even stones as missiles against predators such as leopards. One individual learned that banging empty water cans together made his aggressive display more effective and, quite recently, others have been observed using a leaf 'pestle' and a fibre 'sponge' to get sap from oil palms. There is no evidence yet of them using tools to create new tools (such as chipping a stone hammer with another stone) but they do alter their tools to fit the task; for example, they bite thin, spindly twigs to a required length, peel off the bark, strip the leaves, fray one end, and then use them to fish for termites in termite mounds.

Gorillas have very manipulative hands, and are impressively skilful at opening and eating the palatable parts of many different

the loudness of the call – and many different figures have been published – but, once in full voice, a male can be heard at least 3 km (2 miles) away through the jungle and 5 km (3 miles) away across water. Howling sessions take place at dawn and are a form of territorial defence, to keep neighbouring troops well spaced. From a distance, different species of howler monkey can be recognized by their howls: for example, mantled howlers

or pygmy chimpanzees (*Pan paniscus*), gorillas (genus *Gorilla*) and orangutans (genus *Pongo*), but excludes humans.

Our closest relatives are the chimpanzees. Indeed, the relationship is so close that, genetically, we are almost identical and share 96%–99% of our genes. We also share similar qualities such as empathy, altruism and the ability to work in a team. The gorilla and human lines diverged 6–7 million years ago; chimps and human diverged 4–6 million years ago (humans are genetically closer to chimps than chimps are to bonobos). We are more closely related to all the African apes than they are to orangutans. This is not surprising, since orangs branched off the evolutionary tree about 12–16 million years ago – more than six million years before the

Howler monkey
The mantled howler monkey (*Alouatta palliata*) is one of the loudest mammals in the world.

plants, but do not appear to use tools in the wild. Little (but some) tool use has been observed in bonobos.

★ NOISIEST

Howler monkeys (genus *Alouatta*) of Central and South America are among the noisiest arboreal animals in the world. They have greatly enlarged lower jaws, accommodating an egg-shaped hyoid bone at the top of the windpipe that helps to reverberate the sound of their roaring and growling calls. This chamber is larger in the male, whose call is consequently much louder and deeper. It is difficult to quantify

(*A. palliata*) sound like a cheering crowd in a football stadium, while Venezuelan red howlers (*A. seniculus*) resemble the crashing of surf on a distant shore.

★ CLOSEST RELATIVE

The relationship between humans and all other apes is a much-studied and highly controversial subject. The fact is though that humans are apes: there is no natural category that includes chimpanzees (*Pan troglodytes*), bonobos

Gorillas and chimpanzees have a cluster of sweat glands under their arms and, like humans, tend to have smelly armpits after strenuous exercise.

human and African ape lines parted company and human lines diverged. This is equivalent to half a million generations ago – not long by evolutionary standards.

MAMMALS

★ MOST COLOURFUL

The male mandrill (*Mandrillus sphinx*), a kind of forest baboon from the rainforests of west Africa, is the most colourful mammal in the world. It has an olive-brown coat with pale yellowish underparts; yellowish-orange side whiskers; a whitish moustache and goatee beard; a red and blue naked rump; pink ears; a brilliant red, purple, white and blue face; a black nose; and even a red penis and blue scrotum. All the skin colours become more pronounced when the mandrill gets excited. Females and youngsters are similarly coloured, but much duller in comparison with the male.

★ LEARNING BEHAVIOUR

There are numerous examples of primates learning different forms of behaviour by observing and imitating one another, and then retaining the knowledge for future use. There is very little evidence to suggest active teaching: in most cases, young animals learn by passive observation of adults, followed by trial and error, rather than by direct instruction. The two best-known examples of learning are nut-cracking in chimpanzees (*Pan troglodytes*), which provided the first evidence for behavioural techniques being passed from one group or community to another ; and potato-washing in Japanese macaques (*Macaca fuscata*), which provided the first evidence for cultural transmission of behaviour in a non-human species.

During a study of chimpanzees in west Africa, a 31-year-old female named Yo changed home, from her birth group in the Ivory Coast to a new one 10 km (6 miles) away across the border in Guinea. Her new group was already using a special technique to crack open almond-shaped oil palm nuts, using stones as a hammer and anvil. But when biologists presented them with some spherical coula nuts, which they had not encountered before, they did not know how to adapt this technique to crack them open. Yo, who was already familiar with coula nuts from her time in the Ivory Coast, immediately placed one on her stone anvil and cracked it open ready to eat. Within a matter of days, two youngsters in the group (a five-year-old female and a six-year-old male) had learned the new technique and soon acquired a taste for the coula nuts.

Biologists studying a troop of Japanese macaques on Koshima Islet, in the extreme south of Japan, began to provide the animals with frequent supplies of sweet potatoes. The potatoes were distributed on a beach and, before eating them, the macaques always rubbed off the worst of the sand with their hands. The food must still have been rather gritty to eat until, in September 1953, a two-year-old female named Lino

Male mandrill
The male mandrill's colourful face is believed to be important in sexual selection, its colourful rump is thought to make it more visable (and easier to follow) in thick vegetation.

dipped a potato into a stream that ran across the beach – and immediately had a clean potato. Other animals in the group readily adopted the new behaviour and, by 1962, all but the older adults were potato-washers. Then they discovered that sweet potatoes washed in salty seawater tasted better than those washed in freshwater and, within a few years, most members of the troop were picking up armfuls of potatoes and carrying them down to the sea.

Japanese macaques learnt how to wash sweet potatoes in the sea before eating to rinse off the sand and give them a pleasant salty taste.

★ LONGEST GESTATION PERIOD

Primates have remarkably long gestation periods. The longest are found in the apes: about 220–245 days in the gibbons (*Hylobates*), 230–240 days in both the chimpanzee (*Pan troglodytes*) and bonobo (*Pan paniscus*), 250–270 days in the gorilla (genus *Gorilla*), 260–270 days in the orangutan (genus *Pongo*), and 250–285 days in humans.

★ SHORTEST GESTATION PERIOD

The shortest gestation period known for any primate is 54–68 days, a record held jointly by the brown mouse lemur (*Microcebus rufus*) and the grey mouse lemur (*M. murinus*). Even this is long compared with other similar-sized mammals (22–24 days in the slightly smaller common dormouse (*Muscardinus avellanarius*), for example).

★ MOST INTELLIGENT

Intelligence is a difficult concept to measure in animals, not least because many recognized psychological tests require the use of hands (which some highly intelligent animals, such as dolphins, do not possess); this means

White handed gibbon
White-handed gibbons have one of the longest gestation periods of any primate, lasting for seven months. Young are nursed for over a year and a half, and full maturity comes at about 8 years.

that different species are better at some tasks than others simply because of their adaptations to certain ways of life. But it is generally considered that the great apes are the most intelligent non-human animals. They are quick learners; they can use logic and insight to solve complicated tasks and puzzles; and they can be trained to use symbols or sign language to communicate, albeit in a rudimentary way.

It has not been possible to teach orangutans (genus *Pongo*), gorillas (genus *Gorilla*) or chimpanzees (*Pan troglodytes*) how to speak, because they do not have the necessary vocal apparatus. But attempts to teach them sign language have been more successful. Chimpanzees, in particular, can use abstract terms such as 'like' and 'different', but how far these indicate capacity for thought or language is still open to question. Evolutionary biologists have long pointed to the human brain's much larger frontal lobe as evidence of our superior skills of creative thinking and language. But recent research shows that it does not differ strikingly from other primates: the frontal lobe amounts to 31.7% of a gorilla's brain, 36.1% of a chimpanzee's brain, and 36.8% of a human's. There are more subtle differences, though; for example, within the frontal lobe, humans have a significantly larger 'white body', a structure from which nerve fibres begin to fan out and make contact with other parts of the brain.

★ STRANGEST LOOKING

There are a number of strange-looking primates: for example, the red uakari (*Cacajao rubicundus*), with its bare, bright red face; the long, droopy-nosed male proboscis monkey (*Nasalis larvatus*); the emperor tamarin (*Saguinus imperator*), with its enormous white moustache; and the male orangutan (genus *Pongo*), with its rather splendid 'face mask'. But the rare and elusive aye-aye (*Daubentonia madagascariensis*) of Madagascar is probably the strangest of them all. Once described as having been assembled from bits of other animals, it looks like a large cat with a bat's ears, a beaver's continuously growing incisor teeth, an owl's large eyes, a squirrel's bushy tail, and a middle finger resembling a long, dead twig. In fact, it is a nocturnal lemur (the only member of the family Daubentoniidae) and is the largest nocturnal primate in the world (head-body length 36–44cm (14–17½ in) and tail length 50–60 cm (20–24 in)).

★ MOST ARID HABITAT

In 1986 a troop of 15 chacma baboons (*Papio ursinus*) was discovered living in the most arid environment known to be inhabited by any non-human primate. Conrad Brain of the Desert Ecological Research Unit of Namibia found the animals in the lower reaches of the Kuiseb River Canyon, in the heart of the Namib Desert, southern Africa, and has been studying them ever since. The animals survive in an area where daytime temperatures frequently reach

45°C (113°F) and where there is no surface water for about eight months of the year. The Namib Desert annually receives about 27 mm (⅛ in) of rain, and the Kuiseb River usually runs for only a few weeks between December and March. In the last months of 1992, they were unable to drink for 116 days; they obtained some moisture from wild figs, but even these had come to an end by the time the floods eventually arrived. The baboons were so relieved to see the newly formed river that they drank almost continuously, and even swam.

★ SELF-HEALING

A number of primates are known to eat food that, as well as being nutritious, also has medicinal properties. But it is likely that few of them realize the significance of what they are doing. This does not seem to be true of chimpanzees (*Pan troglodytes*), which are the only animals other than humans known to be able to link consumption of a particular food source with relief from sickness or pain (although recent research on wild gorillas (genus *Gorilla*) suggest they also self-medicate). Indeed, they frequently select the same plants that local people use for similar complaints, and may even know as much about herbal medicine. The best-known example comes from a study of

chimpanzees in the Gombe Stream National Park, Tanzania, by famous chimp watcher Jane Goodall, and Richard Wrangham, professor of anthropology at Harvard University. It was discovered that

In many parts of tropical Africa chimpanzees appear to treat themselves for a range of ailments by seeking out certain leaves and seeds specifically for their medicinal properties.

the animals use a variety of medicinal plants but, in particular, they seek out three species in the genus *Aspilia*. The young leaves of these tall but rather nondescript members of the sunflower family contain high concentrations of a bright red oil called *thiarubrine-A*, which is known to be a potent antibiotic and is also an effective antifungal and deworming agent; among its other properties, it is even more potent than the anti-cancer drug vinblastine in *in vitro* toxicity tests. Normally, when they are feeding, chimpanzees stuff leaves into their mouths as fast as they can; but they select the *Aspilia* leaves very carefully, and at different times of day when the chemistry of the plants varies. They also roll them around in their mouths and swallow them whole instead of chewing and swallowing as usual. It is unlikely that

Baboon
Baboons are capable of living in more environments than any other non-human primate.

RABBITS, HARES & PIKAS

Lagomorpha

83 species (little agreement on classification): 21 rabbits, 32 hares and 30 pikas

the leaves are ingested either for food or to increase fibre intake – since they are passed through the gut undigested – but they are believed to release significant amounts of chemicals before passing out the other end. Perhaps most significant of all, the local Tongwe people make a special tea out of *Aspilia* leaves to treat stomach disorders and a variety of external ailments such as wounds and burns. Scientists are now studying the same plants in the hope that they may prove useful to western medicine but, significantly, the chimpanzees found them first.

The first time a chimpanzee's recovery from an illness could be linked directly to its self-medication was in Mahale Mountains National Park, Tanzania, in the late 1980s. One day, a female being observed by primatologists was noticeably lethargic and clearly suffering from bad diarrhoea. She searched for a plant called *Vernonia amygdalina*, sucked out the bitter-tasting juice from the shoots, and then rested in a tree while her companions stayed nearby. Within 24 hours, she was back in the swing of things and seemed to be fully recovered.

★ MOST DANGEROUS

Before gorillas (genus *Gorilla*) were studied in the wild, they had a reputation as highly dangerous and savage animals. But in recent years, almost by way of an apology, there has been a tendency to portray them as harmless, gentle giants. The truth is somewhere in between: for much of the time, they are peaceful family animals, and yet irate silverbacks are potentially the most dangerous of all the primates, of course with the exception of humans. When defending their families, they rush towards intruders and emit ear-shattering roars; it is these spectacular displays of strength that gave them their legendary reputation. But, it is now known that the vast majority of charges are bluff. Chimpanzees (*Pan troglodytes*) can be extremely dangerous. They hunt in small groups, killing and eating monkeys, wild pigs and small antelopes, and there are several reports of them killing humans in the wild and in captivity.

★ LARGEST

The world's largest lagomorph is the Alaskan or tundra hare (*Lepus othus*), which lives on open tundra in western Alaska and far eastern Siberia. It weighs 3.2–6.5 kg (7–14¼ lb) (average 4.8 kg (10½ lb)) and has a head-body length of 50–60 cm (20–24 in).

The European or brown hare (*Lepus europaeus*), which is found over most of Europe except Ireland, the Mediterranean region and Scandinavia, is often quoted as the largest lagomorph. One particular individual which was shot near Welford, Northamptonshire, UK, in November 1956, weighed 6.83 kg (15 lb 1 oz); however, the normal weight for this species is 3–5 kg (6 lb 10 oz–11 lb) (average 3.8 kg (8 lb 6 oz)). It has a head-body length of 52–60 cm (20½–24 in).

The Arctic hare (*Lepus arcticus*), which lives in Greenland and northern Canada, is also large, weighing an average 4–5 kg (8 lb 2 oz–11 lb).

The largest breed of domestic rabbit is the Flemish giant. Adults weigh 7–8.5 kg (15 lb 7 oz–18 lb 11 oz) (average toe-to-toe length when fully stretched 91 cm (36 in)), but weights up to 11.3 kg (25 lb)

Antelope jackrabbit
The antelope jackrabbit (*Lepus alleni*) lives in the desert in southern Arizona, USA and northwestern Mexico. Its incredibly long ears help it keep cool by acting as radiators.

have been reliably reported for this breed. The largest domestic rabbit on record is a five-month-old French lop doe weighing 12 kg (26 lb 7 oz). It was exhibited at the Reus Fair in northeast Spain in April 1980.

★ SMALLEST

The smallest lagomorphs are the pikas and the record-holder is the tiny Steppe or little pika (*Ochotona pusilla*), which lives in steppe regions from the upper Volga River and southern Ural Mountains south and east to the Chinese border. It has a head-body length of only 18 cm (7 in) and weighs just 75–210 g (2³⁄₄–7¹⁄₂ oz).

Both the Polish and the Netherland dwarf rabbits have a weight range of 0.9–1.13 kg (2–2¹⁄₂ lb). In 1975 Jacques Bouloc of Coulommiere, France, announced a new hybrid of these two breeds that weighed an average of 396 g (14 oz).

★ LONGEST EARS

The antelope jackrabbit (*Lepus alleni*), which lives in the desert regions of southern USA and northwestern Mexico, has longer ears than any other lagomorph. They measure 13.8–17.3 cm (5⁷⁄₁₆–6¹³⁄₁₆ in) from the top of the head to the tip (average 16.2 cm (6³⁄₈ in)).

The longest ears in domestic rabbits are found in the lop family and, in particular, the English lop. The ears of a typical example measure about 60 cm (24 in) from tip to tip (taken across the skull) and 14 cm (5¹⁄₂ in) maximum width, but they can go up to almost 80 cm (31¹⁄₂ in).

★ FASTEST

Some of the larger hares, which tend to live in open habitats and are adapted for running rather than burrowing (in contrast to most rabbits), reportedly reach speeds of 80 km/h (50 mph) when in full flight. They are also good long-distance runners and can maintain speeds of up to 50 km/h (31 mph) for long periods.

★ HIGHEST LIVING

The highest-living mammal in the world is the large-eared pika (*Ochtona macrotis*). It lives in the Himalayas, the Pamir Mountains, the Karakorum Range and other high-altitude mountain ranges in Asia at a height of 2500–6130 m (8200–20,106 ft) (marginally higher than the maximum elevation reached by the yak (*Bos grunniens*). A significant number of other lagomorphs live at elevations higher than 4000 m (13,120 ft). In particular, the Ladak pika (*Ochotona ladacensis*) lives at 4300–5450 m (14,104–17,876 ft) in the mountains of Kashmir, in India, and Qinghai, Xizang and Xinjiang, in China. The woolly hare (*Lepus oiostolus*) lives in the mountains of Tibet, China, Nepal and Kashmir at a height of 2500–5400 m (8200–17,712 ft). There is also a single reliable record of an individual seen at 6035 m (19,800 ft).

★ POPULATION FLUCTUATIONS

Most animal populations fluctuate irregularly or unpredictably. But the best-known exception is the snowshoe hare (*Lepus americanus*), whose populations in the boreal forests of North America undergo remarkably regular fluctuations which peak every 8–11 years. The fluctuations are broadly synchronized over a vast area from Alaska to Newfoundland and are so dramatic that the difference between a population high and a low may be more than 100-fold (normally 10–30-fold). This extraordinary cycle has been documented in fur-trade records kept by the Hudson's Bay Company, Canada, for over two centuries and has been studied in considerable detail. For many years, it was supposed that the predatory activity of the Canadian lynx (*Felis canadensis*) was responsible, because this species also shows population highs and lows at roughly 10-year intervals (lagging a year or two behind those of the hare). But it is now believed that the driving force is a complex interaction between the hare and its food, while the lynx – rather than influencing the cycle – is actually being influenced by it.

European hare
The European hare (*Lepus europaeus*), pictured here running, is one of the largest of the lagomorphs. It is incredibly agile with very long powerful legs.

The enormous ears of the black-tailed jackrabbit are not only for hearing; they also act as radiators, helping this desert animal to lose excess heat.

RODENTS

Rodentia

c. 2280 species (more than 40% of all mammal species) including beavers, squirrels, mice, rats, porcupines, voles and guinea pigs

★ EARLIEST

Rodents first appear in the fossil record in the late Palaeocene, some 57 million years ago, from localities in Asia and North America. They were squirrel-like and belonged to the extinct family Paramyidae. Unfortunately, the evolutionary origin of rodents is obscured by the fact that, by this time, all the main characteristics of the order had developed.

★ MOST PRIMITIVE

The mountain beaver (*Aplodontia rufa*), which lives in coniferous forests in western North America, is the most primitive of all the living rodents. Something of a zoological mystery, it is neither a beaver nor a particularly mountain-loving animal and is classed in a family of its own called the *Aplodontidae*. Unlike most other mammals, it has difficulty regulating its body temperature and, since it is unable to conserve either body moisture or fat, cannot hibernate.

★ SMALLEST

The world's smallest rodent is the tiny Baluchistan pygmy jerboa (*Salpingotus michaelis*), which lives in north-western Baluchistan, Pakistan. It has a head-body length of 3.6–4.7 cm ($1^7/_{16}$ –$1^{13}/_{16}$ in) and a tail length of 7.2–9.4 cm ($2^{13}/_{16}$ – $3^{11}/_{16}$ in). For its size, it has enormous hind feet of some 1.8–1.9 cm ($^{11}/_{16}$–$^3/_4$ in) in length (as an adaptation for jumping).

★ LARGEST

The world's largest living rodent is the capybara (*Hydrochoerus hydrochaeris*) of northern South America, which lives in densely vegetated areas around ponds, lakes, rivers, marshes and other aquatic habitats. It has a head-body length of 1–1.4 m ($3^1/_4$–$4^1/_2$ ft) (the tail is vestigial); a shoulder height of 50–66 cm (20–24$^1/_2$ in); and a weight of 35–66 kg (77–145$^1/_2$ lb). In captivity, this species can attain an even greater weight and there is one record of a cage-fat specimen of 113 kg (250 lb). Some extinct forms of capybara were twice as long and up to eight times as heavy as the modern species.

★ OLDEST

The longest-lived rodents are the porcupines and, in particular, the 11 species of Old World porcupines (family Hystricidae). The greatest reliable age reported is 27 years and three months for a Sumatran crested porcupine (*Hystrix brachyura*), which died in the National Zoological Park, Washington, DC, USA, on 12 January 1965. Many rodents have

Capybara

This capybara (*Hydrochoerus hydrochaeris*) pictured here with its young at the waterside in Llanos, Venezuela, is the giant of the rodent world.

Flying squirrel
The flying squirrel launches itself off the tops of trees and glides by extending the flaps of skin that stretch from its arms to its legs. Once in the air it is very agile and able to make adjustments to its direction.

legs to open the membrane (known as the patagium). They bank and turn by raising and lowering their arms, and use their tail as a stabilizer. Just before landing, they brake by turning their tail and body upwards.

As soon as it lands on a tree trunk, a flying squirrel runs around to the other side in case an owl or another predator has been following its flight.

longer lives in captivity, but in the wild most small species have short lifespans of only 1–3 years and the larger ones fair little better with an average of about ten years.

★ MOST TEETH

All rodents have a single pair of razor-sharp incisors on each jaw and no canines, but the number of molars and premolars varies considerably from species to species. The silvery mole-rat (*Heliophobius argenteocinereus*), from central and east Africa, is the record-holder with 24 (making a total of 28 teeth).

★ LEAST TEETH

The Shaw Mayer's shrew mouse (*Pseudohydromys ellermani*) has four incisors and no canines, like all rodents, but is distinguished from the others by having no premolars and just four molars (making a total of eight teeth altogether).

★ LONGEST GLIDE

Two rodent families have evolved the ability to glide between trees; the flying squirrels (family Sciuridae), which live in Southeast Asia, North America and

northern Europe, and the scaly-tailed squirrels (family Anomaluridae), which live in western and central Africa. There are 38 species of flying squirrels and seven species of scaly-tailed squirrels (although the flightless scaly-tailed squirrel (*Zenkerella insignis*), does not have a gliding membrane and, as its name suggests, is incapable of gliding). The longest recorded glide of any gliding mammal was an outstanding 450 m (1500 ft) for a giant flying squirrel in the genus *Petaurista*. The longest glide of any of the scaly-tailed squirrels was *c.* 250 m (820 ft) by a Lord Derby's flying squirrel (*Anomalurus derbianus*). Some 50–100 m (160–330 ft) is more typical for most species.

Despite their names, these flying rodents are not capable of true flight. But they glide from tree to tree with the help of a furry membrane along each side of the body (stretched between the forelimbs and hindlimbs); this acts as a kind of parachute. It is an economical way to travel through their tall forest homes and an effective means of escaping from tree-borne predators. After climbing to an elevated point in a tree, they carefully judge the distance to the proposed landing site and then leap out into space, extending their arms and

★ LONGEST HIBERNATION

Several ground squirrels in the genus *Spermophilus*, especially those living in areas with a severe climate, spend considerably more than half the year in hibernation. Some not only hibernate during the winter but also sleep during part of the summer, when there is drought and the vegetation is poor. North American populations of the arctic ground squirrel (*Spermophilus parryii*), living in Alaska and northern Canada, are probably the record-holders. They hibernate for nine months of the year and, during the remaining three months, they feed, breed and collect food to store in their burrows.

★ LARGEST COLONIES

As recently as 100 years ago, western North America was teeming with prairie dogs (family Sciuridae) and the total population of all five species was probably more than five billion. The largest single colony or 'town' (indeed, the largest colony of mammals ever recorded) was one built by black-tailed prairie dogs (*Cynomys ludovicianus*) in western Texas. Discovered in 1901, it contained about 400 million individuals and was estimated to cover an area of 61,440 km² (24,000 miles²) (almost the size of The Republic of Ireland). For much of this century, prairie dog populations have declined dramatically as a direct result of shooting, poisoning and destruction of their grassland homes; however, the black-tails and others have been increasing once again in the past 20 years.

★ MASTER ENGINEER

With the exception of humans, no mammal is capable of modifying its environment as dramatically as the North American beaver (*Castor canadensis*) and the European beaver (*Castor fiber*). Beaver dams average about 23 m (75 ft) in length, but many are considerably longer. The largest ever built was probably one recorded on the Jefferson River, in Montana, USA, which measured 700 m (2300 ft) and was so strong it could bear the weight of a rider on horseback. Measurements of up to 1220 m (4000 ft) have also been claimed, although these have not been verified.

Beavers build dams, which obstruct the course of a stream or river, to create artificial lakes. These ensure that the water level around their home or 'lodge' is deep enough for the underwater entrances to be below ice-level during the winter freeze. Dams are made of logs (their massive incisor teeth are so strong that they can fell trees up to 1 m (3 ft) in diameter), as well as branches and twigs, and are shored up by layers of mud, gravel and larger stones. The task of maintaining and extending the dams is continuous and may spread over several generations. In the middle of the new lake, they build a dome-shaped lodge of sticks and mud to avoid being caught by wolves and other predators. Ventilation is provided by looser construction on the top of the mound (which can extend more than 2 m (6 ft 7 in) above the surface of the water and may have a diameter at the base of over 12 m (40 ft)) and access is provided by underwater tunnels.

★ HIGHEST DENSITY

The highest density of rodents ever recorded was an astonishing 205,000 per ha (83,000 per acre) for a population of house mice (*Mus musculus*) in the dry bed of Buena Vista Lake, in Kern County, California, USA, in 1926–7. A similar 200,000 per ha (81,000 per acre) was later recorded for a population of house mice in Central Valley, California, in 1941–2.

North American beaver
The North American beaver is an accomplished engineer, able to construct dams and artificial lakes, and a family home – complete with moat – that is safe from predators and the rigours of winter.

★ MOST PROLIFIC

Many rodents are reproductively prolific: they breed frequently and have short gestation periods and large litters. The youngest breeding mammal is the female Norway lemming (*Lemmus lemmus*) of Scandinavia, which can become pregnant when only 14 days old. Several rodent species have gestation periods of as little as 19–21 days but the shortest, by a small margin, is 15–16 days in the golden hamster (*Mesocricetus auratus*). In terms of frequency, the house mouse (*Mus musculus*) is capable of producing up to 14 litters in a year; and there is a record of a pair of Norway lemmings producing no fewer than eight litters in 167 days, after which the male died.

★ MASS SUICIDES

The compelling image of vast numbers of lemmings (sub-family Arvicolinae) hurling themselves over cliffs in mass suicide attempts is far from the truth. However, their extraordinary migrations – which inevitably result in many deaths – have never been properly explained. They

remain one of the most intriguing puzzles of population ecology. A number of lemming species show dramatic population fluctuations, and migrations, but one of the best-known is the Norway lemming (*Lemmus lemmus*). It is a prodigious breeder and its population peaks roughly every 3–5 years. This leads to overcrowding which, according to one theory, forces many of the animals to leave in search of new places to live (normally in late summer or early autumn). At first, the migrations are fairly modest but, as numbers build up, they become more reckless and the animals seem to have a greater sense of urgency. There have even been reports of columns of lemmings marching across main roads and through busy town centres – with no intention of stopping. Eventually, there is mass panic and, driven on by those behind them, some of the lemmings fall over cliffs to their death or drown while attempting to swim across rivers that are too wide or too fast.

Naked mole rat
Naked mole rats have such a unique social system that, genetically, members of a colony are almost identical – as if they had inbred for 60 generations.

★ MOST UNIQUE SOCIAL ORGANIZATION

Naked mole rats (*Heterocephalus glaber*) are unique among mammals in the way they organize their colonies. There are clear divisions of labour, organized by a single breeding female, in a system which has parallels only in the social insects such as bees, wasps and ants. These almost hairless rodents live in underground colonies of 75–80 individuals (more than 250 have been recorded on occasion) in the dry savannas of Kenya, Somalia and Ethiopia. Breeding is entirely the preserve of a single female (the queen) and one or two male consorts. The other members of the colony are workers (which dig tunnels, transport soil, forage, and carry food and bedding to the communal nest) and the larger non-workers (which spend most of their time in the nest, attending to the needs of the queen, caring for her offspring, defending the colony against snakes and other predators, and mending damaged tunnels). There is a distinct hierarchical system: the queen and the breeding males dominate the non-breeders, and larger animals dominate smaller ones, regardless of sex. The breeding female gives birth to between one and five litters a year, with an average of 14 pups in each, and suckles herself; the record-holder was a captive individual which had 27 pups in a single litter and 108 pups, in five different litters, in a single year. If the queen dies, another female in the

Naked mole rats can build enormous tunnel systems occupying an area greater than 13 soccer (or 18 American football) pitches.

colony, which was previously sexually inactive, quickly becomes active for the first time and takes over. According to research by Hudson Kern Reeve and colleagues at Cornell University, New York State, USA, and Christopher Faulkes and colleagues at the Institute of Zoology, London, this practice can lead to members of a colony being so similar genetically that it is as if they had inbred for 60 generations.

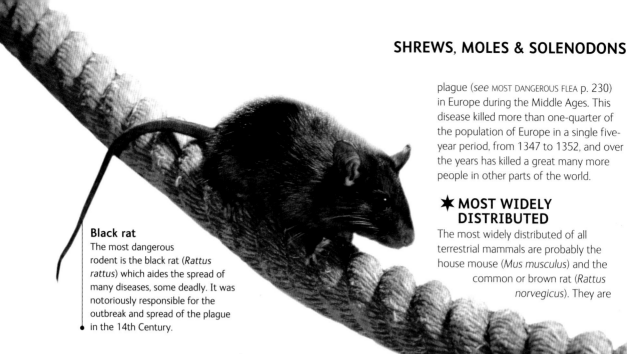

plague (*see* MOST DANGEROUS FLEA p. 230) in Europe during the Middle Ages. This disease killed more than one-quarter of the population of Europe in a single five-year period, from 1347 to 1352, and over the years has killed a great many more people in other parts of the world.

✷ MOST WIDELY DISTRIBUTED

The most widely distributed of all terrestrial mammals are probably the house mouse (*Mus musculus*) and the common or brown rat (*Rattus norvegicus*). They are

Black rat
The most dangerous rodent is the black rat (*Rattus rattus*) which aides the spread of many diseases, some deadly. It was notoriously responsible for the outbreak and spread of the plague in the 14th Century.

Naked mole rats are capable of building the most enormous tunnel systems, largely in their constant search for succulent plant tubers. One record-breaking colony in Tsavo West National Park, Kenya, consisted of more than 3 km (2 miles) of tunnels and occupied an area greater than 100,000 m² (120,000 square yards). The same colony – in an average month – excavated more than 200 m (656 ft) of new burrows (each about 4–7 cm (1⁵⁄₈–2³⁄₄ in) in diameter) and they ejected more than 350 kg (772 lb) of soil through some 40 surface openings.

✷ MOST DANGEROUS

Some rodents are important transmitters of disease and have probably been responsible for more human deaths in the last millennium than all wars and revolutions put together. They carry over 20 pathogens and spread bubonic plague, Lassa fever, murine typhus, *Salmonella* food poisoning, leptospirosis and rat-bite fever, among others. In this respect, the most dangerous are the species that habitually live near humans. The black or ship rat (*Rattus rattus*), in particular, was the main species responsible for transmitting the Black Death or bubonic

found on every continent, including Antarctica, and even on many remote oceanic islands. The house mouse originally came from Asia and Mediterranean Europe, and the brown rat from northern China, but they have been able to extend their ranges by tolerating and, more importantly, by taking advantage of human habitation. Their ability to hitch rides on ships has also been essential.

SHREWS, MOLES & SOLENODONS

Soricomorpha

c. 423 species: 376 shrews. 45 moles and desmans and 2 solenodons

✷ MOST VENOMOUS

Only two groups of mammals are venomous: the monotremes and certain insect-eaters in the families Soricidae and Solenodontidae (order Soricomorpha). The Cuban solenodon (*Solenodon cubanus*), the Haitian solenodon (*Solenodon paradoxus*), the American short-tailed shrew (*Blarina brevicauda*) and the Eurasian water shrew (*Neomys fodiens*) all have venomous bites. They have venom-producing salivary glands which open near the bases of the lower incisors and, when they bite, a special

toxic saliva seeps along a groove in the incisor into the puncture wounds. Once a prey animal has been located, it is normally attacked from behind and quickly bitten on the neck or at the base of the skull, where the neurotoxic venom is most readily introduced into the central nervous system. Even a small amount causes paralysis and enables the animals to tackle prey considerably larger than themselves; the American short-tailed shrew carries enough venom to kill by intravenous injection about 200 mice. The venom is used mainly to subdue large creatures

HITCHING A RIDE
Some shrew families have a habit of 'caravanning' when they are on the move. The young form a line, each holding on to the rump of the animal in front, with the mother leading the way; their grip is so strong that an entire family can be lifted off the ground by holding up the mother.

such as frogs, fish, lizards and small birds. In humans, a bite can cause considerable pain, hypersensitivity and reddening of the skin which may last for several days.

Pygmy white-toothed shrew
The pygmy white-toothed shrew (*Suncus etruscus*) is the world's smallest land mammal and is native to southern Europe, southwest Asia and northern Africa.

★ SMALLEST

The world's smallest land mammal (*see* SMALLEST BAT p.26) is the pygmy or Savi's white-toothed shrew (*Suncus etruscus*), otherwise known as the Etruscan shrew. It has a head-body length of 3.6–5.2 cm ($1^7/_{16}$–2 in), a tail length of 2.4–2.9 cm (1–$1^1/_8$ in), and a weight of just 1.5–2.5 g (around $^1/_{128}$ oz). It is so small, it can even creep into the holes made by large earthworms. It is found along the Mediterranean coast, eastwards as far as Sri Lanka and southwards to Cape Province, South Africa. Several other shrews are almost as small. Two of the closest contenders are probably the least shrew (*Sorex minutissimus*), which occurs from Scandinavia eastwards to Japan, and the Eurasian pygmy shrew (*Sorex minutus*), which occurs from Europe across Siberia into parts of central Asia. They have a head-body length of 3.5–4.5 cm ($1^3/_8$–$1^3/_4$ in) (least shrew) and 3.9–6.4 cm ($1^1/_2$–$2^1/_2$ in) (Eurasian pygmy); a tail length of 2.1–3.2 cm ($^3/_4$–$1^1/_4$ in) (least shrew) and 3.2–4.4 cm ($1^1/_4$–$1^3/_4$ in) (Eurasian pygmy); and an average weight of 3 g (around $^1/_{10}$ oz) (least shrew) and 4 g (around $^1/_7$ oz)

(Eurasian pygmy). The smallest freshwater mammal in the world is the southern or Miller's water shrew (*Neomys anomalus*), which lives in streams and marshes in southern and eastern Europe. It has an overall length of 6.7–8.7 cm ($2^5/_8$–$3^7/_{16}$ in); a tail length of 4–5.2 cm ($1^9/_{16}$–2 in); and a weight of 8–17 g (less than $^1/_2$ oz).

★ SHORTEST LIFESPAN

Shrews (family Soricidae) are the shortest-lived mammals in the world. They are so active they burn themselves out very quickly and, consequently, have an even shorter lifespan than other mammals of a similar size. In the wild, most species live for an average of 9–12 months; however, they can live longer in captivity, the record being four years for a greater white-toothed shrew (*Crocidura russula*).

★ LARGEST APPETITE

Shrews (family Soricidae) have a hectic pace of life and need to consume disproportionately large amounts of food for their body size. To satisfy their energy requirements they have to feed every 2 or 3 hours – day and night – and can die of starvation in as little as 4 hours. Indeed, it is not unusual for them to consume as much as 1.3 times their own body weight in a single day.

TENRECS, OTTER-SHREWS & GOLDEN MOLES

Afrosoricida
c. 51 species: 30 tenrecs and otter-shrews and 21 golden moles

★ LARGEST

The giant otter-shrew (*Potamogale velox*) lives in streams and pools in western and central Africa. Its size can be deceptive as its general appearance closely resembles a small otter. It has a head-body length of 29–35 cm ($11^1/_2$–$13^3/_4$ in) and a tail length of 25–29 cm ($9^3/_4$–$11^1/_2$ in).

The common or tail-less tenrec (*Tenrec ecaudatus*), which lives in Madagascar and the Comoro Islands, is also large. It has a head-body length of 25–39 cm ($9^3/_4$–$15^1/_2$ in), a tail length of 1–1.6 cm ($^3/_8$–$^5/_8$ in), and weighs 0.5–1.5 kg (1 lb 2 oz–3 lb 5 oz) with a maximum of 2.4 kg (5 lb 5 oz) in captivity.

A golden mole can lift 150 times its own weight.

★ YOUNGEST BREEDER

The streaked tenrec (*Hemicentetes semispinosus*) of Madagascar is weaned after only 5 days, and females can breed when they are only 3–5 weeks old

★ LONGEST LIFESPAN

Small mammals tend to have short life-spans (an absolute maximum of 5–8 years for most species). However, the greatest reliable age recorded is over 16 years for a lesser hedgehog-tenrec (*Echinops telfairi*), which was born in Amsterdam Zoo, Netherlands, in 1966, and was later sent to Jersey Zoo, Channel Islands, UK, where it died on 27 November 1982.

★ LARGEST LITTER

The greatest number of young born to a placental mammal at a single birth is 31 (30 of which survived) in the case of the common or tail-less tenrec (*Tenrec ecaudatus*), at Wassenaar Zoo, Netherlands, in 1972. This species is normally found in Madagascar and the nearby Comoro Islands, where individuals inhabiting relatively seasonal woodland

Yellow streaked tenrec
The female of this species is exceptional in that it can breed as soon as three to five weeks after being born.

and savanna regions have an incredible average of 20 young per litter (fewer in habitats with more stable climatic conditions). The females have up to 29 nipples – more than on any other mammal.

TREE-SHREWS

Scandentia

c. 20 species. These superficially squirrel-like mammals are not shrews. They are a little like some early fossil primates and, for many years, were classified as primitive members of the primate order. Although closely related to primates, they are now placed in a group of their own (the order Scandentia). There are now 20 recognized species, living mainly in the tropical rainforests of eastern India and Southeast Asia

★ LARGEST

The longest member of the order Scandentia is the common tree-shrew (*Tupaia glis*), which has a maximum head-body length of 23 cm (9 in), a tail length of up to 20 cm (8 in), and a maximum weight of 185 g (6½ oz). The Mindanao tree shrew (*Urogale everetti*) is shorter, with a maximum head-body length of 22 cm (8¾ in) and a tail length of up to 17.5 cm (7 in), but a fully grown male weighs a relatively hefty 350 g (12½ oz).

★ SMALLEST

The world's smallest tree-shrew is the rare pen-tailed or feather-tailed tree-shrew (*Ptilocercus lowii*), which has a head-body length of 10–14 cm (4–5½ in), a tail length of 13–19 cm (5–7½ in), and a weight of 25–60 g (1–2 oz). There are several close runners-up and, in particular, the pygmy tree-shrew (*Tupaia minor*) and the northern smooth-tailed tree-shrew (*Dendrogale murina*) are both nearly as small.

WHALES, DOLPHINS & PORPOISES

Cetacea
84 species

★ EARLIEST

The first whale-like animals, called *Archaeocetes*, or ancient whales, appeared about 50 million years ago. They were not the direct ancestors of modern whales but were probably very similar. However, they were more primitive in many ways – for example, in having nostrils which had not completely moved to the tops of their heads for easier breathing at the surface. There were many different kinds of *Archaeocete*, ranging in length from 2 m (6½ ft) to 21 m (69 ft), but they all lived in coastal swamps and shallow seas. Their bodies were torpedo-shaped and their front limbs had turned into paddles. Known only from fossils, they eventually died out about 30 million years ago.

The 'missing link' between whales and their four-legged land-living ancestors is believed to have been a creature called *Ambulocetus natans* (Latin for 'walking and swimming whale') which lived some 50 million years ago, just when the first whales were colonizing the seas. The first fossil to be discovered was an incomplete skeleton in the Kala Chitta Hills, Pakistan, in 1993. In some ways, *Ambulocetus* resembled a sea lion, in particular by being able to hobble around on land on its legs and chest. But, unlike sea lions, which swim mainly with their forelimbs, it used its forelimbs for steering and probably swam by beating its enlarged, webbed hind feet and tail up and down. It is uncertain whether *Ambulocetus* was the actual whale ancestor or a hangover from earlier stages of whale evolution.

★ LARGEST

See **Blue whale** on p. 108. The largest toothed whale is the sperm whale (*Physeter catodon*). The average size for a male is about 15 m (49 ft 2 in) and 45 tonnes; females are considerably smaller, averaging 12 m (39 ft 4 in) and 20 tonnes. The largest officially measured was a record-sized male, some 20.7 m (67 ft 11 in) in length, which was captured in the summer of 1950 off the Kurile Islands, in the northwest Pacific. However, the 5 m (16 ft 5 in) long lower jaw of a sperm whale in the possession of the Natural History Museum, London, UK, is reputed to have belonged to a male measuring nearly 25.6 m (84 ft). The heaviest animal reliably weighed was an 18.1 m (59 ft 5 in) male that stranded in the Netherlands on 24 February 1937; it weighed 57 tonnes. Even larger males were reported in the early days of whaling, though there are no authenticated records.

The largest member of the dolphin family is the killer whale or orca (*Orcinus orca*). Males typically grow to 8 m (26 ft 3 in) long, though females are considerably smaller and rarely exceed 7 m (23 ft). The longest individual recorded was a 9.8 m (32 ft) male in the western North Pacific.

Grey whale
The grey whale travels between its feeding and breeding grounds on a yearly basis and takes one of the longest known mammal migrations. The round trip journey takes it along up to 20,000 km (12,500 miles) of coastline.

★ SMALLEST

The black dolphin (*Cephalorhynchus eutropia*), Hector's dolphin (*Cephalorhynchus hectori*), finless porpoise (*Neophocaena phocaenoides*) and vaquita (*Phocoena sinus*) are probably equal contenders for the world's smallest cetacean. All four species can be as short as 1.2 m (3 ft 11 in) when fully grown although, taking average lengths, the shortest are Hector's dolphin and vaquita by a narrow margin. In terms of weight, the finless porpoise is probably the lightest, weighing 30–45 kg (66–99 lb); nearly 3000 finless porpoises would weigh roughly the same as one blue whale. The black dolphin, vaquita and franciscana (*Pontoporia blainvillei*) can all weigh as little as 30 kg (66 lb) when fully grown, though their average weights are higher. Commerson's dolphin (*Cephalorhynchus commersonii*) is also very small; 19 animals off the South American coast ranged from 26–44.5 kg (57–98 lb).

The smallest baleen whale is the pygmy right whale (*Caperea marginata*). The maximum lengths recorded are 6.45 m (21 ft) for a female and 6.09 m (20 ft) for a male. Only two animals have been weighed: a female of 6.21 m (20 ft 4 in) was 3.2 tonnes and a male of 5.47 m (18 ft) was 2.85 tonnes; both were taken from the South Atlantic.

★ LONGEST MIGRATION

The grey whale (*Eschrichtius robustus*) is traditionally believed to undertake the longest known migration of any mammal. Hugging the North American coastline, it swims from its winter breeding grounds in Baja California, Mexico, to its summer feeding grounds in the rich waters of the Bering Sea, and back again, every year. This amounts to a total annual distance of 12,000–20,000 km (7500–12,500 miles). In a grey whale's lifetime of 80 years or more, this is equivalent to two return trips to the moon.

Baleen

Like most of the larger whales, the grey whale has baleen plates. It feeds by scooping up sediments from the sea floor and its baleen then acts like a sieve, capturing the small sea animals taken in.

Recent studies on migrating humpback whales (*Megaptera novaeangliae*) suggest that some populations may possibly travel even further than this. One population makes an incredible migration between the Antarctic Peninsula and Colombia – a minimum distance of 8700 km (5400 miles) each way – every year.

★ BALEEN

Most large whales have hundreds of furry, comb-like structures hanging down from their upper jaws, called baleen plates, or whalebones; these form a sieve to filter food from the sea-water. The size and

Blue Whale

The blue whale (*Balaenoptera musculus*) is the heaviest and largest animal on Earth. The average adult length is 25 m (80 ft) in males and 26.2 m (86 ft) in females, with body weights of 90–120 tonnes. Blue whales in the southern hemisphere tend to be the largest, and females are larger than males of the same age.

No blue whale has ever been weighed 'whole'. All known weights have been obtained either by cutting them into smaller pieces, or by adding up the total number of known-capacity cookers filled with the meat, bone and blubber of individual whales at shore stations or on floating factory ships. The heaviest recorded blue whale was a female, caught in the Southern Ocean on 20 March 1947, which weighed 190 tonnes. Another female blue whale, brought to the shore station at Prince Olaf Harbor, South Georgia, Southern Ocean, in 1931, was 29.5 m (97 ft) long and was calculated to weigh, after adding 6.5% for loss of blood and other body fluids, 199 tonnes.

The longest blue whale ever recorded was another female, landed in 1909 at Grytviken, South Georgia, in the South Atlantic, which measured 33.58 m (110 ft 2 in) from the tip of her snout to the end of her tail.

★ LARGEST APPETITE

A large blue whale eats up to five and a half tonnes of (five million) krill every day, the equivalent in weight to an African elephant. It gorges itself all summer in polar waters and then eats little or nothing for the rest of the year while on migration and at its breeding grounds in warmer waters.

★ LARGEST BABY

In the two months before it is born, the weight of a blue whale (*Balaenoptera musculus*) increases by as much as two tonnes – it grows about 1000 times faster than a human baby in the womb. The newborn calf is a record-breaking 6–8 m (20–26 ft) long and weighs 2–3 tonnes. Every day, the baby drinks about 200 litres (360 pints) of its mother's milk and gains as much as 90 kg (198 lb) in weight (roughly equivalent to the weight of a grown man).

★ WEIGHT LOSS

While nursing her calf, a 120-tonne female blue whale (*Balaenoptera musculus*) can lose up to one tonne per week – equivalent to more than 25% of her body weight during the seven-month lactation period.

★ TALLEST BLOW

A 'blow' or 'spout' is the cloud of water droplets produced above a whale's head when it blows out. The tallest blow belongs to the blue whale (*Balaenoptera musculus*); slender and vertical in shape, it reaches a height of 15m (50 ft) which is clearly visible from several kilometres away.

★ NOISIEST

The low-frequency pulses made by blue whales (*Balaenoptera musculus*) and fin whales (*Balaenoptera physalus*) when vocalizing with each other across enormous stretches of ocean have been measured at up to 188 decibels, making them the loudest sounds emitted by any living source. The sounds themselves are infrasonic (below the range of human hearing) but, using specialist equipment, have been reliably detected from a distance of 3000 km (1850 miles) away. Biologists have established that blue whales calling off the coast of Newfoundland, Canada, can be heard throughout the western North Atlantic possibly as far south as the West Indies; and a fin whale calling off the coast of North Carolina, USA, can be heard off Nova Scotia, Canada; Bermuda; and Puerto Rico.

number of baleen plates varies greatly from species to species and from one individual to another. The longest baleen is found in the bowhead whale (*Balaena mysticetus*): there are many records within the 3–4 m (10–13 ft) range, but lengths of up to 5.18 m (17 ft) have been reported for animals killed during the 19th century. A plate taken from a bowhead killed in 1849 was reputed to be 5.8 m (19 ft), though this claim has been disputed since. The shortest baleen is found in the northern minke whale (*Balaenoptera acutorostrata*), with a maximum length of about 30 cm (12 in). The total number of baleen plates inside the mouth ranges from a minimum of 280 in the grey whale (*Eschrichtius robustus*) to a maximum of 946 in the fin whale (*Balaenoptera physalus*).

★ GESTATION PERIOD

The longest known gestation period is 15–17 months (with a possible record of 18 months 28 days) for the sperm whale (*Physeter catodon*) and up to 17 months for Baird's beaked whale (*Berardius bairdii*). The shortest gestation period is unknown, although 10–12 months is typical in many species and there have been reports of even shorter periods: seven months for a Dall's porpoise (*Phocoenoides dalli*), eight months for a harbour porpoise (*Phocoena phocoena*) and nine months 15 days for a long-snouted spinner dolphin (*Stenella longirostris*); however, these are probably extreme cases. The gestation period is not dependent on body size: in the blue whale (*Balaenoptera musculus*), it is about 11 months.

BEST-SELLING RECORD

Male humpback whales (*Megaptera novaeangliae*) are the only animals that can boast a top-selling record in the pop charts. When their plaintive songs were first heard in the 1970s, many people were captivated by their eerie moans, groans, roars, snores, squeaks and whistles.

★ LARGEST BABY

See **Blue whale** opposite. The blue whale calf is not exceptionally large in proportion to the size of its mother: one-third of the adult length is typical for most newborn cetaceans. Several species give birth to calves that are closer to half their own length, including belugas (*Delphinapterus leucas*), northern bottle-nosed whales (*Hyperoodon ampullatus*), tucuxis (*Sotalia fluviatilis*), Atlantic white-sided dolphins (*Lagenorhynchus acutus*) and Dall's porpoises (*Phocoenoides dalli*).

★ LONGEST SONG

Male humpback whales (*Megaptera novaeangliae*) sing the longest and most complex songs in the animal kingdom. Each song lasts for up to half an hour and consists of several main components; these are always sung in the same order, but are forever being refined and improved. All the humpbacks in one area sing broadly the same song, constantly incorporating each other's improvisations. Those in other parts of the world sing a completely different version. Most of the singing takes place at the breeding grounds, where the whales serenade one another throughout the day and night, with only brief one-minute pauses for breath. The aim of the singing is probably to woo females and to frighten off rival males.

Belugas (*Delphinapterus leucas*) make such a bewildering variety of whistles, squeals, clangs, moos, belches and yelps that early sailors nicknamed them 'sea canaries'. They also make

Humpback whale
Amongst the most acrobatic of whales, humpbacks have been known to leap almost clear of the water 70–80 times repeatedly, a phenomenal achievement considering that each one weighs, on average, the equivalent of 400 people.

resonant bell-like tones, a noise rather like an echo-sounder and even something resembling a giggling crowd of children.

★ LONGEST TOOTH

The male narwhal (*Monodon monoceros*) has two teeth. The one on the right normally remains invisible, but the one on the left grows to a remarkable length. It pierces the animal's upper lip, develops into a long tusk and eventually looks rather like a gnarled and twisted walking stick. When viewed from the root, it always spirals in a counter-clockwise direction. At least a third of all narwhal tusks are broken, but unbroken tusks reach an average length of about 2 m (6 ft 7 in) and weigh 8–9 kg (17½–19¼ lb). In extreme cases, they exceed 3 m (9 ft 10 in) and 10 kg (22 lb) (with a maximum girth of about 23 cm (9 in)). The tusk is probably used in establishing sexual dominance, in a way not dissimilar to the use of antlers in male deer.

★ LARGEST PREY

Killer whales (*Orcinus orca*) have been known to prey on more than 25 different whale and dolphin species, including sperm whale (*Physeter catodon*), southern right whale (*Eubalaena australis*), grey whale (*Eschrichtius*

> The unicorn, a mythical white horse with a horn growing out of its forehead, was really a narwhal, an Arctic-dwelling species of whale.

robustus), humpback whale (*Megaptera novaeangliae*) and several others that are considerably larger than themselves. In one well-documented case, in May 1978, a young blue whale (*Balaenoptera musculus*) was surrounded and attacked by a pod of killers off the coast of Cabo San Lucas, Baja California, Mexico; after sizeable chunks of flesh had been torn

Killer whale
As well as probably being the fastest cetacean, killer whales have been known to prey on animals much larger then themselves.

away, the blue whale escaped as fast as it could, but probably died afterwards.

The largest 'giant squid' known to be taken by a sperm whale (*Physeter catodon*) was 14.5 m (47 ft 7 in) long, including its tentacles; it was caught on Great Bahama Bank, in the Bahamas. Stories of fights between sperm whales and giant squid have probably been exaggerated, though there is little doubt that squid make formidable adversaries and frequently turn on the whales, wrapping their tentacles around the predators' heads to resist capture.

★ FASTEST

On 12 October 1958 a bull killer whale (*Orcinus orca*) was timed swimming at 55.5 km/h (34 mph) in the eastern North Pacific. Similar speeds, albeit in short bursts, have also been reported for Dall's porpoises (*Phocoenoides dalli*).

★ TALLEST DORSAL FIN

The huge, triangular dorsal fin of the bull killer whale (*Orcinus orca*) can reach a remarkable height of 1.8 m (6 ft), which makes it roughly as tall as a man. In comparison, the blue whale's (*Balaenoptera musculus*) dorsal fin is relatively small, rarely reaching more than 40 cm (16 in) in height.

★ LARGEST APPETITE

See **Blue whale** on p.108. There is a report from the mid-1860s, in which a male killer whale (*Orcinus orca*) was found to have no fewer than 13 porpoises and parts of 14 seals in its stomach (although it did not necessarily eat all of these on its own).

A sperm whale (*Physeter catodon*) eats up to a tonne of squid every day, each animal ranging in size from a few centimetres to over 12 m (39 ft 4 in) long. One whale's stomach was reported to contain 28,000 of the smaller species.

★ LONGEST DIVE

Early whalers reported dive times of more than two hours for northern bottle-nosed whales (*Hyperoodon ampullatus*), although their evidence is anecdotal. Sperm whales (*Physeter catodon*) may also be capable of two-hour dives. On 25 August 1969, a male sperm whale was killed 160 km (100 miles) south of Durban, South Africa, after it had surfaced from a dive lasting 1 h 52 min.

Sperm whale

Sperm whales are thought to dive deeper than any other cetacean and there is some indirect evidence which suggests that they may be able to dive to astonishing depths of at least 3000 m (10,000 ft).

★ DEEPEST DIVE

The sperm whale (*Physeter catodon*) is believed to dive deeper than any other cetacean. Most long, deep dives are made by older males and the depths they reach may be limited by time rather than water pressure. The deepest dives known were recorded in 1991 off Dominica,

When whales and dolphins open their eyes underwater, special greasy tears protect them from the stinging salt.

in the Caribbean, by scientists from the Woods Hole Oceanographic Institute. The scientists tagged a pair of male sperm whales and found that they regularly reached depths of 400–600 m (1312–1968 ft), remaining underwater for an average of 30–40 minutes. On one occasion, the bigger of the two – which was some 15 m (49 ft) in length – made a dive of 2000 m (6560 ft) to the seabed; it descended at a speed of up to 4 m/s (8 mph) and spent a total of 1 h 13 min underwater. The other animal managed a maximum dive of 'only' 1185 m (3887 ft), but even this beat previous recorded dive depths.

On 25 August 1969 a male sperm whale was killed 160 km (99 miles) south of Durban, South Africa, after it had surfaced from a dive lasting 1 h 52 min. Inside its stomach there were two small sharks – which experts

estimated had been swallowed about an hour earlier; these were later identified as *Scymnodon* sp., a type of dogfish found only on the sea floor. The water in the area exceeds a depth of 3193 m (10,473 ft) for a radius of some 48–64 km (30–40) miles, suggesting that the sperm whale had been to a similar depth when seeking food.

★ HEAVIEST BRAIN

The sperm whale (*Physeter catodon*) has the world's heaviest brain, although it amounts to only 0.02% of the animal's total body weight. During a Japanese whaling expedition to the North Pacific, in 1949–1950, the brains of 16 mature males were weighed: the heaviest was 9.2 kg (20 lb 5 oz), the lightest 6.4 kg (14 lb 2 oz) and the average 7.8 kg (17 lb 3 oz). This compares with an average 1.4 kg (3 lb 1 oz) for the brain of an adult human.

★ THICKEST BLUBBER

The blubber layer of the bowhead whale (*Balaena mysticetus*) is thicker than in any other animal, averaging 43–50 cm (17–20 in), and providing the whale with protection against the freezing cold waters of its Arctic home.

★ MOST PARASITES

The grey whale (*Eschrichtius robustus*) is more heavily infested with a greater variety of external parasites than any other cetacean. This may be partly because it moves relatively slowly compared to most other species. It carries two

Yangtze river dolphin
The Yangtze river dolphin, or baiji, was officially declared extinct in 2007 – the first cetacean known to become extinct in historical times.

★ MOST RESTRICTED DISTRIBUTION

The vaquita or Gulf of California porpoise (*Phocoena sinus*) probably has the most limited distribution of any marine cetacean. Today it is found within a 50 km (30 miles) radius in the extreme northern end of the Gulf of California (Sea of Cortez), in western Mexico, although it may once have occurred further south along the Mexican mainland. It is most commonly seen around the Colorado River delta.

Several river dolphins also have extremely limited ranges. The Indus river dolphin (*Platanista minor*) lives exclusively

major types: barnacles and whale lice. Each whale may have 100–200 kg (221–441lb) of barnacles attached to its head and body for most of its life; every barnacle is firmly anchored, through the whale's skin and into its blubber, but is really just hitch-hiking and does its host no serious harm. Strangely one species of barnacle, *Cryptolepas rhachianecti*, attaches itself exclusively to the grey whale and the beluga. The whale lice are not lice at all, but tiny crustaceans called amphipods; they actually feed on the skin of the whale and, if it is injured, will congregate in the wound and keep it clean by eating the decaying tissues. One hundred thousand whale lice have been found on a single whale. Perhaps surprisingly, the grey whale has relatively few internal parasites.

Dusky dolphin
The dusky dolphin has a well-deserved reputation as one of the most acrobatic animals in the world.

in the Indus river, Pakistan, with more than 80% of the population living along a 170 km (106 miles) stretch in the lower reaches of the river between the Sukkur and Guddu barrages.

★ YOUNGEST BREEDER

The female harbour porpoise (*Phocoena phocoena*) reaches sexual maturity at about three years old and begins to breed the year afterwards, which is probably younger than any other cetacean.

★ OLDEST BREEDER

Male sperm whales (*Physeter catodon*) reach sexual maturity at about 18–21 years, which is believed to be older than in any other cetacean. Even then, they have to wait until they are 20–25 years old before being strong and large enough to gain access to receptive females. Female short-finned pilot whales (*Globicephala macrorhynchus*) reach sexual maturity when they are around nine years old and, thereafter, have a calf every 4–6 years. They give birth for the last time when they are about 37 years old, but can continue to produce milk and suckle other calves until they are in their early forties.

★ LONGEST LIVING

Cetaceans are long-lived animals. However, it is difficult to assess their ages accurately and the maximum longevity is unknown for most species. The limited information available suggests that larger species tend to have longer lifespans. A giant bowhead whale (*Balaena mysticetus*), caught off the coast of Alaska in May 2007, was found to have an ancient harpoon point embedded in it dating back to 1880. Because the type of harpoon became obsolete a few years later this suggests the whale was as much as 130 years old. Meanwhile, scientists have developed a way of determining the ages of some whales by

examining the amino acids in the lenses in their eyes. Limited evidence from this research suggests that another bowhead whale in Alaska may have been 211 years old when killed.

★ WORST EYESIGHT

Ganges river dolphins (*Platanista gangetica*) and Indus river dolphins (*Platanista minor*) are the only cetaceans with eyes that lack a crystal-line lens. The optic opening is no bigger than a pin prick and barely large enough to allow light to penetrate. Also known as the blind river dolphins, they live in muddy rivers where eyes would be useless; they find their way around by building up a 'sound picture' of their surroundings with a system known as echolocation, similar to bats.

★ MOST ACROBATIC

Many cetaceans are known for their spectacular aerial displays. Among the larger species, southern right whales (*Eubalaena australis*), humpbacks (*Megaptera novaeangliae*) and killer whales (*Orcinus orca*) are particularly well known for their acrobatics. Humpbacks have been known to leap almost clear of the water 70–80 times repeatedly (Hawaii, USA); this is a phenomenal achievement, considering an average-sized humpback weighs the equivalent of 400 people.

Other outstanding acrobats are in the dolphin family. notably the bottlenose dolphin (*Tursiops truncatus*), pantropical spotted dolphin (*Stenella attenuata*), striped dolphin (*Stenella coeruleoalba*) and dusky dolphin (*Lagenorhynchus obscurus*). They have been known to hurl themselves as high as 7 m (23 ft) into the air and turn somersaults before re-entering the water. The most spectacular acrobat is the long-snouted spinner dolphin (*Stenella longirostris*), which hurls itself high into the air, then spins around on its longitudinal axis as many as seven times in a single leap.

★ LONGEST FLIPPERS

The longest flippers belong to the humpback whale (*Megaptera novaeangliae*). They grow to 23–31% of the length of the whale (making a potential maximum of over 5.5 m (18 ft)) but typically measure around 4.6 m (15 ft) in large animals. They are used to herd fish, to manoeuvre while swimming, to touch their young and to slap the surface of the water.

Bottlenose dolphin
Bottlenose dolphins are exceedingly acrobatic mammals and are known to hurl themselves as high as 7 m (23 ft) into the air and frequently turn somersaults before re-entering the water.

BIRDS

★ LARGEST
Ostrich (*Struthio camelus*) (p. 116)

★ SMALLEST
Bee hummingbird (*Mellisuga helenae*) (p. 117)

★ LARGEST WINGSPAN
Wandering albatross (*Diomedea exulans*) (p. 118)

★ LONGEST BILL
Australian pelican (*Pelecanus conspillicatus*) (p. 119)

★ FASTEST WINGBEAT
Horned sungem (*Heliactin bilophus*) (p. 120)

★ FASTEST FLYING
Peregrine falcon (*Falco peregrinus*) (p. 121)

★ LONGEST FLIGHT
Arctic tern (*Sterna paradisaea*) (p. 121)

★ BEST FIELD OF VISION
Eurasian woodcock (*Scolopax rusticola*) (p. 136)

★ BEST HEARING
Barn owl (*Tyto alba*) (p. 137)

★ FASTEST SWIMMER
Gentoo penguin (*Pygoscelis papua*) (p. 139)

★ FASTEST RUNNER
Ostrich (*Struthio camelus*) (p. 140)

★ MOST TALKATIVE
Budgerigar (*Melopsittacus undulatus*) (p. 142)

Peacock
A male peacock displaying
its impressive plumage.

PREHISTORIC

★ EARLIEST

Archaeopteryx lithographica is the earliest unambiguous fossil bird. It displays a mixture of reptilian and avian characteristics, providing paleontologists with their most conclusive evidence that birds evolved from reptiles, and is therefore one of the most important fossils of all time. It was discovered in 1861 and is known from only ten body fossil specimens and the imprint of a feather found a year earlier, which may belong to *Archaeopteryx*. They were all found in the Solnhofen limestone beds of what is now Bavaria, southern Germany. Roughly the size of a magpie, *Archaeopteryx* had many reptilian features as well as two features formerly regarded as distinctive of birds: feathers (which are now also known in many small meat-eating (theropod) dinosaurs), and a wishbone (recently discovered in many advanced theropod dinosaurs). Despite the presence of flight feathers like those of modern birds, it is uncertain whether it was capable of sustained powered flight or was mainly a glider. It lived at the end of the Jurassic period, 147 million years ago.

★ LARGEST PREHISTORIC

The largest and heaviest prehistoric bird was the flightless *Dromornis stirtoni*, a huge emu-like creature which lived in central Australia 6–8 million years ago, in late Miocene times. Fossil leg bones found near Alice Springs, in 1974, indicate that the bird must have stood almost 3 m (10 ft) tall and may have weighed as much as 500 kg (1100 lb).

★ MOST FORMIDABLE PREHISTORIC

The most formidable birds were probably the so-called terror birds or phorusrhacoids. They were the dominant terrestrial carnivorous animals of South America from 58 million years ago until about 2.5 million years ago. At least one species spread north as far as Florida about 3 million years ago. These flightless birds were powerful flesh-eaters and some may have reached a height of up to 3 m (10 ft). It has been suggested that they were capable of speeds of up to 70 km/h (44 mph), although there is no way of estimating this with certainty. Their large heads and laterally flattened eagle-like bills suggest that they fed by tearing flesh and, indeed, they may have been predominantly carrion feeders.

★ LARGEST FLYING PREHISTORIC

The largest prehistoric flying bird was the giant teratorn (*Argentavis magnificens*), which lived on the South American pampas about 6–8 million years ago. Fossil remains were discovered at a site 160 km (100 miles) west of Buenos Aires, Argentina, in 1979. The available evidence suggests that it was probably a soaring bird and flapped its wings only occasionally, but its discovery rocked the bird world and forced experts to re-examine their theories relating to size limitations in flight. *Argentavis* might have weighed as much as 72 kg (158 lb), which

> The vulture-like giant teratorn had a wingspan of over 6 m (20 ft), making it about the size of a small light aeroplane.

is well above the theoretical limit for flapping flight, and had a standing height of 1.5 m (5 ft). Its primary feathers are believed to have been as long as 1.5 m (5 ft) and as much as 18 cm (7 in) wide.

BIRD STATISTICS

Aves

About 9500 to over 10,000 species. In 2003 the latest figure of recognized species was 9721, of which 128 are thought to be extinct

★ LARGEST

The largest living bird is the ostrich (*Struthio camelus*), which is found in Africa (although there is also an introduced population in Australia). Five sub-species are recognized though one, the Arabian ostrich *Struthio c. syrizcus* is now extinct. The tallest is the North African ostrich (*Struthio c. camelus*), which occurs south of the Atlas Mountains, from Chad across to the Sudan and central Ethiopia. Males are larger than females and have been recorded up to 2.75 m (9 ft) (including a head and neck of up to 1.4 m or 4½ ft); the average height is closer to 2 m

Andean condor
This is a young Andean condor soaring in the skies in Peru. It is the one of largest birds of prey in the world with a wingspan of 3 m (10 ft).

Ostrich
The ostrich is the world's largest living bird, with an average height of around 2 m (6½ ft) although specimens have been recorded at heights up to 2.75 m (9 ft).

least 3.6 m (11¾ ft) maybe even 4 m (13 ft). There were 10–15 moa species of varying sizes in New Zealand before the Polynesians and Europeans arrived, but it is believed that they all became extinct before or during the 16th century.

★ SMALLEST

The smallest bird in the world is widely claimed to be the bee hummingbird (*Mellisuga helenae*), from Cuba and the Isla de la Juventud. Males have an iridescent red throat patch with long lateral plumes extending from it, a wingspan of only 65 mm (2½ in), and a total body length of 57 mm (2¼ in), half of which is taken up by the bill and tail; they can weigh as little as 1.6 g (or less than ¹⁄₁₅ oz). However, the little woodstar (*Chaetocercus bombus*) of southwest Columbia, Ecuador and northern Peru is considered by some experts to be slightly smaller.

The bee hummingbird is so tiny that it is dwarfed by many butterflies and moths in its rainforest home.

★ LARGEST BIRD OF PREY

The heaviest individual bird of prey ever recorded was a female harpy eagle (*Harpia harpyja*) called Jezebel. Owned by the former manager of the Dadanawa cattle ranch, Guyana, she weighed 12.3 kg (27 lb). However, this was really exceptional, since the heaviest weight for females of this species from the rainforests of Central and northern South America is 6–9 kg (13–20 lb). Adult females are, however, always larger than males.

(6½ ft). The heaviest sub-species is the southern African ostrich (*Struthio c. australis*) which is reputed to weigh up to 156 kg (344 lb).

The extinct elephant bird (*Aepyornis maximus*), a flightless species related to the ostrich and other ratites, which lived in Madagascar probably until the 17th century, is estimated to have weighed

450 kg (992 lb) (almost three times as heavy as the heaviest ostrich), and reached a height of about 3 m (10 ft).

The tallest bird ever was probably the flightless giant moa (*Dinornis robustus*), from South Island, New Zealand. At 250 kg (550 lb), it was comparatively slender compared to the elephant bird, but attained a maximum height of at

Strictly speaking, condors are not birds of prey and are more closely related to storks. However, they are commonly included as members of the group. With this in mind, the largest, taking average weight as the measure, is the Andean condor (*Vultur gryphus*) which lives in South America, predominantly in the Andes Mountains. The larger males weigh about 11–15 kg (24–33 lb) and have a wingspan of 3 m (10 ft) or more.

★ LARGEST MARINE BIRD

The heaviest marine bird is the emperor penguin (*Aptenodytes forsteri*), which averages 30 kg (66 lb) in weight and 1.15 m (45 in). Its standing height, with the head held horizontal, is about 1 m (40 in). The heaviest ever recorded was 45.3 kg (100 lb). The longest marine bird recorded is the wandering albatross (*Diomedea exulans*) from South Georgia, which has a body length of 1.1–1.4 m (43–55 in) and weighs 6–11.9 kg (13–26 lb).

★ LARGEST OWL

Some of the Siberian races of the Eurasian eagle owl (*Bubo bubo*) are usually regarded as the world's largest owl. Females are larger than males, with a length of up to 75 cm (29½ in), weighing as much as 4.2 kg (9¼ lb) and a wingspan of up to 2 m (6½ ft). They can kill prey as large as foxes and roe deer fawns, and regularly kill other owls and powerful birds of prey such as goshawk (*Accipiter gentilis*) and peregrine falcons (*Falco peregrinus*).

Individual females of Blakiston's fish owl (*Bubo blakistoni*) of the Russian Far East and northeastern China, and of the snowy owl (*Nyctea scandiaca*) found

• **Snowy owl**
A snowy owl landing in snow in Canada. It is one of the largest types of owl and has a strong and steady flight with deliberate, powerful downstrokes and quick upstrokes.

right around the Arctic, may be as big and heavy as the Eurasian eagle owl.

★ LARGEST WINGSPAN

The wandering albatross (*Diomedea exulans*) of the southern oceans has the largest accurately measured wingspan of any living bird. Its wings average 2.54–3.51 m (8 ft 4 in–11½ ft) at full

stretch, but the largest recorded specimen was a very old male with a wingspan of 3.63 m (11 ft 11 in), caught by members of the Antarctic research ship *USNS Eltanin* in the Tasman Sea on 18 September 1965. Unconfirmed measurements of up to 4.22 m (13 ft 10 in) have also been claimed for this species and, since only a relatively small number have ever been measured, lengths of this order may prove to be feasible. The royal albatross (*Diomedea epomophora*), which also lives in the southern oceans, has a similar average wingspan of 3.05–3.51 m (10–11½ ft).

The vulture-like marabou stork (*Leptoptilos crumeniferus*) of tropical Africa has the largest wingspan among land birds. The average length for the male's wingspan is 2.63 m (8½ ft) but up to 2.87 m (9 ft 5 in) is not uncommon, and individuals have been recorded whose wing spanned up to 3.2 m (10 ft 5 in). There is an unconfirmed report of a specimen, shot in 1934, which had an estimated wingspan of 4.06 m (13 ft 4 in).

The Andean condor (*Vultur gryphus*) of South America is a possible rival for this record, with a wingspan that may exceed 3.1 m (10 ft 2 in) in some individuals.

★ LONGEST FEATHERS

The longest feathers grown by any bird are those of the Phoenix fowl or Yokohama chicken (a strain of the domesticated fowl which in turn was derived from the red jungle fowl (*Gallus*

gallus), which has been bred in southwestern Japan for ornamental purposes since the mid-17th century. Its upper tail coverts (small feathers which cover the bottom of the longer feathers), moult very infrequently and can grow continually for up to six years. The longest ever recorded is 12 m (40 ft).

Among flying birds, the tail feathers of the male crested pheasant or crested argus (*Rheinardia ocellata*), from Vietnam and the Malay peninsula of Southeast Asia, regularly reach 1.73 m (5 ft 8 in) in length and 13 cm (5 in) in width. The central tail feathers of Reeves' pheasant (*Syrmaticus reevesii*) of central and northern China have reached 2.43 m (8 ft) in exceptional cases.

The longest feathers relative to body length among wild birds belong to the male ribbon-tailed astrapia (*Astrapia mayeri*), a bird of paradise which lives in the mountain rainforests of New Guinea.

SHORTEST LEGS

The shortest legs belong to several species of swift. The family name (Apodidae), literally translated, means 'lacking legs'. Swifts spend so much of their time in the air that their legs have become almost non-existent and, in some species, only the feet are visible outside the plumage.

astonishing 9–11 cm (3½–4½ in), making it longer than the bird's body length excluding the tail. Its length enables the sword-billed hummingbird to gather nectar from a number of different plants with very deep trumpet-shaped flowers. When perching, the bird (which measures up to 17–23 cm (6¾–9 in) from the tip of its bill to the end of its tail), tilts its head back and slants its bill steeply upwards to support the relatively tremendous weight.

Its ribbon-like central tail feathers, which play a key role in courtship display, measure up to 90 cm (3 ft) long and quadruple the overall length of their 27.5 cm (11 in) owner.

★ LONGEST BILL

The spectacular bill of the Australian pelican (*Pelecanus conspicillatus*) is 34–47 cm (13–18½ in) long and is the longest bill of any bird.

The longest bill in relation to overall body length belongs to the sword-billed hummingbird (*Ensifera ensifera*), an inhabitant of South America that lives mainly in the high Andes from Venezuela south to Bolivia. Its bill measures an

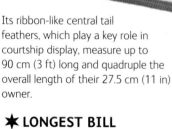

Australian pelican
The record for the longest bill of any bird in the world is held by the Australian pelican here gaping its beak wide open.

★ LONGEST LEGS

The longest legs of any living bird belong to the ostrich (*Struthio camelus*), which is only found in the wild as a native species in Africa (although there is also an introduced feral population in Australia). Males are normally larger than females and, in extreme cases, their powerful legs may be up to 1.3 m (51 in) tall.

The longest legs in relation to body length belong to the black-winged stilt (*Himantopus himantopus*), a striking black-and-white wader with a very wide world distribution from southern Europe and Africa to central and southern Asia, New Guinea, Australia and New Zealand, Hawaii and the Americas. Its long, pinkish-red legs measure 17–24 cm (7–9 in), which is up to 60% of the total body length of 35–40 cm (14–16 in).

★ LONGEST TOES

The longest toes in relation to body length belong to the eight species of jacana or lily-trotter (family Jacanidae), which live in many parts of tropical and sub-tropical Africa, Asia, Australasia and Latin America. Their splayed, long-nailed toes can each be considerably longer than the tarsus (the length of leg between the 'knee' – a bird's ankle joint – and the 'ankle' – a bird's toe joint), and are designed to disperse the birds' weight, enabling them to walk on lily pads and other floating vegetation. Some of the larger species, whose maximum overall adult length is about 30 cm (1 ft), have a 'toespan' of at least half their total length at 15 cm (6 in).

BIRDS IN FLIGHT

★ HEAVIEST FLYING

The world's heaviest flying birds are the kori bustard (*Ardeotis kori*) of northeastern and southern Africa and the great bustard (*Otis tarda*) of Europe, northwest Africa and Asia. Weights of 19 kg (42 lb) have been reported for exceptionally large mature male kori bustards, and there is an unconfirmed record of 21 kg (46 lb 4 oz) for a male great bustard shot in Manchuria, although it was too heavy to fly. The heaviest reliably recorded great bustard weighed 18 kg (39 lb 11 oz).

The mute swan (*Cygnus olor*) can reach almost 18 kg (40 lb) in the wild on very rare occasions, and there is an exceptional record from Poland of a tame cob (male) weighing 22.3 kg (49 lb 10 oz), although it had temporarily lost the power of flight.

★ TALLEST FLYING

The tallest of the flying birds is the sarus crane (*Grus antigone*) of India, Southeast Asia and northern Australia. Males may be up to 1.8 m (6 ft) tall.

★ FASTEST LONG-DISTANCE FLYING

The fastest bird recorded in sustained level flight is a sea duck, the common eider (*Somateria mollissima*) which travelled at 76.5 km/h (47.5 mph).

One of the fastest sustained flights ever recorded was accomplished by six wandering albatrosses (*Diomedea exulans*) moving across the south-western Indian Ocean in the late 1980s. They easily maintained a speed of 56 km/h (35 mph) over a distance of more than 800 km (500 miles). However, in 2003 a grey headed albatross (*Thalassarche chrysostoma*) beat this record; it was recorded by satellite tracking during the course of a foraging trip flying for about nine hours with virtually no rest, at a mean ground speed of 127 km/h (79 mph) It was done with the help of tailwinds during an Antarctic storm.

★ FASTEST DIVE

The male Anna's hummingbird performs a remarkable courtship dive that can reach speeds of up to 80 kph (50 mph). The

Hummingbird
A broad-billed hummingbird female in flight feeding on a sweet william. Hummingbirds have the fastest wingbeats in the bird world.

dive ends abruptly with outstretched wings and a dramatic upturn. It is the fastest aerial manoeuvre for an animal compared to its size. The G-force created when the hummingbird comes out of its dive is the same as the maximum G-force experienced by fighter pilots.

★ FASTEST WINGBEAT

Hummingbirds have the fastest wingbeats in the bird world. As a general rule, the smaller the bird the faster the wingbeat and, in many species, the wings move so fast that they are a blur and impossible to see with the human eye. They have to be measured with a stroboscope or similar sophisticated equipment.

The maximum wingbeat recorded is for the horned sungem (*Heliactin bilophus*), a hummingbird living in tropical South America, at 90 beats per second. Similar rates have been claimed for the amethyst woodstar (*Calliphlox amethystina*), another hummingbird from South America, and several other members of the family have been recorded at 70–80 beats per second. During foraging flights, between 10 and 80 wing beats per second seem to be the normal amount for most hummingbird species. While hovering at these speeds, the wings make the strange humming sound that gives the hummingbirds their family name.

There are claims for wingbeats of up to 200 beats per second during courtship flights of ruby-throated hummingbirds and rufous hummingbirds. These were thought to be for the narrow tips of the primary feathers only though and not for the complete wing.

★ HOVERING

Few species are capable of true hovering flight, although many can hover for short periods or can use the wind in a technique called 'wind-hovering' (to remain stationary relative to the ground, they must fly into a moderate wind at the same speed as they are being blown back). The largest bird able to hover for sustained periods in windless conditions is

WORLD RECORD HOLDER

Fastest flying

The fastest flying bird (and, indeed, the fastest animal of any kind) is the peregrine falcon (*Falco peregrinus*). When 'stooping' or 'plunge diving' from great heights to catch birds in mid-air, or during territorial displays, it is able to reach a maximum speed of at least 200 km/h (124 mph) and probably as much as 250 km/h (155 mph). However, the greatest attained speed is a much-debated figure. It has been calculated, using precise mathematical formulae, that a peregrine weighing just over 1 kg (2¼ lb) (with its wings folded and tail feathers closed to form a sleek projectile), would reach a maximum velocity of 384 km/h (239 mph) in a 1524 m (5000 ft) free-fall. Experiments in both Germany and Russia have recorded a velocity of 270 km/h (168 mph) at a 30° angle of stoop, rising to a maximum of 350 km/h (217 mph) (Germany) and 360 km/h (224 mph) (Russia) at steeper angles; however, there is still some controversy over the accuracy of these figures. Even at lower speeds, no-one knows how this jet fighter among birds manages to pull out of such astonishing dives without blacking out or tearing itself apart.

the pied kingfisher (*Ceryle rudis*) of Africa and Asia, which is 25–29 cm (10–11½ in) in length and hovers with its body almost vertical and its bill pointed downwards while hunting for freshwater fish.

Hummingbirds (family Trochilidae) are the experts at hovering for prolonged periods in still air. Under experimental conditions, one bird hovered continuously for 50 minutes.

★ MOST ACROBATIC

Many birds are built for precision, speed and agility in the air. Even simple manoeuvres, such as landing on a perch or flying in dense flocks, require very fine coordination and split-second timing. The ultimate in flight control is found in predatory birds that have to capture moving targets at high speed, without harming themselves. In this respect, the hobby (*Falco subbuteo*) of Europe, North Africa and many parts of Asia is widely

considered to be one of the best aerial acrobats. It catches nearly all its prey in mid-air and is fast and agile enough to catch a swallow (*Hirundo rustica*), a swift (*Apus apus*), a bat or a dragonfly on the wing.

In terms of aerial manoeuvrability, hummingbirds (family Trochilidae) are probably the record-holders. By tilting their wings, in the same way that a pilot alters the angle of the rotors on a helicopter, they can fly forwards, backwards or sideways, spin on their axis and even turn over to fly upside down. Other birds can do this briefly or momentarily but such aerobatics reach their zenith in hummingbirds.

★ LONGEST FLIGHT

Several bird species are thought to fly continuously between leaving their breeding colonies as youngsters and returning several years later as adults.

Wandering albatross
The wandering albatross takes some of the longest flights ever recorded in search of food for its chick. It is pictured here flying above the Weddell Sea, Antarctica.

Arctic tern
No other animal experiences as much daylight in a year as the globe-trotting Arctic tern, which makes the longest regular migratory journey of any bird, flying from the Arctic to the other side of the world after breeding.

Most notable among these are the sooty shearwater (*Puffinus griseus*), which has made the longest electronically tracked migration of any bird (not non-stop), some 64,000 km (40,000 miles).

Various swifts (family Apodidae) make the longest non-stop flights of any bird. They fine-tune the angle of their wings from spread wide to swept back, so they get the best performance for the smallest amount of energy. It has been calculated that the common swift (*Apus apus*), breeding in Eurasia and wintering in Africa, completes a non-stop flight of 500,000 km (300,000 miles) between fledging late one summer and its first landing at a potential nesting site a minimum of two years later.

The longest recorded non-stop flight was in 2007 by a bar-tailed godwit (*Limosa lapponica*), which flew 11,680 km (7,257 miles) in just over eight days.

The longest one-way migration (assuming a coastal route) was of a common tern (*Sterna hirundo*) which flew 26,000 km (16,210 miles) in January 1997.

Traditionally, the Arctic tern (*Sterna paradisaea*) has been credited with the longest flight and it makes the longest regular migratory journey of any bird. It breeds mainly around the shores of the Arctic Ocean and then flies to the other side of the world to spend the remainder of the year in the Antarctica; a total distance, if it were to travel in a straight line, of at least 15,000 km (9300 miles)

each way. Many individuals travel even further (strangely, birds that nest farthest north also go the farthest south). Terns travel a 70,900 km (44,000 miles) round trip when migrating, this excludes wintering and summer breeding grounds. Recent tracking research has discovered that they make a lengthy stop-over in

In a lifetime, an Artic tern flies approximately three return trips to the moon.

the middle of the North Atlantic about 1,000 km (620 miles) north of the Azores, and do not fly straight to the Antarctic when they leave the Arctic as previously thought. The birds then fly south along the coast of western Europe and western Africa, then either continue their path around Africa or sweep across the Atlantic from the Cape Verde Island to continue the journey along the Brazilian coast. Researchers believe wind patterns might be a contributing factor to which flight path the birds make. When leaving Antarctic waters, where they spend the

winter months, the terns fly back to the Arctic via a different route across the Atlantic Ocean, flying in a giant 'S' shape taking advantage of prevailing winds. Arctic terns can live for 30 years so they could potentially clock up a lifetime mileage of over 2.4 million km (1 ½ million miles), approximately three return trips to the moon.

Other birds travel long distances while foraging but, since they rarely maintain a steady course, the distances covered are difficult to measure. When finding food for their nestlings, swifts (*Apus apus*), for example, are believed to fly up to 1000 km (600 miles) a day and, in a lifetime may easily match or even exceed the distance covered by Arctic terns.

In 1990, six foraging wandering albatrosses (*Diomedea exulans*) were tracked across the Indian Ocean by satellite via miniature radio transmitters. Their results showed that the birds covered 3600–15,000 km (2240–9320 miles), flying at speeds of up to 80 km/h (50 mph), in single feeding trips, each lasting 10–33 days. According to the two researchers, the birds' long journeys were made possible by making the most of the prevailing weather; on the outward journey, they exploited the winds, and on the return journey they tacked their way home to avoid facing directly into the wind. Regularly albatrosses (*Diomedea exulans*) travel up to 10,000 km (6000 miles) or more to find food for the single chick.

★ MOST AIRBORNE

The most aerial of all birds is the sooty tern (*Sterna fuscata*), which is widespread throughout the tropical oceans. After leaving its nesting grounds as a youngster, it is reputed to remain aloft continuously for 3–10 years until it is old enough to breed for the first time. Although this is impossible to prove, research suggests that it does not need to return to land to rest but, as long as there is enough food available, can stay in the air indefinitely. It does not even need to settle on the sea to feed, preferring to catch fish or squid by picking them from the surface while hovering, or by seizing them in mid-air when they jump to escape underwater predators.

The most aerial land bird is the common swift (*Apus apus*), which remains airborne for 2–4 years after fledging, during which time it sleeps, drinks, bathes, eats and even mates on the wing. Its flight is about 70% more efficient than that of other birds of comparable size, because it has long, slender wings, a low body mass in relation to wing area (to reduce energy expenditure) and a shallow, forked tail that reduces drag and increases lift. Like the sooty tern, it has to come to land only when it is ready to breed.

After fledging, royal albatross chicks may not return to land for up to five years.

★ HIGHEST FLYING BIRDS

Most bird species fly at altitudes below 1500 m (4920 ft), even on migration. However, a Rüppell's griffon vulture (*Gyps rueppelli*) collided with a commercial aircraft over Abidjan, Ivory Coast, on 29 November 1973, when it was recorded to be flying at an altitude of 11,277 m (37,000 ft). The impact damaged one of the aircraft's engines, which had to be shut down, but the plane landed safely without further incident. Sufficient feather remains of the bird were recovered to allow the Smithsonian National Museum of Natural

Whooper swan
Whooper swans have been recorded at higher altitudes than nearly all other types of bird.

History in Washington, USA to make a positive identification of this high-flier, which is rarely seen above 6000 m (20,000 ft). No mammal of a similar size could breathe enough air even to remain conscious at such an altitude. It should also be noted that the airliner was flying at an average of 10,000 m (33,300 ft), that the vulture's nearest recorded locality is 500 km (310 miles) to the north, and that in the report of the collision there is no discussion of the location of the strike.

Common cranes (*Grus grus*) have also been recorded at great heights flying across the Himalayas at up to 10,000 m (33,000 ft).

Bar-headed geese (*Anser indicus*) have been seen flying over the Himalayas at altitudes approaching 9000 m (29,500 ft). On 9 December 1967 about 30 whooper swans (*Cygnus cygnus*) were recorded at an altitude of just over 8200 m (27,000 ft), flying in from Iceland to winter at Lough Foyle, which borders Northern Ireland and the Republic of Ireland; they were spotted by an airline pilot over the Outer Hebrides, and their height was confirmed on radar by air traffic control.

BIRD NUMBERS

★ TOTAL NUMBERS

It has been estimated that some 150,000 bird species have inhabited the Earth since birds first evolved. Nearly 94% of them have become extinct. Estimates of the total number of species alive today vary widely between 9500 and over 10,000 though, for the purposes of this book, c. 9720 species are recognized.

★ LARGEST ORDER

The passerines, which include the songbirds, form by far the largest order of birds. According to the system of classification used for this book, there are an incredible 5878 members of the order Passeriformes, which is equivalent to nearly 60% of all the bird species in the world. This order includes all the most familiar garden birds, such as tits, robins and sparrows, as well as a host of other species from a wide range of land habitats.

★ STICKING TOGETHER

Starlings have one rule that enables them to keep the flock together in perfect formation. The secret is for each bird to interact with seven others, irrespective of their distance, keeping the group incredibly cohesive. If the group is attacked this rule enables them to re-form very quickly.

★ MOST ABUNDANT

Excluding domestic fowl, the red-billed quelea (*Quelea quelea*), a seed-eating weaver bird of the drier parts of Africa south of the Sahara, is the most abundant bird alive today. It has an estimated adult breeding population of several billion. Each bird weighs only about 20 g (³/₄ oz) but, when vast flocks descend on trees, they frequently break branches with their combined weight.

The North American passenger pigeon (*Ectopistes migratorius*) is widely believed to have been the commonest bird that has ever lived on Earth. Conservative

Densely packed flocks of red-billed quelea, containing hundreds of millions of birds, are so highly synchronized as they wheel and turn in flight that they look like smoke clouds from a distance.

estimates of the population at its peak suggest that it was almost as many as three billion and maybe as many as ten billion in the first half of the 19th century. At the time, it is likely that 25–50% of all the birds in North America were passenger pigeons. They lived in huge, densely packed flocks (some single flocks containing more than 2000 million birds), which darkened the sky and could take up to three days to pass overhead. But huge numbers were killed for their meat, and by sports hunters, and hunting

competitions were organized in which more than 30,000 dead birds were needed to claim a prize; forest destruction and fragmentation also took its toll. The last passenger pigeon to be seen in the wild was shot by a young boy on 24 March 1900; the species had been hunted to extinction in less than 100 years. The most abundant seabird in the world is probably Wilson's storm petrel (*Oceanites oceanicus*). There are thought to be more than 50 million pairs of this little, sparrow-sized bird nesting in the

Red-billed quelea
The most abundant bird in the world is the red-billed quelea, which has an estimated adult breeding population of several billion. Here a flock is massing to drink on the wing in Tsavo National Park, Kenya.

Antarctic and adjacent sub-Antarctic islands. Outside the breeding season, they range far north into the world's three main oceans.

★ MOST WIDESPREAD SPECIES

Worldwide distribution is extremely rare at the species level, although the barn owl (*Tyto alba*), osprey (*Pandion haliaetus*), swallow (*Hirundo rustica*), Arctic tern (*Sterna paradisaea*), cattle egret (*Bubulcus ibis*), and several others are virtually cosmopolitan. The house sparrow (*Passer domesticus*) naturally breeds in Eurasia, but has been deliberately introduced to many other parts of the world. It continues to spread. The peregrine falcon (*Falco peregrinus*) is generally considered to be the most widespread bird species of all, breeding on every continent except Antarctica and on many oceanic islands. Within its range, it shows great geographical variation, with the northern forms being the largest and generally the palest, and the southern forms being smaller and either darker or brighter in colour. Worldwide distribution does not, of course, imply great abundance, and the peregrine falcon and barn owl still face threats in a number of countries throughout their range.

★ MOST SUCCESSFUL NATURAL SPREAD

The collared dove (*Streptopelia decaocto*) has dramatically increased its range in recent years. It originated in northern India but, by the 16th century, had spread to parts of southeastern Europe. Then there was a lull in the action, for unknown reasons, until about 1930, when it suddenly continued its spread across Europe. It reached Britain in 1952 (the first recorded British nesting was at Cromer, Norfolk, in 1955) and, by the 1970s, was breeding in the Faeroe Islands and Iceland. It has also been travelling in other directions and has already reached southern Asia and Japan.

BIRD DISTRIBUTION

★ MOST SPECIES

Colombia, South America, has over 1760 indigenous breeding bird species, which is more than any other country in the world. In comparison, Canada and the USA combined have over 600 breeding species.

By far the richest avifauna is found in the neotropical region, consisting of tropical Mexico, Central and South America and the Caribbean. With some 3500 indigenous species of breeding birds, it is home to almost twice as many species as any other region and more than a third of the world total. As regular migrants, a further 175 species use the region. Diverse areas of a few square kilometres in the Amazon may hold well over 500 species, about 50% more than a comparable area of tropical Africa or Asia.

★ HIGHEST LIVING

The alpine chough (*Pyrrhocorax graculus*) has been recorded at a higher altitude on land than any other bird species. In the Himalayas, it is found year-round at altitudes of 3500–6250 m (11,500–20,500 ft), but an Everest expedition observed a small party of the birds at a record height of 8235 m (27,010 ft). For comparison, laboratory mice in a pressure chamber are barely able to crawl at the altitude equivalent to 6100 m (20,000 ft). Some Himalayan snowcocks (*Tetraogallus himalayensis*) may nest at heights of more than 5000 m (16,400 ft).

★ MOST SOUTHERLY

Most Antarctic birds breed on islands in the Southern Ocean or along the coastal strip of the continent itself. Few species breed 'inland' on a regular basis. The most southerly breeder is the snow petrel (*Pagodroma nivea*), which nests among the rocky mountain peaks that poke through the ice, up to 240 km (150 miles) inland. Adelie penguins (*Pygoscelis adeliae*) breed almost as far south; the most southerly rookery is just in front of Sir Ernest Shackleton's hut at Cape Royds, Ross Island, where 1600 pairs of Adelies nest at approximately 77° 34'S, 167° 07'E.

The most southerly nests ever recorded belong to Antarctic petrels (*Thalassoica antarctica*), which have bred in the Thiel Mountains, at 80° 30'S, 25° 00'W; snow petrels (*Pagodroma nivea*) on Mount Provender, in the Shackleton Mountains, at 80° 23'S, 29° 55'W; and south polar skuas (*Stercorarius maccormicki*), in the Theron Mountains, at 79°S 30°W. Southern skuas

(*Stercorarius antarctica*) and south polar skuas forage wherever humans leave something to scavenge upon and have even been recorded at the South Pole itself. Penguins may also wander far south: on 31 December 1957, the tracks of an emperor penguin (*Aptenodytes forsteri*) were found by a party of explorers traversing the Antarctic continent, over 400 km (250 miles) from the nearest sea.

Emperor penguin
Although it is the heaviest marine bird, the emperor penguin has the smallest egg in relation to the mother's size.

★ MOST NORTHERLY

On average, the ivory gull (*Pagophila eburnea*) has the most northerly breeding range of all birds. It occurs almost exclusively north of 70°N, with major breeding grounds on Svalbard, Franz Josef Land, Novaya Zemlya, northern Canada and northern Greenland.

Several bird species have been recorded breeding at the extreme northern limits of land, in Greenland at 83°N, including knot (*Calidris canutus*), Ross's gull (*Rhodostethia rosea*), ivory gull and Arctic tern (*Sterna paradisaea*). Some of their nests have been within 750 km (500 miles) of the North Pole. The ivory gull has the record of nesting on the edge of Arctic pack ice at about 650 km (450 miles) south of the North Pole. Turnstones (*Arenaria interpres*), snow geese (*Anser caerulescens*), snow buntings (*Plectrophenax nivalis*) and several other species are regular breeders in the Lake Hazen area, Ellesmere Island, Canada, at 82°N. The gyrfalcon (*Falco ruticolus*) breeds as far north as 82°N in Greenland.

Although some 145 bird species breed regularly in the Arctic, relatively few of these are truly high-Arctic species, and even fewer are year-round residents. The only species which remain in the Arctic, at least in some areas, all year round are: rock ptarmigan (*Lagopus mutus*), common raven (*Corvus corax*), willow grouse (*Lagopus lagopus*), snowy owl (*Nyctea scandiaca*), gyrfalcon (*Falco rusticolus*), common redpoll (*Carduelis flammea*), Ross's gull (*Rhodostethia rosea*), ivory gull (*Pagophila eburnea*), black guillemot (*Cepphus grylle*) and eider (*Somateria mollissima*). When food is available, the snowy owl may live further north than any other bird species during the winter; it has been recorded coping with the darkness and bitter cold of mid-winter on Ellesmere Island, Canada, at 82°N.

Only three birds have been recorded at the North Pole itself: a snow bunting (*Plectrophenax nivalis*) in May 1987; a black-legged kittiwake (*Rissa tridactyla*) in July 1992; and a northern fulmar (*Fulmarus glacialis*) in August 1993.

BREEDING BIRDS

★ SMALLEST NEST

The smallest nests are built by hummingbirds (family Trochilidae). They are typically inconspicuous cups of plant material, held together with silky threads from spiders' webs, and often adorned with tiny pieces of moss or lichen. The shallowest nest is probably that made by the vervain hummingbird (*Mellisuga minima*), which lives in Jamaica and two nearby islets, and is about half the size of a walnut shell. The bee hummingbird (*M. helenae*), found in Cuba and the Isla de la Juventud, has a deeper but narrower nest.

> Bee hummingbirds build nests no bigger than a thimble.

A number of birds make no nest at all or, for example, lay their eggs in a simple scrape in the ground. The guillemot, called the common murre in North America, (*Uria aalge*), lays its single egg on the bare ledge of a sea cliff; the white tern (*Gygis alba*) lays its egg

Anna's hummingbird
This is a female hummingbird (*Calypte anna*) sitting on its nest, in California, USA. Hummingbirds build the smallest nests of all birds, tiny cups of plant material.

directly on to a tree branch, where it is in constant danger of being knocked to the ground; many owls (family Tytonidae) and falcons (family Falconidae) use the abandoned nests of other birds; and king penguins (*Aptenodytes patagonicus*) and emperor penguins (*A. forsteri*) simply keep their single eggs balanced on their feet.

★ LARGEST NEST

A nest measuring 2.9 m (9½ ft) wide and 6.1 m (20 ft) deep was built by a pair of bald eagles (*Haliaeetus leucocephalus*), and possibly their successors, near St Petersburg, Florida, USA; it was examined in 1963 and was estimated to weigh 2722 kg (nearly 3 tons). The golden eagle (*Aquila chrysaetos*) also constructs huge nests, and one 4.5 m (15 ft) deep was reported from Scotland in 1954; it had been used for 45 years.

The incubation mounds built by several species of megapode or mound-builder (family Megapodiidae) are even larger. The male begins by digging a hole in the ground about 1–1.5 m (40–60 in) deep. In the process, he may have to move some very large objects – a 1 kg (2 lb) bird was once seen to shift a rock weighing 6.9 kg (15 lb). Then he fills the hole and makes a huge mound of leaf litter and soil or sand, in which the female lays the eggs. These are incubated by the sun and by fermentation of the decaying vegetation (it is rather like being inside a compost heap). However, the male is still kept busy maintaining the mound in such a way as to ensure a stable temperature inside for the eggs, which have to be kept at a constant 32–35°C (90–95°F). He checks the temperature of the mound at intervals by thrusting his bill – which is equipped with temperature sensing organs – into its surface. The best-known megapode is the mallee fowl (*Leipoa ocellata*) of southern Australia, which builds a huge mound of leaf litter and soil measuring up to 4.5 m (15 ft) in height

and 10.5 m (35 ft) in length. A mound of this size would involve the collection and movement of up to 250 cubic metres (8829 cubic feet) of vegetation and soil weighing more than 300 tonnes in a typical year. The mound is kept in use year after year.

★ STRANGEST NESTING MATERIAL

There are many examples of birds using a variety of strange and unlikely materials to build their nests. In 1909, the 600 kg (1455 lb) nest of a white stork (*Ciconia ciconia*) was removed from the tower of a cathedral in Colmar, France, when it started to lean over; inside the walls of the nest the workmen found 17 ladies' black stockings, five fur caps, three old shoes, the sleeve of a white silk blouse, a large piece of leather and four buttons from a railway porter's uniform. In the Galapagos Islands, Ecuador, mocking-birds (*Nesomimus trifasciatus*)

Bald eagle
The American bald eagle builds enormous nests for its chicks. One is pictured here with its chicks in a nest, in British Columbia, Canada.

occasionally take hair from the heads of passing tourists for their nests; and, in Australia, magpies (*Gymnorhina tibicen*) have a particular fondness for wire off-casts from farm fencing (one nest contained no fewer than 243 pieces of

A pair of house crows in Mumbai, India, made their nest entirely of gold spectacle frames, which they had stolen from an open shop window.

wire with a total length of 100 m (330 ft). Red kites regularly incorporate children's dolls and other toys, rags, bones, handkerchiefs, hats and gloves and, in

one case, two dead kittens into their nest. Many other birds use equally strange, but more natural, nesting materials. The violaceous trogon (*Trogon violaceous*) of Central and South America, for example, takes over a wasp's nest (having eaten all the adult wasps first) and then digs out the comb to make its own nesting cavity. Just as strange is the water thick-knee or dikkop (*Burhinus vermiculatus*) from Africa, which frequently lays its eggs on the sun-dried droppings of large mammals such as hippos.

★ MOST NESTS

Male wrens (family Troglodytidae) and weavers (family Ploceidae) construct large numbers of nests for evaluation by their prospective mates. Marsh wrens (*Cistothorus palustris*) are the record-holders: bigamous males build an average of 25 nests and monogamous males build 22 nests for the obviously fussy females to compare. The nests that are rejected for egg-laying serve as dummy nests that help to confuse potential predators.

★ MOST VALUABLE NEST

The most valuable nests in the world belong to several species of cave swiftlet, in particular the edible-nest swiftlet (*Aerodramus fuciphagus*) from Southeast Asia which nests in huge colonies – as many as 300,000 in the famous Niah Caves in Borneo. All swifts and swiftlets (family Apodidae) use a substance secreted from a pair of enlarged salivary glands situated beneath their tongues to glue their nests together, but in cave swiftlet nests saliva is the principal ingredient. Made into a gelatinous soup, which is essentially a protein-sugar solution, they have been eaten by the Chinese for some 1500 years. Nowadays they are considered a special delicacy (although, to the western palate, 'birds' nest soup' is almost tasteless), and have become extremely valuable. Collecting this so-called 'white gold' from the roofs and walls of deep caves can be very hazardous, but the demand is great, and annual production is about 27 tonnes. Hong Kong, which consumes more than 60% of all the nests taken, imports some

eight million of them. Top-grade nests can fetch as much as £2000 per kg (2 lb 3 oz) (US$4000) in Hong Kong. It takes two nests to make one bowl of soup.

★ MOST POPULOUS NEST

The aptly named sociable weaver (*Philetairus socius*), which lives in the dry grasslands of southwest Africa, builds an enormous communal nest that hangs from a tree or telegraph pole and looks surprisingly like a giant haystack. The 'haystack' contains up to 100 individually woven grass nests, each housing a single pair of weavers and their brood, all of which are clustered under one dome-shaped thatched roof. It provides a home for many more birds than the builders, including the African pygmy falcon (*Polihierax semitorquatus*), which never builds its own nest but usually uses the empty nests in a sociable weaver colony, as do a variety of other birds that do nest elsewhere too – geese, owls, eagles, finches and chats. The communal nest is

Sociable weaver
This giant communal nest hanging from a tree in the Kalahari Gemsbok National Park, South Africa, has been built by the sociable weaver. There are at least 100 individual nests, each with a pair of weaver birds.

constantly being repaired and extended and may be as large as 2 m (6½ ft) high and 8 m (26 ft) long. The main limit to its size is weight; it is not unusual for a sociable weaver nest to get so heavy that the tree collapses. When this happens, the birds simply build a new home elsewhere.

★ QUICKEST TO FLY

Young megapodes (family Megapodiidae) hatch with extremely advanced contour-like feathers, instead of the down of most other young birds, enabling them to fly and escape from predators very soon after hatching. The best-known example is the mallee fowl (*Leipoa ocellata*) of southern Australia. Within an hour, the baby mallee fowl can run confidently, after two hours it can flutter above the ground for 10–15 m (30–50 ft) and, just 24 hours after its escape from the mound, it is capable of strong flight.

★ SLOWEST TO FLY

The wandering albatross (*Diomedea exulans*) has the longest known interval between hatching and being able to fly. On average the chick flies from the nest for the first time some 278–280 days after hatching. It takes so long for the young bird to prepare itself that the adults can breed only once in two years.

★ FASTEST TO MATURITY

Five species of quail in the genus *Coturnix* reach breeding maturity faster than any other bird: they are able to reproduce when only five weeks old. Even so, they are still in immature plumage at this stage and do not attain the full adult plumage for another five to seven weeks.

★ SLOWEST TO MATURITY

The slowest birds to reach breeding maturity are the albatrosses (family Diomedeidae) and, in particular, two species of 'great albatross', the royal (*Diomedea epomophora*) and wandering (*D. exulans*) albatrosses. They become sexually mature at around eight years old but often do not breed until they are ten years old; there are even reports of first

breeding attempts at 17 years old. When they do eventually form pairs, before settling down, they spend a year of 'keeping company'; after that the partners stay together for life. Despite this protracted period of adolescence, in many cases their first breeding efforts are unsuccessful.

★ LARGEST CLUTCH

The number of eggs laid in a single clutch varies markedly from species to species, from individual to individual and according to latitude, habitat, time of year, age of the female, population density and local environmental conditions. The upper limit depends upon how many eggs the female can produce and incubate properly, and how many young the parents can feed at any one time.

Some domestic chickens lay almost daily (i.e. up to 360 eggs per year). Among wild birds, the grey partridge (*Perdix perdix*) is generally considered consistently to lay the most eggs (typically 15–16 but up to 19) in a single clutch.

★ SMALLEST CLUTCH

Many birds lay just one egg. This is a particularly common phenomenon in seabirds such as petrels and albatrosses (families Procellariidae and Diomedeidae), but is also found in several large eagles (family Accipitridae), king penguins (*Aptenodytes patagonicus*), emperor penguins (*A. forsteri*) and a variety of other species.

★ MOST CLUTCHES

In captivity, there are reports of zebra finches (*Taeniopygia guttata*) raising as many as 21 consecutive broods and, indeed, there are other examples of birds laying one brood after another under artificial conditions.

In the wild, the stock dove (*Columba oenas*) in Britain probably has more broods than any other species, frequently attempting up to four a year.

Albatross
Black-browed albatross chicks like this one develop quicker than the royal or wandering albatross. They leave the nest three to four months after hatching and are mature at five-years old.

Eggs

★ LARGEST EGG

An ostrich egg (*Struthio camelus*) measures on average 16 cm (6¼ in) long, by 13 cm (5 in) and weighs 1–1.78 kg (2¼–3 lb) (on average, roughly equivalent in capacity to two dozen hens' eggs). The largest egg on record, reported in September 2006, was laid by an ostrich at the ostrich farm of Gunnar and Kerstin Sahlin near the small central Swedish town of Borlänge – it weighed just over 2.5 kg (5½ lb).

The largest egg ever laid belonged to the extinct elephant bird (*Aepyornis maximus*) from Madagascar. The largest known specimen was collected in 1841 and is currently housed in the Académie des Sciences, Paris, France and measures 39 cm (15½ in) in length and 32.6 cm (12¾ in) in width. It would have weighed about 12.2 kg (27 lb) with its contents.

★ HIGHEST YOLK CONTENT

The eggs of kiwis (family Apterygidae) have the highest yolk content of any bird, around 60%, making them such a rich source of food for the developing chicks that they usually do not have to feed for several days after hatching. Most other birds rarely have as much as 50%, while where nestlings stay in the nest for a long time, it can be down to as little as 15%.

★ SHORTEST INCUBATION

No bird is known to have a normal incubation period of less than ten days. However, a number of small passerines are known to incubate their eggs for as little as ten days, including the great spotted woodpecker (*Dendrocopos major*) 10–16 days, the shorelark or horned lark (*Eremophila alpestris*) 10–14 days, and the lesser white-throat (*Sylvia curraca*) for 10–11 days.

★ SMALLEST EGG

The egg of the vervain hummingbird (*Mellisuga minima*), which lives in Jamaica and on two nearby islets, is barely the size of a pea and is possibly the smallest egg laid by any bird on record. Two specimens measuring less than 1 cm (⁷⁄₁₆ in) in length weighed 0.363 g (¹⁄₄₅ oz) and 0.375 g (¹⁄₇₆ oz). However, the eggs are still unknown for many hummingbird species and, with further research, this record may yet be broken.

★ RAREST EGG

There are several extinct bird species for which only one egg survives. Two good examples are held at the Natural History Museum, UK: *Cabalus modestus* and *Parendiastes pacificus*, both of which are rails.

★ LONGEST INCUBATION

Six species, two albatrosses and four kiwis (families Diomedeidae and Apterygidae), incubate their eggs for longer than 70 days, most averaging between 75–82 days and, exceptionally, 85 days. However, the male emperor penguin (*Aptenodytes forsteri*) has the longest continuous incubation period, incubating its single egg on the top of its feet without relief for 62–67 days. In contrast, the albatrosses and kiwis have the opportunity to leave their nests at intervals to feed.

★ YOUNGEST INCUBATOR

The female white-rumped swiftlet (*Aerodramus spodiopygius*), of New Britain, Fiji, and various other Pacific islands, lays two eggs several weeks apart. By the time she has laid the second one, the first has hatched and the chick has grown enough to do the incubating.

Ostrich egg
This egg is shown at actual size. Although only 1.5 mm (¹⁄₁₆ in) thick, the shell can easily support the weight of an adult man.

BIRDS

★ LEAST CLUTCHES

Many birds have such extended nesting cycles, or such long periods of parental care, that they cannot produce more than one clutch in a year. The Philippine eagle (*Pithecophaga jefferyi*), formerly known as the monkey-eating eagle, has such a slow reproductive rate that it produces only one egg every two to three years.

Several species of albatross (family Diomedeidae) breed only in alternate years; since most of them do not even start breeding until they are 10–15 years old, they also have among the lowest total egg output of any bird.

★ HATCHING TIME

The length of time between the first crack appearing in an eggshell and the emergence of the chick varies within a clutch in order to synchronize hatching, and also varies from species to species. Total hatching time ranges from about 30 minutes in many small passerines to as long as 6 days in some of the larger albatrosses (family Diomedeidae).

★ SHORTEST CHICK-REARING PERIOD

There are basically two kinds of newly hatched chick: altricial and precocial. Altricial species are born blind and with little or no down, they cannot walk or fly and are even unable to regulate their own body temperatures; they are totally dependent on their parents for many days, weeks or even months after hatching. Precocial species, in contrast, hatch from the egg in an advanced state of development, usually leave the nest soon afterwards and are often capable of leading an independent existence within about 24 hours of hatching. The most extreme examples of precocial birds are found among the 21 species of megapode (family Megapodiidae), many of which have chicks that are completely independent and receive absolutely no parental care after hatching; in many cases, they never even see their parent, and there have been observations indicating that, when by chance a parent does see its chick, it completely ignores it.

★ LONGEST CHICK-REARING PERIOD

Frigatebirds (family Fregatidae), king penguins (*Aptenodytes patagonicus*) and California condors (*Gymnogyps californianus*) have longer chick-rearing periods than any other birds. In frigatebirds, the young begin to fly when they are five to six months old, but keep returning to the nest to be fed until they are up to a year old. Endangered California condors feed and tend their young on their nesting cliffs for a year or more. King penguins lay their single eggs early in the sub-Antarctic summer, but their chicks fail to grow and moult in time to fledge before the onset of winter; they survive the bad weather by delaying the moment of independence from their parents, and spend the winter in creches on starvation rations, before fledging the following spring – some 360 days after hatching. A number of other species continue to receive food from their parents for up to a year after hatching, although they are not entirely dependent.

FEEDING BIRDS

★ LARGEST PREY

The largest recorded wild animal killed and carried away by a bird was a 7 kg (15 lb) young, male, red howler monkey killed by a harpy eagle (*Harpia harpyja*) in Manu National Park, Peru, in 1990. This eagle, which lives in the tropical forests of Central and South America, is widely considered to be the world's most powerful bird of prey, although it weighs only 9 kg (20 lb). The harpy is also known to kill and eat 5 kg (11 lb) two-toed sloths on a regular basis. An American bald eagle (*Haliaeetus leucocephalus*) has been reported flying with a 6.8 kg (15 lb) mule deer in its talons.

Lesser flamingo
Flamingoes are the only true filter-feeding birds, employing a system similar to the one used by baleen whales to strain krill or fish from seawater. Here a flock of lesser flamingoes is feeding in Lake Nakuru National Park, Kenya.

American bald eagle
Although capable of carrying prey as large as a 6.8 kg (15 lb) mule deer in its talons the American bald eagle feeds mainly on fish in the breeding season.

Stories of eagles carrying off human babies, children and even adults are generally unsubtantiated and treated with suspicion by most experts. However, there is one well documented case. In 1932, a three and a half year old Norwegian girl, Svanhild Hansen, who was apparently small for her age, was reported to have been taken by a white-tailed sea eagle (*Haliaeetus albicilla*) from near her parents' farmhouse. The eagle was said to have dropped her 1.6 km (1 mile) away, on a narrow ledge below its eyrie, and circled overhead while the girl was rescued, unharmed.

★ MOST SPECIALIZED DIET

Many birds have specialized diets. Some have such highly adapted bills and feet that they are unable to change diet if their normal food supplies are unavailable; these species are particularly vulnerable to fluctuations in their food supply and, not suprisingly, a number of them are threatened. One of the most extreme examples is the snail kite (*Rostrhamus sociabilis*), which eats almost exclusively on snails of the genus *Pomacea*, and the subspecies living in southern Florida (*R. s. plumbeus*) feeds almost exclusively on the large freshwater apple snail (*Pomacea paludosa*). Another good example is the lesser flamingo (*Phoeniconaias minor*), which breeds in Africa, migrates to Madagascar and parts of Africa, southern Asia and India, and is almost totally dependent on the filamentous blue-green algae *Spirulina*.

Pigeons (family Columbidae) and flamingoes (family Phoenicopteridae) of both sexes, as well as male emperor penguins (*Aptenodytes forsteri*), feed their chicks exclusively on a high-protein secretion from the cells lining the crop (or oesophagus in flamingoes); this is similar in composition to mammalian milk.

★ STRONGEST GIZZARD

The gizzard is the part of a bird's stomach that performs the function of mammalian teeth by grinding the food into small pieces; in most birds, it contains sand grains or small stones to aid the grinding process. The strongest gizzard recorded belongs to a turkey (*Meleagris gallopavo*), which was capable of completely crushing 24 walnuts (in the shell) in under four hours and could turn surgical lancet blades into grit in less than 16 hours.

★ BLOOD DRINKING

The sharp-beaked ground finch (*Geospiza difficilis*), which may be the only truly regularly parasitic bird, drinks blood from holes it pecks between feathers in the wings of nesting masked boobies (*Sula dactylatra*) and red-footed boobies (*Sula sula*). Surprisingly, the boobies do not seem to be particularly bothered by its activities. A few finches have even adopted the unpleasant habit of digging their long sharp curved bills into the flesh of sheep, just above the kidneys.

MOST FOOD

Hummingbirds (family Trochilidae) require up to one and a half times their own body weight in food (primarily nectar) every day. With the possible exception of shrews, these tiny frenetically active birds have the highest metabolic rate of any known animal.

Sharp-beaked ground finch
The sharp-beaked ground finch, found only in the Galapagos Islands, is feeding off a live masked booby, drawing out its blood.

★ LONGEST FAST

The longest known period of fasting for any waking bird is endured by the male emperor penguin (*Aptenodytes forsteri*), which spends several months without feeding on the frozen sea ice of the Antarctic. The female lays a single egg in late May or early June and then leaves the male to incubate it for 62–67 days until it has hatched. The longest continuous fast recorded for a male emperor penguin was an incredible 134 days.

Surviving on reserves of subcutaneous fat, which can be 3–4 cm (1¼–1½ in) thick, his weight may drop from 40 kg (88 lb) at the beginning of winter to just

> Having travelled overland from the sea to the breeding colony, courted the female, incubated the egg, waited for the female to return and then travelled back to the open sea, the male emperor penguin may have had to go without food for as long as 115–120 days.

20 kg (44 lb) towards the end. The North American common poorwill (*Phalaenoptilus nuttallii*) fasts for up to 5 months while it hibernates in a rock crevice or under a desert shrub, during the worst of the winter weather. It remains torpid for up to 100 days, reducing its body temperature from the normal 40°C (104°F) to just 10°C (50°F).

★ STRANGEST MEALS

When it died, an ostrich (*Struthio camelus*) that had been living in London Zoo, UK, was found to have swallowed an alarm clock, a roll of film, a handkerchief, 90 cm (3 ft) of rope, a cycle valve, a pencil, three gloves, a comb, part of a gold necklace, a collar stud, a Belgian franc, four halfpennies and two farthings.

BIRD SENSES

★ FIELD OF VISION

The field of vision in birds ranges from only a few degrees to a full 360° and is an excellent indication of whether they are predators or prey. Prey species tend to have eyes on the sides of their heads, giving them 360° vision; this enables them to scan as much of the world as possible to spot approaching danger. The Eurasian woodcock (*Scolopax rusticola*) is the best- known example because, in addition to having complete wrap-around vision horizontally, the position of its eyes, very high up on the head (so high

that they are above the brain case and not behind it as in most birds), mean that it can also see above itself – without having to move its head. All other seven species of woodcock worldwide e.g. the well-known American woodcock, and six lesser-known species, one in New Guinea, one on the Ryukyu Islands and four in Southeast Asia, have similar anatomy with eyes high on the head. The drawback of this arrangement is that the woodcock has only a very limited field of binocular vision (directly in front and behind), which limits its ability to judge size and distance, and to see finer details, and reduces the sensitivity of its eyes when the light is poor. Despite this it has a mainly crepuscular and nocturnal lifestyle, making 'roding' display flights at dusk

and dawn and feeding mainly at night. It is thought that it does this mainly through using touch sensors in its bill. The tawny owl (*Strix aluco*) is an excellent example of a predator, with around 60° of binocular vision in front and an extensive blind area of around 130° behind. The field of vision of most other birds falls within these two extremes.

★ KEENEST VISION

There are many unsubstantiated records of incredible visual acuity in birds; unfortunately, these are mainly based on anecdotal field observations. In reality, not much is known about how well they can see and, although some clearly have an outstanding ability to discriminate fine detail in distant objects, there is surprisingly little definitive data. Birds of prey are believed to have the keenest eyesight, with a slightly magnified area in the centre of their field of view. Large species, with eyes similar in size to our own,

Woodcock
The woodcock has the greatest field of vision. Not only does it have 360° horizontal vision, but the position of its eyes so high on its head also lets it see above itself without moving its head.

can probably resolve details at two and a half to three times the distance we can. To put this into perspective, under ideal conditions a golden eagle (*Aquila chrysaetos*) can detect the slight movements of a rabbit from more than 2 km (1¼ miles) away.

A peregrine falcon (*Falco peregrinus*) can spot a pigeon at a range of over 8 km (5 miles).

✶ SEEING IN THE DARK

Nocturnal birds, such as owls (families Tytonidae and Strigidae) and nightjars (family Caprimulgidae), have eyes with the best light-gathering power, or visual sensitivity. It would be untrue to say that they can literally 'see in the dark', since in total darkness they can see no better than we can; but total darkness rarely occurs in nature and they can see extremely well on nights so dark that we would be utterly helpless. Controlled experiments have shown that several species of owl are able to see lifeless objects at light intensities of as little as 1% of those we would require to see the same objects. Their eyes are not simply giant versions of our own, but actually have more light-sensitive cells on the retina and a variety of other special adaptations.

✶ BEST HEARING

It is very difficult to measure hearing acuity in birds although, in many species, it is certainly very impressive. It is likely that barn owls in the genus *Tyto* have the most exceptional hearing of all birds. They are able to catch live prey, in total darkness, guided by sound cues alone. It has been shown under laboratory conditions that a barn owl (*Tyto alba*) is able to pinpoint the slightest sounds to within one degree in both the vertical and horizontal planes. It does this by measuring the differences in intensity and time of arrival of sounds at its two ears, and can distinguish time delays of as little as 100 microseconds. Not only can the owl hear and locate noises accurately, it

Barn owl
The nocturnal barn owl has very acute hearing enabling it to pinpoint its prey, in this case a mouse, very precisely.

can also identify what is making them. The barn owl and other highly nocturnal owls, such as the long-eared owl (*Asio otus*) and Tengmalm's boreal owl (*Aegolius funereus*) with very acute hearing, have asymmetrical positioned ears. This increases the effect of sound waves, taking slightly longer to reach one ear and thus enabling the bird to pinpoint the sound precisely.

✶ HEARING RANGE

Collectively, birds have a narrower range of good hearing than mammals. However, their sensitivity to sounds of different frequencies is by no means uniform and varies considerably from species to species. Using sensitive equipment in a laboratory, scientists have found that pigeons (family Columbidae) can detect sounds as low as 0.1 Hz (i.e. one vibration every ten seconds). Since pigeons do not seem to have particularly exceptional ears, it seems likely that many other birds can pick up such low-frequency sounds as well (although there is a possibility that the birds cannot actually 'hear' the

BIRDS

sounds but, instead, detect them via touch receptors on other parts of the body). There are several possible advantages in hearing low-frequency sound (infrasound); for example, it may enable the birds to hear the deep sounds generated by storms and thus give them advance warning of bad weather. It possibly may also be of use in finding their way when on migration, e.g. by listening for the sound of a river far below or the waves of the sea over which it needs to pass to stay on course, or the infrasounds caused by small-scale seismic waves generated by oceanic waves against cliffs. All this may enable the birds to build up a navigational map. Interestingly, birds involved in four pigeon races in Europe and northeast USA in June 1997 may have been disorientated by passing through infrasonic shock waves from supersonic Concorde airliners. At the other end of the scale, some owls (families Tytonidae and Strigidae) have a high-frequency hearing limit of around 15–20 kHz, which is essential for detecting prey in almost total darkness. For comparison, the human range of hearing extends from about 20 Hz to almost 20 kHz.

✦ ECHOLOCATION

The only birds known to echolocate are certain cave swiftlets (genus *Collocalia*) living in Southeast Asia, and the oilbird (*Steatornis caripensis*), which lives in South America. Both the cave swiftlets and the oilbird nest and roost in the total

darkness of caves and use a fairly simple system of echolocation to navigate; even in total darkness, and when flying at considerable speed, they can sense the walls of their caves and any other major obstacles in their path in time to take evasive action. As with bats and many cetaceans, they emit pulses of sound and build up a 'sound picture' of their surroundings by analysing the returning echoes. However, unlike echolocating mammals, they are restricted to the use of low frequency sounds (which are within the human range of hearing and can be heard as deep clicks) and, consequently, are not as efficient at finding their way around in the dark. Oilbirds, for example, cannot reliably detect objects less than about 20 cm (8 in) in diameter – a level of performance actually matched by some blind humans, who can also be guided by sound. Cave swiftlets are more sensitive and can avoid objects as small as 6 mm ($^1/_2$ in), though even this does not match the sensitivity of mammals using high-frequency ultrasound.

✦ COLOUR VISION

As a group, birds probably have better colour vision than any other group of animals on Earth. They have a unique combination of light receptors in the retina, which are colour-sensitive, and oil droplets, which act as filters by narrowing the band of wavelengths absorbed and deciphered by each receptor. Together, they create a powerful system for

LARGEST EYES

The ostrich has the largest eyes of any living bird (indeed, of any living land animal). They are up to 5 cm (2 in) in diameter. All birds have relatively large eyes; compared to its body size, the eyes of a starling (*Sturnus vulgaris*), for example, are at least eight times larger than human eyes.

discerning subtle hues. The specific arrangement of these receptors and filters varies from species to species, according to their particular needs, but it is likely that most, if not all, birds have colour vision of one kind or another.

✦ ULTRAVIOLET VISION

There is direct evidence that mallards (*Anas platyrhynchos*), black-chinned hummingbirds (*Archilochus alexandri*), belted kingfishers (*Megaceryle alcyon*) and other species can see into the near-ultraviolet or even ultraviolet part of the light spectrum. This is now known for a total of over 35 species. Given the taxonomic diversity of the species tested to date, the majority of birds probably possess this ability, enabling them to appreciate colours that are not visible to mammals. Ultraviolet vision has several possible advantages. For example, it may help hummingbirds to detect flowers, which often strongly reflect ultraviolet light, and, since ultraviolet light penetrates

thin cloud cover, migrating birds may use it to determine the position of the Sun on cloudy days. It's also shown to be important to birds in influencing their decisions relating to choice of a mate, such as zebra finch (*Taeniopygia guttata*) and European starling (*Sturnus vulgaris*).

★ BEST SENSE OF SMELL

Most birds have a poor sense of smell, although its importance varies markedly between species. Indeed, a small number rely on smell to find food and have large areas of their brain devoted to this sense. The New Zealand kiwis (family Apterygidae), uniquely, are noted for their ability to smell out worms, slugs and other prey animals amongst leaf litter and in the soil; no-one knows how

they prevent the soil from blocking their nostrils, but towards the base of the bill is a valve that allows the kiwi to expel any soil or other matter and water from the nostrils by blowing air through them, producing loud snuffling sounds in the process. The olfactory lobes of kiwis are the biggest in any bird, around ten times the size of those in most other birds. A relatively well-developed sense of smell occurs in some other birds (probably due to the large olfactory centres of their brains), including some of the New World vultures (family Cathartidae) – those in the genus *Cathartes*, i.e. the turkey vulture

The black-footed albatross, which lives in the North Pacific, can be attracted by the smell of bacon fat being poured on to the ocean surface from a distance of at least 30 km (19 miles).

(*Cathartes aura*), the lesser yellow-headed vulture (*C. burrovianus*), and greater yellow-headed vulture (*C. melambrotus*), honey-guides (family Indicatoridae), petrels, shearwaters (family Procellariidae), grebes (family Podicipedidae) and nightjars (family Caprimulgidae).

BIRD ATHLETES

★ FASTEST SWIMMER

The gentoo penguin (*Pygoscelis papua*) is probably the fastest underwater swimming bird in the world and has been recorded at a maximum speed of about 36 km/h (22 mph) during short bursts of 'flying' underwater.

Earlier claims of speeds reaching 60 km/h (37 mph) are now considered to be inaccurate by most authorities.

★ DEEPEST DIVE

The deepest dive accurately measured for any bird was recorded during a study of

emperor penguins (*Aptenodytes forsteri*) in the Ross Sea, Antarctica, from October–December 1990. A team of French and American scientists from the Centre National de la Recherche Scientifique, in Strasbourg, and the Scripps Institution of Oceanography, in San Diego, obtained a complete record of diving depths reached by one particular penguin over a period of 14 days. They found that, although most dives were to mid-water depths, some were at or near the bottom. On day six, the penguin made a series of four dives ranging from

444 to 483 m (1456–1584 ft) over a bottom depth of about 450–500 m (1500–1650 ft). However, the maximum depth of an emperor penguin dive is said to be at least 540 m (1750 ft).

Gentoo penguin
The fastest-swimming bird in the world is probably the gentoo penguin, which literally 'flies' underwater at speeds of up to 36 km/h (22 mph). Here, they are porpoising whilst travelling at high-speed near the Falkland Islands.

BIRDS

★ LONGEST DIVE
The longest dive accurately measured or any bird was recorded in 1969 for a small group of ten emperor penguins (*Aptenodytes forsteri*) at Cape Crozier, Antarctica, by a team of scientists. They recorded a maximum dive time of 18 minutes.

★ WALKING ON WATER
The storm petrels (family Hydrobatidae) are the only birds capable of 'walking on water'. They feed on small animals which they pluck from the sea while pattering on the surface. In fact, they are wind-hovering (flying, slowly into the wind) while trailing their webbed feet in the water like sea anchors. Jacanas (family Jacanidae) are able to walk on floating lily pads (*see* LONGEST TOES p. 119).

★ LONGEST STRIDE
When running, the stride of an ostrich (*Struthio camelus*) is 3–5 m (10–16 ft). It has been claimed that in an all-out sprint its stride may exceed 7 m (23 ft).

★ WORST WALKER
Several bird families are essentially incapable of walking, for example hummingbirds (family Trochilidae), swifts (family Apodidae), tropicbirds (family

ENERGY EXPENDITURE
In relation to their size, hummingbirds expend more energy than any other bird and indeed more fuel than a jet fighter aircraft. If human beings were to expend energy at the same rate, their body temperature would rise to nearly 400°C (750°F).

Phaethontidae) and loons or divers (family Gaviidae). When ashore, a loon rests its weight entirely on its breast and 'leap-frogs' over short distances by kicking its legs out backwards.

★ FASTEST RUNNER
In 1964, a male ostrich (*Struthio camelus*) was timed at 72 km /h (45 mph) over a distance of 732 m (2400 ft); this would be fast enough to win most horse races. Another ostrich has been clocked over a short distance on the Mara plains, Kenya, at a speed of 60 km/h (37 mph). In short bursts, ostriches can probably run even faster than these two records and there are even claims of them reaching speeds

of up to 96 km/h (60 mph), though these do seem excessively high and have yet to be proven. At slightly slower speeds of 50 km/h (30 mph) most ostriches can keep running for about 30 minutes without apparently tiring.

Flying birds are generally slow runners compared to similar-sized mammals, presumably because they have stronger wing muscles and weaker leg muscles. The fastest running flying bird is the roadrunner (*Geococcyx californianus*),

> At speeds of 50 km/h (30 mph) most ostriches can keep running for about 30 minutes without apparently tiring.

a member of the cuckoo family living in the dry, scrubby deserts of southwestern USA. It has been clocked at speeds of at least 42 km/h (26 mph) and can even turn at right angles without slowing down. It straightens out its neck, opens its wings slightly to act as stabilizers and uses its long tail as a rudder in order to dash around the desert catching insects, lizards and rattlesnakes.

BIRD BEHAVIOUR

★ TOOL USING
More than 30 species of birds are known to use tools. Some of the better-known examples include the Egyptian vulture (*Neophron percnopterus*), which throws stones at the thick-shelled eggs of ostriches (*Struthio camelus*) in order to break them and eat the nutritious contents; the woodpecker finch (*Camarhynchus pallidus*), which uses cactus spines held in its bill to remove grubs from holes in trees; the song thrush (*Turdus philomelos*), which cracks the shells of snails using rocks as anvils; and

Song thrush
The song thrush (*Turdus philomelos*) cracks the shells of snails using rocks as anvils to get to the snail inside.

the green heron (*Butorides virescens*) and striated heron (*Butorides striata*) which have been seen angling for fish by throwing small pieces of twig, biscuit or anything else to hand into the water as bait (some individuals have even been seen to fashion twigs into the right shape and size).

Perhaps most remarkable of all, the New Caledonian crow (*Corvus moneduloides*) actually makes a relatively complex tool for extracting grubs from crevices by shaping the leaf of a pandanus (screwpine) palm using its bill while holding it down by the stalk with one foot, and can bend wire provided by experimenters into hooked tools.

★ MOST AGGRESSIVE

Many wild birds are aggressive during the breeding season, when they are defending territories or competing for nest sites and mates. Perhaps surprisingly, one of the most aggressive birds in the world is the European robin (*Erithacus rubecula*). Fights between males can be extremely vicious and not infrequently result in death (up to 10% of adult robins die as a result of territorial disputes).

★ MOST DANGEROUS

Birds are not particularly dangerous to people and most 'attacks' are the result of molestation or provocation. Terns (family Laridae), skuas (family Stercorariidae),

Egyptian vulture
This Egyptian vulture is using a stone to crack open the tough shell of an ostrich egg so that it can get to its rich contents.

owls (families Tytonidae and Strigidae) and many others will vigorously defend their nests, while a great many birds will peck or kick if they are handled. Some owls, notably tawny owl (*Strix aluco*) and great grey owl (*Strix nebulosa*), may attack particularly fiercely.

The only birds known to have attacked in the wild and caused people to die are ostriches (*Struthio camelus*), mute swans (*Cygnus olor*) and, perhaps the most dangerous of all, the three species of cassowary (family Casuariidae). Cassowaries, which live in New Guinea and northeastern Queensland, Australia, are large birds (up to 2 m (80 in) tall) and have dagger-like claws up to 12 cm (4³/₄ in) long. A cornered or wounded bird can be extremely dangerous and will leap into the air and kick, damaging vital organs or causing massive bleeding.

★ GROUP WORK

Pied babblers, a species that lives in small groups from the Kalahari Desert of southern Africa, work communally. While the group forages for food such as small snakes and scorpions one of them stands guard in a tree watching for predators. It sings a special song and makes alarm calls if a predator is spotted.

★ MOST BOSSY

The kea (Nestor notabilis), a rowdy member of the parrot family living in New Zealand, is the only bird known to have a society in which higher-status individuals can force others to work for them. A study on a captive breeding colony of keas at the Konrad Lorenz Institute, Austria, provided the birds with a wooden see-saw with a perch at one end that lifted the lid of a feeding box at the other. It was designed so that the percher could not reach to feed itself and, as

soon as it left the perch, the lid closed. It was found that the dominant birds always fed at the box while their subordinates did the perching. If the subordinates dared to neglect their duties, their superiors would chase them back. There was no evidence of the birds taking it in turns to feed and work the see-saw.

★ MOST AVID COLLECTOR

Male bowerbirds (family Ptilonorhynchidae) go to great lengths to impress the females. In their forest homes in Australia and New Guinea, they spend many months building and maintaining ornate 'bowers' on the ground. These vary in design, depending on the species, from simple clearings and avenues of grass to substantial roofed huts; sometimes the bowers are painted with berry juice. They are all liberally decorated with bright objects such as berries, flowers, mushrooms, stones, shells, bones, kangaroo droppings and even tin foil, pieces of plastic or glass. There is great rivalry between the males and they often steal sought-after objects from each other's

collections. Generally speaking, the duller the male, the more elaborate his bower – apparently to make up for his own shortcomings and there appears to be a correlation between the colour of his

> The male Vogelkop's bower, which is like a thatched hut with a front garden adorned with trophies, was first thought by European explorers to New Guinea to be the work of local tribesmen.

plumage and that of the treasures he collects. When a female begins to show interest, the male cackles and dances around, carefully displaying his decorations as if showing her valuable jewels. If all goes well, they mate inside or near the bower, and the female then goes away to build a nest.

The most elaborate bower is that built by the male Vogelkop bowerbird (Amblyornis inornata), one of the so-called gardener bowerbirds, and one of the plainest, dull brown species.

TALKING BIRDS

★ MOST TALKATIVE

A number of birds are renowned for their talking abilities (i.e. the reproduction of human words), but the grey parrot (Psittacus erithacus) of West Africa excels in this ability. A psychologist, Dr Irene Pepperberg from the USA, has worked with and studied a number of grey parrots and has shown that, as well as straight mimicry, they can use words in novel ways and are capable of categorization and concept formulation. One female, named Prudle, formerly owned by Lyn Logue (who died January 1988) and then in the care of Iris Frost of East Sussex, UK, won the 'Best-Talking Parrot-like Bird' title at the National Cage and Aviary Bird Show in

Budgerigar
Budgies are the most talkative birds, learning to imitate more human words than any other species of bird.

London each December for 12 consecutive years (1965–76). Prudle, who had a vocabulary of nearly 800 words, was taken from a nest at Jinja, Uganda, in 1958. She retired undefeated and was still talking two days before her death, on 13 July 1994. However, the record holder is a budgerigar (Melopsittacus undulatus) called Puck owned by Camille Jordan of Petaluma, California, USA, which had a vocabulary of 1728 words on 31 January 1993. He died in 1994.

Learning to imitate human words is basically a variation of the vocal mimicry that is found among many birds in the wild. Interestingly, some species, such as the marsh warbler (Acrocephalus palustris), are able to mimic a bewildering variety of other birds but have never been known to mimic people. Yet, in contrast, species such as the hill mynah (Gracula religiosa) of India and other parts of south Asia are able to imitate the spoken words of their owners but, in the wild, never mimic the sounds of other birds.

★ BEST MIMIC

Many wild birds are able to mimic the sounds made by other animals, or even human machinery, but few are able to

mimic a broad range of sounds. In this respect, the marsh warbler (*Acrocephalus palustris*) is generally considered to be the world record-holder. Each individual has a song which contains elements of up to 100 different species. A typical male imitates 70–80 species: about half from its European breeding range and the other half from its African wintering range. These appear to be copied indiscriminately from birds in the local community, since marsh warblers living near the coast, for example, have more marine species in their repertoires than those living further inland. Almost the entire marsh warbler repertoire is made up of mimicry, including elements 'borrowed' from a total of more than 200 different species.

Grey parrot
The grey parrot excels in its talking abilities and, as well as mimicry, it has learnt how to associate human words with meaning.

★ LOUDEST SONG

Low-frequency sounds, such as the calls of grouse (family Phasianidae), cuckoos (family Cuculidae) and large owls (family Strigidae) are the most effective for long-distance communication. On the ground, the most far-carrying song of any bird is the deep boom of the male kakapo (*Strigops habroptilus*), an extremely

The male kakapo inflates two enormous air sacs, which swell his breast and throat until he is the size and almost the shape of a football, to make a deep booming sound that reverberates through the night air.

rare nocturnal parrot now restricted to a few small islands off the coast of New Zealand.

By trampling with his strong feet, the male excavates bowl-like depressions, called 'booming bowls', in 'courts' that he occupies on sloping ground around his territory. These bowls amplify the booms, like parabolic reflectors. Groups of males compete for females at a communal lek. He may boom all night, producing a series of 25–40 booms repeated at half-minute intervals or so, every night, for as long as 3 months, in his untiring efforts to attract a female. The song of a booming kakapo can be heard by people up to 1 km (¹/₂ mile) away, and has been heard from a record distance of 7 km (4¹/₂ miles).

The deep boom of the Eurasian bittern (*Botaurus stellaris*), which lives in parts of Europe, Asia and Africa, is also far-carrying and has been heard from as far as 8 km (5 miles) away. Its deep, very distinctive sound is more reminiscent of a distant foghorn, or even a mooing cow, than a bird. It can be imitated reasonably accurately by blowing over the top of an open bottle.

The loudest bird sounds are generally considered to be the advertising calls of the four species of bellbirds, genus *Procnias*, of the exclusively New World cotinga family (Cotingidae). Found in southern Central America and the northern half of South America, they produce extraordinarily loud sounds that peak at up to 100 decibels. The white bellbird (*Procnias alba*) of northeast South America makes a sound of a bell being struck, while others sound more like the metallic 'bonk' sound of a hammer on an anvil.

For its size, the 9–10 cm (3¹/₂–4 in) wren of Eurasia (*Troglodytes troglodytes*) (called winter wren in North America) has one of the loudest songs of any bird. Certain elements of the song, which consists of a loud warble ending in a harsh, rattling trill, can be heard from a distance of up to 1 km (¹/₂ mile) away.

BIRD ODDITIES

★ MOST RECORDED PECKS IN A DAY

The black woodpecker (*Dryocopus martius*) from Europe has been recorded pecking trees at an incredible rate of 12,000 pecks a day.

★ HIGHEST G-FORCE

American experiments have shown that the beak of the red-headed woodpecker (*Melanerpes erythrocephalus*) hits the bark of a tree with an impact velocity of

Black woodpecker
This black woodpecker is pecking out a nest hole in a tree, in Germany. The species has the record for the most recorded pecks in a day, altogether an astonishing 12,000.

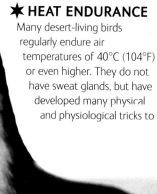

more than 21 km/h (13 mph), subjecting its brain to a deceleration of about 10*g* when its head snaps back. Little research work has been done in this field and other woodpeckers may experience an even higher g-force.

★ HIBERNATION

The only known hibernating bird is the desert-dwelling common poorwill (*Phalaenoptilus nuttallii*) of North America. Its hibernating habits were first discovered by scientists in the Chuckwalla Mountains of the Colorado Desert, California, USA, in December 1946, although the Hopi Indians have always known it as *Holchko*, 'the sleeping one'. With the onset of winter, it chooses a narrow cleft in a south-facing rock, or a comfortable spot under a desert shrub, and stays there for up to five months during the worst of the weather. Its heart and respiration rates drop to almost unmeasurable levels, and its temperature falls from about 41°C (106°F) to as low as 6°C (43°F). After waking, it requires about 7 hours to warm up fully.

Many other birds can enter into a dormant state overnight, or even for a few days at a time, if the weather is particularly severe or if food is in short supply. By allowing their body temperatures to fall, they slow their metabolic rates and consequently make considerable energy savings. A rock ptarmigan (*Lagopus mutus*), for example, can cope with a blizzard by

HEAD TURNING

Some owls (order Strigiformes) can rotate their heads by as much as 280° and then rapidly swivel them round in the opposite direction in order to maintain visual contact. Accounts of them being able to swivel their heads a full 360° have been exaggerated.

settling into a comfortable spot in the snow and allowing its body temperature to drop to within a degree or two above the point of death.

★ POISONOUS BIRD

The only poisonous birds known are three species of pitohui (pronounced 'pitohooey') from New Guinea: the hooded pitohui (*Pitohui dichrous*), the rusty pitohui (*P. ferrugineus*) and the variable pitohui (*P. kirhocephalus*). The hooded pitohui is the deadliest of the three. In 1992 an ecology student from Chicago, USA, who was studying other birds in the pitohui's forest home, was scratched on his hand by a 'particularly feisty' individual as he released it from a mist net. After sucking the wounds, he experienced a 'numb and tingly' sensation in his mouth. It was a year before he caught another specimen and was able to investigate further, initially by licking one of its feathers and then by chemical analysis. He discovered that the skin and feathers of the songbird contain a homobatrachotoxin, almost identical to the chemical toxin secreted by the celebrated poison-arrow frogs in the Amazon. An extract from just 10 mg ($^3/_{10,000}$ oz) of the bird's skin, injected into a mouse, killed the animal in 20 minutes; and tests imply that a single gram ($^1/_{32}$ oz) of the poison would be enough to dispatch roughly 20 million mice. The poison is believed to be a defence mechanism against hawks and snakes, and the birds' striking black and orange-red plumage is probably a warning. It is likely that the birds don't produce the neurotoxin themselves but acquire it by eating beetles of the genus *Choresine*.

★ HEAT ENDURANCE

Many desert-living birds regularly endure air temperatures of 40°C (104°F) or even higher. They do not have sweat glands, but have developed many physical and physiological tricks to

African skimmer
The African skimmer, pictured at its nest with its chick in the Chobe National Park, Botswana, can withstand higher air temperatures than any other bird.

keep their body temperatures below the fatal level (around 46–18°C (115–64°F) in most species). One extreme example is the African skimmer (*Rynchops flavirostris*) nesting on the shores of Lake Rudolph, Kenya, where the ground surface temperature may exceed 60°C (140°F) and the air temperature just above the ground may reach 40°C (104°F).

★ COLD ENDURANCE

The male emperor penguin (*Aptenodytes forsteri*) is one of the hardiest creatures on Earth. It spends the height of the Antarctic winter, when temperatures of -60°C (-76°F) and icy winds gusting up to 200 km/h (124 mph) are not unusual, coping with some of the worst weather the planet can offer. While most other animals are moving northwards, as the surface of the Southern Ocean starts to freeze with the onset of winter, the emperors head south to breed. When the weather gets really bad they huddle together in groups of up to 5000 for warmth, taking it in turns to go inside the huddle (where the temperature can be as much as 60°C (108°F) higher than on the periphery) and then on the leeward side and, finally, on the windward side. In this way, they can reduce their heat loss by as much as 50% compared with standing alone.

Male emperor penguins incubate their single eggs continuously for 62–67 days, much of the time in total darkness, holding them between their feet and a loose fold of skin on their bellies.

The effectiveness of the insulation provided by an incubating emperor penguin was demonstrated in an Antarctic study in which egg temperatures were taken. It was found that if the eggs were exposed to outside temperatures for more than a few seconds, they chilled. But during incubation the heat transfer from the male's brood patch to the egg was so efficient that, when the external temperature was -26°C (-15°F), the internal egg temperature was 31°C (88°F), some 57°C (103°F) higher than the surrounding environment.

★ LONGEVITY

The life expectancy of most small birds in the wild is only 2–5 years and few larger species live for longer than 20–30 years. However, it is very difficult to determine the maximum age of wild birds and, consequently, there are few extreme records. The highest ever reported is an unconfirmed age of about 82 years for a male Siberian white crane (*Grus leucogeranus*) named Wolf at the International Crane Foundation, Baraboo, Wisconsin, USA. Said to have been hatched at a zoo in Switzerland in about 1905, Wolf died in late 1988 after breaking his bill while repelling a visitor who approached too close to his pen.

The greatest irrefutable age reported is over 80 years for a male sulphur-crested cockatoo (*Cacatua galerita*) named Cocky, who died in London Zoo on 28 October 1982. He was presented to the zoo in 1925, and had been with his previous owner since 1902 when he was already fully mature.

The oldest brooding bird and, indeed, the oldest ringed sea bird on record is a female royal albatross (*Diomedea epomophora*) named Blue-White. She was first banded as an adult when she arrived to breed on Taiaroa Head, New Zealand, in 1937. Since most royal albatrosses do not start breeding until they are at least nine years old, she was probably born in 1928 or even earlier. Since then, she came back every other year to breed on the same headland and raised ten chicks of her own and fostered three others with her mate Green White Green. She even laid an egg at the age of 60, in November 1988, when her name was changed to

Grandma. She failed to return to her colony at the end of 1990 and has not been seen since.

★ SMELLIEST

The smelliest bird in the world is probably the South American hoatzin (*Opisthocomus hoazin*), which smells like cow manure. The cause of the smell is believed to be a combination of the hoatzin's diet, which consists almost exclusively of green leaves, and its highly specialized digestive system (which, unique among birds, involves a kind of foregut fermentation that is strikingly similar to the one found in cows, sheep, deer and a number of other ruminant mammals).

There is also the absolutely evil smell of the stomach oil expelled with amazing force by both adults and chicks of the fulmar (*Fulmarus glacialis*). This not only smells incredibly strongly but the stench is impossible to remove from a pullover or other garment despite repeated washing, and even after many years can still be detected, so that most fulmar ringers or others unfortunate enough to have been targeted throw the offending item of clothing away.

The hoopoe (*Upupa epops*) is said to have the foulest-smelling nest. The penetrating stench, which is produced by the large preen gland, is like that of rotting meat and is believed to function as a predator deterrent. In young birds, this gland is active at four days and reaches its maximum size at 12 days, before being gradually reabsorbed as fledging approaches. In addition, however, nestlings are capable, from the sixth day, of squirting copious amounts of liquid faeces and cloacal contents at an intruder in the nest, usually aiming steeply upwards, and with the jet of foul liquid covering a distance of 25–60 cm (10–24 in). Both the cloacal ejection and olfactory defence can occur simultaneously. Moreover, the young birds, holding the crest raised, leaning forward on the breast, and with tail cocked and expanded, emit snake-like hisses, and make sudden sharp jabs with the bill. Such is the stench that arises from the nest that the phrase 'stink like a Hoopoe' is a term of abuse in some rural areas of central Europe.

★ MOST DAYLIGHT

The Arctic tern (*Sterna paradisaea*) spends the northern summer in the Arctic and the southern summer in the Antarctic and, consequently, experiences more daylight per year than any other animal.

South American hoatzin
Hoatzins, pictured here basking in the sun in the Amazonas, Brazil, are the smelliest birds, smelling of cow manure. This is probably due to the food they eat and the fact that they ferment it in their gut.

REPTILES

Aldabra giant tortoise
An enormous Aldabra tortoise pictured here on a beach in its native Seychelles.

CROCODILES & ALLIGATORS

Crocodilia

23 species: 13 crocodiles, 6 caiman, 2 alligators,1 false gharial, 1 gharial

★ EARLIEST

The first crocodilians appeared some 240 million years ago and thrived during the Jurassic period. Apart from birds, the 23 species alive today are more closely related to the dinosaurs than any other creature on Earth.

★ LARGEST

The black caiman (*Melanosuchus niger*), American alligator (*Alligator mississippiensis*), American crocodile (*Crocodylus acutus*), Nile crocodile (*Crocodylus niloticus*), Orinoco crocodile (*Crocodylus intermedius*), saltwater crocodile (*Crocodylus porosus*) and gharial (*Gavialis gangeticus*) have all been known to attain lengths of 5.5 m (18 ft) or more. However, in most cases, such extreme sizes are exceptional.

The largest living crocodilian (and, indeed, the largest reptile in the world) is the saltwater or estuarine crocodile which ranges throughout the tropical regions of Asia and the Pacific. Males are mature when they reach a length of about 3.2 m (10 ft 6 in) and females when they reach about 2.2 m (7 ft 3 in) and they continue to grow for many years afterwards. Extreme lengths of 9–10 m (29½–33 ft) are generally considered to be within the realms of possibility. However, the pressure of hunting has been so great that few have been able to grow to their maximum potential, at least during the 20th century.

The largest specimen in modern times may have been a saltwater crocodile which, in the early part of the 20th century, was considered sacred by the Seluke people of the Segama River, northern Borneo. On one occasion, local rubber plantation owner James Montgomery saw the huge animal on a sandbank in the river and, when it moved off, measured the impression left behind in the sand. This suggested that the crocodile was 10.05 m (33 ft) long.

A leading authority on saltwater

crocodiles, Ron Pawlowski, reportedly measured 10,287 'salties' in his life and all but one measured less than 5.5 m (18 ft). The single exception was an individual shot by his wife, Kris, in Norman River, northern Australia, in July 1957, which reportedly measured 8.64 m (28 ft 4 in). Unfortunately, although a photographic record existed until 1968, it has since been lost; and no skeletal evidence is available to verify the claim, since even the head was apparently too heavy to move. This record is considered by many to have a high probability of accuracy.

The longest authenticated record of recent years is a male saltwater crocodile just over 7 m (23 ft) long, which lives in the Bhitarkanika Wildlife Sanctuary, Orissa State, India. There are three other individuals in the same sanctuary measuring more than 6 m (19 ft 8 in).

Lengths in excess of 6.1 m (20 ft) have also been reliably reported for the gharial or gavial (*Gavialis gangeticus*) which lives in the river systems of India and Pakistan. The largest on record was one killed by Matthew George in the Kosi River, north Bihar, India, in January 1924, which measured 7.1 m (23 ft 4 in).

★ LARGEST PREHISTORIC

The largest ever land predator may have been a caiman found on the banks of the Amazon in rocks dated as eight million years old. Estimates from a skull 1.5 m (5 ft) long (complete with 10 cm (4 in) long teeth) indicate a length of 12 m (40 ft) and a weight of about 18 tonnes, making it larger than the fearsome dinosaur *Tyrannosaurus rex*. It was subsequently identified as a giant example of *Purussaurus brasiliensis*, a species named in 1892.

The longest alligator on Earth was probably the eusuchian *Deinosuchus rio-grandensis* ('terrible crocodile') from the lakes and swamps of what is now Texas, USA, about 75 million years ago. Fragmentary remains discovered in Big Bend National Park, Texas, indicate a skull of over 2 m (6 ft 6 in) and a hypothetical length of 10–12 m (33–40 ft).

> The 'terrible crocodile', *Deinosuchus riograndensis*, was one of the longest predators on Earth at 10–12 m (33–40 ft).

★ BEST NAVIGATION

Crocodiles are capable of navigating their way back home over long distances and through unknown terrain. Three wild crocodiles were taken hundreds of kilometres from their homes in northern Queensland, Australia, before being released. Each crocodile was fitted with a satellite tracking device and each made it back to their home rivers, swimming between 9.7 and 30.6 km (6 and 19 miles) a day. One swam round the northern tip of Australia covering more than 402 km (250 miles) in 20 days.

★ MOST MARINE

Several crocodilians live in coastal habitats and a few have been found far out to sea. The saltwater crocodile (*Crocodylus porosus*) is notable for being able to inhabit saltwater indefinitely and for travelling great distances across the ocean. The record was a 3.8 m (12 ft 6 in) male which was found alive on Ponape, part of the eastern Caroline Islands, in the Pacific Ocean, at least 1360 km (845 miles) away from the nearest known population. Another managed to swim 1100 km (680 miles) from the Andaman Islands, in the Bay of Bengal, to the Krishna Sanctuary in Andhra Pradesh, India. As a protection against becoming overloaded with salt, the saltwater crocodile has special glands at the back of its tongue which secrete a concentrated sodium chloride solution.

★ MOST WIDELY DISTRIBUTED

The saltwater crocodile (*Crocodylus porosus*) is the most widely distributed of all the crocodilians, occurring throughout the tropical regions of Asia and the Pacific, from the west coast of India, through Sri Lanka, Bangladesh, the Malay Peninsula, Indonesia and the Philippines, New Guinea and Australia, to the Solomon Islands and Fiji. It occurs in freshwater localities up to 1130 km (700 miles) inland and has even been found more than 1000 km (620 miles) out to sea.

★ MOST RESTRICTED DISTRIBUTION

The Cuban crocodile (*Crocodylus rhombifer*) has the smallest known natural distribution of any crocodilian. It is currently restricted to the Zapata Swamp in northwestern Cuba. Until recently, a small remnant population still survived in the Lanier Swamp on the nearby Isla de la Juventud, but this has apparently become extinct.

★ MOST DANGEROUS

At least seven of the 23 species of crocodilian have been known to prey on people: black caiman (*Melanosuchus niger*), American alligator (*Alligator mississippiensis*), Nile crocodile (*Crocodylus niloticus*), saltwater crocodile (*Crocodylus porosus*), American crocodile (*Crocodylus acutus*), Orinoco crocodile (*Crocodylus intermedius*) and the mugger (*Crocodylus palustris*). Human remains and jewellery have been found inside the stomachs of gharial (*Gavialis gangeticus*) on a number of occasions, but it is likely the animals feed on human corpses drifting down the Ganges from the burning ghats and that they do not kill people at all. Several other species are large enough to inflict serious or even fatal injuries if they feel threatened; the relatively small Cuban crocodile (*Crocodylus rhombifer*), for example, has a reputation for being

Saltwater crocodile
The most widely distributed — and the most dangerous — crocodilian, the saltwater crocodile (*Crocodylus porosus*) kills up to 2000 people every year. Numbers have been severely depleted throughout much of its range in recent years.

aggressive towards people and therefore children may be vulnerable. However, only the Nile and saltwater crocodiles are justly accused of being regular man-eaters and, on occasion, will even attack small boats; some individuals have been accused of killing up to 400 people, though such reports are probably exaggerated.

The saltwater crocodile probably kills hundreds of people every year, the vast majority of which go unrecorded. There were 62 authenticated and unprovoked) attacks on humans in Australia alone between 1971 and 2004. The largest death toll is reputed to have occurred during the night of 19–20 February 1945, when Allied troops invaded Ramree Island, off the west coast of Burma (Myanmar), in the Bay of Bengal, and trapped 800–1000 Japanese infantry men in a coastal mangrove swamp. During the night, some of the infantrymen fell to gunfire, some drowned and some fell to other causes. But by far the majority are believed to have been taken by crocodiles, which moved in *en masse* as soon as darkness fell. In recent years, the authenticity of this often-quoted account has been questioned, but observers at the time reported that, by morning, only 20 of the men were left alive. In a more widely accepted account, in December 1975, over 40 people were attacked and eaten by

saltwater crocodiles when their holiday boat sank in the Malili River of central Sulawesi (Celebes), Indonesia.

The Nile crocodile (*Crocodylus niloticus*) also has a bad reputation and may also kill hundreds of people every

> Crocodilians can shut their jaws with devastating force, but the muscles for opening them are extremely weak and, for ones up to 2 m (6 ft 7 in) in length, they can usually be kept closed with a rubber band.

year. When this species was more numerous, some estimates put the total number of human deaths as high as 20,000 every year.

★ LARGEST PREY

There are many reliable reports of large crocodilians, in particular saltwater crocodiles (*Crocodylus porosus*) and Nile crocodiles (*Crocodylus niloticus*), tackling enormous prey. A saltwater crocodile has

been reported seizing a stallion and dragging it into the river. Other 'salties' have been known to take feral buffalo and domestic cattle. There are also records of Nile crocodiles successfully tackling fully grown black rhinoceroses, wildebeest, giraffes, lions and other big game. In the 1860s, in Natal, South Africa, a Nile crocodile was observed to seize the hind leg of a fully grown African elephant at a water hole; but the elephant dragged its attacker out of the water where another member of the herd killed it under its feet.

The stomach of a notorious Nile crocodile, which was killed in the Okavango Delta, Botswana, in November 1968, was found to contain the remains of a local woman, two goats and about half a donkey.

★ LONGEST LIVING

Estimates for the maximum lifespan of crocodilians in the wild vary widely from around 50 years to as much as 200 years, although very little is known. In captivity, the greatest claimed age is for a male of unknown species, which was captured in the 1890s as a 5–10-year old juvenile and died in a Russian Zoo in 1997 aged 110–115 years. However, the validity of this record is uncertain. The greatest

Mugger crocodile
Like many crocodilians, the mugger is a formidable predator and has been known to prey on people. It is adapted to terrestrial life more than most of its relatives and can chase prey on land.

authenticated age is 66 years for a female American alligator that arrived at Adelaide Zoo, South Australia, on 5 June 1914, as a two-year-old, and died there on 26 September 1978.

★ LONGEST INCUBATION PERIOD

The incubation period for eggs laid by the dwarf crocodile (*Osteolaemus tetraspis*) can be as long as 115 days, which is longer than for any other crocodilian.

★ LEAST EGGS

Several crocodilian species lay exceptionally small clutches: Schneider's dwarf caiman (*Paleosuchus trigonatus*) rarely lays more than 15 eggs; Johnstone's crocodile (*Crocodylus johnsoni*) lays from just four to 18 eggs; the dwarf crocodile (*Osteolaemus tetraspis*) lays from about ten to 17 eggs; and the Philippine crocodile (*Crocodylus mindorensis*) lays from just seven to 14 eggs.

★ MOST EGGS

The record number of eggs laid in a single clutch by any crocodilian is 97 by a gharial (*Gavialis gangeticus*) in 1982; 69 of the eggs subsequently hatched in a hatcher-incubator. However, the average number of eggs in a gharial clutch is only 40, which is relatively low. The average clutch

size of the black caiman (*Melanosuchus niger*) is larger than for any other crocodilian, being 50–60. Nest-sharing occurs in some species, in which two different females may lay their eggs in the same nest, accounting for unusually large numbers in certain cases.

The Nile crocodile (*Crocodylus niloticus*) and the saltwater crocodile (*Crocodylus porosus*) have both been known to lay as many as 90 eggs in a single clutch.

★ LARGEST EGGS

The female false gharial (*Tomistoma schlegelii*) lays the largest eggs of any crocodilian, typically measuring 10 by 7 cm (4 by 2³/₄ in).

Crocodile and alligator eggs frequently 'talk' to one another, as the young animals communicate by tapping from inside their shells; this may help to synchronize hatching of the clutch.

★ MATERNAL CARE

The female American alligator (*Alligator mississippiensis*) looks after her young for as long as three years or, exceptionally, four years, which is longer than for any other crocodilian. In

Gharial crocodile
The female gharial lays on average 40 eggs. She does not assist her hatchlings into the water (perhaps because her teeth are too sharp) but does protect them from predators.

contrast, young Nile crocodiles (*Crocodylus niloticus*) are left to make their own way in the world after only a few weeks. No maternal care at all has been observed in some species, although this is most likely to be because they have not been studied closely enough in the wild.

★ SKIN TRADE

The peak in the crocodilian skin trade came in the late 1950s and early 1960s when 5–10 million hides entered the world market every year. The figure has dropped to some 500,000 skins, but it is still a serious threat to some populations (other skins come from farms). The main species involved are American alligator (*Alligator mississippiensis*) and Nile crocodile (*Crocodylus niloticus*).

★ MOST VARIABLE

The Nile crocodile (*Crocodylus niloticus*) is the most geographically variable species of crocodilian, with as many as seven sub-species officially recognized: Ethiopian Nile crocodile (*C. n. niloticus*); East African Nile crocodile (*C. n. africanus*); West African Nile crocodile (*C. n. chamses*); South African Nile crocodile (*C. n. corviei*); Madagascan Nile crocodile (*C. n. madagascariensis*); Kenyan Nile crocodile (*C. n. pauciscutatus*);

REPTILES

and Central African Nile crocodile (*C. n. suchus*).

The spectacled caiman (*Caiman crocodilus*) is also highly variable, with three sub-species generally being recognized: Apaporis River caiman (*C. c. apaporiensis*); common caiman (*C. c. crocodilus*); and the brown or American caiman (*C. c. fuscus*). Several other sub-species have been described for the spectacled caiman but are not widely accepted.

★ FASTEST

The fastest crocodilian motion on land is the rarely seen gallop. The hindlimbs push the crocodile forward in a leap, the forelimbs reach out and hit the ground at the end of the leap, then the hind limbs swing forward as the back bends and push once again. Only a few species are capable of galloping. The fastest ever recorded is the freshwater crocodile (*Crocodylus johnsoni*), which can reach speeds of up to 17 km/h (10½ mph).

★ MOST AQUATIC

The gharial (*Gavialis gangeticus*) is arguably the most aquatic of all the crocodilians. Adults have weak legs, cannot walk in a semi-upright stance (as other crocodilians are able to do) and seldom move more than a few metres from the water.

★ LONGEST SUBMERSION

Most crocodilians stay underwater for no more than a few minutes, although many species have the ability to stay under for an hour or even up to eight in cold conditions. In a series of gruesome experiments conducted in 1925, during which animals were held underwater until

• Nile crocodile
Nile crocodiles are capable of tackling enormous prey including, on one occasion, a fully grown black rhino. They are only found throughout sub-Saharan Africa including of course, the Nile River basin.

American alligator
Male alligators bellow loudly to attract mates and warn off other males during the mating season. They do this by sucking air into their lungs and blowing it out in intermittent, deep-toned roars.

they drowned, an American alligator (*Alligator mississippiensis*) survived for six hours five minutes.

★ COLDEST
The Chinese alligator (*Alligator sinensis*) and the American alligator (*Alligator mississippiensis*), live in areas where the temperature can fall below freezing during the winter. Both species excavate burrows into which they can retreat for the worst of the weather. If they remain in water they keep the tip of the snout exposed, enabling them to breathe, but allow the rest of the head and upper body to be frozen into the ice. They can survive like this until the ice melts, even though their internal body temperature may plummet to just 5°C (41°F) (compared with a normal figure of around 33°C (91°F)).

★ NOISIEST
Crocodilians are the noisiest of all the reptiles, capable of making a wide variety of coughs, hisses, roars and bellows. It is even possible to distinguish individuals on the basis of their calls. The most vocal of them all is the American alligator (*Alligator mississippiensis*), possibly because of its habitat, where visual communication may be hard to maintain. Its bellowing, which vaguely resembles the roaring of a lion, can be heard easily from a distance of 150 m (500 ft). Bellows are used during courtship and when the animals are aggravated.

> From a distance of 5 m (16 ft), a male American alligator's bellowing is almost as loud as standing next to a small propeller aircraft.

LIZARDS

Lacertilia
c. 4800 species

★ EARLIEST
The world's oldest fossil reptile, nicknamed 'Lizzie the Lizard', was found in March 1988 by palaeontologist Stan Wood, in a small quarry at Bathgate, near Edinburgh, UK. The 20 cm (8 in) long reptile (whose sex is, in fact, indeterminable) is estimated to be about 340 million years old. 'Lizzie' was officially named *Westlothiana lizziae*, in 1991 and was sold by her finder to the National Museums of Scotland for £195,000 ($375,000). However, recently, painstaking study of the animal's palate, and the discovery of a second specimen, have thrown doubt on its reptilian pedigree. The oldest confirmed reptile is *Hylonomus* ('forest mouse'), which lived in Nova Scotia 315 million years ago.

★ FASTEST
Lizards are renowned as much for their powers of acceleration as for their overall speed; some species can accelerate from a standing start to 95% of their maximum speed within a quarter of a second. The highest speed accurately measured for any reptile on land is 34.9 km/h (21½ mph) for a spiny-tailed iguana (genus *Ctenosaura*) from Costa Rica, in a series of experiments by Professor Raymond Huey from the University of Washington, USA, and colleagues at the University of California, Berkeley, USA. A special lizard racetrack was used, with a series of light beams and a computerized timing device: as the animals dashed down the track, they broke the beams and their times were automatically fed into the computer. The system is so accurate that it is claimed to rival the ones used in the Olympics.

A close runner-up is a six-lined racerunner (*Cnemidophorus sexlineatus*), which was clocked at 29 km/h (18 mph) near McCormick, South Carolina, USA, in 1941. It was being chased by a car and maintained its speed on all four legs for over a minute before darting into the undergrowth by the side of the road.

★ LONGEST
The longest lizard in the world is the slender Salvadori or Papuan monitor (*Varanus salvadorii*) of Papua New Guinea. It is normally shorter than the Komodo dragon (*Varanus komodoensis*), and far less bulky, but has been reliably measured at lengths of up to 4.75 m (15 ft 7 in). Nearly 70% of the total length is taken up by its tail. There are unsubstantiated claims of the Salvadori monitor reaching a length of just over 6.1 m (20 ft), though this is considered highly unlikely by most experts.

★ LARGEST

The largest lizard in the world is the Komodo dragon (*Varanus komodoensis*), otherwise known as the Komodo monitor or ora. Found on the Indonesian islands of Komodo, Rinca, Gili, Motang, Padar and Flores, males average 2.25 m (7 ft 5 in) in length and weigh about 59 kg (130 lb); females are typically about two-thirds this size. Lengths of up to 9.15 m (30 ft) have been claimed for this species, though these are likely to be wild exaggerations.

The largest accurately measured specimen was a male presented to an American zoologist, in 1928, by the Sultan of Bima. In 1937 it was put on display in St Louis Zoological Gardens, Missouri, USA, for a short period, by which time it was 3.10 m (10 ft 2 in) long and weighed 166 kg (365 lb). There are fewer than 5000 Komodo dragons surviving and Komodo itself has been made a national park – one of very few of the world's protected areas set aside specifically for a lizard.

Most geckos (family Gekkonidae) are fairly small, with a maximum length of

about 30 cm (12 in), but there is one dramatic exception: the giant gecko (*Hoplodactylus delcourti*), which measures a staggering 60 cm (24 in) from the tip of its snout to the end of its tail. It was first discovered in the 1980s as a mounted specimen in the Marseilles Natural History Museum, France. No other specimens exist and it is believed to be extinct, but it is thought to belong in the New Zealand genus *Hoplodactylus* and was probably collected in New Zealand by a 19th-century French expedition.

★ SMALLEST

The smallest lizard (indeed the smallest reptile) in the world is the appropriately-named dwarf gecko (*Sphaerodactylus ariasae*), which was discovered in Jaragua National Park, Dominican Republic in 2000. It measures just 1.6 cm (⅝ in) from snout to vent with a tail of approximately the same length. It has two similarly small

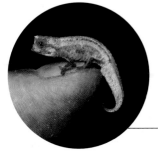

Pygmy chameleon
Pygmy chameleons are found in Madagascar and live in very small ranges in almost unreachable territory. Being the smallest chameleons on record, and given their sensitive nature, they have been relatively poorly studied.

Komodo dragon
The world's largest lizard is the threatened Komodo dragon, which lives only on a handful of islands in Indonesia. The Komodo dragon will eat any animal it can catch and sometimes even tackles local villagers.

★ TAIL SHEDDING

Most lizard species are able to shed their tails (a process called autotomy) when danger threatens. Usually the tail breaks off only when it is grasped by a predator but, in some species, it can be ejected voluntarily. Although the fracture occurs on the spine, it is across a specific fracture-plane and the loss causes the creature little discomfort. Special muscles cause the tail to wriggle on its own, to hold the predator's interest while the lizard makes its escape. Eventually the lost tail regrows (though it is never quite the same as the original and is always supported by cartilage rather than bone); there is no limit to the number of times regrown tails can be lost.

Tail-shedding is completely unknown in all species of chameleons (Chamaeleonidae), beaded lizards (Helodermatidae), monitors (Varanidae) and xenosaurs (Xenosauridae) and in the Bornean earless monitor (*Lanthanotus borneensis*).

The most extraordinary tail shedding probably occurs in the 1.5 m (5 ft) Pallas's glass snake (*Ophisaurus apodus*), which is really a lizard without legs. It is named for

close relatives: *S. parthenopion*, which is up to 1.8 cm ($^{11}/_{16}$ in) from snout to vent, and *S. elasmorhynchus*. The only known specimen of *elasmorhynchus* was an apparently mature female with a snout-vent measurement of 1.7 cm ($^5/_8$ in) and a tail of approximately the same length. This specimen was found on 15 March 1966 among the roots of a tree in the western part of the Massif de la Hotte, Haiti.

The world's smallest chameleon is another close contender. The stump-tailed or pygmy chameleon (*Brookesia peyrierasi*), from Madagascar, has a maximum snout-vent measurement of only 1.9 cm ($^3/_4$ in) and a tail length of 1.6 cm ($^9/_{16}$ in).

★ SLIMMEST

The slimmest lizards in relation to body length are the snake lizards (family Pygopodidae) and the slow-worm (*Anguis* *fragilis*) and glass lizards (family Anguidae), all of which are elongated, slender and limbless. The best example is probably the Australian leg-less snake lizard (*Lialis burtonis*), which attains a length of 50 cm (20 in) or more, but is no thicker than a pencil at mid-body.

★ BROADEST

The broadest lizards in relation to body length are probably the horned lizards in the genus *Phrynosoma*, which grow to about 15 cm (6 in) – and are saucer-shaped. The Latin *Phrynosoma* actually means 'toad-bodied' and they are often called horned 'toads' because of their toad-like shape. There are 14 species, all of which are found in the drier regions of the USA and Mexico.

After an uncomfortably close encounter with a predator, some skinks have been known to return to the spot where they lost their tails and eat them – a unique example of self-cannibalism.

its extraordinary ability to shatter its own tail. If under stress, it fractures its tail (which amounts to two-thirds of its length) at all or most of the joints. Each piece of tail then wriggles convulsively on its own for several minutes, while the 'body' of the lizard makes its escape – sometimes reduced to as little as a third of its original length.

★ MOST VENOMOUS

Two of the most venomous lizards are the gila monster (*Heloderma suspectum*), which lives in the southwestern USA and Mexico and the Mexican beaded lizard (*Heloderma horridum*), which lives in the western coastal region of Mexico south to Guatemala. They both have well-developed venom glands in their lower jaw (venomous snakes have them in their upper jaws). The venom is not injected but seeps into the wound caused by the bite; consequently, in a serious attack, the lizard may continue to hang on and actively chew for several minutes (the powerful jaws may have to be prized open to release the victim). The bite is both unpleasant and potentially dangerous, since the venom contains a pain-producing substance called serotonin, enzymes which break down tissue, anti-clotting agents and a powerful neurotoxin. In the wild both species seem reluctant to bite unless provoked; however, when they are sufficiently aggravated, they can attack

WORLD RECORD HOLDER

Most bizarre defence

Three species of horned lizard (*Phrynosoma solare*, *P. cornutum* and *P. coronatum*) can squirt blood from their eyes over a distance of up to 1.2 m (47 in), by increasing the blood pressure in the sinuses of their eye sockets until the walls burst. However, this is normally a last resort for these strange-looking lizards from western North America: they also have more traditional means of defence at their disposal when they feel threatened. They can change colour to match the desert sand, inflate themselves to look more intimidating and then jump forward and hiss.

Venomous gila monster
The gila monster is a venomous lizard, carrying enough venom to kill two adult humans. It reaches a total length of about 50 cm (20 in), making it the largest lizard in the USA.

with surprising agility – despite their heavy-bodied, plump and rather sluggish appearance. It is believed that the venom is used almost exclusively for defence and isnot needed to subdue the relatively small and harmless invertebrate prey or birds' eggs that are the mainstay of their diet.

The Komodo dragon (*Varanus komodoensis*) from Indonesia also possesses a venomous bite and will eat almost anything from smaller dragons to

Chameleon tongue

Only very high speed photography can catch the tongue of the chameleon in action, since it can spring more than a body length away, hit a tiny and sometimes moving target and reel it back to the mouth in less than half a second – all in the blink of an eye.

water buffalo. Scans of a preserved skull showed the presence of two venom glands in the lower jaw and further research found that the glands secreted venom containing several different toxic proteins.

★ WALKING ON WATER

The plumed basilisk or Jesus Christ lizard (*Basiliscus plumifrons*) can run across the surface of water at speeds of up to 12 km/h (7½ mph). It lives among the dense vegetation lining rivers and streams in Central America and, when threatened, runs away on its hind legs. If it is suddenly confronted with water, it simply keeps on running – and does not sink. It is able to do this by running incredibly fast (it has the most highly developed form of bipedal locomotion of all the lizards) and with the help of its powerful hind legs, which end in long, fringed toes that act like flippers. Normally basilisks will begin to sink after a few paces. When they do

finally sink, they are good swimmers and can hold their breath long enough to avoid most predators.

★ LONGEST TONGUE

All lizards possess well-developed, extendable tongues but the longest by far belong to the 140 known species of chameleons (family Chamaeleonidae). Their tongues can be catapulted forward and extended to a length at least as long as their own bodies (in some species up to 1.5 times their body length). A sticky mucus on the end of the tongue (which can pull in about half the chameleon's own body weight) helps to capture the animal. A special bone with its own muscle is used to propel the tongue forward and different muscles retract it.

★ WORST CLIMBER

Among the tree-living lizards, the western fence lizard (*Sceloporus occidentalis*) is probably the world's worst climber. Researchers working in the Hastings Natural History Reservation in Monterey County, California, USA, have calculated that the lizards fall out of their oak tree homes, landing with a thump on the forest floor, at a rate of around 12000 falls/ha (4860/acre) every year. One clumsy individual fell at least five times in two months, the final fall proving fatal. This lack of surefootedness is probably due to their overenthusiastic pursuit of canopy insects, desperate efforts to escape from predators and, with males, over-vigorous showing off before prospective mates.

★ MOST NORTHERLY

The viviparous or common lizard (*Zootoca vivipara*) lives further north than

One 80 cm (32 in) basilisk was seen successfully running across a 40 m (131 ft) wide lake without sinking.

any other species of lizard, occurring high above the Arctic Circle, at the northern extremes of mainland Norway.

★ MOST SOUTHERLY

Several species of iguana (family Iguanidae) live further south than any other species of lizard. One particular species, the Magellanic lizard (*Liolaemus magellanicus*), occurs on Tierra del Fuego, at the southern tip of Argentina.

★ MOST EFFICIENT THERMO-REGULATOR

Like all reptiles, lizards are unable to produce heat internally and rely primarily on the sun to raise their body temperature to the optimum level. The black-coloured lava lizard (*Liolaemus multiformis*), which lives in the Peruvian

REPTILES

Andes, is believed to be more efficient at absorbing solar radiation than any other lizard. In near-freezing conditions, it can raise its body temperature to 33°C (91°F) after only an hour in the sun, while the surrounding air temperature has barely risen to 1.5°C (35°F). Incredibly, its preferred body temperature is 35°C (95°F) – which is never reached by the surrounding air.

★ MOST TOLERANT TO FREEZING

Only a handful of vertebrate species are known to be able to tolerate freezing: four amphibians, several turtles, one snake and two lizards. The lizards include the European wall lizard (*Podarcis muralis*) of central and southeastern Europe, and the spiny lizard (*Sceloporus grammicus*) which lives at a high altitude on the slopes of Iztaccihuatl Volcano, Mexico. The tolerance of *S. grammicus* was discovered by accident by scientists from the University of Nebraska-Lincoln, USA. On 29 June 1991 they collected a total of 14 lizards from the slopes of Iztaccihuatl Volcano: seven *S. grammicus* and seven members of a closely related species of spiny lizard (*S. mucronatus*). They were all placed in a home freezer (inside temperature about 0°C (32°F)) to kill them prior to preservation. The following day (after 28 hours) all the solidly frozen lizards were removed. However, after

about half an hour of warming at room temperature, the scientists noticed movement among the *S. grammicus* species. When all the lizards had completely thawed, all seven *S. grammicus* were alive and well while all seven *S. mucronatus* were dead.

The alpine water skink (*Eulamprus kosciuskoi*), which lives in the subalpine and montane regions of southeast Australia, can remain active even when its body temperature drops below freezing. Its optimum body temperature is 26–34°C (79–93°F) but, thanks to small amounts of an anti-freeze agent (glycerol) in its blood, it can still move about when the temperature drops to -1.2°C (30°F).

★ MOST MARINE

The only truly marine lizard is the marine iguana (*Amblyrhynchus cristatus*), which lives in the Galapagos Islands, off the coast of Ecuador. This 1.75 m (5 ft 9 in) lizard feeds almost exclusively on seaweed and can dive to depths of up to 9.3 m (30½ ft) and stay underwater for as long as 60 minutes. While foraging, its heart rate and blood flow slow down to about half normal speed to cut down on heat

loss (the waters of the Humboldt Current are extremely cold) and to reduce oxygen requirements to a minimum. It swims gracefully and with ease, using its long laterally flattened tail and feet for propulsion; it also has special glands in its nasal cavity which secrete excess salt.

★ MOST PROLIFIC

There are two major strategies for producing a large number of offspring: lay a single large clutch (or have a large number of young) once a year or have a number of smaller clutches throughout the year. Iguanas (family Iguanidae) and geckos (family Gekkonidae), for example, choose the strategy of laying many small clutches (usually one or two eggs at a time). But the record-holder – the species which regularly lays the most eggs in any given year – is Meller's chameleon (*Chamaeleo melleri*), which lays up to 80 eggs.

A number of females of the same species may lay all their eggs together in a large 'cache'. The largest recorded cache belonged to an unknown number of female teiid lizards (*Kentropyx calcaratus*) and contained a total of 800 eggs (whole and broken). It is believed that the cache had been used over a period of several years.

Marine iguana
Darwin reported in *The Voyage*: 'A seaman on board sank [a marine iguana], with a heavy weight attached to it, thinking thus to kill it directly; but when, an hour afterwards, he drew up the line, it was quite active.'

Chameleon's eyes

Chameleons are believed to have excellent colour vision, and each eye covers 180° so they can see to the side and behind. Each eye operates independently of the other, so when hunting they use one to look for insects while the other keeps a wary lookout for predators. Together the eyes give excellent 3-D vision.

★ BEST EYESIGHT

Many lizards have good eyesight and vision is the most important sense for all but a few species. It is difficult to make direct comparisons but chameleons (family Chamaeleonidae) can probably see better than most other species and have to rely almost entirely on sight to detect rivals, mates, predators and prey. They are unique in having neither an external ear opening nor a middle ear cavity and, consequently, they are so deaf that shouting next to sleeping chameleons will not wake them up (though they can probably sense vibrations); they also have a poor sense of smell.

★ WORST EYESIGHT

Burrowing lizards have the worst eyesight. In particular, blind lizards (family Dibamidae) have only rudimentary eyes which are covered by skin. They are probably unable to distinguish anything other than light from dark.

★ VIRGIN BIRTH

The ability of females to breed and produce viable offspring without the need for males to fertilize their eggs is common among insects and other invertebrates, but rare among vertebrates. Parthenogenesis, as this process is called, is known or suspected in several different lizard species but is most extreme in the whiptail lizards (genus *Cnemidophorus*), which live in North and Central America. Some of the species are exclusively parthenogenetic – for example, males are completely unknown in the Chihuahuan spotted whiptail (*Cnemidophorus exsanguis*) of southern Texas, USA, and northern Mexico – and all-female populations are known for a number of others.

The great benefit of parthenogenesis is obvious in environments where periodic disasters such as floods or devastating fires are likely, because only a single female needs to survive for the population to re-establish itself. The main disadvantage is that the offspring are identical to their mother (they are literally clones of one another) and so, if local conditions should change, there is little chance of them making any necessary adaptions. In 2007, five Komodo dragons (*Varanus komodoensis*) hatched after an eight-month gestation period at Chester Zoo, England. Each hatchling is a product of a virgin birth as their mother produced the eggs without the assistance of a male.

Many lizards, and tuataras, have a 'third eye': a small opening on the top of the skull; this is believed to register daylight and may be used to control activities such as basking, hibernation and seasonal courtship.

★ MOST VOCAL

Sound is an important means of intra-specific communication in the geckos (family Gekkonidae) and the snake lizards

(family Pygopodidae), both of which are primarily nocturnal and use a variety of barks, grunts and squeaks to keep in touch with one another. Several species have reputations for being very loud or for their elaborate vocal repertoires. Barking geckos (*Ptenopus garrulus*), which live in the deserts of southwest Africa, are unique among lizards because the males all call together just as many frogs do in their choruses; at night, and on cloudy days, each male sits in the entrance to his burrow and calls loudly, using the burrow to amplify the sound.

The tokay gecko (*Gekko gecko*), which lives in Southeast Asia and grows to an impressive 50 cm (20 in) in length, has a staccato bark that is so loud it would compete with a barking dog. The appropriately named talkative or barking gecko (*Ptenopus garrulus*) also has a reputation for its varied and loud vocal repertoire.

★ BEST GLIDER

No lizard has the power of flight, although some species are capable of gliding from tree to tree or from a branch or trunk down to the ground. The best-known glider is the flying dragon (*Draco volans*), an inhabitant of the rainforests of Southeast Asia. Like other lizards of the genus *Draco*, which are the most highly adapted lizards for gliding, it even has its own 'wings'. These comprise several pairs of elongated ribs, with a wide flap of skin stretched between them, and can be opened and closed voluntarily. As with all 'flying' lizards, the flying dragon steers with its tail.

Another species to have evolved its own special adaptations for gliding is the African blue-tailed tree lizard (*Holarpis guentheri*). It is known to leap from tree to tree, and its tail and toes are fringed by large flattened scales, which may be an adaptation to reduce air resistance.

Flying gecko

Flying geckos in the genus *Ptychozoon* are from Southeast Asia and have webbed feet, a fringed tail and flaps of skin along their flanks; however, the flaps have no skeletal support and are opened purely by air resistance during gliding.

★ LONGEST LIVING

There is little information on lizard lifespans in the wild and, consequently, most authenticated information relates to species in captivity. However, it is known that few lizards live very long lives and, indeed, some smaller species such as the side-blotched lizard (*Uta stansburiana*) rarely live for more than a year. The average lifespan for the entire group (ignoring the high mortality of newly-hatched or newborn babies) is probably in the region of 5–10 years. Members of the families Anguidae (glass lizards, alligator lizards and the slow worm) and Lacertidae (wall and sand lizards) are exceptional in regularly exceeding 20 years. The greatest age recorded is 59 years old for a Grand Cayman blue iguana (*Cyclura lewisi*) called Godzilla, who died in 2004 at Gladys Porter Zoo, South Texas, USA.

★ FOOD STORAGE

Several desert-dwelling lizards are able to store fat in their tails in preparation for periods of food shortage. The best example is probably the slow-moving gila

When food is scarce the gila monster can survive off the fat it stores in its tail. After a long period without food the girth of its tail can reduced by as much as 80%.

monster (*Heloderma suspectum*), which lives in the southwestern USA and Mexico and feeds on invertebrates, small reptiles, birds' eggs and small rodents. When food is plentiful, the gila monster is able to consume more than 35% of its own body weight in a single sitting. But when food is scarce, it can manage on very few meals by breaking down the fat stored in its tail.

★ MOST SPECIALIZED DIET

Many lizards have highly specialized diets. Most geckos (family Gekkonidae) and chameleons (family Chamaeleonidae), for example, are exclusively insectivorous, while horned lizards (genus *Phrynosoma*) feed mainly on ants and the snake lizard (*Pygopus nigriceps*) on scorpions. But many of these are adaptable and will vary their diets according to local conditions and seasonal changes in the availability of food. However, there are several species with very specific and unwavering diets, including caiman lizards in the genus *Dracaena*, which eat only mollusks and the marine iguana (*Amblyrhynchus cristatus*), which eats only seaweed.

★ LARGEST MEAL

Unlike snakes, lizards cannot dislocate their jaws and therefore the upper limit of food items they can swallow is less than the width of their heads. However, they are able to tear food and many species can chew. As a result, the larger monitors (family Varanidae) will eat any animal they can catch and the record-holder in this respect is the Komodo dragon (*Varanus*

komodoensis). This huge 2.25 m (7 ft 5 in) lizard feeds mainly on carrion, but has been known successfully to tackle animals as large as horses and, in one case, a 590 kg (1300 lb) adult water buffalo. Local villagers on the island of Komodo, Indonesia, also fall prey to the dragons from time to time; and, since the animals have become a tourist attraction, there have been several, well-documented occasions on which the tourists

Thorny devil lizard
One of the most extraordinary of all lizards with a highly specialized diet is the Australian thorny devil, which eats only ants of the genus *Iridomyrmex*.

themselves have been added to their diet. In relation to body size, the largest single meal on record is a 41 kg (90 lb) wild pig which was eaten by a 46 kg (101 lb) komodo dragon in one sitting.

★ TUATARA

In 1867 Albert Gunther of the British Museum announced to a startled scientific community that the lizard-like tuatara (*Sphenodon punctatus*) was not a lizard after all, but the sole surviving member of an ancient order of reptiles called the Rhynchocephalia. The order lived in many parts of the world during

the reign of the dinosaurs and all but the tuatara died out more than 65 million years ago. Recent studies have substantiated Gunther's statement: it is not a lizard because its jaw teeth are not separate, but just simple serrations of the jaw bone, the structure of its skull is different, it does not have an ear drum or a middle ear, and for many other reasons. The studies have also revealed that there are, in fact, two surviving species: the individuals living on North Brother Island, in Cook Strait, between New Zealand's North and South Islands, are genetically distinct and now belong to a new species called Brother's Island tuatara (*Sphenodon guntheri*); the original species is now known as the Cook Strait tuatara. The tuataras are rare animals, that can hold their breath for up to an hour, have a mysterious third eye at the top of

> Tuataras are the sole survivors of the order Rhynchocephalia which could be found in many parts of the world during the reign of the dinosaurs.

their heads and despite being cold-blooded are mainly nocturnal. Tuataras may be under threat due to climate change because females are only guaranteed in nests at temperatures lower than 22.1°C (71.78°F) and if temperatures continue to rise all tuataras may end up being male. They can weigh up to 1.3 kg (2 lb 14 oz) and attain a maximum overall length of 61 cm (24 in) (males are larger than females). They are found only on about 30 remote, windswept islands off the coast of New Zealand. Compared with the lizards, they break a number of significant records: longest period between mating and eggs hatching (37 months); longest incubation period (15 months – which is the longest known for any reptile species); oldest age to reach sexual maturity (20 years); longest period of growth (60 years); longest

Worm lizard
Worm lizards are not true lizards and are believed to feed mainly on burrowing invertebrates and small vertebrates.

lifespan (possibly more than 100 years) and oldest reptile father (at 111 years).

★ WORM LIZARDS

Despite their name, worm lizards are not true lizards but are placed in a separate sub-order Amphisbaenia within the reptilian order Squamata (which includes both snakes and lizards). There are about 130 species altogether – most of them similar in size, colour and general appearance to earthworms. All but three have no legs and they are all believed to feed mainly on burrowing invertebrates and small vertebrates. The majority are 15–35 cm (6–14 in) long, but the largest is a species called *Amphisbaena alba*, from the rainforests of northern South America and the island of Trinidad, which grows to about 75 cm (30 in). The shortest is only 10 cm (4 in) long. As a group, worm lizards are found in North and South America, Africa, the Middle East and extreme southern Europe.

SNAKES

Serpentes
c. 3000 species

★ EARLIEST

Snakes evolved from lizard-like ancestors and are believed to have appeared for the first time some 100–150 million years ago. The earliest known snake is *Lapparentophis defrennei* which lived in the region that is now North Africa. One of the oldest complete snake fossils, found in the Middle East in deposits about 96–98 million years old, measured about 1 m (3 ft 4 in) long and belonged to a species called *Pachyrhachis problematicus*. Another species, *Najash rionegrina*, found in Patagonia, Argentina, in 2003 is at least 90 million years old; however, it had 'hips' and is therefore more significant in the study of snake evolution.

★ OLDEST

The greatest reliable age recorded for a snake is 40 years, three months and 14 days for a male common boa (*Boa constrictor constrictor*) named 'Popeye', which died at Philadelphia Zoo, Pennsylvania, USA, on 15 April 1977. In the wild, the oldest natural longevity known is about 30 years for the black ratsnake (*Elaphe olsoleta*).

★ LONGEST

Giant snake stories abound due to the wild imaginations of many early explorers, the difficulties in estimating or measuring the length of live animals which refuse to stay still and the fact that large snake skins can be deliberately stretched by more than 30% without causing much noticeable distortion. In reality, even among the pythons (family Pythoninae) and boas (family Boinae), giant individuals are very rare. However, there are a few authenticated records of snakes exceeding a length of 9.14 m (30 ft).

The record-holder is the reticulated python (*Python reticulatus*) of Southeast Asia, which regularly exceeds 6.25 m (20½ ft). The greatest proven length for this species is 10 m (32 ft 9½ in) for a specimen shot on the north coast of Celebes, Indonesia, in 1912; it was accurately measured with a surveying tape by civil engineers working at a nearby mining camp. The closest runner-up is an African rock python (*Python sebae*) measuring 9.81 m (32 ft 2¼ in), which was shot in 1932 by Mrs Charles Beart, in the grounds of a school in Bingerville, Ivory Coast, West Africa; however, this particular individual was truly exceptional, since the average length for this species is only 3–5 m (9 ft 10 in–16 ft 5 in).

The largely aquatic anaconda (*Eunectes murinus*) of South America is a close contender for the longest snake record, although it has probably been the subject of more exaggerated claims regarding its size than any other living animal. Early Spanish settlers in South America spoke of individuals measuring 18–24 m (60–80 ft) and even larger specimens have been reported. But, in reality, it rarely exceeds 6.25 m (20½ ft). Perhaps the most famous of the claims that have been taken seriously was made in 1907 by Lt. Col. Percy Fawcett of the Royal Artillery. He shot an unusually large anaconda while navigating the Rio Abuni near its confluence with the Rio Negro, in the Amazon, Brazil, as it made its way out of the water and up a riverbank. He claimed that 'as far as it was possible to measure', a length of 13.7m (45 ft) lay out of the water, and 5.2m (17 ft) lay in it, making a total of 18.9 m (62 ft). Fawcett was very meticulous in all the observations he entered in his journal, but his explorations often read like a comic-book adventure so the reliability of his giant anaconda has often been questioned. The truth will probably never be known for sure.

King cobra
The longest venomous snake in the world is the king cobra. It is found across a wide range over India and Southeast Asia. The king cobra is one of the few snakes known to feed almost exclusively on other snakes.

REPTILES

The longest (and heaviest) snake ever held in captivity was a female reticulated python named 'Colossus' which was 8.68 m (28 ft 6 in) long and weighed 145 kg (320 lb) at her heaviest. She died at Highland Park Zoo, Pennsylvania, USA, on 15 April 1963.

Most modern herpetologists have a healthy scepticism about any snake claimed to be longer than 9.14 m (30 ft). However, it has been calculated, by taking into account the biomechanical and physiological stresses imposed on a large snake moving over land, that the upper length limit is probably about 15 m (49 ft); a longer snake would have to spend most of its time in the water, to support its enormous weight. Unfortunately, reports in 2003 of a 15 m (49 ft) reticulated python captured by villagers on Sumatra, Indonesia, were grossly exaggerated (the snake was 6.5 m (21 ft) in length).

★ SHORTEST

The world's shortest snakes are the thread snakes (family Leptotyphlopidae). There are about 100 species, widely distributed in tropical America, Africa and parts of western Asia, and they are all shorter than 40 cm (16 in). The shortest of all is the

> One type of thread snake has such a small, matchstick-thin body it could slither through the hole left in a pencil after the lead is removed.

very rare thread snake (*Leptotyphlops carlae*), which is believed to be only known on Barbados in the Caribbean. It is about 10 cm (4 in) long and as thin as a spaghetti noodle.

Some worm-like blind snakes (family Typhlopidae), which are widely distributed in the warmer parts of the world, are also very small. *Typhlops fornasinii* of East Africa, *T. caecatus* and *T. hallowelli* of West Africa, and *T. anchietae* of Angola all measure 12.7–15.2 cm (5–6 in). Most blind snakes (there are 130 species in total) feed on small invertebrates, such as ants and termites.

★ LONGEST VENOMOUS

The longest venomous snake in the world is the king cobra (*Ophiophagus hannah*), also called the hamadryad, which averages 3.7–4.6 m (12–15 ft) in length. A 5.54 m (18 ft 2 in) specimen captured alive near Fort Dickson in the state of Negri Sembilan, Malaysia, in April 1937 grew to 5.71 m (18 ft 9 in) in London Zoo, UK. It was destroyed at the outbreak of war, in 1939, to avoid it escaping. The largest spitting cobra, Ashe's spitting cobra (*Naja ashei*), can grow to a length of 9 ft (2.7 m) long and has enough venom in a single bite to kill up to 20 people, but has taken to spitting its venom, with great accuracy, into the eyes of its aggressors when threatened.

Reticulated python
One of the longest snakes in the world, the reticulated python squeezes its prey to death and then devours it whole, digesting the entire animal in its stomach and intestines.

★ LONGEST SEA SNAKE

The longest of all the sea snakes is *Hydrophis spiralis,* from the northern Indian Ocean and many parts of Southeast Asia, which can grow to 2.75 m (9 ft) in length.

★ HEAVIEST

The heaviest snake in the world is the anaconda (*Eunectes murinus*) of tropical South America and Trinidad: it attains a considerably greater body weight than the much more slender reticulated python (*Python reticulatus*); for example, a 5.2 m (17 ft) anaconda would weigh roughly the same as a 7.3 m (24 ft) reticulated python. The record-holder is a female anaconda shot in Brazil in *c.* 1960. It was 8.43 m (27 ft 9 in) long, with a girth of 1.11 m (44 in), and was estimated to have weighed nearly 227 kg (500 lb).

★ HEAVIEST VENOMOUS

The heaviest venomous snake is probably the eastern diamondback rattlesnake (*Crotalus adamanteus*), found in sparse woodland and lowland coastal regions in the south-eastern United States. It averages 5.5–6.8 kg (12–15 lb) (1.5–1.8 m (5–6 ft) in length), although the heaviest on record weighed 15 kg (34 lb) and was 2.36 m (7 ft 9 in) long.

The gaboon viper (*Bitis gabonica*) of tropical Africa is probably bulkier than the eastern diamondback, but its average length is only 1.2–1.5 m (4–5 ft). An exceptionally long 1.83 m (6 ft) female weighed 11.34 kg (25 lb) and another female measuring 1.74 m (5 ft 8½ in) weighed 8.2 kg (18 lb), with an empty stomach.

★ FASTEST

The fastest land snake in the world is the much-feared black mamba (*Dendroaspis polylepis*) of the eastern part of tropical Africa. There are many stories of this species overtaking people on galloping horses but, although moving snakes do give an illusion of speed, such stories are greatly exaggerated. However, top speeds of 16–19 km/h (10–12 mph) have been recorded for black mambas in short bursts over level ground, and speeds of 10–11 km/h (6–7 mph) are probably not unusual.

★ SPERM STORAGE

The females of many species of snake are able to store sperm in their reproductive tracts before using it to fertilize their eggs. These are nature's sperm banks, enabling the females to be fertilized by the best males whenever they happen to be available, regardless of whether it is also the best time for young to be brought into the world. Implantation finally takes place in anticipation of a time when food is plentiful and the weather more suitable.

The world record-holder for storing sperm is the Javan wart snake or elephant-trunk snake (*Acrochordus javanicus*), which can store sperm for up to seven years.

Black mamba
The fastest land snake in the world is the black mamba. This snake could certainly, in short bursts of speed, catch up with a person on foot.

No snake species is known to look after its offspring: once born, they are left to survive on their own.

★ EGG INCUBATION

Several species of snake guard their eggs, but female pythons (family Boidae) are the only ones known to incubate them. Since they are cold-blooded animals, keeping the eggs warm can be difficult. However, some species can raise their temperature by as much as 7°C (13°F) above that of the surroundings, by rapidly contracting their own muscles or by gently shuffling the eggs in and out of the sun.

★ COUNTRY WITH MOST VENOMOUS SNAKES

Australia has more venomous snakes than any other country in the world. Interestingly, it is the only continent with a higher proportion of venomous snakes to non-venomous ones: out of a total of nearly 187 species (including 31 sea snakes) around 120 of them are venomous (roughly 15% of all the world's snakes are venomous and considered dangerous to humans). Some 20–25 of these are considered to be highly dangerous to people, the commonest cause of serious snake-bite being the tiger snake (*Notechis scutatus*).

Even though few parts of Australia are entirely free of

The venom produced by Russell's viper is used to stop bleeding in haemophiliacs.

Brown snakes (genus *Pseudonaja*) and tiger snakes (genus *Acanthophis*) have been responsible for the most deaths. After them come the taipan (*Oxyuranus scutellatus*) and the death adder (*Acanthophis antarcticus*).

★ COUNTRY WITH LEAST VENOMOUS SNAKES

Several countries and islands have no snakes at all, including Iceland, Greenland, Newfoundland, Ireland, New Zealand and the Falkland Islands. Many of the islands of the Pacific Ocean, and many Caribbean islands, have no venomous land snakes, although those in equatorial waters are likely to have poisonous sea snakes just offshore. Madagascar is unusual in having a large and varied population of snakes – a total of nearly 90 species altogether – but no dangerous ones (venomous but rear-fanged).

★ MOST VENOMOUS LAND SNAKE

Some 600 of the world's 3000 snake species are venomous (almost one third of which are harmless to people). By far the most venomous land snake in the world is the 1.7 m (5 ft 7 in) small-scaled or fierce snake (*Oxyuranus microlepidotus*), found in isolated patches over a very large area of central Australia. It appears to be most common in the Diamantina River and Cooper Creek drainage basins, Queensland and western New South Wales, where it feeds mainly on the plague rat. The snake's venom is strongly neurotoxic. The average venom yield after milking is 44 mg (^{3}/$_{2000}$ oz), but one male specimen yielded a record 110 mg (^{4}/$_{1000}$ oz) – enough to kill 250,000 mice (or 100 human adults). Fortunately, because of the remoteness of its habitat and its docile nature, the fierce snake rarely comes into contact with people and, so far, no human fatalities have been reported.

dangerous snakes – and an estimated 3000 Australians are bitten by venomous snakes every year – deaths due to snakebite are relatively uncommon. Fatalities have dropped dramatically over the past 100 years as anti-venoms have become more readily available.

Fierce snake
The small-scaled or fierce snake from Australia is the most venomous land snake. It feeds mainly on the plague rat, and a bitten rat would probably drop dead within a few seconds, since the snake's venom is strongly neurotoxic.

★ MOST VENOMOUS SEA SNAKE

Most of the world's 70 species of sea snakes are venomous, but the most venomous – and indeed, the most venomous snakes in the world – are probably the sea snakes *Hydrophis belcheri* and *Enhydrina schistosa*. They have a neurotoxic venom many times more effective than the venom of any land snake. However, fatalities by sea snakes are rare since the potency of the venom is matched only by the mild temperament of many species. They have to be subjected to severe treatment before they can be induced to bite, and people and sea snakes rarely encounter one other. Most bites are of fishermen handling nets – and even then only about 25% of those bitten ever show signs of envenomation, since the snake rarely injects much of its venom.

★ COUNTRY WITH HIGHEST INCIDENCE OF SNAKEBITE

Certain islands of the Ryukyu group, between Japan and Taiwan in the western Pacific, have the highest incidence of snakebite in the world. On average, 0.2% of the population – 1 in every 500 people – is bitten by a snake every year. Every person in the area has at least a one in seven chance of being bitten by a snake at one time or another during their lives. The snake most responsible is the Okinawa habu (*Trimeresurus flavoviridis*); fortunately, most of its victims recover.

★ COUNTRY WITH MOST DEATHS FROM SNAKEBITE

Around the world, an estimated 2.5 million people or more are bitten by snakes every year. However, few of the snakes responsible are highly dangerous and, indeed, research has shown that in as many as 50% of bites no venom is injected. Consequently, in most countries there is more chance of being killed by a bee than there is of being killed by a snake. Nevertheless, the World Health Organisation estimates that as many as 125,000 people are killed every year by snakes (although this figure is little more than a rough calculation) and, in some areas, the risk is relatively high.

More people die from snakebite in India than in any other country in the world, with the total death toll estimated to average 10,000–50,000 annually. This is

> Snakes inject venom through their fangs, which are specially adapted teeth. The forked tongue is used only for feeling and smelling and cannot sting or harm in any way.

partly due to a high incidence of venomous snakes, but also because in many areas medical care is not always readily available and, consequently, more bites prove fatal. Death can often be prevented by prompt medical treatment and, indeed, most deaths from snakebite occur well away from hospitals and other treatment centres. In some areas, local habits and conditions also encourage a higher incidence of snakebite; in Bombay, for example, poor hygiene attracts large numbers of rats and other rodents which, in turn, attract large numbers of cobras (family Elapidae).

More people die of snakebite in Sri Lanka than in any other comparable area. An average of 800 people are killed by snakes every year on the 65,610 km² (25,332 miles²) island – equivalent to one person every 82 km² (32 miles²) annually. Over 95% of the fatalities are caused by the common krait (*Bungarus caeruleus*), the spectacled cobra (*Naja naja*) and Russell's viper (*Daboia russelli*).

★ MOST ACCURATE SPITTER

Several cobras (family *Elapidae*) are able to spit or, more precisely, to eject their venom over considerable distances, thanks to a slight adaptation of the fangs. When the venom lands on human skin it has a minimal effect (unless it happens to

enter an open wound), but if it hits the eyes it can cause temporary blindness. For this reason, spitting cobras need to be able to aim accurately for maximum effect. A Mozambique spitting cobra (*Naja mossambica*) can aim its venom with remarkable accuracy at the eyes of an approaching person when still 3 m (10 ft) or more away.

★ LARGEST YIELD OF VENOM

The gaboon viper (*Bitis gabonica*) of tropical Africa probably has the highest average yield of venom – up to 600 mg ($^{2}/_{100}$ oz). Just a tenth of that is enough to kill a fully grown man.

★ LONGEST FANGS

The longest fangs of any snake are those of the highly venomous gaboon viper (*Bitis gabonica*) of tropical Africa. In a specimen of 1.83 m (6 ft) in length they measure up to 5 cm (2 in).

Gaboon viper
The venom glands of the gaboon viper are enormous, and produce more venom than any other snake.

★ LARGEST MEAL

Snakes cannot chew or tear their food so they have no choice but to swallow it whole. They are superbly adapted to swallowing prey considerably larger in girth than themselves because, as the wider part of the body enters the mouth, the bones of the lower jaw can be temporarily dislocated and certain bones in the skull are capable of pulling apart. Once the prey has been swallowed, the snake yawns a few times to return the various parts of the skull to their original positions. The largest prey item on record was a 59 kg (130 lb) impala, which was removed from a 4.87 m (16 ft) African rock python (*Python sebae*). One Burmese python (*Python molurus bivittatus*), measuring 3.9 m (13 ft) long tried to swallow a 1.8 m (6 ft) alligator whole – it exploded and was found by rangers at the Everglades National Park, USA, in 2005. There are many examples of snakes swallowing other snakes that are much longer than themselves. In 1955 a captive cottonmouth moccasin (*Ancistrodon piscivorus*), which was 35.5 cm (14 in) long, swallowed a very slender 73.6 cm (29 in) ribbon snake (*Thamnophis sauritus*) sharing the same cage. The stomach of a 1.51 m (59½ in) long file snake (*Mehelya capensis*) killed in South Africa contained a olive grass-snake (*Psammophii sibilans*), an African rock python (*Python sebae*), a brown water snake (*Lycodonomorphus rufulus*) and a ring-necked spitting cobra (*Hemachatus haemachatus*).

★ MAN-EATING

There are many stories of snakes swallowing people, but only a few have been authenticated – and, in most of these cases, the victims have been either young children or babies. One of the best-known examples occurred in November 1979, in northern Transvaal, South Africa, when a young Tswana herdsman was seized by an African rock

African rock python

African rock pythons regularly take large prey such as this impala but, when swollen with food, they are vulnerable to attack by wild dogs and hyenas and so prefer to eat more moderate meals at shorter intervals.

python (*Python sebae*) measuring 4.5 m (14 ft 9 in) in length. His friend ran to get help but when he returned with two elders, about 20 minutes later, the victim had already been entirely swallowed by the snake. The men pelted the snake with stones and attempted to kill it with a

A king cobra (*Ophiophagus hannah*) was once placed by a misguided keeper in a cage with six Indian cobras (*Naja naja*); by the following morning, the king cobra had eaten all its room-mates.

pick-axe until, eventually, it regurgitated its prey; unfortunately, the young man was already dead.

★ LONGEST FAST

Most snakes do not feed every day but, on average, do so about once a week. If necessary, for example when they are hibernating or if they are unable to find suitable prey species due to adverse environmental conditions, they can survive without food for considerably longer. The longest known fasts are carried out by the highly venomous Okinawa habu (*Trimeresurus flavoviridis*), the largest of the Asiatic pit vipers, found in the Ryukyu Islands between Japan and Taiwan in the western Pacific. In 1977, the Amami Kanko Pit Viper Centre in Naze City, Kagoshima Prefecture, Japan, started a fasting experiment with five of these snakes, and one survived for over three years without food.

★ MOST DANGEROUS

It is difficult to identify the most dangerous snake in the world, because

European grass snake
With a sagging jaw, lolling tongue and a deathly expression on its 'face', the European grass snake is very convincing at playing 'dead' when threatened.

the effect of a snakebite depends on the combination of many factors above and beyond the species itself: the age, weight and health of the victim; the size of the snake, the number of bites and the volume of venom injected; and, of course, the speed and efficiency of first aid treatment. However, taking into account the five most widely accepted features for comparison (venom toxicity, venom yield, fang length, temperament and frequency of bite) the saw-scaled or carpet vipers (genus *Echis*) are generally considered to be the most dangerous snakes in the world. Ranging from West Africa through the Middle East to India and Sri Lanka, they probably bite and kill more people in the world than any other species. In Asia they are reported to kill 8000 people annually. The venom is more toxic than in any other viper, they are small and easy to overlook and become extremely aggressive when frightened or disturbed.

The beaked sea snake (*Enhydrina schistosa*) is considered to be the world's most dangerous sea snake. Blamed for many deaths in Southeast Asia, in particular, it normally grows to about 1.2 m (4 ft) long and hunts catfish in shallow estuaries and tidal creeks.

★ PLAYING DEAD

A number of snakes, including the European grass snake (*Natrix natrix*) and the North American hog-nosed snakes

(*Heterodon* sp.), pretend to be dead when they are threatened. The most impressive 'death display' is probably used by the West Indian wood snake (*Tropidophis* sp.) of Cuba. When threatened, this small boa twists itself into a tight coil to mimic the stiffness of death and, with the help of fluids coating its scales, gives off a foul stench of decomposing flesh. To add to the illusion, it even has special blood vessels that burst to flush the eyes with blood and to form a trickle of blood from its gaping mouth. The overall effect successfully convinces most predators that the snake has been dead for some time.

★ RESISTANCE TO VENOM

Some people have a higher than average resistance to snake venom.

A series of bizarre experiments was carried out by Saul Wiener, in 1958, to test the theory that people can develop an immunity to snake venom. His willing human guinea pig was 46-year-old Charles Tanner, animal curator of the Alfred Hospital, in Melbourne, Australia. Tanner had already been bitten several times by venomous snakes and was allergic to anti-venom. The experiments

involved injecting Tanner with venom milked from tiger snakes (*Notechis scutatus*), the dosage gradually being increased over a period of 13 months. The result of his final injection – which, under normal circumstances, would have been enough to kill 30 men – was nothing more than tenderness and muscle stiffness.

August Eichorn, a household name in Australia in the early 1900's, spent many years developing a remedy for snakebite. He was so confident in his new product

All snakes are unable to hear airborne sounds (apart from very low frequencies); instead they detect vibrations on the ground through their bodies. Snake charmers therefore use the movements of their instruments to 'charm' snakes; it is not the music itself.

(which almost certainly gave no immunity at all) that he became quite a performer and coaxed snakes to bite him to demonstrate its efficacy. There are numerous photographs taken at the time, showing Eichorn 'accepting' the bites of some of Australia's most dangerous snakes – tigers (*Notechis scutatus*) and browns (*Pseudonaja textilis*) among them – on his arms, hands and face. There are photographs of tiger snakes clinging to his cheeks and hanging from his throat and he would even allow them to bite him under the tongue. He eventually died in 1943, at the grand old age of 85, from blood poisoning.

In general, venomous snakes are fairly resistant to their own venom and to the venom of other individuals of their own and closely related species. However, the level of immunity is unclear and may even vary from individual to individual.

There are cases of venomous snakes that have been bitten by one of their contemporaries and have suffered little more than a swelling, but there are also cases of venomous snakes accidentally biting themselves and dying within a couple of days. When one venomous snake eats another, it apparently suffers no ill-effects from the venom because of a 'protective factor' in the blood; it is hoped that in the future this factor can be used to help create a 'multipurpose' anti-venom for people that have been bitten by deadly snakes (existing anti-venoms act only against specific snake species). In another twist, garter snakes have developed total resistance to the rough-skinned newts on which they prey. These newts have enough toxin to kill a roomful of people, but the snakes are immune.

★ MOST VARIABLE

Several snake species show a startling degree of variation in their markings. One of the best examples is the common garter snake (*Thamnophis sirtalis*): individuals may have brilliant stripes, bright spots or heavy speckling, they may have rather subtle or even dull markings or, in some parts of their range, they may even be completely black.

★ GLIDING AND JUMPING

A number of snakes can jump or glide. The golden tree snake (*Chrysopelea ornata*), found in Southeast Asia, is able to glide from tree to tree over distances of at least 10 m (33 ft); during the 'flight' it holds its body rigid, like an arrow, and its ventral surface caves in to offer greater resistance to the air.

The jumping viper (*Atropoides nummifer*), from Central America, strikes so fiercely that its entire body moves forward. It is able to clear a height of up to 1 m (3 ft 4 in) high, by curling its body into an S-shape and using it as a spring or coil.

★ HIGHEST ALTITUDE

The Himalayan pit viper (*Gloydius himalayanus*) has been found at greater altitudes, 4900 m (16,072 ft), than any other snake. The ridge-nosed rattlesnake (*Crotalus willardi*) of Mexico is not far behind, frequently being found at altitudes of over 4000 m (13,120 ft).

★ MIMICRY

One of the best examples of mimicry in snakes is probably between a highly venomous coral snake known as the harlequin (*Micrurus fulvius*) and the false coral snake (*Lampropeltis triangulum*). Their physical resemblance – both have black, white, yellow and red bands – is astonishing. Since both species are secretive, nocturnal and occur together in the rainforests of Central America, the harmless harlequin probably benefits because potential predators believe they are dealing with a dangerous animal and consequently do not attack.

TURTLES & TORTOISES

Testudines (Chelonia)
c. 300 species

★ EARLIEST

The first chelonians appeared on Earth during the late Triassic at least 200 million years ago. Fossil species, such as *Proganochelys* and *Proterochersis*, found in Triassic deposits in Germany and Thailand, resemble modern species in many ways. However, they also reveal some significant differences; for example, the fossil animals had small neck spines and a long tail terminating as a club.

Leatherback turtle
The largest living chelonian is the leatherback turtle which nests on tropical beaches in the Atlantic, Indian and Pacific Oceans and forages widely in temperate waters.

★ LARGEST

The largest living chelonian is the widely distributed leatherback turtle (*Dermochelys coriacea*). The overall length from the tip of the beak to the end of the tail is normally 1.8–2.1 m (6–7 ft) (shell length averages 1.5–1.6 m (5–5½ ft)) and the front flipper-span is about 2.1 m (7 ft). Mature specimens typically weigh at least 450 kg (1000 lb). The largest leatherback turtle reliably recorded was a male found dead on the beach at Harlech, Gwynedd, UK, on 23 September 1988. It had an overall length of 2.91 m (9 ft 5½ in) (shell length 2.56 m (8 ft 5 in) and measured 2.77 m (9 ft) across the front flippers. It weighed 961.1 kg (2120 lb). Although most museums refuse to exhibit large turtles

(because they can drip oil for up to 50 years) this specimen was put on display at the National Museum of Wales, Cardiff, on 16 February 1990. There are claims of leatherback turtles reaching 3.7 m (12 ft) in length (in particular, by the crew of a British trawler in 1962) but these have never been authenticated.

The largest freshwater turtle (according to weight) is the alligator snapping turtle (*Macrochelys temminckii*) of the southeastern USA. The really large individuals tend to be most common in the northern extremes of the range, where the species is only rarely encountered. Males are much larger than females and may reach an overall length of 90 cm (35 in) and an upper weight of about 100 kg (220 lb). There is an unconfirmed report of a giant individual living in Fulk's Lake, near the town of Churubusco, Indiana, which was first seen in the summer of 1948; despite repeated attempts, it was never captured and properly measured, but eye-witness accounts described it a being the size of 'a dining-room table' and estimated its weight to be

> No tortoises or turtles have teeth; they rely on the sharp cutting edges of their jaws to tear food.

around 227 kg (500 lb). There is another unconfirmed record of 183 kg (403 lb) for an enormous specimen caught in the Neosho River, Cherokee County, Kansas, USA, in 1937. Several species of soft-shell turtle (family Trionychidae) can match the alligator snapping turtle (*Macrochelys temminckii*) in length, but not in weight. The longest freshwater turtle is Cantor's giant soft-shelled turtle (*Pelochelys cantorii*), now found only in small pockets in Southeast Asia. Its shell length can be as much as 2 m (6½ ft) but its maximum weight is 50 kg (110 lb).

The largest living tortoises are the Aldabra giant tortoise (*Geochelone gigantea*), which is found on Aldabra Atoll, a group of four major islands in the Seychelles (there are also several introduced populations on other

islands in the western Indian Ocean), and the Galapagos giant tortoise (*Geochelone elephantopus*), which is found on a handful of islands in the Galapagos archipelago, in the Pacific. The normal maximum size attained by certain sub-species of the Galapagos giant tortoise (there are 11 surviving sub-species altogether) is greater than that attained by the Aldabra giant tortoise (a shell length of 1.22 m (48 in) and a weight of 270 kg (595 lb) compared with 1.05 m (41 in) and 100–200 kg (220–440 lb). The largest living specimen on record is a Galapagos giant tortoise named 'Goliath', who

Galapagos tortoise
Some of the largest tortoises are the giant tortoises of the Galapagos Islands. In February 1535, a Spanish ship discovered the islands and the sailors named the islands 'Galápagos', Spanish for saddle, after the distinctive shape of the tortoises they found living there.

Alligator snapping turtle
This turtle has the strongest jaws and possesses a worm-shaped appendage on its tongue used to lure fish into its mouth, before closing its jaw with tremendous speed and force.

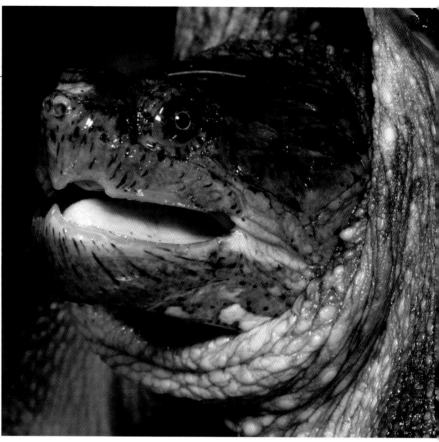

has resided at the Life Fellowship Bird Sanctuary in Sessner, Florida, USA, since 1960. In 1996 he measured 1.36 m (53½ in) long, 1.02 m (40½ in) wide, 68.5 cm (27 in) high and 400 kg (882 lb) in weight. He is still growing. An Aldabra giant tortoise presented to London Zoo, UK, at the beginning of the last century, had a shell length of 1.4 m (55 in); although its weight was never recorded, it was estimated to be in excess of 318 kg (700 lb). A male of the same species, called 'Esmeralda', a long-time resident of Bird Island in the Seychelles, weighed 304 kg (670 lb) in early 1995.

★ LARGEST PREHISTORIC

The largest prehistoric chelonian was a turtle called *Archelon ischyros*, which lived about 70 million years ago in a shallow sea that covered most of central North America. It attained a length of at least 3.5 m–4.5 m (11½–15 ft) and weighed an estimated 2200 kg (4850 lb). A close runner-up is *Stupendemys geographicus* (family Pelomedusidae), which lived about five million years ago. Fossil remains indicate that this turtle had an overall length of about 3 m (9 ft 10 in) (shell length 2.18–2.30 m (7 ft 2 in–7 ft 6½ in)) and weight of 2040 kg (4500 lb).

The largest prehistoric tortoise was probably *Geochelone atlas*, which lived in what is now northern India, Myanmar (Burma), Java, the Celebes, and Timor about two million years ago. It had a total length of 2.44 m (8 ft) and is computed to have weighed 850 kg (2100 lb).

★ SMALLEST

The world's smallest chelonian is the southern speckled padloper tortoise (*Homopus signatus cafer*), which lives in the Karoo of southwestern South Africa. It grows to an average shell length of 6–8 cm (2³/₈–3¹/₈ in) with a maximum of 9.6 cm (3¹/₄ in). The typical weight is about 140 g (5 oz). The adults are so small that even birds attack them.

The smallest turtle is the stinkpot or common musk turtle (*Sternotherus odoratus*), which ranges from southern Canada to northern Mexico and has an average shell length of 7.62 cm (3 in) when fully grown and a weight of only 227 g (8 oz); it is named for the offensive smell it emits when feeling threatened. A sub-species of the freshwater striped mud turtle (*Kinosternon baurii baurii*), which ranges from southern Georgia in a southerly direction through the Florida Keys, USA, is also very small with a maximum shell length of only 9.7 cm (3³/₄ in).

The smallest of the seven species of sea turtle (and, indeed, the most critically endangered) is the Atlantic or Kemp's ridley (*Lepidochelys kempii*), which nests mainly at Rancho Nuevo, on the Gulf coast of Mexico. It has an average shell length of 50–70 cm (20–28 in) and a maximum weight of around 80 kg (176 lb).

Local Indians claim that the Chiapas cross-breasted turtle, from Central America, is able to eat its way out of a crocodile.

★ STRONGEST JAWS

The strength in the jaws of a large alligator snapping turtle (*Macrochelys temminckii*) is almost legendary. There are stories of individuals biting broomsticks in half and, although such claims may well be exaggerated, there is more than a little truth in them. The species is certainly quite capable of removing a human finger or toe if given the opportunity.

FREEZING

Young painted turtles, adult box turtles and garter snakes freeze in the cold winter months. After hatching in late summer, painted turtles stay put, well hidden from predators, and freeze until the following spring. When frozen, they show no movement, respiration, heart beat or blood circulation, and barely any neurological activity.

★ SLOWEST

The land-based tortoises (family Testudinidae) are notoriously slow and laborious creatures simply because their large, cumbersome shells severely restrict mobility. Unfortunately, it is very difficult to identify the slowest of them all because speed has to be measured over a sensible distance to be meaningful. However, tests carried out on the Californian desert tortoise (*Gopherus agassizii*) revealed an walking speed of 3–8 metres (10–26 feet) a minute. Similar tests carried out on a captive Aldabra giant tortoise (*Geochelone gigantea*) in Mauritius revealed that, even when hungry and enticed by a cabbage, it could not exceed 4.5 metres (15 feet) a minute. Interestingly, Charles Darwin clocked a Galapagos giant tortoise (*Geochelone elephantopus*) at 6.4 km (4 miles) per day which, when spread over a 24-hour period, is equivalent to an average speed of 4.5 m (15 feet) a minute.

★ FASTEST

The fastest chelonians are the sea turtles (families Cheloniidae and Dermochelyidae). The highest speed claimed for any reptile in water is 35 km/h (22 mph) by a frightened Pacific leatherback turtle (*Dermochelys coriacea*). The UK National Tortoise Championship record is 5.48 m (18 ft) up a 1:12 gradient in 43.7 seconds by 'Charlie' at Tickhill, South Yorkshire, UK, on 2 July 1977. However, limited evidence suggests that wild tortoises regularly exceed this speed.

★ LONGEST HIBERNATION

Many chelonians enter a state of dormancy when the temperature drops or during prolonged periods of drought. The length of time spent hibernating depends on local environmental factors and varies from a few days to many months. Certain populations of Horsfield's tortoise (*Testudo horsfieldii*) in Kazakhstan, on the border with Russia, are active for only about three months of the year, from the end of March to the middle of June. Apart from a very brief appearance at the end of the summer, they spend the remainder of the year buried underground hibernating or aestivating.

★ UNDERWATER NESTING

Most reptiles lay their eggs on dry land for the simple reason that the developing embryos need oxygen to survive and would drown underwater. But the northern long-necked turtle (*Chelodina rugosa*) of Australia is unique in laying its eggs underwater, usually in holes that have been dug into the muddy bottom at depths of 15–20 cm (6–8 in). The eggs survive in a state of arrested development until the floodwaters have subsided and then they start developing under the hardened mud. Tests have shown that, once they have started developing, the embryos cannot survive immersion underwater.

★ LONGEST NECK

A number of species of snake-necked turtle (family Chelidae), as their name suggests, have exceptionally long necks in relation to the size of their bodies. The most notable are members of the Australian genus *Chelodina* (eight species) and the South American genus *Hydromedusa* (two species), in which the neck can be almost as long as the shell. The giant snake-necked turtle (*Chelodina expansa*), for example, has a shell size of up to 30 cm (12 in) but its overall length is nearly doubled when its head and neck are fully extended.

WORLD RECORD HOLDER

Longest living

The greatest authenticated age for a chelonian and, indeed, the oldest authenticated age for any land animal is 175 years for a Galapagos giant tortoise (*Geochelone elephantopus*) called Harriet, who died at her home in Australia Zoo on 23 June 2006. DNA testing suggested that she had been born in 1830, when Charles Darwin was developing his theory of evolution. In fact, it is believed Harriet was one of three animals Darwin brought back from his trip to the Galapagos Islands in 1835.

Aldabra giant tortoises (*Geochelone gigantea*) are close contenders. Five individuals were brought from the Seychelles to Mauritius in 1766 by Marion de Fresne, the French explorer, and were presented to the army garrison at Port Louis, the island's capital. When the British captured Mauritius in 1810, the tortoises were officially handed over, along with the island, by the surrendering French forces. The last survivor of the five became the British mascot. It went blind in 1908 and was accidentally killed in 1918 when it fell through a gun emplacement. Since it was fully mature at the time of its capture, this ancient animal could have been nearly 200 years old at the time of its death – although any estimate beyond 152 years is purely speculation.

There have been many unauthenticated claims of tortoises living for nearly 200 or even 300 years. Perhaps the most famous was a much-battered radiated tortoise (*Astrochelys radiata*), known affectionately as 'Tu'imalilia' (King of the Malilia), which reputedly reached the grand old age of 193 years. It was said to have been a gift from Captain Cook to the King of Tonga in 1773 and, after an eventful life during which it was run over by a cart, kicked by a horse and escaped from two forest fires, it eventually died on 19 May 1966. Even if the story is true (unfortunately, there is no record of the original gift in Captain Cook's journals) the record may have been the composite of two or more tortoises living on the island in sequence.

Stories of pet tortoises staying 'in the family' for generations are difficult to authenticate. A large size and well-worn shell are not reliable indications of great age; neither are the growth rings in the shell, since the number laid down each year varies according to weather conditions and the availability of food. Many 'record-holders' are probably the result of dead animals secretly being replaced by thoughtful parents keen to avoid unnecessary upset and, since some tortoises undoubtedly outlive their original owners, the continuing existence of one individual is very difficult to prove one way or the other. Nevertheless, there are numerous reliable records of Mediterranean spur-thighed tortoises (*Testudo graeca*), European pond tortoises (*Emys orbicularis*) and several other species living for more than 100 years.

The oldest turtle on record was an alligator snapping turtle (*Macrochelys temminckii*) at Philadelphia Zoo, Pennsylvania, USA, at 58 years old.

Aldabra giant tortoises
Many Aldabra giant tortoises are thought to live to more than 100 years of age.

★ LONGEST MIGRATION

Sea turtles (families Cheloniidae and Dermochelyidae) are renowned for making prodigious migrations between their feeding grounds at sea and their nesting beaches thousands of kilometres (miles) away. Evidence has been found indicating that sea turtles can read the magnetic map of their native area (each ocean has a different magnetic signature) and imprint it into their memories so that they can always find their way home. A female leatherback turtle that was tagged using a satellite-tracking system was recorded to have covered over 20,558 km (12,774 miles) on a trip from a beach in Papua, Indonesia, where she laid her eggs, across the Pacific to Oregon on the northeast coast of America. Adults migrate from their temperate feeding and foraging areas to tropical breeding grounds. The record-holders are probably loggerhead turtles (*Caretta caretta*) born in Japan, which are known to travel 10,000 km (6200 miles) across the Pacific to feed off the coast of Mexico.

★ LONGEST DIVE

In 2007 a loggerhead turtle (*Caretta caretta*) was recorded diving for 10 hours and 14 minutes – a marine vertebrate record. It is thought that the turtles rest or even sleep underwater and that they can hold their breath for long periods by slowing down their internal systems and so reducing their need for oxygen.

Loggerhead turtle

Loggerhead turtles make long migrations, some leaving Japan as hatchlings and, after being swept along by strong ocean currents, arriving in Mexico two years later. They feed and grow for the next five years and swim back to Japan as adults.

★ MOST RESTRICTED RANGE

The black soft-shell turtle (*Aspideretes nigricans*) exists only as a single semi-captive population in an artificial pond forming part of the sacred shrine of the Islamic saint Hazrat Bayazid Bostami, at Nasirabad, near the town of Chittagong, Bangladesh. The pond is currently 100 m (330 ft) long and 50 m (165 ft) wide and

DEEPEST DIVE

In May 1987 it was reported by Dr Scott Eckert that a leatherback turtle fitted with a pressure-sensitive recording device had reached a depth of 1200 m (4000 ft) off the Virgin Islands, in the West Indies. Leatherbacks are believed to dive to depths of more than 1500 m (5000 ft) to reach dense aggregations of jellyfish.

5–6 cm (2–2³/₈ in). Among the species that lay elongated eggs, the largest are laid by the Malaysian giant turtle (*Orlitia borneensis*), which has a carapace length of about 80 cm (31½ in); on average, its eggs measure 7.6 cm (3 in) in length and 4.05 cm (1½ in) in diameter, but can be as much as 0.5 cm (¼ in) longer in both directions. However, there are exceptions in the relationship between body size and egg size and the largest eggs in relation to body size are laid by the black wood turtle (*Rhinoclemmys funerea*); this species has a maximum shell length of about 33 cm (13 in) and yet lays eggs which, on average, are 6.7 cm (2⁵/₈ in) in length and 3.7 cm (1½ in) in diameter; one female, herself only 20 cm (8 in) long, laid eggs with a length of 7.5 cm (3 in).

★ MOST EGGS

All turtles and tortoises lay eggs. The largest clutches are laid by sea turtles (families Cheloniidae and Dermochelyidae), which lay anything from a little under 70 to more than 180 eggs in multiple clutches at intervals of 9–30 days. The overall record-holder for a single clutch is a hawksbill turtle (*Eretmochelys imbricata*), which nested on Cousin Island, in the Seychelles, and laid a total of 242 eggs. However, the most prolific – and, indeed, the most prolific of all reptiles – are the green turtles (*Chelonia mydas*) that nest on Sarawak, Borneo; in a single breeding season, each female lays up to a record of 11 clutches, each containing over 100 eggs – a total of more than 1100 eggs in less than five months.

★ LEAST EGGS

The pancake tortoise (*Malacochersus tornieri*) and the big-headed turtle (*Platysternon megacephalum*) are among many species that lay just one egg (sometimes two) in a clutch.

★ MATERNAL CARE

The Burmese brown tortoise (*Manouria emys*) is the only species of tortoise or turtle known to show any degree of maternal care. After laying, some species spend up to an hour concealing their eggs and the nest site, but then take no further interest. In contrast, the female Burmese brown tortoise is unique in remaining close to her nest site for several days afterwards.

> The incubation temperature of turtle and tortoise eggs directly influences the sex of the hatchlings in many species.

contains fewer than 400 turtles. The animals depend almost entirely on food provided artificially by people. The origin of the population is unknown (although it was described as long ago as 1875) and no specimens of the black soft-shell turtle have been found anywhere else in the world.

★ LARGEST EGGS

Most turtles and tortoises lay eggs which are either spherical or elongated. Since egg size tends to increase with body size, it is not surprising that the largest spherical eggs are laid by leatherback turtles (*Dermochelys coriacea*) and Galapagos giant tortoises (*Chelonoidis nigra*); these have an average diameter of

Hawksbill turtle

The hawksbill turtle lays the largest clutch of eggs, typically around 140, in sand-covered nests on tropical beaches. After 60 days the eggs hatch and the newborn turtles make a perilous night-time scurry to the sea.

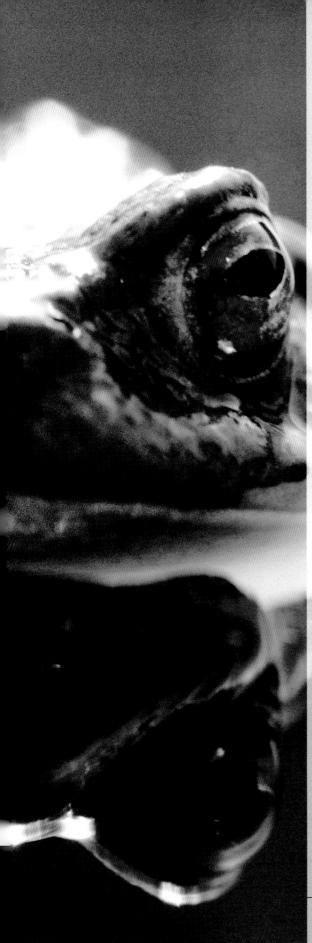

AMPHIBIANS

European toad
A female common
European toad (*Bufo bufo*).

CAECILIANS

Gymnophiona

176 species (exclusively in the tropics and sub-tropics)

★ EARLIEST

Until recently, the fossil record of caecilians was almost non-existent and consisted of just two vertebrae (one from the Palaeocene of Brazil and the other from the late Cretaceous of Bolivia). However, the exciting discovery of an extensive series of early Jurassic caecilians in Coconino County, Arizona, USA, was announced by scientists from Harvard University and the University of London in 1993. The 200 million-year-old fossils are believed to belong to a prehistoric species known as *Eocaecilia micropodia* and reveal numerous features, such as limbs, unlike modern caecilians (which are tropical, limbless amphibians that look like large earth worms). This find is also exciting because it provides evidence of substantial evolutionary divergence between caecilians and other modern amphibian groups. The new species is older than the earliest known salamanders but younger than the earliest known frogs, confirming that the three groups were well differentiated by Jurassic times.

★ LARGEST

The world's largest caecilian is a species called *Caecilia thompsoni*, which lives in Colombia and attains a maximum length of about 1.5 m (60 in) and a width of up to 3 cm (1¼ in). This size is really exceptional and most caecilian species are within the 30–70 cm (12–28 in) range.

A number of other species are shorter but much bulkier than *C. thompsoni*. For example, *C. nigricans* is 80 cm (32 in) long and has a body diameter of 4 cm (1¾ in). Body shapes vary between caecilians, with some stout-bodied species having a length:diameter ratio of 15:1, and more slender-bodied species having a length:diameter ratio of 100:1.

★ SMALLEST

One of the world's smallest caecilian is a species in the genus *Idiocranium*, which lives in West Africa and attains a maximum length of about 14.4 cm (5½ in) from the end of the snout to the tip of the tail. Adults as small as 5.1cm (2 in) have been found.

FROGS & TOADS

Anura

5818 species (typically 75–100 new species formally described every year)

★ EARLIEST

Our knowledge of early frogs and toads is almost non-existent. The earliest frog-like creature known is a species called *Triadobatrachus massinoti*, which has been found in Madagascar in deposits dating from the early Triassic period some 210–225 million years ago. It was about 10 cm (4 in) long and had a wide, flat skull (like modern frogs) as well as a short tail. The first species believed to be almost identical to modern frogs appeared during the early Jurassic, about 150 million years ago.

★ MOST PRIMITIVE

The world's most primitive frogs are members of the genera *Ascaphus* and *Leiopelma*. Four species live in New Zealand and two in northwestern North America (which alone is circumstantial evidence that these frogs are survivors of an ancient time when the continents were joined together to form great land masses). A number of curious anatomical features (such as the presence of a tail or tail-wagging muscles) suggest that these frogs are survivors of a time when frog evolution was still in its infancy.

★ LARGEST

The largest of all frogs and toads is the African giant or Goliath frog (*Conraua goliath*) of West Africa, which frequently attains a snout-to-vent length of 30 cm (12 in). A specimen captured in April 1989 on the Sanaga River, Cameroon, had a snout-to-vent length of 36.8 cm (14½ in) (87.6 cm (34½ in) overall with legs extended) and weighed 3.66 kg (8 lb 1 oz) on 30 October 1989.

There are a small number of records of longer frogs, though none exceed the

Cane toad
The largest toad ever recorded is a cane toad. Weighing an incredible 2.65 kg (5 lb 13½ oz), it measured over half metre long at 53.9 cm (21¼ in) fully extended.

Sanaga River specimen in weight. The longest authenticated record is of an American bullfrog (*Lithobates catesbeiana*) which was caught in Martha Lake, Alderwood Manor, Washington, USA, in 1949. It reportedly measured 91.4 cm (36 in) in overall length (with legs extended) and weighed 3.29 kg (7 lb 4 oz).

The largest toad ever recorded was a male cane or marine toad (*Bufo marinus*) named Prinsen ('The Prince'), owned by Hakan Forsberg of Akers Stvckebruk, Sweden. It weighed 2.65 kg (5 lb 13½ oz) and measured 38 cm (15 in) snout-to-vent (53.9 cm (21 in) when extended) in March 1991. The largest female ever recorded was a cane toad nicknamed 'Totally Awesome' and owned by Blank Park Zoo, Des Moines, Iowa, USA; she attained a peak weight of 2.31 kg (5 lb 1½ oz) and a snout-to-vent length of 24.1 cm (9½ in) on 19 November 1987. (She died on 8 April 1988, most probably from old age). However, the average size of the cane toad (which is native to Central and South America and has been introduced elsewhere) is considerably smaller; an average specimen weighs 453 g (1 lb) and measures about 15 cm (6 in) (snout-to-vent). Several toad species exceed this average size; in particular, Blomberg's toad (*Bufo blombergi*) of Colombia frequently attains a length of 24 cm (9½ in).

★ SMALLEST

The world's smallest frogs – indeed the smallest known amphibians – are the tiny Cuban frog (*Euhyas limbata*) and the gold frog (*Brachycephalus didactylus*) which are both about 0.8–1.2 cm (⅓–½ in) long (snout-to-vent) when fully grown. A number of other species vie for this title: several *Eleutherodactylus* spp. (which range from northern Mexico, south into Argentina and across to the West Indies), the smallest members of the widely distributed family Microhylidae, and *Brachycephalus didactylus*, from Brazil, all have an average adult length (snout-to-vent) of just under 10 mm (⅓ in).

The world's smallest toad is *Bufo beiranus*, which lives in Africa and attains a diminutive 2.4 cm (1 in) in length (snout-to-vent).

★ MOST POISONOUS

Frogs and toads are incapable of inflicting a poisonous bite or sting to deter their predators, but instead some secrete a toxic or distasteful substance from their skin. The most deadly toxins are produced by the 60 or so species of poison-arrow frogs in the genera *Dendrobates* and *Phyllobates*. These brightly coloured species (the garish colours warn potential predators that they are highly poisonous and should be disregarded as potential meals) are found in Central and South America. Several of them secrete some of the most deadly biological toxins known to science and, indeed, their secretions are so toxic that a tiny smear is enough to kill a horse.

The skin secretion of the golden poison-arrow frog (*Phyllobates terribilis*) of western Colombia is the most poisonous. This brilliant yellow or orange species, which was not discovered until 1973 and was first described in 1978, grows to a length of about 3.5 cm (1½ in). The

Golden poison-arrow frog
Golden poison-arrow frogs produce such a highly toxic skin secretion that scientists have to wear thick gloves when handling them.

combination of batrachotoxins and homobatrachotoxins found in its secretion is 20 times more toxic than that produced by any other poison-arrow frog. An average adult specimen carries enough poison that scientists have to wear thick gloves to protect themselves when they pick it up. The golden poison-arrow frog has only two enemies: the frog-eating snake (*Leimadophis epinephelus*), which is believed to be immune to its toxin; and Choco Indians, who use the toxin to poison their blowpipe darts which can then kill large prey in a matter of seconds (in the past they also used poisoned darts to kill neighbouring hostile tribesmen).

> **The golden poison-arrow frog carries enough poison to kill nearly 20,000 mice.**

BIGGEST SIZE DIFFERENCE BETWEEN NEWBORN AND ADULT

The aptly named paradoxical frog, which lives in the Amazon and on the island of Trinidad, metamorphoses from a giant tadpole into a tiny frog. The tadpole grows to a length of 16.8 cm (6½ in) but then its whole body, including all its vital organs shrinks into a tiny frog (5.6–6.5 cm (2¼–2½ in) or less.)

For many years, it was assumed that poison-arrow frogs produce the toxins themselves. But recent research suggests that, although they do synthesize some of their own, they also obtain significant quantities of toxins from the food that they eat.

★ STOMACH BROODING

The only animals in the world known to brood their young in the female's stomach are the northern or Eungella gastric brooding frog (*Rheobatrachus vitellinus*) and the gastric brooding platypus frog (*R. silus*), both of which live in Australia and are now possibly extinct. They certainly show the most remarkable form of parental care among anurans. It is not known if the female swallows fertilised eggs or tadpoles, but these then develop into froglets inside her stomach. After a 'gestation period' of six or seven weeks, she eventually gives birth to the froglets through her mouth. For the whole of this period the female is unable to feed (the tadpoles have sufficient yolk to be able to feed themselves) and the mechanism for digestion is 'switched off', with the help of a chemical that is produced by her youngsters to ensure that their mother's

digestive juices do not break them down. The gastric brooding platypus frog was first discovered in 1972 but, within a few years, seemed to have become extinct and has not been seen alive since 1983. Strangely, the northern gastric brooding frog was discovered just a couple of months later, although there is now concern that it has also become extinct (it was last seen in 1985).

★ MOST EGGS

The female cane or marine toad (*Bufo marinus*) lays as many as 30,000–35,000 eggs per spawning. However, she leaves them to the mercy of the weather and predators, so the mortality rate is extremely high.

A wild African bullfrog once entered a snake enclosure at Pretoria Zoo, in South Africa, and ate 16 live ringhal cobras; it was caught in the act whilst eating the 17th.

★ LEAST EGGS

The tiny female Cuban frog (*Euhyas limbatus*) lays just a single egg, but does everything possible to make sure that it survives. A number of other anuran species (particularly small terrestrial ones) lay only three to six eggs.

★ MOST RESTRICTED RANGE

Hamilton's frog (*Leiopelma hamiltoni*), is thought to be found only on Stephens Island, an offshore island in Cook Strait, New Zealand. Discovered in 1919, the frogs live among a pile of rocks known as Frog Bank. A second and far larger population (discovered in 1958), was thought to exist in a small patch of forest on the neighbouring Maud Island. However, it's now known that the Maud Island population is a different species of frog, the Maud Island frog (*L. pakeka*).

The Mallorcan midwife toad (*Alytes muletensis*) also has a severely restricted range, occurring only in six or seven colonies in crevices in limestone cliffs on the island of Mallorca, in the Mediterranean.

★ BREATHING THROUGH SKIN

All frogs and toads have functional lungs in the adult stage, but they are also able to absorb oxygen through their skin (either from water or air). The species most efficient at breathing through its skin is the Lake Titicaca frog (*Telmatobius culeus*). It has a very folded and wrinkled appearance, because the surface area of its skin has been greatly increased to maximize the area over which oxygen can diffuse. This enables the frog, if it so wishes, to stay underwater for very long periods of time.

✸ COLOUR VARIATIONS

Some frogs and toads have a number of contrasting colour phases. One of the best examples is the African reed frog (*Hyperolius marmoratus*), which has three very distinctive phases: brilliantly striped, heavily speckled, and plain-coloured. All of these may occur within the same population – often side-by-side with other species sharing similar phases. The colour phases are so different that it is hard to believe they all belong to *H. marmoratus*. This can make identification extremely difficult, since two similarly striped frogs from the same pond may belong to different species, while a striped frog and a heavily speckled one may belong to the same species.

There is little sexual dimorphism (in terms of colour) among frogs and toads; in most species, the males and females are very similar. The main exceptions are several toad species in the genus *Bufo*, an African reed frog called *Hyperolius hieroglyphicus* and Couch's spadefoot toad (*Scaphiopus couchi*).

✸ LONGEST LEAP

There is tremendous variation in jumping ability both between species and between individuals. It is not necessarily the largest ones that make the longest jumps. In one detailed study of the performance of 82 different species from around the world, the longest jumps were recorded by some of the smallest individuals. Indeed, the world record-holder is the South African sharp-nosed frog (*Ptychadena oxyrhynchus*), which is only 5.5 cm (2$\frac{1}{4}$ in) (male) and 6.6 cm (2$\frac{1}{2}$ in)

African sharp-nosed frog
The African sharp-nosed frog (*Rana mascareniensis*) is one of a number of frogs with great jumping ability. The current world record holder is its relative, the South African sharp-nosed frog (*Ptychadena oxyrhynchus*).

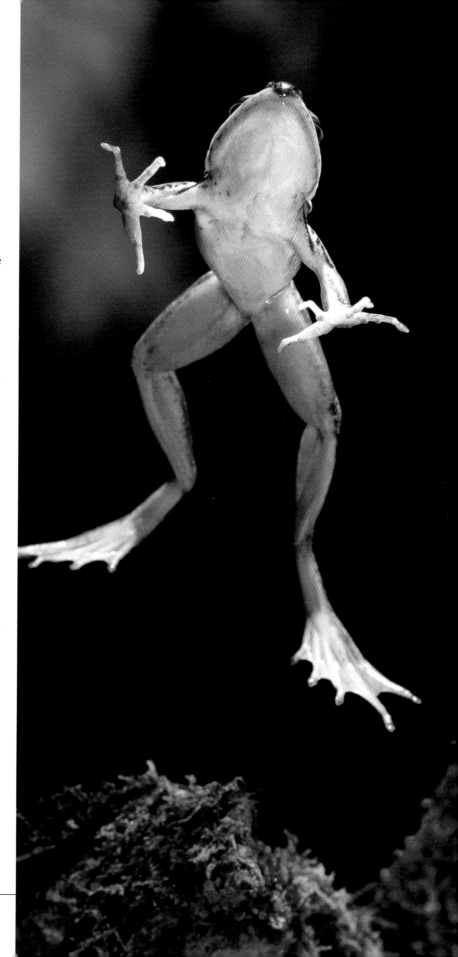

AMPHIBIANS

(female) in length. In 1975, at the annual Calaveras County Jumping Frog Jubilee held at Angels Camp, California, USA, an individual named 'Ex Lax' jumped an amazing 5.35 m (17 ft 6 in), the longest single leap recorded for any amphibian.

Competition frog jumps are normally taken as the aggregate of three consecutive leaps. The greatest distance covered by a frog in a triple jump is 10.3 m (33 ft 5½ in) by a South African sharp-nosed frog (*Ptychadena oxyrhynchus*) named Snotjie at a frog Derby held at Lurula Natal Spa, Paulpietersburg, Natal, South Africa, on 21 May 1977.

★ WORST SMELLING

The worst smelling of all the anurans is the aptly named Venezuela skunk frog (*Aromobates nocturnus*) which was described as new to science in 1991. Found in the cloud forests of the Venezuelan Andes, it attains a length of 6.2 cm (2½ in) and is the largest of the poison-arrow frogs (family Dendrobatidae). Unlike other members of the family, which rely on toxic secretions from their skin for defence, the skunk frog releases a vile-smelling secretion instead. Appropriately enough, the chemical responsible for the smell is the same organosulphur compound as the one emitted by more familiar mammalian skunks.

★ MOST TRANSPARENT

Some glass frogs (family Centrolenidae) look as if they were made of frosted glass and are partially transparent when seen from below. Found in the cloud and rainforests of Central and South America, these rather delicate frogs are usually green in colour above but have such transparent skin on their bellies that all their bones, muscles and internal organs are readily visible.

★ FASTEST SPREAD

The cane or marine toad (*Bufo marinus*), a native of Central and South America, has spread throughout eastern and northern Australia in the space of just 50 years. In 1935, 100 adult toads were imported to control the grey back cane beetle, (*Dermolepida albohirtum*), which was devastating sugar cane in Queensland. The toads laid more than 1.5 million eggs of which 62,000 hatched and reached young adult stage. These were released into the wild and the species quickly established a niche in Australia – a country with no native toads – and began to spread at a rate of up to 35 km (21¾ miles) per year. In some areas, it has reached plague proportions and hundreds of squashed bodies litter the roads. Many experts are concerned for the native wildlife, because the toad eats not only pests but also has an appetite for almost anything of a suitable size that moves. It is also poisonous to eat, and has been known to kill small crocodiles, koalas, goannas, lizards, snakes and many other animals (in some cases within minutes of being swallowed).

> Fire-bellied toads are unusual in having eyes with heart-shaped pupils.

Glass frog
As the name suggests glass frogs have transparent skin allowing their internal organs, including the heart, liver, and digestive tract, to be seen by the naked eye.

★ HIGHEST SPECIES DIVERSITY

The highest species diversity known for frogs and toads is found in a small outpost called Santa Cecilia, in Ecuador's Amazon basin. A recent survey revealed a total of 81 species inhabiting a little over 1 ha (2½ acres) of rainforest; this is approximately the same number of species known to be living in the entire USA. A team of scientists working in the Santa Cecilia area once collected an incredible 56 different frog and toad species in a single evening.

★ HIGHEST AND LOWEST ALTITUDE

The common toad (*Bufo bufo*) holds two amphibian records – for living at both the highest and the lowest altitude. The highest altitude record is held by an individual found at a height of 8000 m (26,246 ft) in the Himalayas. The lowest is for another individual found at a depth of 340 m (1115 ft) in a coal mine. A third possible record is of a common toad found in a flooded quarry in Leicestershire, UK, at a depth of 22.5 m (71 ft), where the water temperature was 7°C (46°F).

★ ANTIBIOTICS

The toxins secreted by two species of toad – the African clawed toad (*Xenopus laevis*) and the yellow-bellied toad (*Bombina variegata*) – have been found to have antibiotic properties. These appear to be effective against a broad spectrum of disease-carrying bacteria that cause problems to other animals, including the famous food-poisoner found in the human gut, *Escherichia coli*. The secretions may enable the toads to be protected by their own medicines; the yellow-bellied toad, for example, lives in

Common toad
The common toad survives in both high and low altitudes and can be found in Britain, Europe, Africa and Asia.

A chemical extracted from an Ecuadorian frog is a painkiller 200 times more potent than morphine.

stagnant water and may need to protect itself against skin infections. The slimy skin of the South American paradoxical frog (*Pseudis paradoxa*) has been found to contain a substance that protects the frog from infection.

NEWTS & SALAMANDERS

Caudata

584 species (*c.* 530 salamanders and 30 newts)

★ EARLIEST

The earliest known 'amphibian' – and indeed, the earliest known land vertebrate – is a species belonging to the genus *Ichthyostega*. Looking rather like a modern salamander (with four well-formed limbs and a long tail) but with many fish-like features as well,

Ichthyostega appeared towards the end of the Devonian period some 360 million years ago. Found in Greenland, it was about 1 m (39 in) in length .

Despite many similarities between *Ichthyostega* and newts and salamanders, it was not the direct ancestor of modern amphibians. In 2003, scientists discovered

the earliest examples of true salamanders – some up to 165 million years old – in Mongolia and China.

★ LARGEST

The largest amphibians are the giant salamanders (family Cryptobranchidae) of which there are three species. The record-holder is the Chinese giant salamander (*Andrias davidianus*) which lives in mountain streams in northeastern, central and southern China. The average adult measures 1.14 m (45 in) in length and weighs 25–30 kg (55–66 lb). One specimen collected in Hunan Province measured 1.8 m (71 in) in length and weighed 65 kg (143 lb). Unfortunately, this species is considered to be a great delicacy in China and, as a result of hunting, has become highly endangered.

The Japanese giant salamander (*Andrias japonicus*), which lives in southwest Honshu and central Kyushu, Japan, can grow to a similar length but has a proportionately longer tail and therefore weighs considerably less. The third species is the hellbender, (*Cryptobranchus alleganiensis*) which is the largest of the North American salamanders. However, it is less than half the size of its two Asian relatives, reaching a maximum length of only 74 cm (29 in).

The largest land salamander is the tiger salamander (*Ambystoma tigrinum*), which can attain an overall length of 33 cm (13 in).

★ LARGEST PREHISTORIC

During the late Triassic period, around 200 million years ago, there were a number of giant amphibians far exceeding modern species in size. The largest was the crocodile-sized *Mastodonsaurus*, which attained a length of 4 m (13 ft) from the tip of the snout to the end of the tail. Its skull alone was 1.25 m (49 in) long.

★ SMALLEST

The smallest of the world's caudates is the arboreal minute salamander (*Thorius arboreus*), an endangered species found in Mexico, which has an average length of 1.7 cm (³/₄ in).

> Female alpine salamanders start with as many as 60 fertilised eggs. But the first embryos to develop eat the rest so only one to four young are actually born.

★ LONGEST LIVING

The greatest age reliably recorded for an amphibian is 55 years for a Japanese giant salamander (*Andrias japonicus*) which died in Amsterdam Zoo, Netherlands, in 1881. Another individual at the same zoo was born there on 10 November 1903 and died on 6 July 1955 aged 51 years 7 months and 2 days.

★ LONGEST GESTATION

The beautiful gold- and black-coloured alpine salamander (*Salamandra atra aurorae*), which lives in the alpine regions of Europe, notably in Switzerland, Bosnia, Croatia and Albania, has a gestation period of up to 38 months, the longest of any vertebrate. Individuals at high altitudes (above 1400 m (4600 ft)) tend to have the longest gestation period; those living at lower altitudes (below 600 m (2000 ft)) have the shortest recorded for this species of 24–26 months. One or two young are born on land, usually within a few hours of each other.

★ CANNIBALISM

The alpine salamander (*Salamandra atra*), which lives in the alpine regions of Europe, is the only amphibian whose young are cannibalistic before birth. The female carries as many as 60 fertilized eggs in her body, but most of them are devoured by the first few embryos as they develop. She finally gives birth to between one and four young.

The Arizona tiger salamander (*Ambystoma tigrinum nebulosum*) is often cannibalistic. The individuals which eat their own kind (some grow into relatively benign omnivores while others are predominantly carnivorous) are more heavily armed with elongated, curved teeth and a wider head than their unfortunate contemporaries. Strangely, the cannibals are quite choosy about who they eat, preferring to dine on their more distant relatives than their next of kin.

Chinese giant salamander

The Chinese giant salamander holds the record as the largest amphibian in the world; one outstanding specimen measured 1.8 m (71 in) in length.

★ MOST POISONOUS

Many newts and salamanders secrete poisons from numerous poison glands in their skin. In some species, this poison is quite mild and either acts as an irritant or simply makes the animal taste unpleasant. But in other species it can be extremely toxic. The skin, muscles and blood of the California newt (*Taricha torosa*) contain the highly toxic substance tetrodotoxin, a powerful nerve poison also found in puffer fish and some other animals.

★ POISON SPRAYING

The painted salamander (*Ensatina eschscholtzi*) of the western USA is the only caudate known to spray noxious chemicals to repel its predators. The 15–18 cm (6–7 in) long animal secretes a powerful, milky neurotoxin from glands at the base of the tail which it can squirt with considerable accuracy over a distance of at least 2.1 m (7 ft). It shifts its body to direct the spray, frequently towards the attacker's face and, in particular, the eyes; in people, a direct hit causes excruciating pain and can even lead to temporary blindness.

California newt

The toxin produced by the California newt is so powerful that one tiny drop is sufficient to kill several thousand mice (although the newt itself is immune to extremely high concentrations).

The painted salamander is currently the only amphibian known to do this though no doubt others will be discovered as research progresses.

★ LEAST DEVELOPMENT

In some newts and salamanders, the larval stage never develops into a 'normal' adult capable of living on land, although it does become sexually mature and can reproduce (a condition called neoteny). The best-known example is the axolotl (*Ambystoma mexicanum*) which was once common in highland lakes of Mexico (it is rarer nowadays due to hunting for food, lake drainage and predation by introduced trout). This species looks rather like a giant newt tadpole (up to 25 cm (10 in) in length) and has small limbs, a vertically flattened tail and bright red, feathery gills. It is capable of metamorphosing into an adult terrestrial form – for example, if its water source dries up – but normally breeds in its aquatic form.

Other species with similar development restrictions include the North American mudpuppy (*Necturus maculosus*) and the European olm (*Proteus anguinus*) which lives in cold, underground limestone caves and rivers along the Adriatic coast of Italy and Croatia.

A small group of eel-like amphibians, called sirens, are permanent larvae which retain external gills throughout their lives and have small front legs but no hind legs. They are so strange that some scientists classify them as being in a completely separate, fourth group of amphibians; normally, however, they are classified with the newts and salamanders (in the family Sirenidae). There are only three species, all of which live in the southeastern USA and Mexico, and they range in size dramatically from about 25 cm (10 in) in the tiny dwarf siren (*Pseudobranchus striatus*), to more than 90 cm (36 in) in the greater siren (*Siren lacertina*).

★ HARDIEST

Many salamanders are capable of withstanding extremely cold conditions. But the 10 cm (4 in) long Siberian salamander (*Salamandrella keyserlingii*) is exceptional and can survive winter temperatures as low as -56°C (-69°F). It is unable to burrow deep into the soil to escape the cold because of the permafrost and so is frequently trapped in the frozen soil and water near the surface. When warmer weather arrives, it 'thaws out' and lives in the same way as other salamanders.

★ MOST VEGETARIAN

The Santa Cruz climbing salamander (*Aneides flaxipunctatus niger*), which lives in the Santa Cruz Mountains on the west coast of the USA, is the only salamander known to eat vegetable matter intentionally (although it eats insects and other animals as well).

It feeds on pieces of fungus which it rips off from the bark of trees. It is uncertain whether this unlikely food is itself a direct source of nutrients or whether the salamander is benefiting more from the numerous bacteria which coat the fungus.

> When many species of salamander lose an eye, limb or tail, their missing pieces may regenerate within a few months (though possibly in a different colour and shape).

Axolotl
The strange-looking axolotl is unusual because it becomes sexually mature, and can reproduce, in the larval stage. The name 'axolotl' stems from an Aztec word meaning 'water monster'.

WORLD RECORD HOLDER

Strangest ribs

The sharp-ribbed salamander (*Pleurodeles waltl*), which lives in Morocco and parts of the south and west of the Iberian peninsula, has a row of wart-like protruberances along its flanks. These mark the points where the ends of the ribs push against the animal's skin. In some individuals the ribs actually poke through the skin (looking like rows of teeth) and the ends may be so sharp that they can easily draw blood if the salamanders are handled.

The spiny newt (*Echinotriton andersoni*), which lives in China, has a similar system. If it is grabbed by a predator, its long, sharp-pointed ribs push out through poison glands in the skin and give the attacker an intense painful injection in the mouth.

Sharp-ribbed salamander
The sharp ribs protruding from the skin may be a form of defence to prevent the 30 cm (12 in) long salamander being swallowed by its many predators.

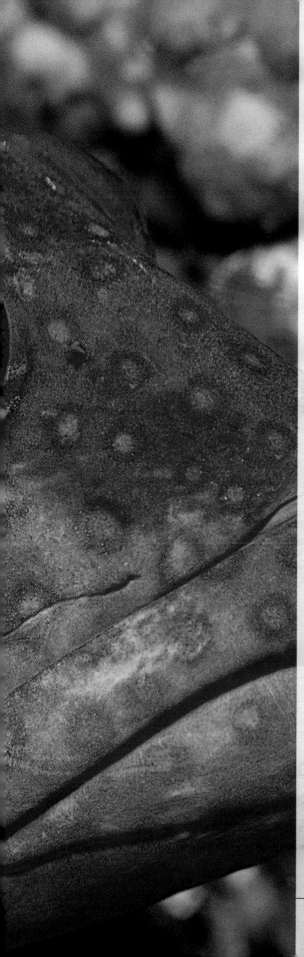

FISH

Coral grouper
A brightly spotted and colourful coral grouper (*Dephalopholis niniata*).

FISH

*Chondrichthyes,
Osteichthyes and Agnatha*

c. 28,000 species (approximately 100
new species discovered every year)

★ EARLIEST

In 2007, scientists working on the
Swedish island of Gotland, in the
Baltic Sea, announced the discovery
of fossils of sardine-sized fish some
420 million years old. The fossilised
jaws and teeth are believed to belong
to the earliest bony fishes ever found
with jaws. Two species have been
identified: *Andreolepis hedei* and
Lophosteus superbus.

★ LARGEST

The world's largest fish is the whale
shark (*Rhincodon typus*), which is found
in tropical and warm temperate waters
of the Atlantic, Pacific and Indian
Oceans. There have been many
unsubstantiated claims of specimens in
the 17–18 m (56–59 ft) range. However,
most experts believe that whale sharks
generally do not exceed a length of
12 m (40 ft). Relatively few have actually
been caught and weighed or measured
and, consequently, the majority of
records are based on visual assessments
(which are notoriously unreliable). It is
especially difficult to estimate the length
of a large animal in the water and,
unfortunately, the tendency is to
overestimate. The largest accurately
measured specimen was captured off
Baba Island, near Karachi, Pakistan, on
11 November 1949. It was 12.65 m
(41½ ft) long and 7 m (23 ft) around the
thickest part of the body; its weight was
estimated to be 15–21 tonnes. Despite
its enormous size, the whale shark feeds

on plankton and is harmless and
unaggressive by nature.

The basking shark (*Cetorhinus
maximus*), which is most common in the
North Atlantic but can also be found in
temperate waters in the South Atlantic
and Pacific, is probably the world's
second largest fish. Circumstantial
evidence suggests a maximum length of
approximately 14–15 m (46–49 ft) but,
despite several claims for specimens of

Whale shark
The world's largest fish is the whale
shark, which has been verified at
lengths of more than 12 m (40 ft) and
may even approach 18 m (59 ft) in
exceptional cases.

this length and even longer, there are no
authenticated records. The best evidence
shows that basking sharks can reach
lengths of at least 12.3 m (40¼ ft).

★ LARGEST BONY

The longest of the bony fish (class Osteichthyes) is the oarfish (*Regalecus glesne*), which has a worldwide distribution in temperate and tropical seas. A specimen seen swimming off Asbury Park, New Jersey, USA, by a team of scientists from the Sandy Hook Marine Laboratory on 18 July 1963, was estimated to measure 15 m (50 ft) in length. Although this is purely an estimate, it is noteworthy because it was seen by experienced observers who, at the time, were aboard the 26 m (85 ft) research vessel *Challenger*, which gave them a yard stick for measuring the fish's length. With regard to scientifically measured records, there are a number of oarfish exceeding 7 m (23 ft) in length; for example, in 1885, a specimen 7.6 m (25 ft) long, weighing 272 kg (600 lb), was caught by fishermen off Pemaquid Point, Maine, USA.

The heaviest and broadest bony fish in the world is the ocean sunfish (*Mola mola*), which is found in all tropical, sub-tropical and temperate waters. The average size of an adult specimen is 1.8 m (6 ft) from the tip of the snout to the end of the tail fin (horizontal length) and 2.4 m (7 ft 10 in) between the tip of the dorsal fin and the tip of the anal fin (vertical length); the average weight is up to 1 tonne. On 18 September 1908 a specimen was accidentally struck by the *SS Fiona* off Bird Island about 65 km (40 miles) from Sydney, New South Wales, Australia, and towed to Port

• Oarfish

The oarfish is a striking fish, looking rather like a flattened silvery band with a red crest and a long red fin along its back; it is the longest bony fish in the world.

GREATEST SIZE DIFFERENCE

With the ocean sunfish (*Mola mola*), the adult measures up to 4 m (13 ft) across (though usually a little under 1 m (39 in)) and yet the newborn is smaller than a pea (only 2.5 mm (1/8 in) in length). It is believed that the eggs are laid in the open ocean.

Jackson. It measured 3.1 m (10 ft) in horizontal length and 4.3 m (14 ft) in vertical length and weighed 2235 kg (4927 lb) – and was the largest specimen ever recorded.

The Russian sturgeon or 'beluga' (*Huso huso*) has also been known to grow to an enormous size, especially in former times when it was more abundant. The largest specimen on record was a gravid female caught in the estuary of the Volga in 1827, which measured 7.3 m (24 ft) in length and weighed 1474 kg (3249 lb), though the average size for this species is considerably less.

★ LARGEST FRESHWATER

The largest fish spending its whole life in fresh or brackish water is the Mekong giant catfish (*Pangasianodon gigas*), found only in the Mekong River and its major tributaries in China, Laos, Cambodia and Thailand. It is known locally as pla buk and the largest specimen, captured in northern Thailand in May 2007, was 2.7m (9 ft) long and weighed 293 kg (646 lb).

However, the individual record for the largest freshwater fish is held by a European or wels catfish (*Silurus glanis*),

which was caught in the Dnieper River, Russia, in the 19th century, and was 4.57 m (15 ft) length and weighed 336.3 kg (720 lb).

The European catfish used to grow to an exceptional size before it was heavily fished – there were often sinister reports of the largest specimens eating small dogs and even children – but nowadays anything over 1.8 m (6 ft) and 90 kg (200 lb) is considered large.

Sturgeons (family Acipenseridae) are also strong contenders, although some live in the sea and only breed in freshwater. The largest species are the white sturgeon (*Acipenser transmontanus*) of North America, the beluga sturgeon (*Huso huso*) and the kaluga sturgeon (*Huso dauricus*). A female beluga sturgeon, caught in Russia's Tikhaya River in 1924, weighed 1227 kg (2706 lb). A white sturgeon caught in the Columbia River, USA and Canada, in 1912, was 3.8 m (12 1/2 ft) long. There are reports of individuals, of several species, growing to be 8.6 m (28 ft) and 2700 kg (5940 lb) but they are not authenticated.

The arapaima or pirarucu (*Arapaima gigas*), from the Amazon and other South American rivers, is often claimed to be the largest freshwater fish in the world. However, the largest authentically recorded specimen, which was caught in the Rio Negro, Brazil, in 1836, measured 'only' 2.48 m (8 ft 1 1/2 in) in length and weighed 147 kg (325 lb). The average size

for this species is 2 m (6½ ft) in length
and 68 kg (150 lb) in weight.

The longest eel ever recorded was
a 3.7 m (12 ft 2 in) leopard moray eel
(*Gymnothorax flavimarginatus*) found in
the Coomera River, Queensland, Australia.
Its body was said to be as thick as a
man's thigh.

★ LARGEST PREHISTORIC

No known prehistoric fish grew
significantly larger than either the whale
shark (*Rhincodon typus*) or the basking
shark (*Cetorhinus maximus*), the two
largest species alive today. However,
a prehistoric shark called megalodon
(*Carcharadon megalodon*) – an extinct
relative of the modern great white shark
(*Carcharodon carcharias*) – was by far
the largest predatory (as opposed to
plankton-feeding) shark known to have
lived on Earth. Recent studies suggest
that it attained a maximum length of
15 m (50 ft), although the size of
megalodon has been a subject for
discussion since the first fossil teeth were
found in the early 1800s. Some estimates
have ranged up to about 37 m (120 ft),
but many of the early assumptions made

are now known to have been in error.
All estimates are based on ratios from
fossil teeth (which are up to 18 cm (7 in)
measured from the tip along one edge
to the base) since these are the only
evidence currently available for the
existence of such an extraordinary
species. Megalodon abounded in the
world's oceans during the middle and late
Tertiary, some 2–50 million years ago.

★ LARGEST PREDATORY

There are a number of sharks that are
thought to reach a length of about 6
m (20 ft) but the largest predatory fish
(excluding plankton-eaters) is currently
thought to be the Greenland shark
(*Somniosus microcephalus*) at 6.4 m
(21 ft). It is closely followed by the
great hammerhead shark (*Sphyrnan
mokarran*) at 6.1 m (20 ft), the great
white shark (*Carcharodon carcharias*)
at 6.1 m (20 ft), the thresher shark
(*Alopias vulpinus*) at 6 m (19 ¾ ft)
(almost half of which is tail) and the
tiger shark (*Galeocerdo cuvier*) at 5.5
m (18 ft). Many consider the great
white to be the predatory fish that
grows consistently to the largest size.

Great white shark
The great white shark is the largest
predatory fish. This one is photographed
breaching off the coast of South Africa.

It is most abundant in cold to warm
temperate waters worldwide. Adult
specimens (females are larger than
males) average 4.3–4.6 m (14–15 ft) in
length and generally weigh 522–771
kg (1150–1700 lb). Stories about the
size of great whites have often been
greatly exaggerated and there are
many claims of huge specimens in
the 6–7.5 m (20–25 ft) range; some
writers and fishermen even quote
lengths in excess of 10 m (33 ft).
However, under close scrutiny, all
of these claims prove to be either
wild exaggerations or genuine
mistakes. The longest was no more
than 6.4 m (21 ft).

★ SMALLEST

The shortest and lightest recorded
species of fish (and, indeed, the shortest
and lightest known vertebrate) in the
world is *Paedocypris progenetica* from
acidic peat swamps in Southeast Asia.

Paedocypris progenetica
This is the smallest species of fish in the world and it is shown here at approximately seven times bigger than lifesize.

Females mature at just 7.9 mm ($^5/_{16}$ in). The parasitic male of a species of angler fish (*Photocorynus spiniceps*) can be even smaller (6.2 mm ($^1/_4$ in)), but it is debatable whether it qualifies as a fish as many of its organs are reduced and females of the species are typically 46–50 mm ($1^3/_4$–2 in) long.

★ MOST VARIED DIET

The tiger shark (*Galeocerdo cuvier*) probably has the most varied diet of all fish. It will eat literally anything it encounters in the water: all kinds of bony fish as well as other sharks; seabirds including cormorants, pelicans and frigatebirds; marine mammals such as dolphins and seals; marine reptiles including sea turtles, sea snakes and marine iguanas; a wide variety of invertebrates such as lobsters, crabs and octopuses; chickens, rats, dogs, cattle and a variety of other domestic animals (some alive and some dead) that happen to fall in the water; and even apparently inedible objects. Not surprisingly, they have been given the nickname 'garbage-can sharks'.

★ HUMAN PARASITISM

The 2.5 cm (1 in) long candiru (*Vandellia cirrhosa*) is the only vertebrate known to be an internal parasite of people, although it enters human bodies only accidentally. This tiny South American catfish has the unpleasant habit of entering the human urinary tract (if the victim urinates in the water).Once inside, it cannot be pulled out because of the erectile spines on its head and gill covers; the only way it can be removed is by surgery. It also parasitizes other fish (passing under the gill cover and between the gills) and even uses its spines to pierce the skin of potential hosts to drink their blood.

Unusual items found in the stomachs of tiger sharks include car tyres, sacks of nails, leather coats, canned fish, wristwatches, car number plates and paint cans.

★ SAME SPECIES PARASITISM

Kroyer's deep-sea anglerfish (*Ceratias holboelli*) is one of about 20 species in the family Ceratiidae in which the male is a parasite of the female. This is believed to be unique among vertebrate animals (although parallels can be found among the invertebrates). Once the male has made contact with a female, he fastens on to her body with his jaws; eventually his blood supply becomes connected to that of his mate and he becomes wholly dependent on her for nourishment and oxygen. There is no fixed place where attachment occurs: the male may be fastened to her side, belly or back, and occasionally two or more males are attached to a single female. In some species, the males and females pair bond for life and remain attached to one another throughout; in others, the males attach themselves to the females only briefly, leaving to resume a free-swimming existence after mating. Female Kroyer's deep-sea anglerfish can grow to 1.2 m (47 in), but the males are rarely longer than 13 cm ($5^1/_8$ in).

★ STRONGEST BITE

Experiments carried out with a 'Snodgrass gnathodynamometer' (shark-bite meter) at the Lerner Marine Laboratory in Bimini, Bahamas, revealed that a 2 m (6 ft $6^3/_4$ in)

Deep sea angler
With most deep sea anglers the female is enormous in comparison to the male, which oftens lives as a parasite on the female. This female is from the family Himantolophidae.

long dusky shark (*Carcharhinus obscurus*) could exert a force of 60 kg (132 lb) between its jaws. This is equivalent to a pressure of 3 tonnes/cm^2 (or 19$^3/_5$ ton/in^2) at the tips of its teeth. The bite of a larger shark such as the great white (*Carcharodon carcharias*) must be considerably more spectacular, but it has never been measured.

✶ LONGEST FAST

The longest known fast by any fish has been recorded in the African lungfish (family Protopteridae), which can remain dormant inside a deep burrow in the muddy bottom of a dried-out swamp for up to four years (*see* SURVIVAL OUT OF WATER opposite).

Sharks are capable of long periods of fasting and even the most active species can survive for six weeks or more without food. The record observed in captivity is for a 1 m (39 in) swell shark (*Cephaloscyllium ventriosum*), which survived for 15 months without eating.

✶ LONGEST TAIL FIN

All three species of thresher shark (family Alopiidae) have a huge scythe-shaped caudal fin (tail fin) which is roughly as long as the body itself. The largest and commonest species, *Alopias vulpinus*, which is found worldwide in temperate and tropical seas, may grow to a length of 6 m (20 ft) of which almost 3 m (10 ft) consists of this greatly elongated

upper tail fin; the body itself is rather sleek and relatively small. Also known as the thrasher or whiptailed shark, it is believed to use its extraordinary tail to herd and then stun schools of milling fish, before turning back to swallow their stunned or dead victims.

✶ SLOWEST

The slowest-moving marine fish are the sea horses (family Syngnathidae) of which there are about 44 species. Their swimming ability is severely limited by a rigid body structure and, indeed, the only parts that can be moved rapidly are the pectoral fins on either side of the back of the head and the dorsal fin along the back. The major source of propulsion is the wave motion of the dorsal fin: this makes a ripple which drives the fish forward in an erect posture. In still water, some of the smaller species such as the dwarf sea horse (*Hippocampus zosterae*), which reaches a maximum length of only 4.2 cm (1$^{11}/_{16}$ in), probably never attain speeds of more than 0.016 km/h ($^1/_{100}$ mph). Sea horses are incapable of swimming against strong currents and, to avoid being swept away, hang on to coral and marine plants with their prehensile tails.

✶ LONGEST MIGRATION

Many fish species undertake long annual migrations, for example between their breeding grounds and favoured feeding grounds. However, it is very difficult to ascertain the maximum distances covered either by different species or by record-breaking individuals. The longest straight-line distance known to have been covered by a fish is 9335 km (5800 miles) for a bluefin tuna (*Thunnus thynnus*) which was dart-tagged off Baja California, Mexico, in 1958, and caught 483 km (300 miles) south of Tokyo, Japan, in April 1963. During its journey, its weight increased from 16 kg (35 lb) to 121 kg (267 lb).

✶ LONGEST FLIGHT

Flying fish in the family Exocoetidae, which have specially adapted pectoral (and sometimes pelvic) fins, are the record-holders in terms of long-distance gliding flight. Depending on the wind and sea conditions, some species are able to remain airborne for as long as 30–40 seconds, can reach a height of up to 10 m (33 ft) (when they catch good air currents) and are able to cover a distance of more than 400 m (1300 ft). They normally fly when they are being pursued by predators and can launch themselves into the air at speeds of up to 30 km/h (20 mph) with a rapid flick of the tail; if they are still being chased when they begin to fall back into the water they flick their tail again and are quickly launched into another flight. When flying fish are swimming, their enormous fan-like pectoral fins are folded away against the body.

Small river-dwelling South American hatchet fishes in the family Gasteropelecidae possess powerful pectoral fin muscles and have been reported beating their fins up and down as if they were flapping true wings in true flight as opposed to the gliding flight of flying fish. However, hatchet fish rarely travel for distances of more than about 10 m (33 ft) above the surface.

★ SURVIVAL OUT OF WATER

The six species of lungfish (families Lepidosirenidae, Protopteridae and Ceratodidae), which can reach a length of up to 1.5 m (5 ft), live in freshwater swamps that frequently dry out for months or even years at a time. One species is found in the Amazon region of South America, one in the Mary and Burnett Risers of northern Queensland, Australia, and four in west, central and southern Africa. In adverse conditions, they can all survive for long periods out of water, but two of the African lungfish

Thresher shark
This thresher shark, in the Philippine Pacific Ocean, has a tail fin roughly equal in length to the rest of its body.

WORLD RECORD HOLDER

Fastest

The sailfish (*Istiophorus platypterus*) is considered to be the fastest species of fish over short distances, although practical difficulties make accurate measurements extremely difficult to secure. This large oceanic fish has a torpedo-shaped body and is streamlined for fast swimming. In a series of speed trials carried out at Long Key Fishing Camp, Florida, USA, one sailfish took out 91 m (300 ft) of line in three seconds, which is equivalent to a velocity of 109 km/h (68 mph) (cf. 96km/h (60 mph) for the cheetah on land).

Some American fishermen believe that the bluefin tuna (*Thunnus thynnus*) is the fastest fish in the sea, and bursts of speed up to 104 km/h (65 mph) have been claimed for this species; however, the highest authenticated speed recorded to date is 70 km/h (44 mph) in a 20 second dash. The marlin (*Makaira sp.*), yellow fin tuna (*Thunnus albacares*) and the wahoo (*Acanthocybium solandri*) are also extremely fast, having been timed at 80 km/h (50 mph), 75 km/h (47 mph) and 77 km/h (48 mph) respectively during 10–20 second sprints.

Most sharks are slow swimmers (even the larger species normally cruise at 1–4 km/h ($^3/_5$–2$^1/_2$ mph) but many of them are capable of rapid bursts of speed when chasing prey. The fastest shark is believed to be the 2.4–3.9 m (8–13 ft) shortfin mako (*Isurus oxyrinchus*), which may be able to attain speeds of up to 88 km/h (55 mph).

Sailfish
The sailfish is probably the fastest fish over short distances.

are the real experts. As the water recedes, they burrow deep into the ground and secrete a mucus to form a moisture-saving cocoon around their bodies. Then they build a porous mud plug at the entrance to the burrow, curl up and wait. As water fills the swamp again, they come to life within the space of a few hours, wriggle out of their burrow and swim away. The mangrove killifish (*Rivulus marmoratus* Poey), found along the east coast of America from Florida to Brazil, spends several months of every year out of water, living inside trees. By altering the way they breathe the killifish can survive by changing their gills to retain

Abandoning gill-breathing in favour of their air-breathing lungs, some lungfish can live for up to four years in a dormant condition during periods of drought.

Frogfish

Frogfish can eat faster than any other vertebrate. They suck their prey into their cavernous mouths much like a vacuum cleaner.

Mudskipper

Mudskippers live in the tropical mudflats and mangrove swamps of Africa, Southeast Asia and Australasia, where they scurry and leap about on the mud and will even climb up the roots of mangrove trees.

water and nutrients, and they excrete nitrogen waste through their bodies. Other fish are able to survive varying lengths of time out of water, provided their skin can remain moist. The European eel (*Anguilla anguilla*), the walking catfish (*Clarias batrachus*) and the climbing perch or gourami (*Anabas testudineus*) are among them. Mudskippers (family Gobiidae) are probably the best known and spend most of their time out of water. They survive by storing water in their large gill chambers so preventing their gills drying out, and can also absorb some oxygen directly from the air through their moist skin. This means that they have to return to the water every few minutes to wet their skin and to take a mouthful of water.

★ FASTEST EATER

Frogfish (family Antennariidae) are voracious predators that can open their mouths and engulf their prey faster than any other vertebrate. There are more than 40 different species, widespread in

tropical and sub-tropical waters around the world. The first spine of the dorsal fin acts as a lure as they lie in wait for any fish or crustacean to pass within striking distance (the strike zone is an area with a radius roughly two-thirds the length of the frogfish). Then they suck the unsuspecting prey into their cavernous mouths as effectively as if they were using a vacuum cleaner. It happens so quickly, opening the mouth and engulfing the prey in just under six milliseconds.

★ LONGEST LIVING

There is little reliable information on the maximum attainable age of fish in the wild and, consequently, most records are for individuals that have been kept in captivity for extended periods. The oldest fish on record is an 88-year-old female European eel (*Anguilla anguilla*) named 'Putte', which used to live in the aquarium at Halsingborg Museum, Sweden. She was allegedly born in 1860 in the Sargasso Sea, North Atlantic, and was caught in a river as a three-year-old elver. She died in 1948.

It is possible to *estimate* the age of wild fish through long-term tagging studies or by counting the growth rings in their scales and bones. Growth ring research suggests that the lake sturgeon (*Acipenser fulvescens*) of North America is one of the longest-lived species in the wild. In one study of the growth rings in the largest ray of the pectoral fin of 966 specimens caught in the Lake Winnebago region, Wisconsin, USA, between 1951 and 1954, the oldest sturgeon was found to be a male (length 2.01 m (6 ft 7 in)), which gave a reading of 82 years. There are several unauthenticated claims for even older lake sturgeon.

In July 1974 a growth-ring count of 228 years was reported for a female ornamental koi (*Cyprinus carpio*), named Hanako, living in a pond in Higashi Shirakawa, Gifu Prefecture, Japan, but the greatest authoritatively accepted age for this species is little more than 50 years.

Most sharks are believed to have a lifespan of approximately 20–40 years, but the spiny dogfish (*Squalus acanthias*) has been reasonably estimated to live for more than 70 years and may even reach 100 years in certain North Pacific populations. There is even one population in which females do not reach sexual maturity until they are 35 years old. Whale sharks may live even longer – up to 150 according to some experts.

★ MOST RESTRICTED RANGE

The devil's hole pupfish (*Cyprinodon diabolis*) is confined to a small part of a spring-fed pool (known as Devil's Hole) in Ash Meadows, Nevada, western USA (although a small number have been recently translocated to another spring nearby). It is believed to have the most restricted range of any vertebrate on Earth. Measuring about 20 m (65½ ft) long and 2.5–3.1 m (8¼–10 ft) wide, the pool is in the middle of an otherwise waterless desert. It is about 15 m (50 ft) below ground level and was once part of a water-filled cave – until the roof collapsed many years ago and exposed it to the desert sun. The pupfish depends

for its food on a limited supply of invertebrates living in the algae on a rock shelf just 6 m (20 ft) long and 3 m (10 ft) wide, which lies just below the water surface. The total population varies from 200–500, depending on local conditions.

★ LONGEST ABSENCE

The coelacanths (*Latimeria chalumnae*) are large, deep-water fish that 'went missing' for about 70–80 million years. Formerly known only from fossilized remains some 70–400 million years old, they were presumed to have become extinct at around the same time as the dinosaurs. Then completely out of the blue, on 22 December 1938, a coelacanth was captured in a trawler's net off the mouth of the Chalumna River, near East London, South Africa, at a depth of 67 m (220 ft). The scientific world was stunned: the discovery was almost equivalent to finding a living dinosaur and many

Coelacanth
The coelacanth 'went missing' for about 70-80 million years: formerly known only from fossilized remains, it was unexpectedly rediscovered in 1938 and nearly 200 specimens have been found since.

experts considered it to be the zoological find of the century. Several years passed before another specimen was caught, this time by a fisherman 1600 km (1000 miles) away off the coast of the Comoros, an isolated archipelago northwest of Madagascar in the Indian Ocean. Further research revealed that the local fishermen had been hauling in the odd coelacanth for many years and, indeed, almost all 300 coelacanths found since 1938 have come from the Comoros. None of those caught alive have survived for more than a few minutes or, rarely, a few hours.

Live coelacanths have been observed on a number of occasions since the first sighting in the Comoros Islands in 1987. In 2000, six of them were spotted by divers while they were exploring a reef in Sodwana Bay, South Africa.

Living coelacanths, which grow up to 1.9 m (6¼ ft) in length, do not differ significantly from their fossil counterparts and have been dubbed as 'living fossils'. Some scientists believe that their muscular, paddle-like fins may hold clues to the crucial stage of evolution when aquatic creatures first developed limbs and took to the land.

★ LARGEST EGG

The largest egg produced by any living fish is that of the whale shark (*Rhincodon typus*). The largest on record measured 30.5 x 14 x 8.9 cm (12 x 5½ x 3½ in) and contained a live embryo 35 cm (13¾ in) long, although this particular specimen may have been aborted. It was found on 29 June 1953 by a shrimp trawler in the Gulf of Mexico fishing about 200 km (125 miles) south of Port Isabel, Texas, USA.

★ LONGEST GESTATION PERIOD

Sharks have some of the longest gestation periods known in the animal kingdom, with a minimum of about five months. The longest recorded is 20–22 months in the piked dogfish (*Squalus megalops*), which gives birth to an average of ten 25 cm (10 in) pups.

★ MOST FEROCIOUS

The razor-toothed piranhas of the genera *Serrasalmus* and *Pygocentrus* are reputed to be the most ferocious freshwater fish in the world. They live in the sluggish waters of the large rivers of South America, and will attack any creature, regardless of size, if it is injured. Carnivorous piranhas live mainly

South American Indians sometimes use the jaws of piranha fish as razor blades.

on fish, but their razor-sharp teeth and powerful jaws mean that, given a chance, they can also tear mammalian flesh. The danger piranhas represent to humans has been greatly exaggerated over the years

Piranha
Piranhas have a reputation for being the most ferocious freshwater fish in the world: their razor-sharp teeth and powerful jaws are certainly capable of tearing flesh to shreds in seconds.

and, indeed, not all of them are voracious predators: some of the 40 or so species are almost exclusively vegetarian, feeding on seeds, fruits, leaves and flowers. Nevertheless, some of the larger members of the genus *Serrasalmus*, in particular, can be a hazard and may attack *en masse*. On 19 September 1981 more than 300 people were reportedly killed and eaten when an overloaded passenger-cargo boat capsized and sank as it was docking

at the Brazilian port of Obidos. According to one official, only 178 of the estimated number of people aboard the boat survived.

The bluefish (*Pomatomus saltatrix*) is often described as the most ferocious marine fish. Found in tropical and warm temperate seas in many parts of the world, it grows to a length of 1.2 m (47 in) and is best known for its strong conical teeth. A schooling fish, it sometimes hunts in packs of thousands that form feeding frenzies, attacking schools of mackerel, herring and other fish – by snapping at their prey indiscriminately and leaving a trail of dead and dying fish in their wake.

★ HIGHEST

The world's highest living fish is the Tibetan loach (family Cobitidae), which is found at an altitude of 5200 m (17,000 ft) in the Himalayas.

★ DEEPEST

Brotulids of the genus *Abyssobrotula* are regarded as the deepest-living vertebrates. The deepest ever recorded was a specimen of *Abyssobrotula galatheae* captured in 1970 at a depth of 8370 m (27,450 ft) in the Puerto Rico trench, by the vessel *John Elliot Pillsbury*.

Dr Jacques Piccard and Lt Don Walsh of the US Navy reported seeing a sole-like fish about 33cm (1 ft) long (tentatively identified as *Chascanopsetta lugubris*) from the bathyscaphe *Trieste* at a depth of 10,918 m (35,820 ft) in the Challenger Deep (Marianas Trench) in the western Pacific on 24 January 1960. This sighting, however, has been strongly challenged by many authorities.

More than 125 species of fish, belonging to over a dozen different families, spend their entire lives in lightless, underground caves or even in

Stingray
This colourful ribbontail ray pictured here in the Red Sea is one of the most venomous fish in the world.

aquifers (water-bearing rock). Most of them live in tropical or warm temperate countries and tend to be colourless and have minute eyes or no eyes at all. Some of the better-known 'cave-dwellers' include the Mexican blind cave tetra (*Astyanax mexicanus*) and a subterranean loach (family Cobitidae) that lives in Iran.

★ MOST ELECTRIC

More than 250 species of fish have evolved the capacity to generate electrical pulses from specialized 'electric organs'. These are used variously for communication (the pulses emitted are recognized by other members of the same species); in a form of electrical echolocation (small electrical pulses are emitted and then bounce back from objects in the water to special electro-receptors in the skin); and to stun or kill both prey and predators (many species can deliver a painful or even fatal electric shock). The most powerful electric fish is the electric eel (*Electrophorus electricus*) from the slow, turbid rivers of northern South America. Despite its name, it is not a true eel but is related to characins in the order Cypriniformes. It has three electric organs (which are derived from muscle tissue and innervated by spinal

nerves) occupying up to 80% of its body. An average-sized specimen can discharge 1 amp at 400 volts, but measurements of up to 650 volts were recorded for a 41 kg (90 lb) individual in the New York Aquarium in the 1930s. This would be sufficient to kill a person on contact or to stun a horse at a distance of 6 m (20 ft).

★ MOST VENOMOUS

Many fish are venomous, including the stingrays (family Dasyatidae), chimaeras (family Chimaeridae), catfish (families Ariidae, Clariidae and Plotosidae), weaverfish (family Trachinidae), toadfish (family Batrachoididae), surgeonfish (family Acanthuridae), stargazers (family Uranoscopidae), scorpionfish (family Scorpaenidae) and the stonefish (family Synanceiidae). The most venomous are the

Stonefish
The most venomous fish is the stonefish, whose spiny dorsal fins release a venomous toxin which inflicts excruciatingly painful wounds often proving fatal.

stonefish, whose spines inflict excruciatingly painful wounds which often prove fatal. Most injuries are caused by people accidentally treading on the fish, which erect their spines when danger threatens; they are so well camouflaged that they are almost impossible to see.

The most venomous of all the 30 or so species of stonefish is the 60 cm (24 in) Indian stonefish (*Synanceia horrida*), which is found in shallow waters throughout the Indo-Pacific, Australia, China and India. It has the largest venom glands of any known fish, each of which is connected to one of 13 grooved dorsal spines. These spines are so sharp that they are capable of piercing the sole of a beach shoe – and inject the strong neurotoxin poison into the wound as efficiently as a hypodermic syringe.

Two species of shark are known to be venomous (*see also* MOST POISONOUS p. 204*)*, the 1.5 m (5 ft) spurdog or spin dogfish (*Squalus acanthias*) and the similar-sized Port Jackson shark (*Heterodontus portusjacksoni*), both of which have specially adapted venomous spines located at the front part of each of their two dorsal fins.

The pain of stonefish venom is so intense that victims frequently become delirious and frenzied, striking or biting anyone trying to help them.

Death puffer
This whitespotted puffer, found near Borneo, Indonesia, is the most poisonous fish. Its viscera, gonads and skin are all highly toxic.

★ MOST POISONOUS

Many species of fish are poisonous to eat, but the most poisonous are the puffer fish (family Tetraodontidae), named for their ability to inflate themselves into a balloon shape by swallowing water or air whenever they feel threatened. The overall record-holder is the notorious death or white-spotted puffer or maki-maki (*Arothron hispidus*), which is found in a broad stretch of ocean from the Red Sea across the Indian Ocean and into much of the South Pacific. Its ovaries and eggs, blood, liver, intestines and, to a lesser extent, its skin contain a virulent poison (called tetrodotoxin) which can kill anyone who eats even a moderate amount. Less than 0.1 g ($^4/_{1000}$ oz) is enough to kill an adult in as little as 20 minutes.

Sufferers of tetrodotoxin poisoning experience extremely unpleasant symptoms: they may remain conscious but cannot swallow, see, speak or move.

In Japan, where the puffer fish is known as *fugu*, its flesh is considered to be a great delicacy and affluent Japanese pay high prices to eat it in specially licensed restaurants. After a three-year apprenticeship, highly qualified chefs remove the poisonous parts without contaminating the rest of the fish: their objective is to retain just enough of the poison to produce a numbing sensation in the lips and tongue – and, of course, the thrill of flirting with death – but not enough to cause tetrodotoxin poisoning. Unfortunately, many non-experts also prepare the fish; consequently, there are about 30 deaths every year – making tetrodotoxin the number one cause of fatal food poisoning in Japan.

The liver (and sometimes other internal organs) of many sharks can be poisonous and may cause 'elasmobranch poisoning'. However, the flesh of only one species of shark is known to be poisonous to eat: the Greenland shark (*Somniosus microcephalus*), which is an inhabitant of the Arctic and cold temperate waters. It is most toxic when fresh but can be eaten if dried and prepared by an expert.

BEST SENSE OF SMELL

Sharks have a better sense of smell and more highly developed scent organs than any other fish. Well known for detecting blood from great distances, they can detect the equivalent of a few drops of blood in an olympic-sized swimming pool. It is said they can even smell other fish's fear.

★ MOST VARIATIONS

Freshwater fish have a greater tendency than almost any other animal to become divided into separate populations, because connecting waterways frequently become impassable. Therefore many species have a range of ecologically and physically distinct variations. The best known example is the brown trout (*Salmo trutta*) of northern Europe, whose breeding habit (returning to the river of birth to spawn) ensures that each population remains genetically isolated as surely as if it were living on an island; consequently, the trout has a great many widely differing populations, both in way of life and appearance. In the past, these have all been divided into as many as 50 different species but, in theory, they are still sufficiently similar genetically to be able to interbreed and so modern biologists classify them all as a single species.

★ MOST VALUABLE

The world's most valuable fish is the beluga sturgeon (*Huso huso*). Rubbed gently to remove the mucus, washed in wine or vinegar, and then dried or salted, the sturgeon's eggs become caviar – the most expensive fish dish in the world. One 1227 kg (2706 lb) female caught in the Tikhaya River in 1924 yielded 245 kg (540 lb) of best-quality caviar, which would be worth nearly £1.2 million (US$2.4 million) on today's market. The sturgeon is also one of the largest freshwater fish in the world, frequently growing to a length of 5 m (16½ ft) and a weight of 1524 kg (3360 lb): a large fish produces up to five million eggs in one spawning. Sturgeon numbers have decreased greatly in recent years and there is now serious concern for the future of the species.

★ BEST SHOT

The archer fish (*Toxotes jaculator*) and its relatives are able to spit drops of water at insects perched on overhanging leaves and branches and shoot them down. The water is ejected in little droplets, rather

Archer fish
The highly accurate archer fish is pictured here spitting a jet of water at a spider to try and make it fall off its leaf.

like pellets from an airgun, and hits the insects with incredible force and accuracy. An experienced adult can score a direct hit on a victim more than 1.5 m (5 ft) above the water's surface – sometimes even when it is in flight. When the insect or spider falls into the water, it is promptly eaten. Living in muddy salt and freshwater habitats in India, Malaysia and northern Australia, the archer fish is almost invisible as it swims towards its prey just below the surface.

✴ FRESHWATER SHARKS

Sharks are geared to life in the sea but several are able to tolerate brackish water for short periods and two are known to spend a significant amount of time in freshwater: the bull shark (*Carcharhinus leucas*) and the Ganges shark (*Glyphis gangeticus*). The bull shark is found further from the sea – up to 3700 km (2300 miles) away in the upper Amazon – than any other member of the family. It is found in many other rivers, including the Hooghly, the Zambezi and the Mississippi, and was once believed to be land-locked in Lake Nicaragua, Central America, but is now known to negotiate rapids and return to the sea. The relatively rare Ganges shark is known only from the Ganges and Hooghly Rivers in India, and possibly in nearby inshore waters; it has a terrible reputation for man-eating, but most human deaths attributed to it are probably caused by the bull shark.

✴ COUNTRY WITH MOST SHARK ATTACKS

An analysis of cases in the *International Shark Attack File* (ISAF) reveals that the 522 unprovoked shark attacks recorded worldwide in the 1990s were centered on very few locations: Florida (185), South Africa (55), Brazil (49), Hawaii (33), Australia (28), California (26), New Zealand (17) and the rest of the world (129). As in most recent years, the majority of attacks were in the USA – no less than 47%. However, many go

Most dangerous shark

Sharks have a bad public image that is largely undeserved. There are no fewer than 410 known species and most of them are harmless to people; indeed, more people die each year from bee stings than from shark attacks. However, nearly 42 species have been known to attack people (or are suspected of attacking people) and about half of these are considered to be highly dangerous. A number of others have the potential to be dangerous. The most dangerous species are those that habitually attack people: the great white shark (*Carcharodon carcharias*), the tiger shark (*Galeocerdo cuvier*), the bull shark (*Carcharinus leucas*) and, in some situations, the oceanic white tip (*Carcharhinus longimanus*).

More attacks on humans are attributed to the great white shark than to any other species. However, in reality, the identification of the shark in many of these attacks is suspect: telling one species from another can be very difficult at the best of times, but it is not surprising that the great white is often the first shark that comes to mind in an attack situation. The fact is that most attacks occur in the tropics, whereas the great white is normally found in cool, temperate waters. It is also relevant that the great white is not a particularly common animal; in recent decades it has suffered from a bad press (particularly after the release of the film *Jaws*) and the resulting human predation has caused population declines in many parts of its range. But none of this detracts from the undeniable fact that the great white accounts for a significant proportion of all fatal shark attacks (20–35% depending on which estimates are to be believed) and that it is certainly one of the world's most dangerous sharks.

Many experts believe that the bull shark has probably attacked more people than any other species of shark. This certainly seems possible. It is a large shark with massive jaws; it has an indiscriminate appetite with a propensity for large prey; it occurs close to shore in tropical waters and therefore is more likely to come into contact with human swimmers and divers; and it is far more common than the great white.

Like most animals, even small sharks will retaliate aggressively if they are provoked or feel threatened and many attacks on people are by sharks that are as little as 2 m (6 ft 7 in) long: these species have been dubbed 'man-attackers' rather than 'man-eaters'. The attacks normally consist of quick 'keep-your-distance' bites – normally aimed at divers who deliberately approach or try to touch the animals. In this category, the blacktip reef shark (*Carcharhinus melanopterus*) and the sand tiger shark (*Carcharias taurus*), which reach lengths of 1.8 m (6 ft) and 3.2 m ($10^1/_2$ ft) respectively, are responsible for the largest number of bites.

It is estimated that only about 50–100 people are attacked by sharks every year, and on average 5–15 of these attacks prove fatal (these figures do not include the victims of shipwrecks that succumb to unknown numbers of shark attacks). There is little documentation for many parts of the world and it is likely that more attacks and fatalities go unrecorded. There are three distinct kinds of shark attack: hit-and-run attacks (the most common) are rarely life-threatening and likely cases of mistaken identity; bump-and-bite attacks (rarer but more dangerous) are probably active feeding or territorial; and sneak attacks, which are active feeding and involve repeated biting and multiple injuries.

Great white shark
More attacks on humans are attributed to the great white shark than to any other species, although it is not always to blame.

unrecorded, especially after shipwrecks or around the coasts of developing countries.

Worldwide, there are typically 50–100 shark attacks every year, resulting in about 5–15 deaths. The number of unprovoked shark attacks has grown at a steady rate over the past century. There were more confirmed unprovoked attacks during the 1990s than during any previous decade on record. But this does not reflect a change in the per capita rate of attack and does not mean that sharks are getting more dangerous. There are simply more people in the sea these days, so more attacks are to be expected. Also, the scientific network and techniques used to discover, investigate and file shark attacks have improved enormously in recent years. In the past decade, in particular, greater interest in shark attacks worldwide, coupled with the ISAF's strong web presence, has resulted in many shark attacks being reported that could easily have been missed in the past.

★ WORST SHARK ATTACK BEACH

New Smyrna Beach, Volusia County, Florida, has more shark attacks than any other beach in the world. Some 10–15 surfers are bitten here in an average year and there were no fewer than six attacks over a single weekend in August 2001. Most of these are not too serious, believed to be by sharks mistaking the soles of the surfers' feet and the palms of their hands for the flashing white flesh of fish.

Florida usually accounts for the most attacks worldwide – making it *the* shark attack hotspot. There are several possible reasons why: it has 2054 km (1277 miles) of coastline, it is home to many potentially dangerous species of shark, and there are huge numbers of people (residents and tourists) in the water at any one time.

★ WORST SHARK ATTACK

It is believed that sharks killed hundreds of men during one attack on 28 November 1942. When a German U-boat

Tiger shark
This is one of the potentially most dangerous sharks for humans, known to attack and eat nearly anything. However, many people have dived with them safely.

fired a salvo of torpedoes into the hull of the Liverpool steamer *Nova Scotia* some 48 km (30 miles) off the coast of Zululand, South Africa, the ship went down in seven minutes and 900 men (including 765 Italian prisoners of war) were thrown into the sea. According to the 192 survivors, who were rescued by a Portuguese sloop, at least half of the men that died were taken by sharks. This fatality rate seems quite possible as the Portuguese sailors had to keep huge numbers of sharks away with boat hooks during the rescue operations; also it is unlikely that the men simply drowned because they were young, fit and the sea was warm enough for them to survive. This is one of the worst attacks on record but there were a substantial number of other shipwrecks during the War where hundreds were also killed by sharks.

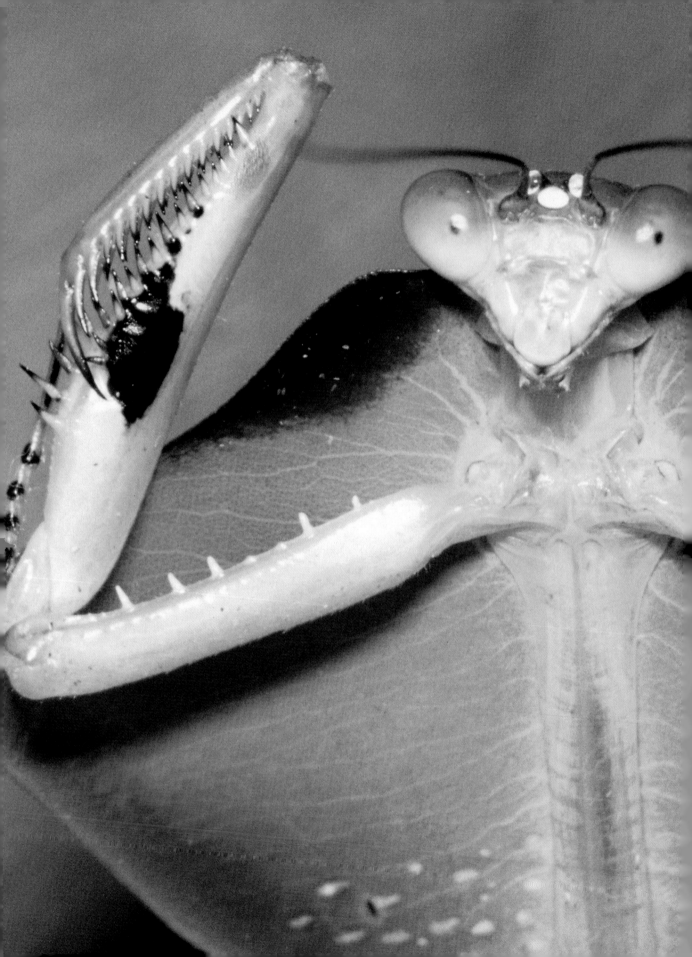

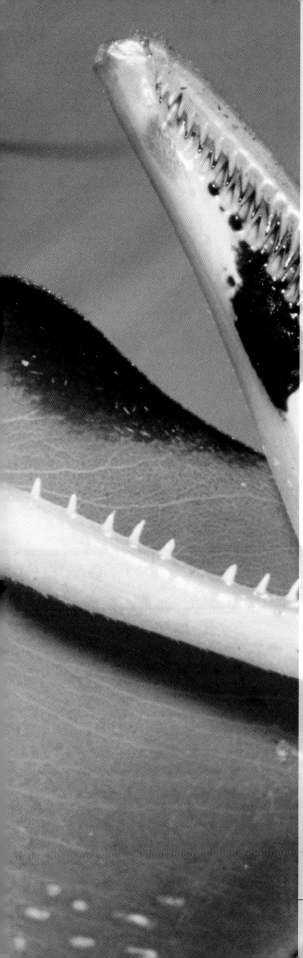

INVERTEBRATES

Tropical shield mantis
This is a tropical shield mantis
(*Choeradodis stalii*) in a typically
aggressive threat display.

ARACHNIDS

Arachnida

c. 70,000–100,000 species. The class Arachnida consists of spiders and ten other orders – harvestmen, ticks and mites, wind spiders, tailless whip spiders, whip spiders, scorpions, palpigrades, pseudoscorpions, schizomids and ricinuleids – nearly all have eight legs and two parts to their bodies

SCORPIONS

Scorpiones

c. 1520 species

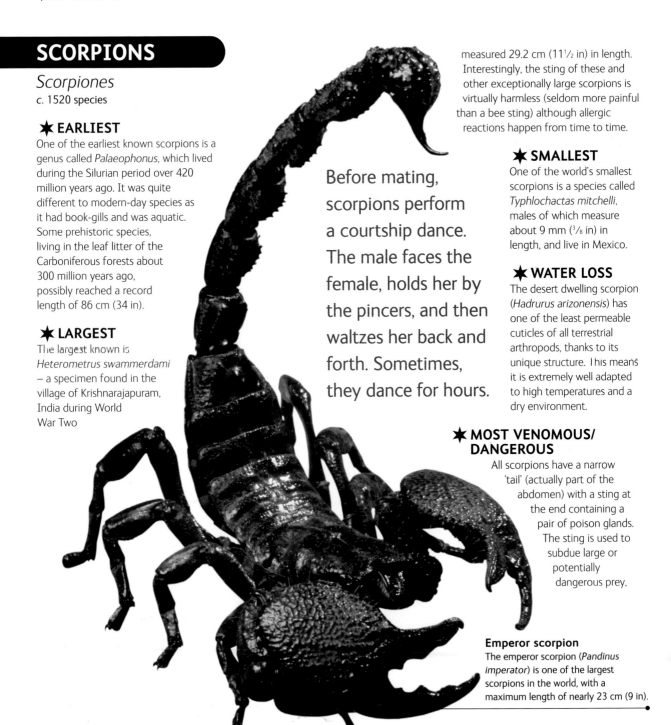

★ EARLIEST

One of the earliest known scorpions is a genus called *Palaeophonus*, which lived during the Silurian period over 420 million years ago. It was quite different to modern-day species as it had book-gills and was aquatic. Some prehistoric species, living in the leaf litter of the Carboniferous forests about 300 million years ago, possibly reached a record length of 86 cm (34 in).

★ LARGEST

The largest known is *Heterometrus swammerdami* – a specimen found in the village of Krishnarajapuram, India during World War Two

Before mating, scorpions perform a courtship dance. The male faces the female, holds her by the pincers, and then waltzes her back and forth. Sometimes, they dance for hours.

measured 29.2 cm (11½ in) in length. Interestingly, the sting of these and other exceptionally large scorpions is virtually harmless (seldom more painful than a bee sting) although allergic reactions happen from time to time.

★ SMALLEST

One of the world's smallest scorpions is a species called *Typhlochactas mitchelli*, males of which measure about 9 mm (³/₈ in) in length, and live in Mexico.

★ WATER LOSS

The desert dwelling scorpion (*Hadrurus arizonensis*) has one of the least permeable cuticles of all terrestrial arthropods, thanks to its unique structure. This means it is extremely well adapted to high temperatures and a dry environment.

★ MOST VENOMOUS/ DANGEROUS

All scorpions have a narrow 'tail' (actually part of the abdomen) with a sting at the end containing a pair of poison glands. The sting is used to subdue large or potentially dangerous prey,

Emperor scorpion
The emperor scorpion (*Pandinus imperator*) is one of the largest scorpions in the world, with a maximum length of nearly 23 cm (9 in).

and in self-defence. Most scorpions are not aggressive and will only sting if they are touched or frightened. The venom of most species, while sufficiently toxic to kill small animals, is innocuous to people and causes little more than a sharp burning sensation. However, a number of species could kill a human. The most dangerous scorpions have small, slim claws and thick tails, and are in the family Buthidae.

The sting of an Indian red scorpion can cause death in minutes.

The world's most venomous scorpion is the Palestine yellow scorpion (*Leiurus quinquestriatus*), which is often called the 'death stalker'. It is found from the eastern part of north Africa through the Middle East to the Red Sea. Fortunately, the amount of venom it delivers with each sting is small and adult lives are seldom endangered. Symptoms after being bitten include respiratory difficulties, excessive sweating and fluid in the lungs.

Other notoriously dangerous scorpions include the hector scorpion (*Androctonus australisi*) from the drier parts of northern Africa including parts of the Sahara, several species in the genus *Centruroides* from Mexico and southern USA, several species in the genus *Tityus* from South America and Trinidad, *Buthus occitanus*, which occurs in many countries around the Mediterranean as well as north Africa (although individuals in southern Europe are not considered dangerous to people), and the Indian red scorpion (*Mesobuthus tamulus*) from India. In fatalities involving *M. tamulus*, the interval between the sting and death varies from several minutes up to a gruelling 30 hours.

The number of fatalities due to scorpion stings varies according to the species and the age of the victim: mortality is much higher among children than adults, due to their smaller body size. For example, in Trinidad 0.25% of adults die after a scorpion sting compared to 25% of children under five years old.

Golden orb-web spider
The world's largest and strongest webs are built by golden orb-web spiders. They have been known to measure up to 1.5 m (5 ft) in circumference, with considerably longer (6.1m (20ft)) supporting guy-lines. The colourful females in the genus *Nephila* are giants compared to the tiny brown males.

SPIDERS

Araneae
c. 40,000 species

✸ EARLIEST
Since spiders are soft-bodied creatures they are not easily fossilised and, consequently, there are huge gaps in our knowledge of prehistoric species. The earliest known spider has been identified from fossils dating back to the Devonian period, some 350–400 million years ago. As a group, spiders are believed to have been abundant for the first time during the Carboniferous period, about 300 million years ago.

✸ LARGEST
The world's largest spider is not a tarantula as you might expect. It is a species of huntsman spider (*Heteropoda maxima*, family Sparassidae), found in Laos. Males have a huge leg span of 30 cm (12 in) – not one to share a bath with.

SIZE DIFFERENCE
The greatest size difference between the sexes is in golden orb-web spiders of the genus *Nephila*. The massive silver, black and yellow females are giants compared to the diminutive brown males; in some tropical species, the females weigh hundreds of times more than their mates.

✸ SMALLEST
The smallest known spiders are the so-called midget spiders (family Symphytognathidae), the tiniest of which is probably the pale yellow *Patu morplesi* of Western Samoa, southwest Pacific. A male specimen was found in moss at an altitude of *c.* 600 m (2000 ft) in Madolelei, Upolu, in January 1965, and measured 0.43 mm ($^1/_{64}$ in) overall – smaller than a pin head.

The smallest known female spider belongs to a new species *Anapistula caecula*, recently discovered in leaf-litter

in the Ivory Coast, West Africa. This white, blind spider measures just 0.46 mm (^{1}/₆₄ in) long. Since male spiders are generally smaller than their mates, the undiscovered male *A. caecula* may yet beat the current champion as the world's smallest spider.

★ LARGEST WEB

The largest spider webs are built by tropical golden orb-web spiders in the genus *Nephila*. Allegedly, the largest properly measured was found in the Karrakpur Hills, near Monghyr, central Bihar, India, and was 1.5 m (5 ft) in circumference. It had long supporting guy-lines up to 6.1 m (20 ft) in length.

The largest communal web is built by a communal spider (*Ixeuticus socialis*), from Australia, and can apparently measure up to 3.7 m (12 ft 2 in) in length and 1.2 m (3 ft 11 in) in width.

★ SMALLEST WEB

The smallest spider webs are built by midget spiders from the family Symphytognathidae and may be less than 10 mm (^{3}/₈ in) wide.

★ STRONGEST SILK

Spider silk is the strongest of all natural and human-made fibres – much stronger than silk from the delicate webs spun by silkworms and even stronger than steel. The dragline of a European garden spider (*Araneus diadematus*), for example, can support a weight of 0.5 g (^{1}/₅₀ oz) without snapping, whereas a steel strand of similar thickness will snap under the strain of just 0.25 g (^{1}/₁₀₀ oz). Golden orb-web spiders in the genus *Nephila* are believed to produce the strongest of all spider silks.

★ SILK ELASTICITY

Spider silk has a unique combination of strength and elasticity that no existing human-made fibre can match. The most elastic silk of all is produced by the ogre-faced or gladiator spiders (family Dinopidae), which can be stretched six-fold without snapping and then revert to

Garden spider

Spider silk has a unique combination of strength and elasticity that no existing human-made fibre can match. The silk of this garden spider is stronger even than steel.

Spider silk is so strong that catching a fly in flight with a web is equivalent to stopping a jet aircraft with a net made of strands a few centimetres (an inch) thick.

their normal length without any obvious sign of distortion. For comparison, a steel thread snaps when it is stretched to barely 8% of its original length.

A team of engineers and molecular biologists from Massachusetts, USA, is working to produce a synthetic spider's silk as good as the real thing – to use in medical, industrial and military markets such as making stronger bullet-proof vests. Army vests are currently made of Kevlar, which can stretch by up to 4%

before breaking, while spider silks can stretch by considerably more before breaking. Spider silk can absorb much more energy (from a bullet, for example) without the vest failing.

★ LARGEST MEAL

It is unusual for spiders to tackle prey much larger than themselves, although some crab spiders (family Thomisidae) ambush and kill animals several times their own size. For example, an individual no more than 6 mm (1/4 in) will tackle prey as large as bees and butterflies. They use a fast-acting venom, which immobilises the prey quickly and reduces the risk of the spider getting hurt. The large tarantulas of South America, particularly those in the genera *Grammostola* and *Lasiodora*, are known to kill and eat pit vipers and rattlesnakes. In the early 1920s, a captive spider in the genus *Grammostola* reportedly killed and ate two frogs, a small rattlesnake and a highly venomous Jararaca snake within just four days.

There is a report from 1919 of a 'barking' spider (*Selenocosmia* sp) in Australia dragging a chicken a distance of 16 m (52½ ft) to its hole.

★ EGGS

The number of eggs laid in a single batch varies from just two by *Oonops domesticus*, a small pinkish spider no longer than 2 mm (1/16 in), to over 2000 by *Cupiennius*, a wandering spider (family Ctenidae). The eggs range in size from only a fraction of a millimetre across, in the case of *Oonops* and many other species, to the size of a small pea in the case of some of the bird-eating spiders.

★ FASTEST RUNNER

Spiders are capable of moving swiftly, even after long periods of inactivity, but normally cannot sustain their speed for more than a few seconds at a time. Allegedly, the fastest recorded spider was a female house spider (*Tegenaria atrica*) which reached a maximum speed of 1.9 km/h (1¼ mph) over short distances during a series of experiments held in the UK in 1970. This is exceptionally fast considering that, effectively, the spider covered a distance equivalent to 330 times her own body length in just 10 seconds.

★ HEAVIEST

The heaviest spiders are female bird-eating spiders (family Theraphosidae). A female scarlet bird-eater (*Lasiodora klugii*) was quoted as one-time record holder, although females of the goliath bird-eating spider (*Theraphosa blondi*) are usually thought of as the heaviest. There is a record of a captive *T. blondi* that weighed in at 155 g (5½ oz).

Goliath bird-eating spider
The heaviest spider is the female goliath bird eating spider from South America. Despite the name, it does not normally eat birds, instead eating mostly invertebrates and sometimes vertebrates such as mice, snakes and lizards.

★ BEST EYESIGHT

Most spiders have relatively poor eyesight and are able to distinguish little more than day from night. They rely mainly on touch and vibrations to tell them what is happening in the world. But some day-active species can see surprisingly well at close range. The best eyesight probably belongs to the tropical jumping spiders (family Salticidae). They have eight eyes. The two biggest – which are in the middle of the front row – have a very narrow field of vision, but can perceive sharp images of objects as far as 30 cm (12 in) away. The smaller, secondary ones have a much greater field of vision and enable them to judge distances with a high degree of accuracy. Jumping spiders are also believed to have good colour vision.

★ LARGEST EYES

Ogre-faced or gladiator spiders (in the genus *Dinopis*) have probably the largest simple eyes of any arthropod, measuring up to 1.4 mm ($\frac{1}{16}$ in) across. They do not produce very clear images, but do have excellent light-gathering power for night work (equivalent to an f-number of 0.6 and therefore better than most camera lenses). When staring at a bright light, their eyes shine like a pair of headlamps.

Spitting spider

Many of the spitting spiders literally spit a quick-setting glue over their prey or potential predators from their fangs, so the prey is left rooted to the spot unable to escape.

★ SPITTING

There are over 100 species of spitting spiders in the genus *Scytodes*, found mainly in the tropics. The glue is produced (in very small amounts) in modified poison glands and then fired in sticky streams from the two fangs. It happens so quickly that it is impossible to see with the human eye – the spider simply seems to shake its head region and the prey is covered. During aggressive encounters, spitting spiders will also spit over one another, typically covering their opponent's head and forelegs with glue. Sometimes, the spat-upon spiders are unable to remove the glue, and die. This remarkable hunting and defence technique is unknown in any other group of spiders.

★ MOST SOCIAL

Very few spiders are social. However, around 40 species demonstrate varying levels of sociality, from mutual tolerance and simple mother-offspring relationships to living in shared nests and working together to build webs, looking after the young and catching prey.

Probably one of the most social species is a lynx spider (*Tapinillus*) belonging to the family Oxyopidae. It was discovered in 1994 by an American zoologist working in the rainforests of Cuyabeno Nature Reserve, Ecuador, where dozens or even hundreds of the spiders live together. Their three-dimensional communal webs are woven around the ends of tree branches and accommodate equal numbers of adults of both sexes as well as juveniles of different ages. Interestingly, research has revealed all the spiders in a web (apart

> Spiders are generally solitary creatures and if they happen to meet they tend to eat one another.

Black widow spider
The venom of the black widow spider is claimed to be 15 times more potent than the venom of a rattlesnake, and it is this spider which has caused some of the most serious bites across the world.

from a few males) are the offspring of a single pair, suggesting parallels with ants and other social insects.

★ MOST SERIOUS BITES

The largest number of serious bites are probably caused by the 30 or so species of widow spiders (*Lactrodectus* sp) which are found in North, Central and South America, southern Europe, north Africa, Asia, Australia and New Zealand. They are extremely common and widespread and frequently come into contact with people.

Australia's Sydney funnel-web spider (*Atrax robustus*) and a number of other species are also close contenders. The funnel-web is remarkable in that the male is most dangerous to people. In all other highly poisonous spiders it is the female.

★ MOST DANGEROUS

Spiders are feared and hated far beyond their power to do harm. All (except a small number in the family Uloboridae) are venomous – the venom is used for defence and for killing and digesting their prey. But by far the majority are incapable of biting people. In the spiders that do sometimes inflict injuries (several hundred species altogether), the venom typically causes little more than a small amount of discomfort, normally felt as a slight stinging sensation and persistent irritation, or like a wasp or bee sting.

Only a very small number of these (around 30 of the 40,000 known species) are really dangerous to people, and even then few bite unless they are provoked. When they do, it can be very painful: in some cases the intensity is almost unbearable. The development of antivenoms has dramatically reduced the number of deaths caused by spider bites, although a small number of people (usually young children and the elderly) die every year. Thousands of others are laid up for days or even weeks after serious bites.

The world's most venomous spiders are the Brazilian wandering spiders of the genus *Phoneutria*. In particular, the Brazilian huntsman (*P. fera*) is widely believed to have the most active neurotoxic venom of any living spider. This spider is very aggressive and will certainly bite if provoked. Symptoms include excruciating pain, sweating and hypothermia, hallucinations, spasms and finally respiratory paralysis. Fortunately, an effective antivenom is available and deaths are now rare.

★ LARGEST VENOM GLANDS

The wandering spider (*Phoneutria nigriventer*), the largest and probably the most aggressive spider in South America, also has the largest venom glands. They each measure up to 10.2 mm ($\frac{1}{2}$ in) in length and 2.7 mm ($\frac{1}{8}$ in) in diameter and can hold up to 1.35 mg ($\frac{1}{100,000}$ oz) of venom. That's enough to kill 225 mice.

★ LONGEST FANGS

Fang length is not linked with the seriousness of a spider's bite. It's the venom that counts. Indeed, most spider fangs are relatively short. The longest belong to the bird-eating spider (*Theraphosa blondi*) and reach a maximum length of only 10.2 mm ($\frac{1}{2}$ in). By comparison, the fangs of the black widow spider (*Latrodectus mactans*) are much smaller, yet its bite is far more dangerous than the bite of almost any other spider in the world.

★ MOST FEARED

The enormous, furry bird-eating spiders (family Theraphosidae) have a fearsome reputation thanks to the popular press and to their starring roles as the great hairy monsters in numerous feature films. Known as baboon spiders in Africa and tarantulas in America, they certainly look dangerous. But most of the 900 known species, which live mainly in the tropics and sub-tropics, are fairly placid creatures. They are normally reluctant to bite (unless being roughly handled or provoked) and, when they do become aggressive, their bite can be extremely painful but is rarely dangerous.

★ LONGEST LIVING

Most spiders have an average lifespan of around a year, although there are some dramatic exceptions. The longest-living of all spiders are the tropical bird-eating spiders (family Theraphosidae). As in most spiders, the females live longer than the males. A 20 to 25-year lifespan is not

Jumping spider

The jumping spiders not only have the highest number of species (5077) in their family but also live at the highest altitude, as high as 6700 m (22,000 ft) on Mount Everest.

unusual for female theraphosids, and it has been estimated that Brazilian tawny red spiders (*Grammostola mollicoma*), for example, can live up to 30 years.

It's not only the very large spiders that live a long time. Certain trapdoor spiders (family Ctenizidae) may also live up to 20 years.

★ LARGEST FAMILY

The largest and most varied of all the 108 known spider families is the Salticidae, or jumping spiders. There are 5077 known species, mostly living in the tropics. Jumping spiders tend to be nomadic daytime hunters and don't spin webs because they do not need them to catch food.

★ HIGHEST LIVING

Jumping spiders (family Salticidae) hold the world altitude record for spiders. In 1924 the naturalist and explorer R. W. G. Hingston collected several specimens living under stones frozen to the ground at a height of 6700 m (21,980 ft) on Mount Everest. One of these was later named as a new species: *Euophrys omnisuperstes*, meaning 'highest of all'. They are believed to feed on tiny creatures that have been blown up by the wind from lower altitudes.

★ LIVING UNDERWATER

The only spider known to live almost entirely underwater is the water spider (*Argyroneta aquatica*), which can occasionally measure 20 mm (³/₄ in) long. It inhabits ponds and slow-moving streams in many mild parts of Europe and Asia. Bubbles of air cling to a mat of special hairs on its body enabling it to breathe in the normal way as it moves around. The spider lives underwater in a 'diving bell'. This diving bell is formed from a mass of air bubbles trapped under threads of silk anchored to aquatic vegetation. Although the spider goes on long hunting expeditions, breathing the

air trapped on the hairs on its body, it has no obvious anatomical adaptations for its unlikely underwater life (although close up it is possible to see long fine hairs on its third and fourth pairs of legs, which enable it to swim well).

★ MOST MARINE

No spider lives in the open sea, but several species live along the seashore.

For example, the intertidal spider (*Desis marina*) lives on exposed coral reefs and on intertidal rocks in Australia and New Zealand. At low tide it hunts sand hoppers and then, when the tide comes in, hides in a disused worm burrow – keeping the water out by blocking the entrance with a woven lid of silk. It is able to survive for several days under water, without a diving bell or a bubble of air.

CENTIPEDES & MILLIPEDES

Myriapoda
c. 12,800 species (2800 centipedes and 10,000 millipedes)

★ EARLIEST

The earliest known land dwellers known from complete fossils were two centipedes and an arachnid found in a layer of rock called the Ludlow Bone Bed, Shropshire, UK. About 414 million years old, all three were thought to be fairly advanced predators. That means there must have already been animals on land for them to prey on before they got there. Indeed, the world's oldest known terrestrial footprints, found in 450-million-year-old rocks in the Lake District, UK, suggest animals were wandering around on dry land nearly 50 million years earlier. Although no fossils of the creatures themselves have yet been found, the tracks were probably made by animals similar to modern centipedes and millipedes.

★ LEAST LEGS

Some centipedes in the sub-class Anamorpha have as few as 15 pairs of legs. Pauropods, which are closely related to centipedes and millipedes, usually have nine pairs of legs.

★ FASTEST

The world's fastest myriapod is probably the house centipede (*Scutigera coleoptrata*), a native of the Mediterranean. With the help of its extremely long legs, it can allegedly run at speeds of up to 50 cm/s (20 in/s), 1.8 km/h (1 mph). In warm weather, it can keep this kind of speed up for several metres. Millipedes are significantly slower.

★ SHORTEST

The shortest myriapod in the world is the millipede *Polyxenus lagurus*, which measures 2.1–4.0 mm ($^5/_{64}$–$^{10}/_{64}$ in). The shortest recorded centipede is an unidentified species that allegedly measures only 5 mm ($^1/_4$ in).

★ LONGEST

The longest recorded centipede is in the Paris Museum of Natural History. It is the aptly named Amazonian giant centipede (*Scolopendra gigantea*), which measures 37 cm ($14^1/_2$ in) in length and was probably about 35 cm ($13^3/_4$ in) long when alive in its Central and South American home. The longest millipede in the world is owned by the lucky Jim Klinger of Coppell, Texas, USA. It is an African giant black millipede (*Archispirostreptus gigas*) and measures a staggering 38.7 cm ($15^1/_4$ in) in length, is 6.7 cm ($2^1/_2$ in) in circumference and has 256 legs.

★ MOST DANGEROUS

All centipedes have venom glands for paralysing or killing their prey. The venom is injected into the prey through a pair of fangs modified from the first pair of legs.

Most bites are harmless to people. However, the bites of certain larger species can cause excruciating pain. Symptoms can include swelling around the bite and lymph nodes and chest pain. The appendages at the end of the tail do not inject venom – they may be modified for defensive or sensory functions.

Millipedes do not have fangs, but most have toxic glands on the sides of the body that can release nauseous fluids containing hydrogen. These fluids repel most of the millipede's enemies. On humans, the fluids released by some large tropical species can cause severe irritation when they come into contact with the skin and may even cause temporary blindness if they touch the eyes. However, a species of capuchin monkey (*Cebus olivaceus*) actually wipe millipede secretions on their fur, probably as an insect repellent.

WORLD RECORD HOLDER

Most legs

Despite their names, centipedes do not have 100 feet (or legs) and millipedes do not have 1000. Nevertheless, millipedes do tend to have more legs than centipedes. They appear to have two pairs per body segment (although, in reality, these are fused segments) compared with just one pair in centipedes. The record is 375 pairs (750 legs) reported for a millipede called *Illacme plenipes*, found in California, USA. The centipede with the most legs is a species called *Gonibregmatus plurimipes* that has 191 pairs (382 legs) from the Fiji Islands. When looking at actual size, one of the largest millipedes in the world is the African giant black millipede (*Archispirostreptus gigas*). When mature they can grow to an incredible length of up to 38.7 cm ($15^1/_4$ in).

INSECTS

Insecta

c. 1 million described (c. 8–10,000 new species discovered annually and an estimated 5–30 million yet to be found), including beetles, ants, bees and wasps, true flies, fleas, butterflies and moths, true bugs, lice, stick insects and leaf insects, grasshoppers, bush-crickets and crickets, cockroaches and termites, earwigs, dragonflies and damselflies, aphids, cicadas, hoppers, mayflies, stoneflies, alderflies, lacewings, caddisflies, mantids etc. In general the body of a typical insect is divided into head, thorax and abdomen and it has six legs and generally one or two pairs of wings. Insects do not have backbones or any other internal bones – they wear their skeletons on the outside. According to some estimates, nearly 90% of all animal species are insects, making them by far the most successful organisms on Earth.

The Natural History Museum in London, UK, has the largest collection of insects in the world. In 2007, it included nearly 30 million specimens.

ANTS, BEES & WASPS

Hymenoptera

Over 250,000 species, including horntails, sawflies, fairyflies, velvet ants, wasps, ants, bees, ichneumon flies, parasitic wasps

★ LARGEST BEE

The world's largest bee is the rare Wallace's giant bee (Chalicodoma pluto), found only on the islands of Bacan, Soasiu and Halmahera, in the Moluccas, Indonesia. Females are larger than males and attain a maximum length of 4 cm (1½ in). Males average about 2.5 cm (1 in). First discovered in 1858, it was not seen again until 1981.

★ SMALLEST BEE

The smallest bee is a Brazilian species of stingless bee Trigona duckei, which measures only 2–5 mm (¹/₁₆–³/₁₆ in) in body length.

★ LARGEST WASP

The largest known wasps are spider hunting wasps of the genus Pepsis, which are found in tropical South America and are known as tarantula hawk wasps. The largest tarantula hawk is probably Pepsis heros, which has a body length of up to 5.7 cm (2¼ in) and a maximum wingspan of 11.4 cm (4½ in).

★ SMALLEST WASP

Together with the 'feather winged' beetles of the family Ptiliidae, the parasitic wasps known as battledore-wing

Orchid bee
Bees are among the most advanced insects, with complex social behaviour. The male orchid bee collects scents from orchid flowers and other sources to attract females.

fairy flies (family Aiymaridae) are the world's smallest recorded insects. With lengths of as little as 0.21 mm ($1/128$ in), they are even smaller than some species of protozoa (single-celled animals) and much smaller than a pin-head — and yet retain all the external characteristics of insects as well as a full complement of internal organs.

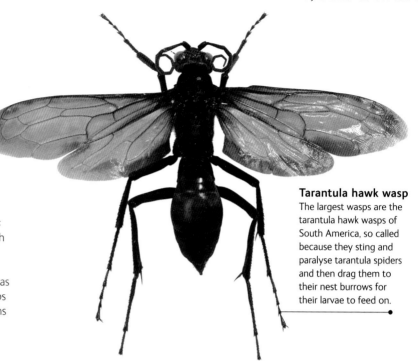

Tarantula hawk wasp
The largest wasps are the tarantula hawk wasps of South America, so called because they sting and paralyse tarantula spiders and then drag them to their nest burrows for their larvae to feed on.

★ LIGHTEST

The parasitic wasp *Caraphractus cinctus* is the lightest insect in the world, though it shares the title with the male blood-sucking banded louse (*Enderleinellus zonatus*). Each wasp may weigh as little as 0.005 mg (equivalent to 5,670,000 wasps to an ounce) and each of its eggs weighs 0.0002 mg (141,750,000 to an ounce).

★ LARGEST WASP NEST

The world's largest wasp nest was discovered on a farm at Waimaukau, New Zealand, in April 1963. Made of a kind of papier mache consisting of wood scrapings mashed up with saliva, it measured 3.7 m (12 ft 2 in) in length and 1.75 m ($5^1/4$ ft) in diameter and was so heavy it had fallen to the ground and broken in two pieces. The species responsible is unknown, but is likely to have been the introduced German wasp *Vespula germanica* which, in New Zealand, builds much bigger nests than the same species in its native Europe.

★ LARGEST ANT

The longest ants in the world are the wingless queens of a species of driver ant (*Dorylus fulvus*), which live in South Africa and have a maximum recorded length of 5 cm (2 in).

The longest workers are bulldog ants (*Myrmecia brevinoda*), which live in Australia and have been measured up to 3.7 cm ($1^1/2$ in).

Workers of the ponerine ant (*Dinoponera gigantea*), which live in Brazil, are bulkier than *Myrmecia*. However, they are shorter and have been known to reach a maximum length of 'only' 3.3 cm ($1^1/4$ in) from the tip of the relatively short mandibles to the end of the abdomen.

★ SMALLEST ANT

The smallest ant in the world is the minor worker of a Sri Lankan species called *Carebara bruni*. It can measure as little as 0.8 mm ($1/32$ in) long.

★ MOST ADVANCED

The most advanced insects are generally considered to be the social ants, bees and wasps of the order Hymenoptera. All ants and some families of bees and wasps have evolved complex cooperative social hierarchies in which there is a clear division of labour between different castes.

The main categories within the hierarchy are the workers (these are wingless, sterile females which care for the eggs, larvae and pupae, maintain the nest, gather food and deal with intruders); the males (these are winged and have only one function: to mate with the queen); and the queen herself (whose main function in the colony is to lay eggs).

★ SLAVE-TAKING

In a very few ant species, the workers do none of the work themselves, but enlist the help of other species by taking slaves. One well-known example is the western slave-making ant (*Polyergus brevicepsi*), which has been studied in the Chiricahua Mountains, in southwestern Arizona, USA. Half a dozen *Polyergus* workers go off in search of potential slave nests (their favourite slave species is *Formica gnava)*, and, as soon as they have found one, return to fetch their contemporaries. As many as 1000 workers follow the original search party back to the *Formica* nest and, instead of killing the inhabitants,

> The western slave-making ants steal pupae from other species and give them to their own slave workers to raise them as slaves.

spray them with a chemical that causes them to flee. They steal as many of the pupae as they can, carry them back to their own nest and then hand them over to the slave workers of their own species, who raise the *Formica* ants to serve their *Polyergus* masters.

★ MOST DANGEROUS ANT

Worker ants of most species have venomous stings or acid-squirting glands, but most are too small to be dangerous to people. However, at least two Australian species have been responsible for fatalities: the jumper ant (*Myrmecia pilosula*), which grows to 3 cm (1 in) and can jump as far as 20 cm (8 in), and a species of bulldog ant (*M. pyriformis*), which gained its name because of its ferocity and determination during attack. Both species are highly aggressive, show little fear of people and will sting a number of times in quick succession. In an attack, the ant holds on to its victim with long, toothed mandibles, curls its

★ LONGEST COLUMN OF ANTS

Army ants (genus *Eciton*) from Central and South America, and driver ants (genus *Dorylus*) from Africa, have a reputation for travelling in highly organised columns. *Dorylus* ant columns can be up to 100 m (110 yd) long and over 1 m (3 ft 4 in) wide and may contain as many as 700,000 individuals in *Eciton* and up to 20,000,000 in *Dorylus*. They frequently take several hours to pass one

★ LARGEST ANT COLONY

In Europe, a vast colony of Argentine ants (*Linepithema humile*) is thought to stretch 6.000 km (3,700 miles) along the Mediterranean coast. Another in the USA extends over 900 km (560 miles) and a third colony exists on the west coast of Japan. These 3 super-colonies belong to one single global megacolony as they refuse to fight one another, which ants from separate colonies usually do.

★ FASTEST SELF-POWERED PREDATORY STRIKE

The trap-jaw ant (*Odontomachus bauri*), a species of ant native to South America, is able to close

abdomen underneath and then thrusts its long, barbless sting into the skin. The sting of both species is extremely painful and, on a few occasions, has been known to kill adults within 15 minutes. A major concern is that in recent years increasing numbers of people in Australia are becoming allergic to the stings, which then produce a much more severe reaction. Several deaths have occurred through anaphylaxis. There have been many claims of huge numbers of ants swarming over people and eating them alive. Columns of army ants (genus *Eciton*) and driver ants (genus *Dorylus*) have certainly killed people in isolated incidents – but there is no evidence of them being a serious threat.

> The sting of both the jumper and bulldog ant has on a few occasions caused death in 15 minutes.

spot. The reputation these ants have for devouring any animal that is too slow to get out of the way is accurate: they will eat, for example, everything from poisonous snakes to tethered horses, but their reputation for swarming over people and tearing at their flesh is grossly exaggerated. They move so slowly (about 14 m/h or 46 ft/h) that it is easy for everyone to get out of harm's way. There is a report of a column of army ants 1.6 km (1 mile) long and half as wide marching on the town of Goiandira, in central Brazil, in December 1973. Supposedly, it devoured several people before being driven back into the jungle with the help of a team of people armed with flame throwers. However, most experts disregard this story and it is highly unlikely ant columns ever reach anything approaching such a size.

Driver ants
Driver ants (*Dorylus* sp.) on the march in Ghana. The central lane of worker ants is carrying food, protected by soldier ants. These columns can reach 100 m (110 yd) in length.

its mandibles at 35 to 64 m (115 to 210 ft) per second. The average duration of a strike was measured at a mere 0.13 milliseconds, 2300 times faster than the blink of an eye.

★ TEMPERATURE TOLERANCE

When temperatures in the central Sahara reach 46°C (115°F), and most creatures are hiding from the midday sun, silver ants (*Cataglyphis bombycinus*) leave their nest holes to search for the corpses of other insects that have succumbed to the blazing heat. They spend as long as half an hour dashing about in search of their prey – occasionally seeking relief in shade or at the top of dried vegetation where the air is slightly cooler – before returning to the safety of their burrows. Their predators, such as lizards, can't cope with such extreme heat and are safely hidden underground while the ants go about their business. If the temperature rises above 53°C (128°F), the ants start to suffer, they become disoriented and lose their co-ordination.

★ MOST USEFUL

The most useful insects in the world and, possibly, the most useful of all animals are the bees (superfamily Apoidea). They are major pollinators of flowering plants which, in turn, feed the world's terrestrial animals and replenish the planet's oxygen. Many plant species are completely dependent upon bees for pollination. Honey bees perform elaborate dances in the hive to tell their nest mates about new sources of food; they are able to pass on information about the distance, direction, type and even quality of food.

★ MOST DANGEROUS BEE OR WASP

Most bees and wasps are able to sting. Although many of their stings can be quite painful, the majority are not particularly dangerous. There are a number of cases of people being stung more than 2000 times by angry swarms of bees, and surviving. The main risk is to people

BEST MEMORY

In an experiment by French biologists at the University of Paris, in Villetaneuse, worker ants of two different species *Formica selysi* and *Manica rubida* were reared together for three months and then separated. It was found they could recognise one another, probably by the odours on their bodies, as much as 18 months later.

who are allergic to the venom, in which case a single sting by a relatively harmless species can prove fatal. Consequently, many thousands of people die from bee and wasp stings every year.

The most dangerous bee is probably a cross between the notoriously ferocious African honey bee (*Apis mellifera scutellata*) and various subspecies of honey bee found in Europe (*Apis melifera* sp.). In 1957, 26 queen African honey bees escaped from a biological research station at the University of Sao Paulo, Brazil. By mating with the more docile local bees, their numbers increased rapidly and they began to spread northwards at a steady rate of about 400 km (250 miles) per year. They had reached Panama by 1982, Mexico by

1986 and the USA by 1990 (the first official acknowledgement that the so-called 'killer' bee had arrived in the US was in October 1990, when US Department of Agriculture officials found a swarm on a farm in southern Texas, a stone's throw from the Mexican border). They are now found in much of the southern US states. In fact, the sting of the Africanised honey bee is no more potent than the stings of many other bees. But their behaviour is different: they attack people approaching their nests more readily (even if they are more than 1 km (³/₅ mile) away) and in far greater numbers. The number of fatalities caused by these bees is unknown.

★ MANTLE OF BEES

During a record-breaking attempt on 29 July in 1991, Jed Shaner was covered by a mantle of *c*. 343,000 bees weighing 36.3 kg (80 lb) at Staunton, West Virginia, USA.

• Western honey bee
The Western honey bee (*Apis mellifera*) plays a crucial role in stimulating life on earth. Through its widespread pollination of flowering plants it drives the plant life cycle which provides food for both animals and humans alike.

BEETLES

Coleoptera

Nearly 400,000 species (almost one
quarter of all described animal species)

★ SMALLEST

The 'feather-winged' beetles of the family
Ptiliidae are, together with parasitic
wasps, the world's smallest recorded
insects. With lengths of as little as 0.21
mm ($\frac{1}{128}$ in), they are even smaller than
some species of protozoa (single-celled
animals) and much smaller than a pin-
head – and yet retain all the external
characteristics of insects as well as a full
complement of internal organs.

★ HEAVIEST

The heaviest and bulkiest of all insects
are the *Megasoma* beetles (family
Scarabaeidae) of South America. The
heaviest species in this genus is
Megasoma actaeon, a fully grown larva of
which has weighed in at 205 g (7$\frac{1}{4}$ oz).

★ LONGEST

The longest beetles in the world are two
species of hercules beetle: *Dynastes
hercules* and *D. neptunus*, which are
found in Central America, northern South
America and on some Caribbean islands.
Males have been reliably measured up to
19 cm (7$\frac{1}{2}$ in) in *D. hercules* and 18 cm
(7 in) in *D. neptunus*. However, in both
species more than half the length is taken
up by the long opposing horns, one on
the head, the other on the prothorax.
With this in mind, the title for the world's

Megasoma
As the heaviest and bulkiest of all
insects, rhinoceros beetles (*Megasoma*
sp.) are proportionally some of the
strongest animals on the planet,
lifting up to 850 times their own weight.

longest beetle should perhaps go to the
fittingly named the titan beetle (*Titanus
giganteus*), from the Amazon region. It
does not have long horns and is still up to
16.7 cm (6$\frac{1}{4}$ in) long.

★ STRONGEST

In proportion to their size, the strongest
animals in the world are the larger beetles
of the family Scarabaeidae, which are
found mainly in the tropics. In tests carried
out on a rhinoceros beetle of the sub-
family Dynastinae, it was found it could
support 850 times its own weight on its
back. As a comparison, in a trestle lift a

human can support only 17 times his or
her own body weight. The dor beetle
(*Geotrupes stercorosus*) has been
observed shifting a load weighing 80 g
(2$\frac{3}{4}$ oz) or 400 times its own body weight.

★ LONGEST SNOUT

The long-snouted South African cycad
weevil (*Antliarhinus zamiae*) has the
longest snout, relative to body size, of
any known beetle. On average, the weevil
itself is about 1 cm ($\frac{1}{2}$ in) long and its
snout can add a further 2 cm ($\frac{3}{4}$ in) to its
overall length (although the snout of the
male is only 1 cm ($\frac{1}{2}$ in)). It's thought the
long snout is needed to drill holes for
laying eggs inside cycad seeds.

★ STRANGEST DEFENCE

The bombardier beetle (genus *Brachinus*)
stores two relatively harmless chemicals
in a special chamber in its abdomen.
When it feels threatened, the chemicals
are released into a second chamber,
where they mix with an enzyme, causing
a violent chemical reaction and

Hercules beetle
The world's longest beetles are the
hercules beetles found in Central and
South America, and on some Caribbean
Islands. This individual is from Dominica, in
the Lesser Antilles.

considerable heat. The concoction can reach boiling 100°C (212°F) and is sprayed from the anus as an explosive puff of irritating gas (which the beetle can aim with remarkable accuracy). The spray can be turned on and off 500 times a second.

★ LARGEST FAMILY

With more than 60,000 species known, the weevils or snout beetles (family Curculionidae) form the largest family in the animal kingdom. All are plant eaters, and many are pests.

★ HIGHEST G-FORCE

The highest g-force endured by any insect is an average of 400 g by the click beetle (*Athous haemorrhoidalis*). When the beetle is placed (or falls) on its back it can right itself by jumping into the air. It arches its back, holding this position for a moment with the help of a tiny peg resting on a ridge on the

If a click beetle is placed or falls on its back, it can right itself by jumping in the air. It does not necessarily land the right way up, but will keep on trying until it does.

Jewel beetle
Jewel beetles lay their eggs under bark and, once hatched, the larvae feed on the wood of the tree. The larvae may take many years to reach maturity – 47 years in one case.

underside of the body. Then, as tension builds up in the body muscles, the peg slips. There is a loud click – and the beetle is suddenly thrown into the air. The jump is nearly vertical and may reach a height of 30 cm (11¾ in). One individual measuring 1.25 cm (½ in) in length and weighing 0.04 g (1/10,000 oz) jumped to a height of 30 cm (11¾ in) and endured a peak deceleration of 2300 g (5 lb) by the end of the movement.

★ FASTEST ON LAND

The world's fastest running insect is the Australian tiger beetle (*Cicindela hudsoni*), which can run 9 km/h (5½ mph). It is a voracious predator of other invertebrates, chasing them down at high speed before devouring them.

★ LONGEST LIVED

There are many authenticated records of splendour or jewel beetles (family Buprestidae) surviving for 30 years or longer. They lay their eggs under the bark of a living tree and, after they have hatched, the young larvae tunnel into the tree and feed on the wood. If the tree is felled, it is not unusual for some of the larvae to survive and then be transported around the world in timber; since some species take many years to reach maturity, the adults may eventually emerge from furniture. The record was broken on 27 May 1983, when a specimen of *Buprestis aurulenta* appeared from the staircase timber in the home of Mr W. Euston, of Prittlewell, Southend-on-Sea, Essex, UK, after at least 47 years as a larva.

TRUE BUGS

Hemiptera
Nearly 90,000 species, including shield bugs, bed bugs, aphids, water boatmen, cicadas, hoppers, pond skaters

✹ LARGEST
The largest true bugs are giant water bugs (*Lethocerus maximus*) in the family Belostomatidae, which can be up to 115 mm (4½ in) long, with a wing span of 216 mm (8½ in). They eat both invertebrate and vertebrate prey.

Cicadas (family Cicadidae) have smaller bodies, but are longer from head to wing tips – up to 10 cm (4 in) long, with 20 cm (8 in) wing span. The largest cicada is the Malaysian emperor cicada (*Pomponia imperatoria*) which has a wingspan of up to 210 mm (8 in).

✹ LONGEST LIVED
In the northern parts of its range, the periodic or seventeen-year cicada (*Magicicada septemdecim*) is known to live underground in the juvenile stage for as long as 17 years (13 years is more typical in the southern parts of its range). The adult cicada lays her eggs in a twig and, when they hatch, the nymphs make their way to the ground where they begin to burrow with their spade-like front legs; they feed underground, on root sap, until they reach the adult stage and then dig their way back up to the surface. They live as adults for no more than a few weeks before dying. Periodic cicadas are found in the woodlands of North America.

✹ MOST FERTILE
The most fertile animal in the world (excluding bacteria, which are not really

Giant water bug
The largest of the true bugs, the giant water bug (*Lethocerus maximus*) is found in South America and feeds off animals as large as salamanders and small fish.

animals) is the cabbage aphid (*Brevicoryne brassicae*). This tiny, pear-shaped, sap-sucking bug is able to reproduce either sexually or by 'virgin birth', a process in which the eggs develop without fertilisation by a male and hatch into exact genetic replicas of the mother. As a result, billions of offspring can originate from just one female aphid. It has been calculated that, in a year with unlimited food and no predators, a single cabbage aphid could theoretically give rise to a mass of descendants weighing 822 million tonnes, or more than twice the weight of the world's human population. The Earth would be covered by a layer of aphids 150 km (93 miles) deep. Fortunately, a variety of natural enemies such as ladybirds, lacewings and insectivorous birds ensure that the aphid's mortality rate is very high.

✹ LOUDEST
The loudest of all insects is the male cicada (family Cicadidae). Its 'song' is made by the rapid movement of a

membrane or 'tymbal', which oscillates several hundred times a second; behind the membrane is a resonating chamber to amplify the sound. Officially described by the US Department of Agriculture as 'Tsh-eeEEE-e-ou', the song of many species is detectable from more than 400 m (¼ mile) away. To put this into perspective, a study by scientists at Princeton University, New Jersey, USA, measured the noise produced by thousands of cicadas in a single tree and found it to be 80–100 decibels at a distance of 18 m (60 ft) (compared with 70–90 decibels for a pneumatic drill at a similar distance). The song is designed to attract a female: each of the 1500 species of cicada has its own version. Most female cicadas are mute.

BUTTERFLIES & MOTHS

Lepidoptera

190,000 known species, including *c.* 20,000 butterflies and 170,000 moths

★ LARGEST

The largest known butterfly is the rare Queen Alexandra's birdwing (*Ornithoptera alexandrae*) of the Popondetta Plain area, in Northern Province, Papua New Guinea. Females are larger than males and they can reputedly have a front wingspan of more than 28 cm (11 in) from tip to tip (average 21 cm (8¼ in)) and a weight of up to 12 g (½ oz) The larvae feed on two species of *Pararistolochia* vines.

There are several moths which match – and may even be bigger than – the Queen Alexandra's birdwing. The Hercules moth (*Cosinocera hercules*) of tropical Australia and Papua New Guinea has a wingspan of up to 28 cm (11 in). The owlet or white witch moth (*Thysania agrippina*), which lives in Central and South America, is of a similar size: the record is a female with a wingspan of 30.8 cm (12¼ in). She was taken in 1934 and is now in the collection of John G. Powers in Ontario, Canada. The enormous Atlas moth (*Attacus atlas*) is often mistaken for a bird while flying around its rainforest home in Southeast Asia, and has a wingspan of up to 25 cm (10 in). There are, however, unauthenticated records of wingspans up to 30 cm (11¾ in) – the male has huge feathery antennae, the largest of any butterfly or moth.

★ SMALLEST

The smallest of the known moths is *Trifurcula ridiculosa*, which lives in the Canary Islands. It has a wingspan of 2 mm (¹⁄₁₆ in) and a similar body length. The world's smallest butterfly is the dwarf blue (*Brephidium barberae*) of South Africa. It has a wingspan of 1.4 cm (⁵⁄₈ in) and weighs less than 10 mg (³⁵⁄₁₀₀,₀₀₀ oz).

★ NOISIEST

Butterflies and moths are normally the essence of peace and quiet, but male butterflies in the genus *Hamadryas* make a loud clickety-clickety-clack sound that can be heard up to 30 m (100 ft) away. Analysis of high-speed photographs and sound recordings has revealed the males produce the sound when their forewings collide during vigorous flight. This is normally at times of courtship, as they jostle for space along female flight paths.

Some moths make loud ultrasonic clicking sounds (beyond the range of human hearing) to distract bats on the prowl (which use echolocation sound signals of their own to find prey). It's unclear exactly how these noises affect the bats, but they may startle them or jam their echolocation systems, or they could even be the acoustic equivalent of warning colours (telling the bats the moths taste unpleasant).

★ GREEDIEST

In the first 56 days of its life, the caterpillar of the polyphemus moth (*Antheraea polyphemus*) of North America eats 86,000 times its birthweight in oak, maple and birch leaves. That's the same as a 3.17 kg (7 lb) baby munching through 273 tonnes of food.

Queen Alexandra's butterfly
The largest butterfly is the Queen Alexandra's birdwing butterfly from Papua New Guinea. This male specimen measures 18.8 cm (7½ in) across the wingtips, but females can reach more than 28 cm (11 in).

INVERTEBRATES

★ STRANGEST DIET

Several hundred tropical and sub-tropical moth species (belonging to six different families) drink the tears of hoofed mammals such as cattle, deer, horses, tapirs, pigs and elephants. They have even been known to drink the tears of people and birds, but have yet to be seen visiting carnivores, marsupials or any other group of vertebrates. This preference for certain hosts may indicate differences in the taste – or it may simply be that the most frequent victims are the most placid and tolerant. Tears are a source of protein and salt, and for most moth species form only part of a much broader diet. However, nearly ten species feed exclusively on tears and one of the most highly evolved of these is a southeast Asian moth called *Lobocraspis griseifusa*, which actively sweeps the victim's eyeball with its proboscis to stimulate a flow of tears.

★ BLOOD DRINKING

A number of moths lap up the blood from open wounds as and when they find them, but the vampire moth (*Calyptra eustrigata*) of Malaysia takes this a stage further. It is the only lepidopteran to make its own wound to drink blood. It uses its unusually short, sturdy proboscis to gouge the skin of large mammals to draw blood. This gruesome behaviour possibly evolved from the fruit-piercing habit of many moths with a similar kind of proboscis.

★ GREATEST CHEMISTS

Recent research suggests butterflies may be nature's greatest chemists. A team of German and British scientists have found that African milkweed butterflies from the

RECORD FLY-PAST

In 1928/29, an enormous flock of African migrant butterflies *Catopsilia florella* took three months to fly past the house of an entomologist living in East Africa. The fly-past was apparently continuous: there was always a steady stream and, at times, even huge swarms.

genera *Danaus*, *Tirumala* and *Amauris* can make no fewer than 214 compounds from 14 different groups of chemical.

Individual milkweed species each have a quite distinct mixture of compounds (some unique to the species) with anywhere from 12 to 59 chemicals each. Until this study, some of the chemicals had never been found in nature before. They are produced in the male scent glands and go to make pheromones (helping the female make sure her potential mate belongs to the right species) and to make the butterflies extremely poisonous to birds and other potential predators.

★ BEST RECOVERY

The blue moon butterfly (*Hypolimnas bolina*) of the Samoan islands of Savaii and Upolu has developed a gene that confers resistance against a bacterial parasite that kills male embryos. Attacks by the bacterial parasite caused the number of males to drop below 1%, but now because of the spread of the gene throughout the butterfly population, the male population has now recovered.

★ LONGEST TONGUE

A characteristic feature of adult lepidopterans is the sucking proboscis or tongue, which is generally rolled up underneath the head when resting and has to be unrolled to feed. It works like a straw and is used mainly for sucking nectar out of flowers. The longest tongues belong to the hawk moths (family Sphingidae), which use them to feed on the nectar deep inside tubular-flowered orchids. The longest of all the hawk moth tongues belongs to the Madagascan hawk moth (*Xanthopan morganii praedicta*), whose discovery was predicted by Charles Darwin. After examining one of Madagascar's native orchids, a species called *Angraecum sesquipedale*, whose nectar-producing organs are almost 30 cm (12 in) deep, he concluded that Madagascar must be home to a butterfly or moth with an exceptionally long proboscis to reach the nectar (and thereby effect pollination). As Darwin suspected, the Madagascan hawk moth has a record-breaking 28 cm (11 in) proboscis, just enough to reach the nectar deep in the orchid.

★ LONGEST MIGRATION

It's extremely hard to study the migratory flights of butterflies and moths, because they are too small, fragile and short-lived to trace with standard 'mark and recapture' techniques used so successfully in bird research. However, there have been a few extraordinary successes. The record-holder is a tagged female monarch or milkweed butterfly (*Danaus plexippus*). It was released in Ontario, Canada, on 6 September 1986, and recaptured 3432 km (2133 miles) away, on a mountain near Angangueo, Mexico, on 15 January 1987. This is the straight line distance between release and recapture, but the actual distance travelled could have been much longer. A study has found that the

Madagascan hawkmoth
The longest tongue or sucking proboscis belongs to the Madagascan hawkmoth. Its proboscis can be as long as 28 cm (11 in) to reach deep inside orchids and get at the nectar at the base.

monarch butterfly (*Danaus plexippus*) has a gene that acts as an internal biological clock, timing the 24-hour cycle of day and night when migrating north or south. It allows the butterfly to calculate its direction of flight by using the sun as a compass.

Research by scientists in Iowa, USA, suggest two moths, the black cutworm or dark swordgrass (*Agrotis ipsilon*) and the armyworm (*Pseudaletia unipunctata*), are extreme long-distance fliers. By tracing the origins of the pollen stuck on 5755 of these moths, it turns out they had flown at least 1600 km (994 miles) and, in some cases, as far as 2200 km (1366 miles).

Vast numbers of painted lady butterflies (*Cynthia cardui*) migrate northwards from the deserts of north Africa and Arabia across Europe and, in some years, as far north as Iceland and beyond. In exceptional summers they go far above the Arctic Circle, more than 3000 km (1865 miles) north of their winter breeding grounds. It is unknown if these long-distance migrations occur in one flight or over several generations.

★ HIGHEST MIGRATION

The greatest height reliably reported for migrating butterflies is 5791 m (19,000 ft) for a small flock of small tortoiseshells (*Aglais urticae*) seen flying over the Zemu Glacier in the eastern Himalayas. The Queen of Spain fritillary (*Issoria lathonia*) has reputedly been seen flying at about 6000 m (19,685 ft) in the Himalayas.

WORLD RECORD HOLDER

Most acute sense of smell

The most acute sense of smell belongs to the male emperor moth (*Saturnio pavonia*) which, according to German experiments in 1961, can detect the sex attractant of the virgin female at an almost unbelievable range of 11 km (6¾ miles). Only the minutest portion is released into the air at any one time. The chemoreceptors on the male moth's antennae are so sensitive they can detect a single molecule of the scent. They can also detect its strength and, as it increases, the moth is able to move along in the direction of the female.

A male Saturniidae moth
The male moths detect the odour of the females through their feathery antennae.

★ LONGEST LIVING

The entire life cycle of a butterfly or moth – from egg to caterpillar and chrysalis to adult – can last for as long as several years. But the lifespan of the adult is usually much shorter than any of the other stages. Most adult butterflies, for example, live for an average of two to three weeks (some for as little as one week), giving them little time to complete courtship, mating and egg-laying. A few

Heliconius **butterfly**
Most adult butterflies live for only a few weeks, but species in the genus *Heliconius* can live much longer, in some cases up to nine months.

in their path. The largest recorded swarm contained an estimated 10 billion individuals and covered a densely packed area of 200 km² (77 miles²).

The insect species that formed the largest swarms in recorded history is the rocky mountain locust *Melanoplus spretus* which became extinct in 1902. One swarm which passed over Nebraska in 1875 was estimated to have covered 512,817 km² (198,000 miles²) and it probably contained 3.5 trillion locusts.

★ HEAVIEST

The heaviest orthopteran in the world is the rare wetapunga (*Deinacrida heteracantha*) from New Zealand. Females can have bodies up to 90 mm (3¹⁄₂ in) long and one pregnant female was found to weigh 71 g (2¹⁄₂ oz), three times the weight of an average house mouse!

★ LARGEST WINGSPAN

The orthopteran with the largest reliably measured wingspan is the emperor bush-cricket, *Arachnacris tenuipes* (*Macrolyristes imperator*), from Malaysia and Indonesia. A female in the collection of the Academy of Natural Sciences of Philadelphia was found to have a wingspan of 274 mm (10³⁄₄ in).

★ HIGHEST LIVING

The orthopteran which lives at the greatest altitude is an un-named grasshopper species which was found between 5182 and 5486 m (17,000 and 18,000 ft) on Mount Everest. It is only known from immature specimens which were collected by the ill-fated 1924 British Everest Expedition, on which George Mallory and Sandy Irvine died.

DRAGONFLIES & DAMSELFLIES

Odonata

5574 species

★ EARLIEST

The Protodanata appeared during the Carboniferous period, between 300 and 350 million years ago. But the Odonata appeared in the Permian between 300 and 250 million years ago, making them (along with mayflies, order Ephemeroptera) the most ancient of flying insects.

★ LARGEST PREHISTORIC

Fossil remains (impressions of wings) of the dragonfly *Meganeura monyi*, discovered at Commentry, France, indicate a wingspan of up to 75 cm (29¹⁄₂ in). This giant insect lived about 300 million years ago.

★ LARGEST

A damselfly, *Megaloprepus caerulatus*, of Central and South America, has a wingspan of up to 191 mm (7¹⁄₂ in) and a body length of 120 mm (4³⁄₄ in).

★ SMALLEST DRAGONFLY

The world's smallest dragonfly is *Agriocnemis naia* of Myanmar (Burma). A specimen in the Natural History Museum, London, UK, has a wingspan of 17.6 mm (¹¹⁄₁₆ in) and a body length of 18 mm (¹²⁄₁₆ in).

★ FASTEST FLYING

Acceptable modern experiments have established that the highest maintainable air speed an insect can attain is a maximum of 58 km/h (36 mph) for the Australian dragonfly (*Austrophlebia costalis*), for short bursts.

The best way to tell dragonflies and damselflies apart is by their wings: dragonflies hold theirs out when resting, while damselflies hold theirs together over their back.

Calopteryx

The European beautiful demoiselle damselfly (*Calopteryx virgo*) is a representative of one of the most ancient groups of insects, the order Odonata (dragons and damselflies).

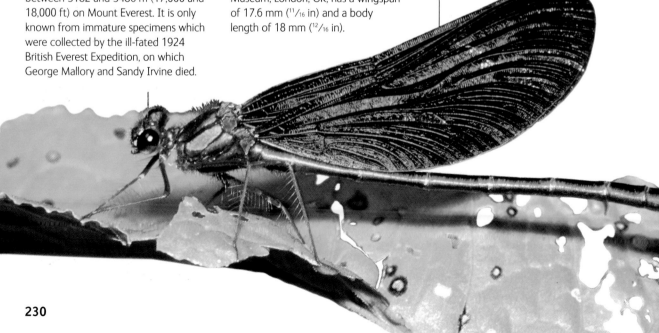

monarch butterfly (*Danaus plexippus*) has a gene that acts as an internal biological clock, timing the 24-hour cycle of day and night when migrating north or south. It allows the butterfly to calculate its direction of flight by using the sun as a compass.

Research by scientists in Iowa, USA, suggest two moths, the black cutworm or dark swordgrass (*Agrotis ipsilon*) and the armyworm (*Pseudaletia unipuncata*), are extreme long-distance fliers. By tracing the origins of the pollen stuck on 5755 of these moths, it turns out they had flown at least 1600 km (994 miles) and, in some cases, as far as 2200 km (1366 miles).

Vast numbers of painted lady butterflies (*Cynthia cardui*) migrate northwards from the deserts of north Africa and Arabia across Europe and, in some years, as far north as Iceland and beyond. In exceptional summers they go far above the Arctic Circle, more than 3000 km (1865 miles) north of their winter breeding grounds. It is unknown if these long-distance migrations occur in one flight or over several generations.

✖ HIGHEST MIGRATION

The greatest height reliably reported for migrating butterflies is 5791 m (19,000 ft) for a small flock of small tortoiseshells (*Aglais urticae*) seen flying over the Zemu Glacier in the eastern Himalayas. The Queen of Spain fritillary (*Issoria lathonia*) has reputedly been seen flying at about 6000 m (19,685 ft) in the Himalayas.

WORLD RECORD HOLDER

Most acute sense of smell

The most acute sense of smell belongs to the male emperor moth (*Saturnio pavonia*) which, according to German experiments in 1961, can detect the sex attractant of the virgin female at an almost unbelievable range of 11 km (6$\frac{3}{4}$ miles). Only the minutest portion is released into the air at any one time. The chemoreceptors on the male moth's antennae are so sensitive they can detect a single molecule of the scent. They can also detect its strength and, as it increases, the moth is able to move along in the direction of the female.

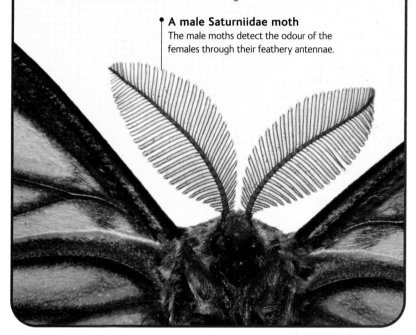

A male Saturniidae moth
The male moths detect the odour of the females through their feathery antennae.

✖ LONGEST LIVING

The entire life cycle of a butterfly or moth – from egg to caterpillar and chrysalis to adult – can last for as long as several years. But the lifespan of the adult is usually much shorter than any of the other stages. Most adult butterflies, for example, live for an average of two to three weeks (some for as little as one week), giving them little time to complete courtship, mating and egg-laying. A few

Heliconius **butterfly**
Most adult butterflies live for only a few weeks, but species in the genus *Heliconius* can live much longer, in some cases up to nine months.

species that hibernate over winter may live as long as 12 months, such as the brimstone (*Gonepteryx rhamni*) and peacock (*Inachis io*). But few remain active for so long. The main exceptions are the 38 species of long-winged butterflies in the genus *Heliconius*, which live in the tropical rainforests of the Americas. They can live 25 times longer than most other butterflies, and the oldest on record was about nine months when it died.

★ LARGEST COLONY

Every November, some 300 million monarch or milkweed butterflies (*Danaus plexippus*) gather in the mature fir, pine and cypress forests along the coasts of California, USA, and Mexico. They spend the winter in the same places year after year, with only slight shifts in the precise trees chosen depending on weather conditions. Crowded together in dense masses, they often cover every available space on the trunks and branches. The Californian colonies each contain a maximum of approximately 100,000 individuals, but the Mexican ones are

considerably larger and may be in their many millions (concentrations reach 10 million/ha or 4 million/acre). As spring approaches, they begin to leave their roosts and mate before departing in late February or early March to begin their migration north (sometimes flying as far as 3000 km or 1860 miles or more).

★ GREATEST DIVERSITY

The greatest diversity of butterflies known anywhere in the world is in the rainforests of South America. Scientists have recorded no fewer than 1209 species within an area of 55 km (21¼ miles) in the Tambopata Reserve, southeastern Peru. In a similar study at Fazenda Rancho Grande, western Brazil, 800 species have been identified in a much smaller forest patch (several sq km) and estimates suggest there are about 1500–1600 in all. This compares with fewer than 440 species in the whole of Europe.

★ LOWEST TEMPERATURE

During the winter, hundreds of insects are able to survive long periods of freezing

Monarch butterfly
Californian colonies of milkweed or monarch butterflies can contain up to 100,000 individuals, though colonies in Mexico may reach millions.

without apparent harm and then thaw in the spring. The record-holder is probably the woolly bear caterpillar (*Gynaephora groenlandica*) of the high Arctic, which is the larval stage of a moth in the family Lymantriidae. The caterpillar spends as much as ten months of the year frozen solid at temperatures that drop to -50°C (-58°F) or even lower.

★ FASTEST FLYING

The fastest-flying lepidopterans are hawk moths (family Sphingidae) – notably, the death's hawk moth (*Acherontia atropos*). These moths have a complex wingbeat (consisting of at least four different wing movements for maximum uplift) and have been credited with bursts of speed of nearly 54 km/h (33½ mph). Speeds as fast as 39 km/h (24 mph) have been witnessed in several species of tropical butterflies (family Hesperiidae).

COCKROACHES

Blattodea

4500-plus species

★ LARGEST WINGSPAN

The world's largest-winged cockroach is *Megaloblatta blaberoides* from Central and South America, which has a wingspan up to 185 mm (7¼ in).

★ HEAVIEST

The world's heaviest cockroach is the wingless rhinoceros cockroach, (*Macropanesthia rhinoceros*), from northern Australia which weighs up to 33.5 g (1 oz) and has a body length of up to 84 mm (3⅓ in).

★ SMALLEST

The world's smallest cockroach is the North American *Attaphila fungicola*, which lives in the nests of leafcutter ants, and has a body length of less than 3 mm (⅛ in).

Megaloblatta longipennis
This cockroach has the second largest wingspan of all cockroaches, only marginally less than its close relative, *Megaloblatta blaberoides*, which can be up to 185 mm (7¼ in).

CRICKETS, GRASSHOPPERS & LOCUSTS

Orthoptera

More than 20,000 species, including grasshoppers, crickets, bush-crickets and wetas

★ MOST DESTRUCTIVE

The single most destructive insect in the world is the desert locust (*Schistocerca gregaria*), which lives in the dry and semi-arid regions of Africa, the Middle East and western Asia. Each locust is 6–9 cm (2³⁄₈–3¹⁄₂ in) long (females are slightly larger than males) and is capable of eating its own weight in food every day. Specific weather conditions induce unimaginable numbers of locusts to crowd together in huge swarms that devour almost every piece of vegetation

Desert locust
A 'small' swarm of some 50 million desert locusts (*Schistocerca gregaria*) can eat, in a single day, roughly the amount of food that would sustain 400 people for a year.

in their path. The largest recorded swarm contained an estimated 10 billion individuals and covered a densely packed area of 200 km² (77 miles²).

The insect species that formed the largest swarms in recorded history is the rocky mountain locust *Melanoplus spretus* which became extinct in 1902. One swarm which passed over Nebraska in 1875 was estimated to have covered 512,817 km² (198,000 miles²) and it probably contained 3.5 trillion locusts.

★ HEAVIEST

The heaviest orthopteran in the world is the rare wetapunga (*Deinacrida heteracantha*) from New Zealand. Females can have bodies up to 90 mm (3¹⁄₂ in) long and one pregnant female was found to weigh 71 g (2¹⁄₂ oz), three times the weight of an average house mouse!

★ LARGEST WINGSPAN

The orthopteran with the largest reliably measured wingspan is the emperor bush-cricket, *Arachnacris tenuipes* (*Macrolyristes imperator*), from Malaysia and Indonesia. A female in the collection of the Academy of Natural Sciences of Philadelphia was found to have a wingspan of 274 mm (10³⁄₄ in).

★ HIGHEST LIVING

The orthopteran which lives at the greatest altitude is an un-named grasshopper species which was found between 5182 and 5486 m (17,000 and 18,000 ft) on Mount Everest. It is only known from immature specimens which were collected by the ill-fated 1924 British Everest Expedition, on which George Mallory and Sandy Irvine died.

DRAGONFLIES & DAMSELFLIES

Odonata
5574 species

★ EARLIEST

The Protodanata appeared during the Carboniferous period, between 300 and 350 million years ago. But the Odonata appeared in the Permian between 300 and 250 million years ago, making them (along with mayflies, order Ephemeroptera) the most ancient of flying insects.

★ LARGEST PREHISTORIC

Fossil remains (impressions of wings) of the dragonfly *Meganeura monyi,* discovered at Commentry, France, indicate a wingspan of up to 75 cm (29¹⁄₂ in). This giant insect lived about 300 million years ago.

★ LARGEST

A damselfly, *Megaloprepus caerulatus*, of Central and South America, has a wingspan of up to 191 mm (7¹⁄₂ in) and a body length of 120 mm (4³⁄₄ in).

★ SMALLEST DRAGONFLY

The world's smallest dragonfly is *Agriocnemis naia* of Myanmar (Burma). A specimen in the Natural History Museum, London, UK, has a wingspan of 17.6 mm (¹¹⁄₁₆ in) and a body length of 18 mm (¹²⁄₁₆ in).

★ FASTEST FLYING

Acceptable modern experiments have established that the highest maintainable air speed an insect can attain is a maximum of 58 km/h (36 mph) for the Australian dragonfly (*Austrophlebia costalis*), for short bursts.

The best way to tell dragonflies and damselflies apart is by their wings: dragonflies hold theirs out when resting, while damselflies hold theirs together over their back.

Calopteryx
The European beautiful demoiselle damselfly (*Calopteryx virgo*) is a representative of one of the most ancient groups of insects, the order Odonata (dragons and damselflies).

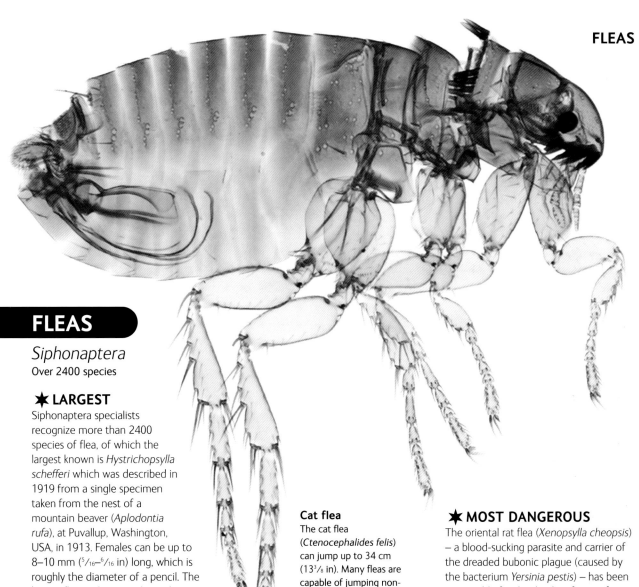

FLEAS

Siphonaptera
Over 2400 species

★ LARGEST

Siphonaptera specialists recognize more than 2400 species of flea, of which the largest known is *Hystrichopsylla schefferi* which was described in 1919 from a single specimen taken from the nest of a mountain beaver (*Aplodontia rufa*), at Puvallup, Washington, USA, in 1913. Females can be up to 8–10 mm (5/16–6/16 in) long, which is roughly the diameter of a pencil. The largest flea in the United Kingdom is the mole flea (*Hystrichopsylla talpae*), the females of which can measure up to 6 mm (1/4 in) long.

★ BEST JUMPER

The cat flea (*Ctenocephalides felis*), is believed to be the champion jumper among fleas and has been known to reach a height of 34 cm (13 3/8 in) in a single jump. However, other species are capable of equivalent or similar feats. In one American experiment carried out in 1910, a human flea (*Pulex irritans*), allowed to leap at will, performed a long jump of 33 cm (13 in) and a high jump of 19.7 cm (7 3/4 in). The fleas do not only use muscle power when jumping, but make use of a pad of rubber-like material called resilin at the top of the back legs. This pad, when squeezed by the leg

Cat flea
The cat flea (*Ctenocephalides felis*) can jump up to 34 cm (13 3/8 in). Many fleas are capable of jumping non-stop for many hours, or even several days, without a rest.

The cat flea jumps with an acceleration equivalent to over 20 times that needed to launch a space rocket.

muscles can store huge amounts of energy. In around a millisecond, they can release as much as 97% of this stored energy for a massive leap (or a series of leaps) whenever it is required.

★ MOST DANGEROUS

The oriental rat flea (*Xenopsylla cheopsis*) – a blood-sucking parasite and carrier of the dreaded bubonic plague (caused by the bacterium *Yersinia pestis*) – has been responsible for the deaths of tens of millions of people in past centuries. Many rodent fleas can carry plague, but this particular species is believed to be responsible for the majority of the world's most catastrophic pandemics. The worst was the Black Death, in the 14th century, which caused the deaths of 25 million people in Europe alone – approximately one-quarter of the population. Even today, plague still breaks out periodically in human populations.

MOST SPECIALIZED DIET

All fleas live on a diet exclusively of blood. Some are highly adaptable and can choose from a variety of hosts, but many are much more specialized; consequently, there is a beaver flea, a human flea, a penguin flea and even a Tasmanian devil flea.

FLIES

Diptera

120,000 species, including midges,
craneflies, mosquitos, gnats, houseflies,
bluebottles, horseflies and hoverflies

★ LARGEST

The world's largest fly is *Midas heros*
(*Mydas herosi*), from tropical South
America, which has been recorded with a
body length of 6 cm (2³/₄ in) and a
wingspan of about 10 cm (4 in). This
powerful predator tackles prey as
formidable and well-armed as bees and
wasps by biting them on the neck.

Craneflies (family Tipulidae) have very
elongated bodies and long legs (thus the
common name 'daddy long legs') but
have very little bulk. The body length
of some species may reach a
maximum 6.5 cm (2¹/₂ in) and the
wingspan can exceed 10 cm
(4 in). However, with the legs
extended, the overall length
(measured from the tips of
the front legs to the tips of
the hind legs) of species
such as *Holorusia
brobdignagius* can
probably exceed
23 cm (9 in).

★ FASTEST
FLYING

The deer botfly (*Cephenemyia
pratti*) is one of the fastest
insects, reaching estimated speeds
of about 39 km/h (24 mph). The
widely publicized claim by an American
scientist in 1926 that the deer botfly
could attain a speed of 1316 km/h
(818 mph) was wildly exaggerated; if true,
the fly would have had to eat one and a
half times its own weight in food every
second to acquire the energy that would
be needed and, even if this were possible,
it would still be crushed by the resulting
air pressure. Coupled with their speed,

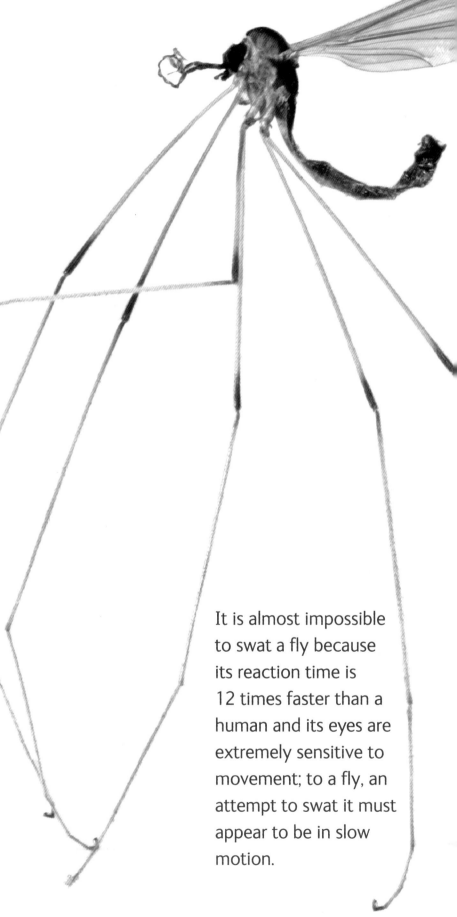

It is almost impossible
to swat a fly because
its reaction time is
12 times faster than a
human and its eyes are
extremely sensitive to
movement; to a fly, an
attempt to swat it must
appear to be in slow
motion.

flies are almost impossible to swat because they have a reaction time 12 times faster than that of a human, and their eyes are extremely sensitive to movement; to a fly, an attempt to swat it must appear in slow motion.

★ FASTEST WINGBEAT

The fastest wingbeat of any insect under natural conditions is an astounding 62,760 per minute (1046 per second) by a tiny midge of the genus *Forcipomyia*. The muscular contraction-expansion cycle that is necessary for such rapid wingbeats also represents the fastest muscle movement that has ever been measured.

★ MOST PROFOUND INFLUENCE

It is difficult to identify a specific record-holder in this case, since there are so many possibilities. For example, five species of tsetse fly in the genus *Glossina* have had a profound influence on human ecology in Africa. They transmit sleeping sickness (a disease confined to Africa and caused by the protozoan *Trypanosoma gambiense*) which is endemic in the large herds of wild grazing animals and also affects domestic cattle. As a result, it has made cattle ranging impossible in vast tracts of the continent.

★ MOST DANGEROUS

The world's most dangerous animals (excluding people) are the single-celled parasites of the genus *Plasmodium*, carried by mosquitos of the genus *Anopheles*, which cause malaria. Excluding wars and accidents, these two creatures combined have probably been responsible directly or indirectly for 50% of all human deaths since the Stone Age. Even today, despite major campaigns to eradicate malaria, at least 500 million people are afflicted by the disease each year. One person dies of malaria, somewhere in the world, every 30 seconds and 80% of the fatalities are in Africa. The most dangerous strain is cerebral malaria – which can strike one day and, unless treated, kill the next. Mosquitos can also transmit diseases such as yellow fever, encephalitis and elephantiasis.

The common housefly (*Musca domestica*) is also highly dangerous since it is able to transmit more than 30 parasites and diseases to people, including bubonic plague, cholera, leprosy, typhoid, dysentery, smallpox, diphtheria, scarlet fever and meningitis. In the developing world, contamination of food by houseflies and related species (one moment they may be feeding on excreta, the next on food) accounts for more than a million infant deaths every year due to dehydration associated with severe diarrhoea.

★ MOST FERTILE

If a pair of houseflies were left to their own devices for a summer, and all the succeeding generations survived, there would be enough flies to cover an area the size of Germany in a mound six storeys high.

LICE

Phthiraptera

5000 species, including biting lice, sucking lice

★ LIGHTEST

The male bloodsucking banded louse (*Enderleinellus zonatus*) may be the lightest insect in the world, though it shares the title with the parasitic wasp (*Caraphractus cinctus*). Each louse may weigh as little as 0.005 mg (equivalent to 5,670,000 lice to an ounce.

Cranefly

Craneflies have elongated bodies and exceptionally long legs as seen here in this close-up of *Lipsothrix nervosa*.

MANTIDS

Mantodea

Praying mantids, nearly 2400 species (most in the tropics)

★ LARGEST

The world's longest mantid is from Africa and is called *Ischnomantis gigas*. The longest known specimen is an adult female which is held in the Natural History Museum, London, UK. It has a body length of 170 mm (6¹⁄₂ in).

★ HEAVIEST

It is unclear what the heaviest species of mantid is as very few have been weighed. However, the likely contenders are *Plistospilota* from Africa or *Macromantis* from Central and South America.

★ SMALLEST

The smallest praying mantid is the Australian *Bolbe pygmaea*, which is about 1 cm (³⁄₈ in) in length.

CANNIBALISM

To some female praying mantids, the male is just another potential meal, so he has to be very careful when approaching her to avoid being seized and eaten. If he is careless (or she is very hungry), she will eat him from the head downwards, though fortunately male mantids continue mating even when headless.

STICK & LEAF INSECTS

Phasmatodea
More than 2500 species

★ LONGEST
The longest recorded insect in the world is the stick insect *Phobaeticus chani* (Chan's megastick) from the rainforests of Sabah, Borneo. The longest known specimen is an adult female in the Natural History Museum, London. It has a body length of 357 mm (14 in) and an overall length of 566 mm (22¹⁄₂ in) with its front legs stretched out. Its total length would have been about 6 mm (¹⁄₄ in) more if the specimen was complete. The species was only formally named in October 2008. Currently only two adult females and one adult male are known.

★ EGG-LAYING
Females of the species *Acrophylla titan*, a 27 cm (10¹⁄₂ in) stick insect from northern Australia, can lay more than 2000 relatively large eggs – more than any other species of stick insect.

★ LARGEST EGG
The largest egg laid by an insect in terms of volume belongs to the 16 cm (6¹⁄₄ in) Malaysian stick insect (*Heteropteryx dilatata*). Eggs typically measure 9 mm (³⁄₈ in) in length, with a height of 6 mm (¹⁄₄ in) and a width of 6 mm (¹⁄₄ in).

★ MOST DANGEROUS
Although most stick insects are harmless creatures, some hiss alarmingly, others attempt to slash predators with their sharp-spurred hind legs, and a few can bite. One of the most 'dangerous' is probably the two-striped walking stick (*Anisomorpha buprestoides*), from the southern USA, which is able to squirt a milky spray over a distance of up to 40 cm (15³⁄₄ in) that can cause temporary blindness in humans.

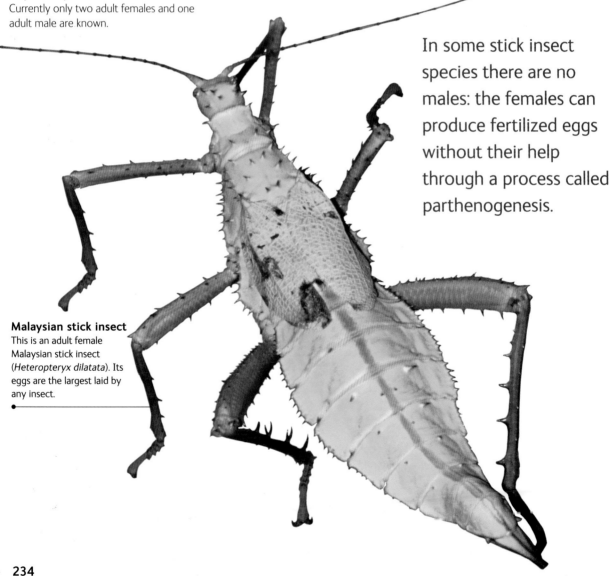

In some stick insect species there are no males: the females can produce fertilized eggs without their help through a process called parthenogenesis.

Malaysian stick insect
This is an adult female Malaysian stick insect (*Heteropteryx dilatata*). Its eggs are the largest laid by any insect.

TERMITES

Isoptera
2600 species

★ EARLIEST

Fossil termite nests that were discovered in rocks in Arizona's Petrified Forest National Park, USA, have been dated at 220 million years old. This was a very significant find since the previous earliest indication of their existence came from a fossilised termite wing fragment which was just over 100 million years old and evidence of termite damage in 70-million-year-old wood. However, without fossil termites (as well as the nests) it is hard to be 100% certain of their identity. The earliest evidence of other social insects – bees, wasps and ants – comes from the Late Cretaceous period, about 70 million years ago.

★ LARGEST

The largest termite in the world is the African species *Macrotermes bellicosus*. The workers are relatively small, but the queens have hugely swollen bodies (which are basically giant egg-producing machines, capable of

Termites
This is a termite mound in Botswana. In proportion to their size, termites build the largest structures of all land-living creatures.

making and laying over 30,000 eggs a day) and have been measured up to 14 cm (5½ in) long and 3.5 cm (1⅜ in) wide. The queens can barely move and spend their entire lives in a 'royal cell' in the centre of the colony – and do little other than feed and reproduce.

★ SELF SACRIFICE

When the nests of some termite species are invaded by marauding ants, the soldiers block off the tunnels by swelling up and then exploding – covering their attackers with all their insides.

★ LARGEST TERMITE MOUND

In proportion to their size, termites build the largest structures of all non-human land-living creatures (coral reefs are considerably larger). The bulkiest termite mounds are found in northern Australia, where they can be as much as 6.1 m (20 ft) high and 31 m (102 ft) in diameter around the base. However, the tallest mounds are built by the African species *Macrotermes bellicosus*; the world record was a mound discovered in The Democratic Republic of the Congo which was 12.8 m (42 ft) high (but a maximum of only 3 m (9 ft 10 in) in diameter). To offer a comparison, the tallest office building in the world is Taipei 101, Taipei, Taiwan: it rises to 509 m (1671 ft) or about the height of 300 people; in contrast, the highest termite mound is taller than 2000 termite workers laid end to end.

★ LONGEST LIVING

A lifespan of 50–100 years has frequently been claimed for queen termites in the genus *Isoptera*, but recent research suggests a more realistic lifespan of up to 25 years.

CRUSTACEANS

Crustacea

c. 42,000 species, including crabs, lobsters, shrimps, prawns, crayfish, barnacles, water fleas, fish lice, woodlice, sandhoppers, krill

★ EARLIEST

The earliest known crustacean is a 12-legged sea spider called *Karagassiema*, which was found in 650 million-year-old rocks in the Sayan Mountains, along the frontiers of east-central Russia and Mongolia.

★ LARGEST

The largest of all crustaceans (although not the heaviest) is the Japanese spider crab (*Macrocheira kaempferi*), named for its superficial resemblance to spiders. Also called the takaashigani (which means 'tall-leg') or the stilt crab, it is found in deep waters off the south-eastern coast of Japan. Its average body size is 25 x 30 cm (10 x 12 in) – though some individuals attain a length of 45 cm (18 in) – and the average leg

span is 2.4–2.7 m (8–9 ft). The record-holder is a specimen with a leg-span of 3.69 m (12 ft 1½ in) and a weight of 18.6 kg (41 lb). Unconfirmed measurements of up to 5.79 m (19 ft) have been reported. Some crayfish and lobsters have longer bodies but are much smaller overall.

The world's heaviest crustacean, and the largest species of lobster, is the American or North Atlantic lobster (*Homarus americanus*), which frequently attains a length of about 60 cm (24 in). On 11 February 1977 a specimen weighing 20.14 kg (44 lb 6 oz) and measuring

Japanese spider crab
The largest of all the crustaceans is the Japanese spider crab (*Macrocheira kaempferi*), which lives on sandy or muddy bottoms in water 30–50 m (100–160 ft) deep off the coast of Japan. It feeds on other crustaceans, echinoderms, worms and molluscs.

1.06 m (3½ ft) from the end of the tail-fan to the tip of the largest claw, was caught off the coast of Nova Scotia, Canada, and later sold to a New York restaurant owner.

The largest (and heaviest) land-living crustacean is the robber or coconut crab (*Birgus latro*), which lives on tropical islands and atolls in the Indo-Pacific. Weights of up to 4.1 kg (9 lb) (the average weight is around 2.5 kg (5 lb 8 oz)) and a leg-span of up to 1 m (39 in) (the average leg-span is 91 cm (36 in)) have been recorded. Unauthenticated weights of up to 15 kg (33 lb) have also been reported. The robber crab is almost entirely terrestrial (although females have to return to the sea to release their eggs) and drowns when submerged in water for any length of time. It feeds mainly on rotting coconuts on the ground, but will eat a variety of other food if coconuts are not available. It has been hunted almost to extinction on many islands in the Indian and Pacific Oceans, because of its sheer size and the fact that it is apparently good to eat.

The largest freshwater crustacean is the crayfish or crawfish (*Astacopsis gouldi*) found under logs and

vegetation in the deep, slow-moving streams and pools of northwest Tasmania, Australia. The average length is less than 40 cm (16 in) and the average weight less than 3 kg (6 lb 9½ oz); however, measurements of up to 60 cm (24 in) and 4.1 kg (9 lb) are not unusual. In 1934 an unconfirmed weight of 6.35 kg (14 lb) was reported for a 74 cm (29 in) individual caught at Bridport, UK. The population size has decreased in recent years, probably as a result of habitat alteration.

★ SMALLEST

Many crustaceans are planktonic and less than 1 mm (³/₆₄ in) in length. The smallest of all are the water fleas of the genus *Alonella*, which may measure less than 0.25 mm (¹/₆₄ in) in length. They are normally found in freshwater.

The smallest crabs in the world are the aptly named pea crabs (family Pinnotheridae), which are parasitic and live in the mantle cavities of oysters, mussels and other bivalve molluscs; they feed on food collected by the gills of their hosts. Some species have a shell diameter of only 6.3 mm (¹/₄ in), including the oyster crab (*Pinnotheres pisum*), which is found in British waters.

The smallest known lobster is the Cape lobster (*Homarus capensis*) of South Africa, which is 10–12 cm (4–4³/₄ in) long.

★ LONGEST LIVING

Little is known about the maximum lifespan of most crustaceans. Large species tend to live longer than small ones and it is believed that very large specimens of the American lobster (*Homarus americanus*) may live to 50–100 years.

SELF SACRIFICE

The female fish louse, an ant-sized crustacean, sacrifices her own life when she gives birth. To make room for up to 100 offspring inside her body she gradually loses all her internal organs until, when the youngsters are old enough, she simply explodes, releasing them into the water and dying in the process.

Coconut crab
The robber or coconut crab, which is almost entirely terrestrial, is the world's largest and heaviest land living crustacean.

★ HIGHEST

Amphipods and isopods have been collected in the Ecuadorean Andes at a height of 4053 m (13,300 ft).

★ DEEPEST

The greatest depth recorded for any living crustacean is 10,913 m (35,802 ft) for an unidentified red shrimp observed by Lt Don Walsh and Jacques Piccard from the bathyscaphe *Trieste* in the Marianas Trench, near Guam, in the western Pacific in 1960.

The greatest depth from which a crustacean has been recovered is 10,500 m (34,450 ft) for live shrimp-like amphipods from the Marianas Trench, by the US research vessel *Thomas Washington* in 1980.

★ MATERNAL CARE

The bromeliad crab, from the mountain forests of Jamaica, is the only crab known to take care of its young after hatching. For three months after hatching, in one of the puddles of rainwater that collect in large leaves of bromeliad plants, the female protects them by chasing away any predators – and fetches them cockroaches, beetles and other food to eat.

★ MOST TERRESTRIAL CRAB

The world's most terrestrial crab is the marsupial crab or side walker (*Austrothelphusa transversa*), which lives more than 1600 km (1000 miles) from the sea, in the deserts of the Australian outback. It survives the long dry season in a burrow, living on the little amount of moisture in the air inside and breathing with the help of lungs. When the rains finally come, it immerses itself in the flooded pools and rivers and breathes through its gills.

★ BEST NIGHT VISION

A deep-sea crustacean called *Gigantocypris* sp., which belongs to the class *Ostracoda*, has better night vision than any other known animal. It surveys its dimly lit world with two parabolic reflectors, each of which directs light on to a retina at their centre. The f-number of its eyes is an incredible f-0.25 (the f-number is a measure of light sensitivity used by photographers – the smaller the number the wider the aperture of the lens and therefore the more light will reach the sensor). For comparison, the f-number of human eyes is about f-2.55 – which makes them many times less sensitive to light than the eyes of *Gigantocypris*. However, *Gigantocypris* has only small eyes and this limits the quality of its vision.

★ BEST COLOUR VISION

Certain species of mantis shrimp (order Stomatopoda) are believed to have better colour vision than any other animal. Their eyes perceive colour through a system based on ten visual pigments, compared with only three in the human eye and up to five in certain fish and insects. It is believed that their ability to distinguish colours well is important in recognizing other mantis shrimps: each shrimp has distinctive coloured markings inside its 'elbow' and, before a fight, they show their elbows to one another to avoid taking on the wrong opponents.

★ LARGEST CONCENTRATION

The largest single concentration of crustaceans ever recorded was an enormous swarm of shrimp-like krill (*Euphausia superba*) estimated to weigh ten million tonnes, which was tracked by US scientists off Antarctica, in March 1981. Vast swarms of this 6.5 cm (2½ in) crustacean – which is one of the most abundant animals in the world – can often be seen in their Southern Ocean home from satellites in space. Their total weight probably exceeds that of any other animal on Earth. Krill is the staple food of a wide variety of Antarctic animals, including baleen whales, seals, penguins and many fish (the word 'krill' actually comes from a Norwegian word meaning 'whale food').

The highest density of crabs in the world is probably on Christmas Island, some 360 km (225 miles) south of Java in the Indian Ocean. An estimated 100 million red crabs (*Gecarcoidea natalis*) live on the 135 km² (52 miles²) island. They

Christmas Island red crabs
Christmas Island red crabs are famous for their annual migration to mate and lay their eggs in the ocean. During the migration the crabs cover the ground so densely that they can be seen from high in the air.

When a mantis shrimp attacks its prey, using its club-like forelimbs, it can deliver a punch that reaches the impact velocity of a .22 calibre bullet.

occur nowhere else in the world. The crabs inhabit the tropical rainforests, feeding on flowers and fruit on the forest floor. Every year (appropriately enough from around November until Christmas) millions of them swarm out of their forest burrows and move down to the coast to mate and spawn. Many die on the way, and others are swept away by the waves, but most survive and return to the forest.

Spiny lobster
When spiny lobsters migrate, as many as 60 travel together, walking along the seabed in single file. They are able to cover distances of up to 50 km (30 miles) without a rest.

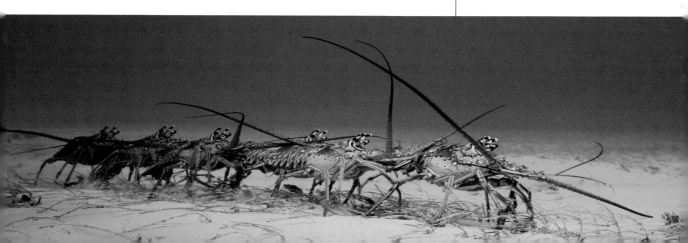

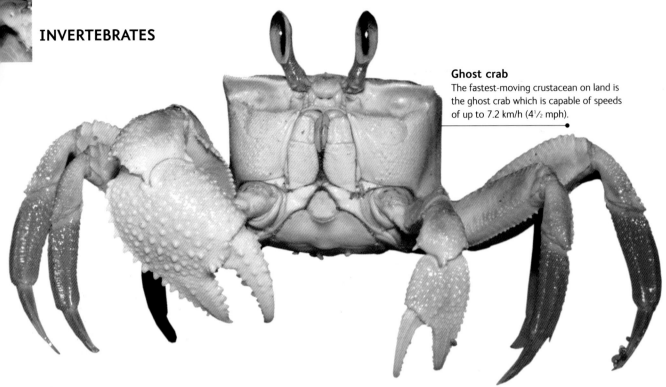

Ghost crab
The fastest-moving crustacean on land is the ghost crab which is capable of speeds of up to 7.2 km/h (4½ mph).

★ FASTEST

The world's fastest-swimming crustaceans are certain lobsters in the genera *Palinurus* and *Homarus;* when escaping from predators, they leap backwards at speeds of up to 8 m/s (26 ft/s) or (29 km/h (18 mph)). However, this is not considered to be true swimming and therefore the fastest-swimming crustaceans are crabs in the family Portunidae, in which the fifth pair of legs is adapted for swimming and flattened into broad paddles to help them chase

and catch fish in the open sea. Most crabs cannot swim, but members of this family are exceptional: they can swim sideways, backwards and sometimes forwards with great rapidity. The current record-holder is Henslow's swimming crab (*Polybius henslowi*), which is found in the eastern Atlantic and has been timed at 1.3 m/s (51 in/s) (4.7 km/h (3 mph)), although it is likely that this and other species attain much greater speeds in the wild.

The fastest-moving crustaceans on land are tropical ghost crabs which

belong to the genus *Ocypode* and live in burrows above the high-tide mark on sandy beaches and among dunes. Some species have been timed at speeds of 2 m/s (79 in/s) (7.2 km/h (4½ mph)). They always travel sideways and, at top speed, the body is raised well off the ground while two or three pairs of legs do all the running. Strangely, to rest the different muscles in their legs, they frequently stop abruptly and turn around 180° before continuing to run in the same direction.

HORSESHOE CRABS

Merostomata
Four species (Atlantic coast of North America and Southeast Asia)

★ SMALLEST

The smallest horseshoe crab is the Southeast Asian species *Carcinoscorpius rotundicauda*, which reaches a maximum length (including the tail) of about 30 cm (12 in).

★ LARGEST

The largest horseshoe crab is the North American species *Limulus polyphemus*, which has an average length (including the tail) of about 50 cm (20 in) and can attain a length of 60 cm (24 in). The

largest individuals are found in estuaries from Georgia to New Jersey, USA.

The largest of all fossil arthropods were the eurypterids, or giant water scorpions, which also belong to the class Merostomata. They lived from 300–450 million years ago and some reached a length of 3 m (9 ft 10 in).

★ EARLIEST

Horseshoe crabs or king crabs are among the oldest of the Earth's inhabitants and are often described as 'living fossils'. Their

heyday was in the Carboniferous period, some 300–355 million years ago, when there were dozens of different species in existence. It is believed their appearance has changed very little in about 200 million years (fossils of an almost identical animal are known from late Jurassic rocks).

★ FURTHEST INLAND

Horseshoe crabs are primarily marine creatures, but *Carcinoscorpius rotundicauda* sometimes occurs in rivers and, on one occasion in India, was reported 145 km (90 miles) from the sea.

JELLYFISH & CORALS

Cnidaria
c. 9700 species including jellyfish, hydroids, sea anemones, corals etc.

★ EARLIEST
Coral reefs are probably the oldest ecosystems on the planet and, indeed, primitive forms existed at least 450 million years ago. The first 'modern' reef-building corals appeared nearly 230 million years ago and, since evolution on coral reefs is a much more gradual process than in many other less stable environments, they have changed surprisingly little since then. In fact, some fossil reef animals dating back to the age of the dinosaurs, about 100 millions years ago, are represented by creatures in the same genera which are still alive today.

★ LARGEST JELLYFISH
Most jellyfish have a bell or body diameter ranging from 2–10 cm (³/₄–4 in), but some species grow considerably larger. The largest is the Arctic giant jellyfish (*Cyanea capillata arctica*) of the northwest Atlantic. One huge specimen washed up in Massachusetts Bay, USA, had a bell diameter of 2.28 m (7¹/₂ ft) and tentacles stretching to 36.5 m (120 ft).

★ LARGEST SEA ANEMONE
The world's largest sea anemone is of the species *Stichodactyla mertensii* which are over 100 cm (40 in) in diameter. They can be found in the Indian and Pacific oceans. A species in the genus *Discoma*, which is found on the Great Barrier Reef, Queensland, Australia is also large. When expanded, its oral disc measures up to 60 cm (24 in) in diameter.

★ MOST DANGEROUS HYDROID
The Pacific Portuguese man-of-war (*Physalia utriculus*) and the Atlantic Portuguese man-of-war (*P. physalis*) both carry a virulent poison and are the only hydrozoans known to endanger human life. All stings are extremely painful but massive ones can prove fatal – and dead animals can sting almost as effectively as live ones. The Pacific form usually has a single tentacle, while the Atlantic has several; each tentacle may be 30 m (100 ft) long and is transparent. In one length of tentacle measuring 9 m (30 ft), scientists counted about 750,000 nematocysts (stinging organs). Also known as bluebottles, both species are widely distributed, although they are most abundant in warm waters. Although they look like jellyfish, each man-of-war is actually a complex colony of hydrozoans; individual hydrozoans perform different functions within the colony: for example, some are adapted for feeding and others for defence.

★ LARGEST STRUCTURE
The largest structure ever built by living creatures is the Great Barrier Reef, off Queensland, northeast Australia, which is over 2000 km (1242 miles) long. Covering an area of 207,000 km² (80,000 miles²), it has been built by countless millions of stony corals (the only animals capable of building massive geological formations). It is not actually a single reef, but consists of thousands of smaller reefs, built over a period of about 18 million years.

★ LARGEST ATOLL
The world's largest coral atoll (a round or horseshoe-shaped reef with a central sheltered lagoon) is Kwajalein in the Marshall Islands: the 283 km (175 miles) long arc of coral encloses a lagoon of 2850 km² (1100 miles²).

A group of jellyfish is called a 'smack'.

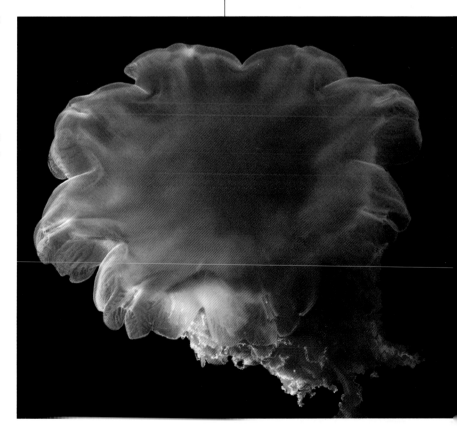

Arctic giant jellyfish
Also known as Arctic lion's mane, this is the largest jellyfish in the world and mainly lives in the northwest Atlantic. Its tentacles can grow up to 36.5 m (120 ft).

WORLD RECORD HOLDER

Most venomous

While all jellyfish are capable of stinging, only a few are considered to be really dangerous to people. The beautiful but deadly sea wasp or box jellyfish (*Chironex fleckeri*) is one of the most dangerous and, indeed, probably the most venomous animal in the world. Found in the near-shore waters of northern Australia and parts of Southeast Asia, its bell can be as a large as a football and it may have as many as 60 stinging tentacles each up to 4.6 m (15 ft) long. Millions of stinging capsules cover the tentacles and discharge venom into the skin of any creature that touches them; other capsules produce a sticky substance to ensure that the tentacles stick to the victim. It takes approximately 3 m (10 ft) of tentacle to deliver a fatal dose of venom to a human, but the pain of the sting from just a couple of centimetres is normally instant and has often been described as unbearable. In the past century, the box jellyfish's cardiotoxic venom has caused the deaths of at least 70 people in Australia alone – more than the combined toll taken in the same region by sharks and crocodiles – and some of the victims have died within four minutes of being stung. A large box jellyfish has enough venom to kill no fewer than 60 adults but, fortunately, an anti-venom was developed in 1970 and this has reduced the number of deaths. Strangely, the stings cannot penetrate women's tights and, until proper 'stinger suits' became widely available, lifesavers patrolling problem beaches used to wear them (top and bottom) unashamedly.

Box jellyfish

The box jellyfish gives an excruciatingly painful and sometimes fatal sting; many beaches along the north coast of Australia are effectively closed during the stinger season.

★ DISCRETE CORAL

The world's largest known example of discrete coral is a stony colony of *Galaxea fascicularis* found in Sakiyama Bay off Iriomote Island, Japan, on 7 August 1982, by Dr Shohei Shirai of the Institute for Development of Pacific Natural Resources. It has a long-axis measurement of 7.8 m (23 ft 9 in), a height of 4 m (13 ft 1½ in) and a maximum circumference of 19.5 m (59 ft 5 in).

★ LONGEST LIVING

The longest-lived cnidarians are certain species of sea anemone, including *Actinia mesembryanthemum*, *Actinia equine* and *Cereus pedunculatus*, which have lived in fish tanks (in captivity) for between 60 and 90 years. Many coral reefs are extremely old. In the 1970s, it was discovered that the age of a reef can be estimated by passing an X-ray through it to reveal annual growth rings like those found in trees. Using this technique, it has been demonstrated that some stony corals (order Madreporaria) on the Great Barrier Reef, in Australia, are 800–1000 years old. However, it is the coral skeletons that attain this age – not the living corals themselves. The skeletons are created by succeeding generations of little animals called polyps (average 1– 3 mm (³/₆₄–¹/₈ in) in diameter), which look rather like miniature sea anemones; each polyp builds a rigid skeleton of almost pure calcium carbonate around itself and, after it dies, the next polyp generation continues the building work.

Beadlet sea anemone

This beadlet anemone is one of the longest lived cnidarians. It looks like an underwater flower but it is really an animal – with poisonous tentacles instead of petals.

MOLLUSCS

Mollusca

More than 90,000 species, including squid, cuttlefish, octopuses, snails, slugs, sea slugs, limpets, bivalves

★ MOST DANGEROUS OCTOPUS

The world's most dangerous octopuses are the blue-ringed octopuses. Their genus includes *Hapalochlaena maculosa*, which is found along the coasts of Australia, and the slightly larger *H. lunulata*, another Australian species which is also found in Indonesia and the Philippines. The relatively painless bite of these deceptively pretty creatures can kill in a matter of minutes although, strangely, some people are only mildly affected. The octopuses carry a venom which includes a component called tetrodotoxin (a paralysing poison identical to the one found in the tissues of pufferfish). They are small animals, with a radial spread of just 10–20 cm (4–8 in), and bite with a parrot-like beak situated at the junction of their eight arms. Victims are often unaware that they have been bitten until the penetration site begins to swell, and they feel a tingling numbness around the mouth. Fortunately, blue-ringed octopuses are not considered to be aggressive and normally 'attack' only when they are taken out of the water and provoked.

In the rare event of other octopus species biting people, the result may be some swelling, soreness and numbness, because they all secrete powerful salivary compounds designed to subdue and digest their prey. However, only the blue-ringed octopuses carry a venom which is dangerous to humans. The suckers on all octopus tentacles are harmless.

★ MOST DANGEROUS SNAIL

Tiny aquatic snails in the genera *Biomphalaria, Bulinus, Physopsis* and *Oncomelania,* form a crucial link in the development of the tropical disease schistosomiasis (bilharzia). Caught by contact with infected water, schistosomiasis is one of the commonest diseases in the world, affecting hundreds of millions of people every year in many parts of Africa, Southeast Asia and South America. It can prove fatal. The disease is caused by infestation of the body with the larvae of parasitic flatworms in the genus *Schistosoma*. These flatworms require two hosts in their lifecycle: the larvae undergo part of their development in the body of the snail; then they enter the water and attach themselves to (and then penetrate) the skin of their second host, which is a human or another mammal. The flatworm larvae mature, mate and lay their eggs, which eventually leave the body of the mammalian host in the urine or faeces, and the cycle continues.

The most venomous gastropods are the cone shells in the genus *Conus*, all of which can deliver a fast-acting neurotoxic venom. There are some 600–700 species altogether, ranging from about 1–20 cm ($^3/_8$–8 in) in length – the largest on record is 25 cm ($9^3/_4$ in) long and is a species called *Conus pulcher*. Several species are capable of killing people, but the geographer cone (*Conus geographus*), found in the Indo-Pacific, is considered to be one of the most dangerous. The venom is injected with the help of disposable darts (which are quickly replaced), and symptoms include impaired vision, dizziness and nausea, sometimes leading to paralysis and death. In the larger species, each dart may be up to 1 cm ($^3/_8$ in) long.

No bivalve molluscs are particularly dangerous to people and, despite the harrowing scenes in many adventure films, giant clams (genus *Tridacna*) do not trap people and hold them under water. Some are certainly big enough to trap a person's leg, and they possess tremendous muscular power to lock their shells shut. But they move so slowly that it usually takes several minutes for them to close properly, so a diver or swimmer would have to be asleep to get caught.

> Each blue ringed octopus is thought to carry enough venom to paralyse ten adult men

Blue-ringed octopus
Despite its beauty, the blue-ringed octopus has a bite that can kill in minutes

243

INVERTEBRATES

★ LARGEST INVERTEBRATE

The Atlantic giant squid (*Architeuthis dux*) is the world's longest invertebrate (excluding worm-like species). Most of the exceptional records came from a series of animals which were washed ashore in Newfoundland, Canada, during the period 1870 to 1889, with the longest reaching 16.8 m (55 ft 2 in). Another 16.8 m (55 ft 2 in) giant squid was washed ashore on Lyall Bay, Cook Strait, New Zealand, in October 1887. Its two long slender tentacles each measured 15.1 m (47 ft 7 in), but its body was a relatively short 1.7 m (5 ft 7 in) in length. Many squid scientists believe however, that this reported length may be exaggerated by the stretching of the delicate tentacles. Unconfirmed reports of giant squid off the coast of Labrador, Canada, measuring in excess of 24 m (79 ft) have never been authenticated.

In terms of the body size and weight, the colossal squid (*Mesonychoteuthis hamiltoni*) is larger. A squid caught in Antarctic waters in February 2007 measured 10 m (33 ft) in length and weighed 495 kg (1089 lbs). Some scientists think it possible that colossal squid may in fact reach longer lengths than giant squid as well.

★ LARGEST GASTROPOD

The largest known gastropod is the trumpet or baler conch (*Syrinx aruanus*) of Australia. One specimen collected off Western Australia in 1979, and now owned by Don Pisor of San Diego, California, USA (who bought it from a fisherman in Kaohsiung, Taiwan, in November 1979) had a shell 77.2 cm (30⅓ in) long with a maximum girth of 1.10 m (39¼ in). It weighed nearly 18 kg (40 lb) when alive.

Giant squid
Reaching a maximum recorded length of 16.8 m (55 ft), including tentacles, the giant squid is the world's largest invertebrate. This example, nicknamed Archie, is on display in the Darwin Centre at the Natural History Museum, London.

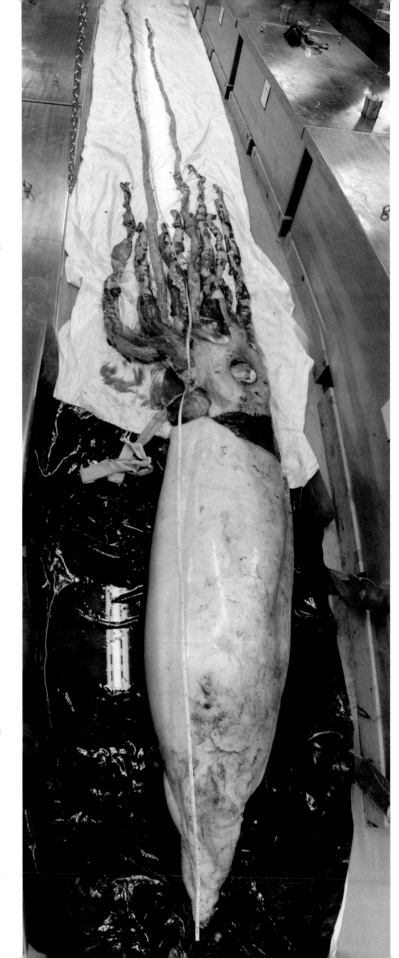

★ MOST VARIABLE COLOUR

All cephalopods (squid, cuttlefish and octopuses) have the ability to change colour, but cuttlefish (order Sepioidea) are the real experts. They have thousands of small contractible pigment sacs in their skin. Each of these is one of three colours and can be enlarged or reduced in size at will, to produce rapid or long-term colour changes. Specific patterns have a variety of uses: to deter predators, in courtship displays and to distract prey animals. Ironically, cuttlefish themselves do not have colour vision.

★ LONGEST GASTROPOD

The longest gastropod is the parasitic eulimid (*Thyonicola dogieli*), which lives inside holothurians and lacks a shell. The longest found was in a holotype 128 cm (50³/₈ in) long.

★ SMALLEST SQUID

The world's smallest squid is said to be *Parateuthis tunicata*, which is known only from two larval specimens collected by the German South Polar Expedition of 1901–03. The larger of the two, which was collected in the Antarctic Ocean at a depth of about 3000 m (10,000 ft), was 1.27 cm (¹/₂ in) in length, including tentacles of 5 mm (³/₁₆ in).

• Cuttlefish

The cuttlefish (*Sepia* sp.) is famous for its ability to change colour and has thousands of small pigment sacs in its skin, all one of three colours. Each sac can be enlarged or reduced in size to change colour.

9.6 m (31¹/₂ ft) and an estimated weight of 272 kg (600 lb). Despite earlier reports, there is no evidence for the existence of *Octopus giganteus*, which supposedly spanned 60 m (200 ft) from tentacle to tentacle. Remains washed up on beaches in Saint Augustine, Florida, USA (1896) and Bermuda (1988) are now considered to be a whale and a fish respectively.

★ LARGEST SEA SLUG

The largest known nudibranch sea slug (nudibranchs have no shells as adults) is an individual found by Tamara Double in May 1991, off Les Sept Frères, a group of islands in the Red Sea belonging to the Republic of Djibouti. It belonged to a small population of brilliant pink and peach-coloured nudibranchs, which were previously unknown to science. The largest was 52 cm (20¹/₂ in) long and 37 cm

★ LARGEST LAND SNAIL

The largest known land snail is the African giant snail (*Achatina achatina*), which looks like an outsize version of many common garden snails. On average its shell is about 20 cm (8 in) in length. The largest recorded specimen measured 39.3 cm (15¹/₂ in) snout-to-tail when fully extended (shell length 27.3 cm (10³/₄ in)) in December 1978 and weighed exactly 900 g (2 lb). Named Gee Geronimo, this snail was owned by Christopher Hudson of Hove, East Sussex, UK, and had been collected in Sierra Leone in June 1976. African giant snails have been introduced to many parts of the world outside Africa, mainly for their food value, but they have become serious crop pests, particularly in Southeast Asia.

★ SMALLEST OCTOPUS

The Sri Lankan species *Octopus arborescens* has an average arm-span of less than 5 cm (2 in) and is the smallest known octopus in the world.

★ LARGEST OCTOPUS

The Pacific giant octopus (*Enteroctopus dofleini*), which lives in an area from California, USA, northward along the coast to Alaska and off eastern Asia as far south as Japan, is the largest octopus in the world. Its average arm-span is believed to be about 2.5 m (8 ft 2 in) and, on average, males weigh about 23 kg (51 lb) and females about 15 kg (33 lb). The world record-holder is a Pacific giant octopus found off western Canada in 1957, with an exceptional arm-span of

(14¹/₂ in) wide; it weighed an estimated 2 kg (4 lb 6 oz). The smallest was 33 cm (13 in) long and 21 cm (8¹/₄ in) wide. It is unclear whether the population represents an extraordinarily large variation of the so-called Spanish dancer (*Hexabranchus sanguineus*) or if it is an entirely new species of *Hexabranchus*. Previously, the world's largest recorded sea slug was believed to be a rather compact species called *Tochuina tetraquetra*, which is found off the northwestern Pacific coast of the USA and reaches a maximum length of 30 cm (12 in). The largest known non-nudibranch sea slug is the giant sea hare (*Aplysia vaccaria*) found in the waters off California. It can reach up to 75 cm (30 in) in length and can weigh up to 13.6 kg (30 lb).

Largest eye

The giant squid (*Architeuthis dux*) has long been thought to have the largest eye of any known living animal. However, in 2007 a specimen of colossal squid (*Mesonychoteuthis hamiltoni)* was caught with an eye measuring 27 cm (11 in) in diameter, which would have been 30–40 cm (11 ¾–15 ¾ in) when it was alive. The specimen was accidentally caught in the Ross Sea off the northern coast of Antarctica. This is the only intact eye of a colossal squid ever found.

★ SUSPENDED ANIMATION

In 1846 two 'dead' specimens of the desert snail (*Eremina desertorum*) were presented to the Natural History Museum, UK. They were glued on to a small wooden tablet and placed on display. Four years later, in March 1850, the Museum staff, suspecting that one of the snails was still alive, removed it from the tablet and placed it in tepid water. The snail moved and later began to feed. This hardy little creature lived for a further two years before it fell into a torpor and died.

★ LONGEST LIVING

The longest-lived mollusc is believed to be the mahogany clam or ocean quahog (*Arctica islandica*), a thick-shelled clam found on both sides of the North Atlantic and in the North Sea. In 2007 a live specimen dredged off the north Icelandic coast was dated to between 405 and 410 years old, using the growth rings in its shell. Unfortunately the mollusc died soon after being caught.

★ FASTEST LEARNER

Squid, cuttlefish and octopuses (all in the class Cephalopoda) are believed to be more intelligent than any other invertebrate. It is very difficult to measure intelligence but, as an example, one recent experiment illustrates how the octopus (*Octopus vulgaris*) can learn simple tasks by observing other octopuses in action. Italian scientists Graziano Fiorito and Pietro Scotto trained a number of individuals to attack either a red ball or a white ball (since octopuses are colour blind, these differed in brightness rather than colour). When they had learned which ball to attack (they were given food rewards each time they got it right), a second octopus in an adjoining tank was allowed to watch. As a result, the observers learned which ball to attack in less time than it had taken the original octopuses to learn by trial and error. The results of this experiment are highly significant because it is the first time anyone has demonstrated that an invertebrate can learn in a way neurologists consider preliminary to conceptual thought.

Octopuses are capable of opening screw-top jars and stoppered bottles to get at food placed inside.

★ SLOWEST GROWTH

The deep-sea clam (*Tindaria callistiformis*), found in the North Atlantic, is believed to have a slower growth rate than any other animal. Scientists at Yale University, Connecticut, USA, calculated that it may take about 100 years to reach a length of just 8 mm ($^5/_{16}$ in).

★ SMALLEST SHELL

The smallest known shell-bearing mollusc is the marine gastropod *Bittium* sp, which

Squid
Squids are renown for their large eyes, and the largest found to date belong to a colossal squid.

INVERTEBRATES

Marine giant clam
The giant clam (*Tridacna gigas*) is the largest species of bivalve in the world, photographed here in the Great Barrier Reef, Australia.

was collected by Mr Zheng Gen Hai from reefs near the Nansha Islands, China. It measures 0.4 mm (¹/₆₄ in) long and 0.3 mm (³/₂₅₆ in) wide.

★ MOST POPULAR SHELL
The most popular shells among shell collectors are generally considered to be the cowrie shells (family Cypraeidae), which have a very smooth, glossy, porcelain-like texture, as well as vivid patterning and coloration. There are more than 200 known species and many local variations. The cowries are closely followed in popularity by cone shells (family Conidae), volutes (family Volutidae) and rockshells (family Muricidae).

★ LARGEST PEARL
The world's largest natural pearl was taken from a giant clam (*Tridacna derasa*) off the coast of Palawan, in the Philippines, on 7 May 1934. Known as the 'Pearl of Laotze', it weighs 6.4 kg (14 lb 2 oz) and measures 24.1 cm (9¹/₂ in) in length and 10.2–14 cm (4–5¹/₂ in) in diameter. It was auctioned in San Francisco, USA, in 1980, for US$200,000 (then £85,000).

★ LARGEST BIVALVE
The largest of all recent bivalve shells is that of the marine giant clam (*Tridacna gigas*), found on Indo-Pacific coral reefs. One specimen measuring 1.15 m (45¹/₄ in) in length and weighing 333 kg (734 lb) was collected off Ishigaki Island, Okinawa, Japan, in 1956, but was not scientifically examined until August 1984. It probably weighed just over 340 kg (750 lb) when alive – the soft parts weigh up to 9.1 kg (20 lb) – and was therefore the heaviest on record. The longest bivalve mollusc was another giant clam, collected at Tapanoeli (Tapanula) on the northwest coast of Sumatra, Indonesia, before 1817, and now preserved at Arno's Vale, which measures 1.37 m (48 in) in length and weighs 230 kg (507 lb).

SPONGES

Porifera
c. 5000 described species (only c. 150 live in fresh water) although it is thought that there may be double that number in existence

★ LARGEST SPONGE
The largest known sponge is the barrel-shaped loggerhead sponge (*Spheciospongia vesparia*), found in the West Indies and in the waters off Florida, USA, which measures up to 1.05 m (42 in) in height and 91 cm (3 ft) in diameter. Neptune's cup or goblet (*Poterion patera*) of Indonesia grows to 1.20 m (48 in) in height, but is far less bulky.

Loggerhead sponge
This is the largest known species of sponge. It has been known to reach 1.05 m (42 in) in height.

★ SMALLEST SPONGE

The widely distributed *Leucosolenia blanca* is just 3 mm (¹/₈ in) tall when fully grown.

★ DEEPEST SPONGE

The deepest living sponges known are members of the family Cladorhizidae, which have been found at depths of up to 8840 m (29,000 ft).

★ HEAVIEST SPONGE

In 1909 a wool sponge (*Hippospongia canaliculata*) measuring 1.8 m (6 ft) in circumference was collected off the Bahamas. When first taken from the water, it weighed 36–41 kg (80–90 lb), but this fell to 5.44 kg (12 lb) after it had been dried and relieved of all excrescences. It is now preserved in the US National Museum, Washington DC, USA.

★ EARLIEST

Sponges were the first multi-cellular organisms to evolve on Earth, appearing some 570 million years ago. The simplest and most primitive multi-cellular animals alive today, they have neither true tissues nor organs, and their cells display a considerable degree of independence.

★ REGENERATION

Sponges are little more than clusters of individual cells, with very limited coordination or dependence between them. Not surprisingly, they have more remarkable powers of regeneration of lost parts than any other animal – and are capable of regrowing from tiny fragments of their former selves. For example, if a sponge is forced through a fine-meshed silk gauze, the separate fragments can reform into a full-size sponge. Also, if a sponge is separated into several different pieces, these will reorganise themselves into one or more new sponges.

STARFISH & THEIR RELATIVES

Echinodermata

c. 7000 species, including starfish, brittle stars, sea urchins, sea cucumbers, feather stars, sea lilies

★ EARLIEST

The earliest echinoderms are believed to have resembled the sea lilies or feather stars (class Crinoidea), which are the most primitive living members of the group. Their origins go back at least to the Cambrian Period, 510–570 million years ago.

★ LARGEST SEA CUCUMBER

The bulkiest of the world's 1000, possibly 1500, species of sea cucumber is *Stichopus variegatus*, which is found in the Philippines; when fully extended, it can be up to 1 m (40 in) in length and 24 cm (10 in) in diameter. The longest sea cucumbers belong to the genus *Synapta* and can reach almost 2 m (78 in) in length when full extended, although they are worm-like in appearance and measure only about 1.2 cm (¹/₂ in) in diameter.

★ SMALLEST SEA CUCUMBER

The smallest known sea cucumber in the world is called *Psammothuria ganapatii*, which is found off the coast of southern India. It rarely exceeds a length of 4 mm (⁵/₃₂ in).

★ LARGEST STARFISH

The largest of the 1600 known species of starfish is the fragile brisingid (*Midgardia xandaros*). A specimen collected by the Texas A & M University research vessel *Alaminos* in the southern part of the Gulf of Mexico, in 1968, measured a maximum 1.38 m (4¹/₂ ft) from the tip of one arm to the tip of another, but its disc was only 2.6 cm (1 in) in diameter. Its dry weight was 70 g (2¹/₂ oz).

★ HEAVIEST STARFISH

The heaviest species of starfish is the five-armed *Thromidia catalai* of the western Pacific. One specimen collected off Ilot Amedee, New Caledonia, in the Pacific, on 14 September 1969, and later deposited at Noumea Aquarium, New Caledonia, weighed an estimated 6 kg (13 lb 4 oz). Its total armspan was 63 cm (24³/₄ in).

Sea cucumber
The sea cucmber *Stichopus variegatus* from the Philippines can grow up to 1 m (40 in) when fully extended.

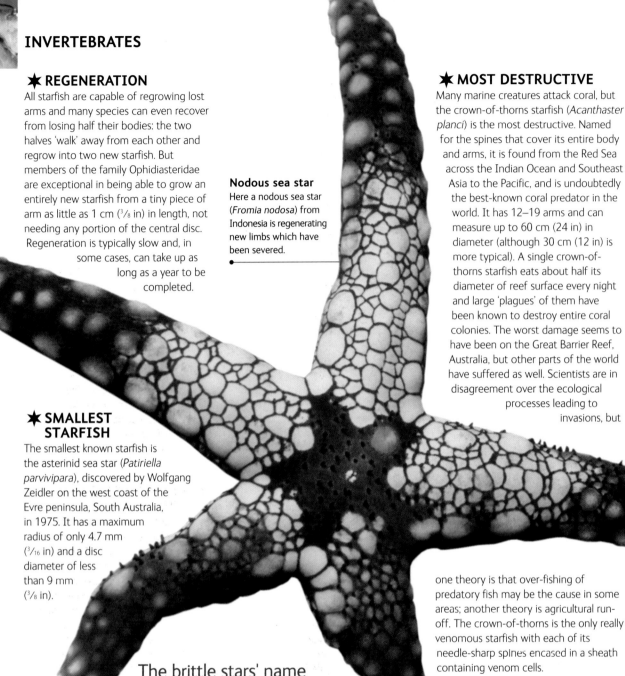

INVERTEBRATES

★ REGENERATION

All starfish are capable of regrowing lost arms and many species can even recover from losing half their bodies: the two halves 'walk' away from each other and regrow into two new starfish. But members of the family Ophidiasteridae are exceptional in being able to grow an entirely new starfish from a tiny piece of arm as little as 1 cm (³/₈ in) in length, not needing any portion of the central disc. Regeneration is typically slow and, in some cases, can take up as long as a year to be completed.

Nodous sea star
Here a nodous sea star (*Fromia nodosa*) from Indonesia is regenerating new limbs which have been severed.

★ SMALLEST STARFISH

The smallest known starfish is the asterinid sea star (*Patiriella parvivipara*), discovered by Wolfgang Zeidler on the west coast of the Evre peninsula, South Australia, in 1975. It has a maximum radius of only 4.7 mm (³/₁₆ in) and a disc diameter of less than 9 mm (³/₈ in).

The brittle stars' name reflects their readiness to cast off their long, thin arms easily when attacked or roughly handled.

★ MOST ARMS

The majority of starfish and brittle stars have five arms, but a few have more; members of the starfish genus *Heliaster*, living along the west coast of North America, have as many as 50. Feather stars are not directly comparable, as they have a different body structure; some primitive species have five arms, but the majority have a total of ten and a few have as many as 200 (resulting from the repeated forking of each original arm).

★ MOST DESTRUCTIVE

Many marine creatures attack coral, but the crown-of-thorns starfish (*Acanthaster planci*) is the most destructive. Named for the spines that cover its entire body and arms, it is found from the Red Sea across the Indian Ocean and Southeast Asia to the Pacific, and is undoubtedly the best-known coral predator in the world. It has 12–19 arms and can measure up to 60 cm (24 in) in diameter (although 30 cm (12 in) is more typical). A single crown-of-thorns starfish eats about half its diameter of reef surface every night and large 'plagues' of them have been known to destroy entire coral colonies. The worst damage seems to have been on the Great Barrier Reef, Australia, but other parts of the world have suffered as well. Scientists are in disagreement over the ecological processes leading to invasions, but one theory is that over-fishing of predatory fish may be the cause in some areas; another theory is agricultural run-off. The crown-of-thorns is the only really venomous starfish with each of its needle-sharp spines encased in a sheath containing venom cells.

★ LARGEST SEA URCHIN

The world's largest sea urchin is *Sperosoma giganteum*, which is found in deep waters off the coast of Japan. The diameter of the test or shell (measured horizontally) averages 32 cm (12¹/₂ in).

★ SMALLEST SEA URCHIN

The smallest known sea urchin is *Echinocyamus scaber*, which is found off the coast of New South Wales, Australia. The diameter of the test or shell (measured horizontally) averages only 5.5 mm (¹/₄ in).

★ LONGEST LIVING

Very little is known about longevity in starfish, although four years is considered to be a good age for most species. The genus *Pisaster* is, however, thought to live up to 20 years. The red sea urchin (*Strongylocentrotus franciscanus*) and,

based on its slow growth rate, the starfish (*Odontaster validus*) are by far the oldest and can live for more than 100 years.

★ DEEPEST

The greatest depth for any echinoderm is an amazing 10,710 m (35,130 ft) for

Myriotrochus bruuni, which was collected by the Soviet research ship *Vityaz* in the Marianas Trench, western Pacific, in 1958. The greatest depth for a starfish is 7584 m (24,881 ft) for a specimen of *Porcellanaster ivanovi,* collected by the *Vityaz* in the same place, in 1962.

WORMS & WORM-LIKE INVERTEBRATES

Nemertea, Annelida, Platyhelminthes, Echiurida & Nematoda

c. 65,000 species, including earthworms, leeches, flukes, ribbon worms, tapeworms, roundworms

★ LONGEST WORM

The longest known worm is the boot-lace worm (*see* box on this page). The world's largest leech, the Amazonian species *Haementeria ghilianii,* can grow up to 40 cm (16 in) .

The longest known species of segmented worm (phylum Annelida) is the giant earthworm *Michrochaetus rappi* (also known as *M. michrochaetus*) of South Africa, which has an average length of 1.36 m (54 in).

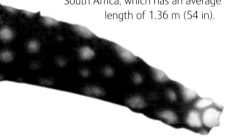

A record-breaking giant earthworm of this species, measuring 6.7 m (22 ft) in length (when naturally extended) and 2 cm (¹³/₁₆ in) in diameter, was collected in the Transvaal in 1937.

Another exceptional individual (presumed to be *Michrochaetus*) was reported in South Africa in 1969 to be about 7 m (23 ft) in length, with a diameter of 7.5 cm (3 in). However, such reports are regarded with considerable doubt by experts since an earthworm of that size is probably impossible physiologically. It seems unlikely that the internal hydraulic pressures necessary to move such a large animal could be sustained without the internal organs being badly damaged and blood circulation being prevented.

★ SHORTEST WORM

Chaetogaster annandalei measures less than 0.5 mm (¹/₆₄ in) in length and is the shortest of the world's known annelids. It lives in freshwater, in close association with several species of snail, and is carnivorous (feeding on amoebas, ciliates, rotifers and trematode larvae).

★ WORM CHARMING

The world record for worm charming was set in 1980, at the Willaston County Primary School, Nantvich, Cheshire, UK, when Tom Shufflebotham raised an astonishing 511 earthworms from a 3 m² (32 ft²) plot. His record-breaking attempt took place during the annual World Worm Charming Championship, which has just two basic rules: no refreshment, stimulation or drugs permitted, and no digging. The contestants are allowed 30 minutes to entice as many worms out of the ground as possible.

Shufflebotham used a traditional technique called 'twanging', in which a four pronged pitchfork is placed in the ground and then wiggled back and forth. The movement is designed to cause special vibrations that apparently persuade the worms to emerge.

★ GENDER DIFFERENCE

The most striking difference in size between the sexes in any known animal is in the marine echiurid worm (*Bonellia viridis*), which is found throughout the Mediterranean. The females are 5–12 cm (2–4¾ in) long but have an extendable proboscis which, when fully stretched, may be over l m (39 in) long. This compares with 1–3 mm (³/₆₄–⁷/₆₄ in) for the males, thus making the females thousands of times heavier than their mates. The males live on or even inside the females.

★ MOST SPECIFIC PARASITE

The hippopotamus leech (*Placobdelloides jaegerskioeldi*), is the only leech known to be specific to one mammal. It feeds only on hippo blood. This is more difficult than it sounds because hippos spend much of their time in deep, fast-flowing water, their skin is thick and they allow birds to search their bodies for tasty ectoparasites such as leeches. One of the leech's many adaptations for this difficult lifestyle is its dark red colour, making it difficult to see against the red viscous fluid that hippos secrete to protect their skin from the burning sun.

WORLD RECORD HOLDER

Longest

The longest known animal is the boot-lace worm (*Lineus longissimus*), a kind of ribbon worm or nemertine (phylum Nemertea) found in the shallow waters of the North Sea. A specimen washed ashore after a severe storm at St Andrews, Fife, UK, in 1864, measured more than 55 m (180 ft) long.

INDEX

INDEX

ACKNOWLEDEMENTS

A great many people around the world have helped with the research for this book. Some shared their knowledge, others read and commented on early versions of the text and provided moral support and encouragement. I am indebted to everyone who has been involved.

For the original work, I would like to thank (in no particular order): Alwyne Wheeler; Jo Taylor and Carolyn Slicer at the Information Service of the World Conservation Monitoring Centre; Chris Wemmer, Chairman, ICUN Deer Specialist Group; Tom Langton and all the staff at Herpetofauna Conservation International Ltd; Colin Harrison; John Burton, the World Wide Land Conservation Trust; Ian Redmond; Alison Smith; Chris Stroud and Erich Hoyt at the Whale and Dolphin Conservation Society; John Gooders; Tony Huston, the Bat Conservation Trust; Nick Garbutt; Robert Burton; Peter Jackson, Chairman, ICUN Cat Specialist Group; Randall Reeves, Deputy Chairman, ICUN Cetacean Specialist Group; Mark Simmonds, University of Greenwich; Paul Thompson, University of Aberdeen; David Lavigne and Chris Mattison; and Jonathan Elphick.

At the Natural History Museum, London I would like to thank the scientists who have checked through the whole of the book, updating and validating the text for this new edition. With a special thanks to the Zoology department and Katrina Cook, Robert Prys-Jones, Mark Adams, Judy White, and Douglas Russel from the Bird Group at Tring, Jerry Hooker and Angela Milner from the Palaeontology department, George Beccaloni and Stuart Hine from the Entomology department, and Steve Swaby.

Space does not permit me to list all the sources of references used for this book. However, having consulted many thousands of journals, magazines and books over a period of several years, I would like to acknowledge the fact that I have drawn freely on the painstaking and pioneering research work of others.

Mark Carwardine

PICTURE CREDITS